9/05

P9-DTC-286

# LEGION COMPANION

CURT SWAN '93
STEVE LIGHTLE '03

TwoMorrows Publishing • Raleigh, North Carolina
www.twomorrows.com

Superboy and the Legion of Super-Heroes TM & © DC Comics.

# Dedication:

*This book is dedicated to the memory of the members of the Legion family, both fans and professionals, who have graced us with their presence and have since moved on. It is on their shoulders that we stand.*

THE LEGION OF SUPER-HEROES and all related characters and indicia are TM and © DC Comics. All Rights Reserved. Used with permission.

TwoMorrows Publishing
1812 Park Drive
Raleigh, North Carolina 27605
www.twomorrows.com • e-mail: twomorrow@aol.com

First Printing • October 2003 • Printed in Canada

Softcover ISBN 1-893905-22-5

## Special Thanks

The author would like to thank the following for their contributions of artwork to this volume:

Miki Annamanthadoo, Alan Bahr, Spencer Beck, Scott Bierworth, Simon Bollinger, Harry Broertjes, Royd Burgoyne, Dylan Clearbrook, Dave Cockrum, Fred L. deBoom, Bertil Falk, Vladimir Fiks, Tom Fleming, Kevin Gould, Mike Grell, Neil Hansen, Peter Hansen, Bryan Hawkins, Allan Heinberg, Greg Huneryager, Scott Johnson, Paul Michael Kane, Scott Kress, Greg LaRocque, Ted Latner, Michael Lieb, Steve Lightle, Jonathan Mankuta, Richard Martines, Bob McLeod, Kevin McConnell, Al Milgrom, Steve Mohundro, Jim Mooney, David Morefield, Mike Napolitano, Al Plastino, Steve (Greybird) Reed, Terry Shoemaker, Chris Snorek, Brian Tidwell, Steven Weill, Edward Zeno

Without their efforts, it would merely be a collection of words.

**The Legion Companion** is published by TwoMorrows Publishing, 1812 Park Drive, Raleigh, NC 27605, USA. 919-833-8092. Glen Cadigan, Editor. John Morrow, Publisher. The Legion of Super-Heroes and all related characters are TM and © DC Comics. All other characters are TM and © 2003 their respective owners, as noted where they appear. "How I Spent My Summer Vacation" by Jim Shooter © 2003 Jim Shooter, as originally published in **The Legion Outpost** #10, 1981. All reprinted text in the Otto Binder, Mort Weisinger, Murray Boltinoff and Cary Bates sections © 2003 Harry Broertjes, as originally published in **The Legion Outpost** #'s 8, 6, & 4, respectively. All reprinted text in the Edmond Hamilton section © 2003 the Estate of Edmond Hamilton, as originally published as "Fifty Years of Heroes" in **Weird Heroes** Vol. 6, 1977. The first interview in the Curt Swan section © 2003 Krause Publications, as originally published in **Comics Collector** #1, 1983. The second interview in the Curt Swan section © 2003 Attic Books, as originally published in **Comics Values Monthly Special**, 1992. All reprinted text in the E. Nelson Bridwell section © 2003 John G. Pierce, as originally published in **Whiz Kids** #2, 1981. John Forte article © 2003 Peter Hansen. Mark Waid interview © 2003 Chris Companiak. Editorial package © 2003 Glen Cadigan and TwoMorrows Publishing.

741.5973
CAD
2003

# Foreword

## by Glen Cadigan

### A lot can happen in forty-five years.

In 1958, America's space program was just getting off the ground, both literally and figuratively. On television, people were still tuning in every week to watch *The $64,000 Question* and *Father Knows Best*. In Vietnam, things were beginning to heat up. And on the home front, Dwight D. Eisenhower was still President.

In the world of comics, it was an interesting time to be a fan. Just two years prior, the Silver Age of comics had begun with the reintroduction of the Flash in *Showcase* #4. Over in the *Superman* office, all sorts of new ideas were being introduced. That same year, both Superman's Fortress of Solitude and the Bizarros would make their first appearances, as would one other idea: The Legion of Super-Heroes.

Originally conceived of as a throwaway gimmick for a Superboy story, the Legion would prove to be one of the most successful concepts to come out of the Weisinger office. Introduced in *Adventure Comics* #247, the Legion would inspire readers to write in and demand more.

Since letter writing was still somewhat of a novelty in those days, the letters were taken to accurately reflect the mood of the public. Delayed sales figures proved the same thing: it turned out Mort Weisinger and company had an accidental hit on their hands.

So another Legion story was ordered. And another. And another. And then, eventually, what was obvious to all could no longer be denied: the Legion deserved its own title.

Taking over as the back-up feature in *Adventure Comics* with #300, the Legion would eventually rise to become the lead in the title, then would move over to the back-up spot in *Action Comics* before migrating over to *Superboy*. There they would displace the Boy of Steel in his own title for the second occasion, having previously done so in *Adventure Comics*. The title was renamed *Superboy and the Legion of Super-Heroes* before the *Superboy* part was dropped altogether. After twenty-one years, the *Legion* finally had a title to call its own.

Many different people have worked on the *Legion of Super-Heroes* over the years. From Jerry Siegel and John Forte through Paul Levitz and Keith Giffen (and beyond), each *Legion* generation has had a version of the team to call its own. While they may not agree on which is best, they can agree on one thing: the Legion of Super-Heroes, in any incarnation, is in a league of its own.

Throughout the years, the focus on the *Legion* has always been on the characters themselves, not the people who have given them life. This book hopes to correct that. The purpose of this book is to tell the creators' stories, in their own words. It is about the people behind the *Legion of Super-Heroes*, and their legacy on the title. It is about the numerous writers and artists (and even a few editors) who have contributed to the Thirtieth Century's greatest super-heroes over the course of forty-five years. After four and a half decades, their work is celebrated here. It may have been a long time in coming, but hopefully it'll be worth the wait. After forty-five years, their time has come.

So let's turn the page, shall we, and see what they have to say? We wouldn't want to keep them waiting any longer.

CURT SWAN + Alan Hutchinson '80

Superboy and the Legion of Super-Heroes TM & © DC Comics.

# Introduction
by Jim Shooter

# How I Spent My Summer Vacation

The title of this piece is pretty strange for a retrospective on the **Legion of Super-Heroes**, I'll admit. I suppose I should have called this "Looking Back at the Legion," or "My Years with the LSH," or even "I Remember Mon-El." But I chose the title for a reason.

Of course, everyone who's ever attended grammar school has had to write at least one composition entitled "How I Spent My Summer Vacation." Most of my friends *suffered* through the ordeal, begrudging every word that flowed like molasses from their Eberhard Faber #2's. I, on the other hand, rather enjoyed writing my composition. I thought it was easy. It occurred to me, at a rather tender age, that if one could somehow get paid for this sort of thing, one had, indeed, discovered a legal racket. Thus were the seeds of my writing career sown.

Sure enough, eventually I sold a script for a "Legion of Super-Heroes" story to the late, great Mort Weisinger, who edited the exploits of that august group back then in 1966, thereby fulfilling my childhood dream of raking in big bucks just for putting words on paper.

Still, you ask, why the stupid title? Well, I wrote that first script in the *summer* of 1965, laboring long and hard up in my hot, stuffy little room while other 13-year-old kids were out playing baseball, swimming, hanging around and otherwise enjoying their vacations. Ergo, the origin of Jim Shooter, Professional Writer and "Legion" Scripter Emeritus is precisely How I Spent My Summer Vacation in 1965.

So what? So who should care about my beginnings as scripter for the Legion, much less the fulfillment of my childhood dreams? No one. What might be of interest, however, is the unique situation my rather young debut as Legion scripter created: I was about the same age as my characters. I was also about the same age as my audience. Better still, my *friends*, who were also my audience, were the same age as my characters, so my friends *became* my characters who were my audience, who...

You get the drift. Now for the really sweet part—*we all aged together*, characters, friends/audience and me. I can vouch for the fact that working with a teen-aged writer aged Mort a few zillion years, too, but the point is that the Legion grew up with me from early 1966 to early 1970. That may not mean much to anyone else, but to my point of view, it made those characters very special, and good, bad or indifferent, I feel responsible for the characters of the Legionnaires I wrote in that period.

You see, before I happened along, "The Legion of Super-Heroes" was very much a plot-oriented book with very little space devoted to characterization. The eminently capable gentlemen who preceeded me on the strip, working with Mort, had given the title a sweeping, science-fiction space-opera identity, which suited it. All too often, though, six planets in four pages made for lines of dialogue like, "My home world...*choke*...*destroyed!*" That just wasn't enough *angst* for me. Being a 13-year-old makes one a leading authority on angst, and I strove to add some to the series.

Something had to give, of course, to fit the angst. Sadly, it was some of the plot, and five of the six planets per four pages. Some readers missed the outrageous space-operas, but most applauded the advent of characterization. A new age was upon us, after all—the *Marvel Age*. Stan Lee was King. Old directions *had* to change, or—dare we say it?—National Comics was in trouble. Thus, with Mort's blessing I struggled to find *raison d'etre* for a character called Bouncing Boy, who previously had been offered up at face value, and played straight and serious.

I found my Bouncing Boy among my Bethel Park Senior High classmates, in the person of a friend whose initials, T.K., and slightly rotund body had earned him the nickname "Teakettle." Going through high school coping with a weight problem and the name Teakettle is not a whole lot different, I think, than being Bouncing Boy in the Legion of Super-Heroes. Thus, in my mind, they became one, and BB grew into a bright-but-insecure, self-effacing, lovable guy who was resigned to the role of comic relief and once described himself as the Legion's "...self-appointed chief of morale." I found similar models for the other Legionnaires. It was easy. Everyone is a character in high school, because no one has learned to hide it yet.

Naturally, the high school "character" I knew best was the tall skinny kid with the armload of science books who was renowned for "drawing cartoons," so there was quite a bit of me scattered among my 20-odd Legionnaire charges. When Karate Kid did something impulsive and got himself in trouble, believe me, I knew *just* how he felt.

So we all progressed—my friends/audience/characters/self thundered toward adulthood together. Together, we abandoned the shy uncertainty of our first dates and slowly learned about love. In my first Legion script ever (**Adventure Comics** #348, "Target—21 Legionnaires") Duo Damsel girlishly flirts with Superboy, eager to hold hands with the "most powerful" Legionnaire, eager to be seen with the Legion's equivalent of the Big Man On Campus. Didn't all freshman girls want to hang out with the football stars? Her crush on Superboy grew as issues passed, while he noticed her less and less. The tension built to the kind of cataclysmic heartbreak that only a sophomore girl, shattered by unrequited love, can know.

Just like the classmate she was modeled after, Duo Damsel went on to discover that just as her love had gone unnoticed by Superboy, someone else's love for

her had gone unnoticed. He was a bright-but-insecure, self-effacing, lovable guy, more than a bit on the plump side, but that was okay. She had learned, and grown, and was able to find in Bouncing Boy things that mattered, things that made him special to her. Their relationship blossomed... they were seniors at the Sweethearts Ball, truly in love.

I left the Legion and comics late in 1969 to pursue other things. One way and another, I ended up back scripting the **LSH**

in 1974. Murray Boltinoff had taken over as editor, and things were a bit different. For one thing, he insisted that the Legionnaires were "all about 15 years old."

Now the editor is responsible for a book's success or failure, and so, by definition, he's always right. Murray's editorial approach was highly successful, making the **LSH** a top book for DC. But frankly, I couldn't adjust to this newfangled angle on that old gang of mine. It showed. My stories were heavily edited and often had to be rewritten (both new experiences to me). Finally, it just seemed best to look for greener pastures elsewhere. I took an offer from Marvel Comics, where I am today, as editor-in-chief. I've been at Marvel for four years now—and still, the characters I'm most identified with are the Legion of Super-Heroes... and I have to admit, I miss them.

A final note—I've been thinking about Duo Damsel and Bouncing Boy being married now. For a time, I didn't like the idea, but I've changed my mind. I figure Teakettle would like it that way.

A final, final note, to Jack, and whomever his future successors may be—take care of 'em, willya? After all, they're my friends. *choke*!

[Originally printed in **The Legion Outpost** #10 in 1981, the above piece is presented here with the permission of the author. For an entirely new interview with Jim Shooter, turn to page 50.]

Superboy and the Legion of Super-Heroes TM & © DC Comics.

# Table of Contents

**Editor**
Glen Cadigan
**Layouts and Design**
Christopher Day
**Publisher**
John Morrow

**Front cover by Dave Cockrum & Joe Rubinstein**
**Front cover colored by Tom Ziuko**

**Cover logo by P. C. Hamerlinck**
**Back cover art by Jim Mooney**

Legion of Super-Heroes TM and © DC Comics.

# Otto Binder

A prolific writer during both the Golden and Silver Age of comics, Otto Binder played a role in the creation of much of the Marvel Family mythos, including Mary Marvel, Uncle Marvel, and Mr. Tawky Tawny. When Fawcett Comics ceased publication in 1953 due to a lawsuit filed by DC (then National) Comics, Binder moved over to DC, where he wrote "Tommy Tomorrow," "Superboy," and "Supergirl," among other features, the latter of which he helped to create. Although he would only write a handful of Legion tales, it was Binder who, along with Superman family editor Mort Weisinger and artist Al Plastino, created the super-hero team from the future, and it was from his typewriter that their first adventure sprang. While it may never be certain as to who came up with what, it is indisputable that nearly half a century later, their creation lives on.

The following interview was conducted by Matt Lage and originally appeared in the *Legion Outpost* #8, Summer, 1974. Thanks go out to Harry Broertjes, former editor of the *Outpost*, for allowing it to be reprinted here.

**TLC:** *You originally wanted to be a pulp writer. Did you want this more than writing for the comics?*

**OB:** Well, as of today when it's far too late, I wish I had stuck to the pulps, especially writing book lengths—today some would be reprinted and I'd be getting royalties. Unfortunately, I dropped the pulps around 1941 because comics paid much more. I was able to double and triple my income for the next twelve years. But who would guess that the bonanza—at Fawcett, anyway—would end abruptly, plus the possibility that [Captain Marvel] would have gotten into the syndicates with myself as writer and [C.C.] Beck as artist. It was pretty well

being set up just after the court case, but of course that ended when Cap was forbidden to appear anywhere else after that. So I lost out on a good thing in the comics and also had abandoned the pulps and sci-fi markets. So it goes...

**TLC:** *Why couldn't you have gone back to the pulps after the demise of Cap? The pulp publishers knew of your talents from years before—so why weren't you rehired?*

**OB:** I did try the pulp field for awhile, and sold about a half-dozen short stories to **Science Fiction Plus**, edited by Sam Moskowitz. I also sold a story here and a story there to other mags, but the rates at one cent and two cents a word were miserable: sci-fi has always been a miserable paying field, as any writer can tell you. Compared to comics, where I get from $10 to $15 a page, it seemed to pay about five times as much in comparison to the time and effort involved. So I took up Mort Weisinger's offer to work at DC—I had held off a few months—and went back into comics which then took up my full

*Superboy meets the Legion of Super-Heroes for the first time in this panel from* **Adventure Comics** *#247. Art by Al Plastino.* Superboy and the Legion of Super-Heroes TM and © DC Comics.

time and paid well. As I mentioned before, I wish now that I had stuck to sci-fi and written book-length stories as the book market at that time was starting to expand nicely. Today I would be getting reprint royalties, as other writers are, from sci-fi. Who can look into the future?

**TLC:** *With your writing, was there any set story formula?*

**OB:** No, decidedly not. There was no set pattern of any kind. In fact, we [at Fawcett] avoided any suggestion of repetition or similarity. Each story was to have its own unique approach. The stories in each book were tailored to be as unlike as possible, for variety.

**TLC:** *Were there any problems in writing particular stories?*

**OB:** Problems? You have to be jesting. Many stories were problems because they were too crammed with plotting so that the writer had to squeeze and make rapid transitions, etc., to the detriment of the final story. Some scripts required too much wordage, both captions and dialogue, that all panels were crowded and created a problem for the artist to depict anything. All the writer could do was to cram it in and let the editor cut where he could, which sometimes hacked up a story

**OTTO BINDER IN THE GOLDEN AGE**

*Above: Binder by longtime Fawcett collaborator C.C. Beck. Top of page: Binder at home in 1974, courtesy of Bertil Falk.*

*Superboy attends his first Legion meeting, from* **Adventure Comics** *#247.*
Superboy and the Legion of Super-Heroes TM and © DC Comics.

badly. Sometimes I would write a script halfway through and then see it could never be finished in the panels left, so I had to rip it up and start all over, grinding my teeth. With difficult stories I would often make a panel-by-panel breakdown for myself, just indicating the scenes briefly and a few key words. That way I avoided leaving myself hanging in the air at the end with more panels needed to finish the story. That's about one hundredth of the problems that came up. None of the scripts were "easy" to write, as most people seem to think, deceived by the story's "simplicity."

**TLC:** *A rather controversial question, especially now after Beck sent a story in to DC and it was rewritten by [E. Nelson] Bridwell. Do you think the editor has the right to rewrite a story, supplied to, but not assigned by, him?*

**OB:** Oh boy! If Bridwell did rewrite a story of Beck's, I'll bet the fur is flying! I doubt Beck took to that kindly, and his relationship with DC must be deteriorating, to put it mildly. As to whether the editor has a right, yes and no. He has the legal right, as a company employee, to alter a script in any way he chooses. As to his ethical right to tamper with a writer's idea and manner of writing is another story—with a good editor, I never felt disturbed if he changed the script around somewhat. With a lousy editor— and I've had many outside Fawcett—you feel resentment as they have ruined your story, so to speak. However, as long as they paid, what the hell?

DC is notorious, of course, for hashing up scripts as they please. Hardly a script of mine went in exactly as I wrote it, though some came close. DC

simply had a rigid pattern or formula to which every story in every book had to conform. Their editing, however, was carefully and responsibly done so that the writer could never complain as to the final quality. It was reasonably good, but with most of the original life—inspiration—in it blue-penciled out. That, I think, is why the stereotyped style of Superman couldn't compete with the free and open writing of Captain Marvel, which consistently outsold Superman during the war years.

**TLC:** *As a movie and comics fan, I know Hollywood had a "blacklist" during the "Red Scare" of the '50s. And comics had a scandal of their own—the Wertham book and Senator Estes Kefauver's hearings. But what I'm trying to make a point of is this: Do you believe in censorship? And do you think such companies as EC should have been able to keep publishing their mags?*

A BINDER PLAYLET WAS A FEATURE AT NEW YEAR PARTIES

*Another Binder cartoon by Beck. Originally published in* **The Legion Outpost** *#9, Fall, 1975.*

**OB:** I am totally against any and all form of censorship in the arts. We all thought Wertham was a big fart who was merely capitalizing on his books, knowing that any anti-comics work would be enthusiastically bought by mothers who thought comics were warping their kids. Nobody has proven that lurid comics or sexy books or even porno material has ever changed a person, unless he was already unstable to begin with. I, too, thought EC horror comics were great and wrote a modest number of them... yes, some actual shockers of that ilk, where I could let my imagination into uninhibited horror and sci-fi. Fun writing them. At every story confab, Bill Gaines would be in on it and every once in a while when we were stalled, he'd whip his arm around and say, "Give 'em the chain!" He acted bloodthirsty but was actually the opposite—very generous in paying his staff and freelancers, for instance. The only reason I regretted that EC went on with the horror comics was because of the gathering storm I knew was being cooked up by Wertham and his cohorts. I didn't want them to get a toe-hold against banning comics, which, of course, happened after the Congressional investigation—that is, with the comics thereafter emasculated to the point of being insipid. Someday, the EC stuff may be called the only true literature that ever came out of the comics medium.

**TLC:** *Today comics will deal with everything from super-heroes, straight sci-fi, horror and juvenile comedy. Would you think this is good or bad, especially when you take into consideration that none of them are like the comics that belonged to the Whiz gang?*

**OB:** Well, I suppose most comics will have to play it straight and use realism. There wouldn't be room for the many humorous types. Actually, the [Captain] Marvel stories aren't humor in the strictest sense of the word, but rather satire and parody of life situations and the doings of humans, good and bad. One might say the tone of Captain Marvel is "whimsy," a series of fantasies reflecting life through funny mirrors like those at amusement parks. The subject matter is recognizable but distorted by exaggeration, spoofing, or running jokes. The secret of it all was that Captain Marvel and Billy were dead serious and never made

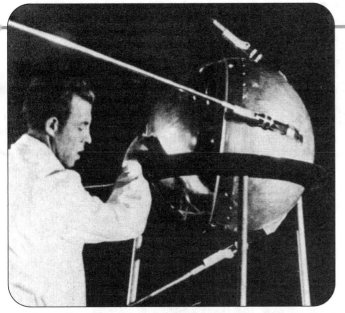

*On October 4, 1957, history was made with the launch of Sputnik, the world's first satellite. Note the use of a satellite in the first Legion story elsewhere on this page, from an issue cover-dated April, 1958. Photo courtesy of the NASA archives.*

**TLC:** *Just out of morbid curiosity—are you getting any residuals from the old Fawcett stories that DC is reprinting?*

**OB:** Not as yet. There was a rumor—via Tom Fagan, or perhaps Marty Griem—that DC was planning to pay residuals once they got the listings of who wrote what, presumably from Jerry Bails or somebody. Nothing has happened so far. I would, of course, welcome any such payments even if small—will be for sure—as DC robbed me of a young fortune by killing off Captain Marvel and Company.

**TLC:** *The inevitable question: are you writing these days?*

**OB:** Yes, of course. I'm far from retired, simply because I can't afford it. All the money I made from the Marvels and had saved up went down the drain when, in 1960, I invested as a junior partner in publishing **Space World**, a magazine about astronomics. Maybe you never ran across it, but I think it was a good job I did as editor-in-chief—although the public stayed away from it in droves.

Though it was the exciting time when the first manned flights occurred, and the moon shots, somehow the public interest was low. It didn't really charge up until the Apollo flights. Result: a loss every month on low sales. The mag lasted some 16 issues, during which time Bill Woolfolk and I had put in more money—I mortgaged my house—all paid up by Cap—and borrowed, etc., but we never got the lucky break. So that left me without money reserves and it was back to the comics until 1967, when my daughter—our only child—was killed by a car at age 14. For reasons difficult to

a joke at all. It was how we played up the slapstick and puns and situation comedy that made it all funny.

But remember this: Young kids usually don't get the joke at all. They take it seriously, namely the battle between good and evil with the good guy—Cap—always winning. In a sense, Captain Marvel was like Jonathan Swift's satires of political situations, and also like **Alice in Wonderland**, which to the adult is a study of human nature. I always felt I was exploring and exploiting human nature too, digging out the zany aspects to show that much of life was a joke and plenty full of craziness.

Despite the humor whimsy, Captain Marvel was pretty close to real life. Witness Mr. Tawny and his typically human situations. I guess that's why Anthony Boucher, many years ago, wrote me letters telling how brilliant certain stories were. Some of the best fantasy-satire in the world, he said. He and his sons followed Captain Marvel faithfully throughout his career. Yet of course I often met people who found out what I did for a living and said, "What?! You write that childish drivel?" So it goes...

*Every good story has a happy ending. Superboy is inducted into the Legion of Super-Heroes in* **Adventure Comics #247.** Superboy and the Legion of Super-Heroes TM and © DC Comics.

*Otto and Jack Binder with their wives circa 1945. It was through his brother Jack, who was then foreman at Harry 'A' Chesler's studio, that Binder entered the comic book field. Picture provided by Peter Hansen.*

*A Depression-era photo of Binder. Courtesy of Peter Hansen.*

explain, my wife and I moved from Englewood, New Jersey to upstate New York where Jack [*Binder, Otto's brother* —**Ed.**] lived. I was pretty broken up and found it difficult to write again up here, but went back to sci-fi, this time as the market hit.

From 1969 to 1972 I had about 15 books published—some fresh, some reprints of my old stuff—the full-lengths I had done. But sci-fi, if you know anything about the field, was subtly changing, veering away from regular plotted stories to God knows what. I still haven't figured it out yet. Into some *avant garde* wild yonder of impressionism or exosociology or what-

ever left me hanging out on a limb. I just couldn't write that stuff and my market dried up. Meanwhile, I had begun writing articles about UFOs for **Saga** magazine, also UFO paperback books. They were followed by two fresh novels—completely different than anything I had done before. Two sold so far. I have another book making the rounds of the publishers right now that is my "big one" as far as I'm concerned. Deals with UFOs but in a direct way, by proving that mankind is a hybrid of early humans and star-people who came ages ago in flying saucers. The proof lies in evolutionary clues—you'd have to read it to get the gist.

So, to sum up, I'm out of sci-fi and the comics. I'm in UFOs, historical novels, and a bit of psychic stuff. The only comics I've done were for **Classics Comics**, adaptations from literary classics, for Vince Fago, several a year.

*From science-fiction to science fact: America's space program took flight during the 1950s. From the NASA archives.*

*Superboy displays his latest achievement.*
Superboy and Pa Kent TM and © DC Comics.

# Al Plastino

A longtime "Superman" artist, Al Plastino was sometimes called upon to also draw "Superboy," and the April, 1958 issue of **Adventure Comics** was one such occasion. Unbeknownst to Plastino at the time, the inaugural appearance of the Legion of Super-Heroes would prove to be one of the Silver Age's most important stories, and would lead to the continuing adventures of the first super-hero team at DC since comic's Golden Age. Although it would be Plastino's only Legion story, his contribution to Legion history cannot be overstated. He was interviewed by Glen Cadigan on February 18, 2003, and copyedited the following interview.

**TLC:** *When did you start working for National Comics?*

**AP:** Ohh...'48, '49, [something] like that. I had a studio in New York on 43rd and Lex with two other cartoonists, and I was doing other commercial art when someone suggested that they were looking for someone to do "Superman." Of course, I thumbed my nose to it. [*laughs*] Someone told me what they were paying—at that time, Wayne Boring was getting $55.00 a page—and they talked me into doing some samples, [which] I did, and they liked them. They offered me $35.00 a page. [*laughs*] Of course I said, "No, no. I can't do that. You're paying fifty-five." They said, "We can't pay *you* fifty-five. You're just a beginner." So we compromised on fifty a page.

I started out bringing the work in, and it got a little hectic. I had to bring it in for the letterer, 'cause I did my own work. No one ever penciled or inked for me. I did everything myself. In fact, if you look in the books, you'll only see one name: Al Plastino. The only thing they had was a colorist, which everybody had, so I convinced them into doing the whole thing at my

*Above: the very first appearance of the Legion of Super-Heroes, from **Adventure Comics** #247. Top of page: Plastino sketching in front of an audience, courtesy of the artist.*
Superboy and the Legion of Super-Heroes TM and © DC Comics.

*Some samples of Plastino's **Ferd'nand** work.* Ferd'nand TM and copyright 2003 United Features Syndicate.

studio. I left the studio [in New York] and went on my own and had a studio at home. I used to go in once or twice a week, just to go over the artwork. Then I got to a point where I said—[and] I'm not bragging now—"I don't change my artwork."

At the beginning I had to copy Wayne Boring's style, so I did that for a while, then I did my own style. I did something like forty-eight covers while I was doing the regular strip, and I was pretty happy there, and it was going pretty good. Then at the same time I was also offered a strip called ***Ferd'nand*** for United Features. [Henning Dahl] Mikkelsen needed an assistant, so I went ahead and helped him out. When he passed away, I got the strip. So I not only did "Superman" [*chuckles*], I did ***Ferd'nand***, which were two opposites. One was a real cartoon, the other was semi-illustration. So I was pretty busy there for a while, meeting deadlines.

**TLC:** *Did you do much comic work before you got on "Superman"?*

**AP:** I did some comic work for Funnies, Inc. I helped out with "Sub-Mariner," I did some inking on ***Captain America***—this was during the war.

**TLC:** *So you were in the service?*

**AP:** No, I was a civilian in the Pentagon. I was there a couple of years. Then when I came out, I was offered the "Superman" strip. But Funnies, Inc., I was with them quite a while. I was just seventeen years old, something like that, and I did a few things during the war. I've got one cover that I'm pretty proud of with ***Blue Bolt Comics***. I have the original, in fact, of this cadet beating up on Mussolini, Hitler, and Hirohito. Then I went into the Pentagon. Of all things, I designed a real plane that was

way beyond its time, and it looked like the space shuttle. That's 1941, and they sent me to the Inventor's Council with the model and the blueprints, and they sent me to 90 Church St. Then they sent me to Grummond, and they didn't know what the hell to do with me. So finally I said, "Look, I don't want anything for the airplane." I had my two brothers in the service. [I said,] "I just want to help out." I used to build model planes. I knew a little about aeronautical engineering. Not too much.

Several days later I received a telegram saying, "Report for Duty." I was assigned to the graphic arts office in the Pentagon. I was drawing war posters for the Pentagon building and producing them in silkscreen. My next assignment was with the Adjutant General's Office, working on illustrations for Army training manuals. When the Germans started the Battle of the Bulge, I had to come back to New York for reassignment and continued my artwork for FM manuals for Steinberg Studios. Mr. Steinberg said DC Comics was looking for someone who could draw "Superman," [and] I said, "No way." I had enough of comics, but the price was right per page. That's how I started working for DC Comics.

**TLC:** *Were you always interested in art growing up?*

**AP:** Oh, yes. Since I was a

little kid. In grade school I had an art teacher who was kind of a grotesque person—people were afraid of her—but she took an interest in me, and helped me out. I'd do the work for their monthly magazines, and she helped me out a lot. Miss Davis her name was. Then when I was in high school, I entered a couple of contests for a magazine called Youth Today. First prize was fifty dollars. I won two first prizes and one second, so they hired me. The art director's name was Mr. Kuden, and I was doing... you know ***Reader's Digest***? The little pen drawings? That's what I was doing. Little black-and-whites. And that's how I got started with the black-and-whites.

Then there was an ad [in the paper]. Harry Chesler was advertising for an artist to do black-and-whites. Well, I didn't realize it was comics. [*laughs*] I went up there and saw about thirty guys doing comics, and I said, "Geez, this is pretty good stuff. Let me try it for a while." So I fooled around. I was doing Pratt work—you know, inking and ruling up pages for the guys?—and I'd

*The cover to **Blue Bolt Comics** Vol. 4, #1, June, 1943. Courtesy of the artist.*

Plastino with friend Jackie Gleason after a golf tournament at Shawnee on the Delaware during the 1950s. Courtesy of the artist.

watch these guys work, and they were all pretty good. To draw something out of your head, you gotta be pretty good. So I got interested in that, but I stayed with the commercial art. We had an agency, a woman that went out and got us work. I did some pulp covers. I got one I'm looking at now on the wall here. **Fifties Love Story**, **Leading Love**, and all that baloney. I was a pretty busy guy. Then I finally settled down with the [comics], 'cause I had young kids then, and I had to make money. I had to make a steady salary. I couldn't fool around with the commercial art. [It] was a rat race. So I settled down doing comics, and also doing painting and whatever.

**TLC:** *Who hired you to do "Superman"?*

**AP:** I think I saw Mort Weisinger, and I think [Whitney] Ellsworth was the head of the department then. The one that wrote [the] **Batman** [newspaper strip]. I had a falling out with one of the editors [in 1970], and Ellsworth said, "Look, do you want to do **Batman**?" and I said, "I'll try **Batman**." I did that for eight or nine years. I did the dailies and the Sunday, and left "Superman." By that time I'd been with "Superman" maybe eighteen years, and from time to time I did special stories for

them. Then eventually, just after **Batman** demised in the papers, I stuck with **Ferd'nand**. I just did **Ferd'nand** and some commercial art. Not too much. I did that for quite a while, and I finally retired in '84, '85.

**TLC:** *Was Mort the editor you fought with?*

**AP:** N-o-o, Mort and I had an understanding a long time ago. It was Murray Boltinoff I didn't get along with. We had a big argument! I said to Murray, "I will not work with you if you are the editor of **Superboy**!"

**TLC:** *So you got along with Mort?*

**AP:** Only professionally, that's all! I worked on "Superboy" and "Superman" with Mort.

**TLC:** *How well did you get to know the other "Superman" artists?*

**AP:** Curt [Swan] I knew pretty well. Poor Curt, he was a workhorse. All he did was pencil stories. We worked together at the beginning on a couple of things, but I didn't want to work with anybody, because then you're involved with going back and forth. I said, "I want to work at home. I don't want any of this baloney." Not that I

was cocky, [but] I knew that I was good enough to do the work.

They wanted me to pencil [tight], and I can't pencil tight. I pencil very rough. I said, "You want me to pencil like Curt? Anybody can ink Curt's stuff." Everything was there—the blacks, the lines—all you hadda do was take a brush and follow his lines, put a little smaltz to it. I said, "If I'm gonna pencil that tight, I might as well finish it." I purposely didn't pencil tight, so [Mort] said, "No, no, you can't pencil," and I said, "I know. I told you I can't pencil so other artists can ink my art!"

What used to turn me off was when [Joe] Shuster and [Jerry] Siegel used to come in and Mort would talk to them like they were dirt. I could never understand that. I told Mort one time, "Mort, you're working because they created Superman." "Oh," he says, "I have other things to do." I said, "But you're still [here]." I said, "If it was me, you would never talk to me that way." They talked down to everybody. I don't understand these guys. They don't do it anymore. The fellas up at [DC] now are a different type of people. They're great people to work for!

**TLC:** *Did you know many of the other cartoonists working back then?*

**AP:** I met some of the most famous cartoonists of the '40s. We would meet at

A **Superman** cover by Plastino.
Superman TM and © DC Comics

[Fred Waring's] golf tournaments at Shawnee on the Delaware [*A popular golf resort in the Poconos* —**Ed**]. I won the tournament sixteen years in a row [*laughs*], and I played with Jackie Gleason, a guy I loved! I would play golf with other celebrities from time to time.

**TLC:** *When you were working on "Superman," what sense did you have of how important the Superman titles were to DC? Were they DC's most important comics?*

**AP:** I think so. Mort was responsible for really building it up with those crazy ideas. I thought they were crazy at the time, like Bizarro and different gimmicks to get things a little different, get [things] a little interesting so they could sell books. In those days you'd go and buy one at the stand. Now it's all by mail-order and whatnot. It's a different business.

**TLC:** *You drew the first appearance of Supergirl.*

**AP:** Yeah, I did.

**TLC:** *What do you remember about that assignment?*

**AP:** I did the first story—I think I did two stories—then I did Super-Dog. I did so much crap. Mort was responsible for all this. I guess you gotta be a little nuts to write that stuff. I never thought it was gonna be anything, but it turned out to be real good.

**TLC:** *Did you come up with Supergirl's costume?*

**AP:** Well, they wanted her to look like Superman, [so] you put a skirt on her, put the red boots on her, and the red cape. The only discussion was, "Should she be blonde?" and I thought that was a good idea.

**TLC:** *Do you remember him telling you about it? The idea they had for it?*

**AP:** I think they discussed it with other editors, then I would come in and they'd say, "Al, I want you to blah blah blah." I said, "Okay, I'll work on it." I don't remember specifically what he said. I got along fairly well with

him, but I always kept him in his place. If you let an editor jump on your back and get you shakin' in your boots, you're dead! You're dead in the comic business. They treat you like dirt! They treat you like you're nothing. And that's when Murray just annoyed me one time. I said, "Who the hell do you think [you are]? You talk to me like a man or I don't want to even look at you."

And he went wild. He went on and on and on. I said, "Okay, let's go in your office." I got him in the office, closed the door and said, "Don't you ever talk to me that way again." 'Cause we were in the artroom with a bunch of guys. And most of the guys took it. They would take it. I mean, imagine talking to Shuster like he's a piece of dirt. And the poor guy was so humble, and so afraid of Mort. I said, "What the hell is he afraid of?" And finally they consented to give the guy $20,000 a year for life. He worked at a post office. They were making millions on him. That rubbed me the wrong way.

**TLC:** *There was one other feature that you drew the first appearance of, and that was "The Legion of Super-Heroes."*

**AP:** I think so, yeah.

**TLC:** *Did looking at that issue bring back any memories?*

**AP:** I looked at it, but I still don't

YOU SEE, WE'RE FROM THE **FUTURE!** NATURALLY, WE KNOW YOUR LIFE STORY FROM HISTORICAL RECORDS! WE WORE 20ᵗʰ-CENTURY CLOTHES TO HAVE A BIT OF FUN WITH YOU!

SO THAT'S IT! WHAT A RELIEF THAT MY SECRET IDENTITY IS STILL SAFE HERE IN SMALLVILLE!

COSMIC BOY   SATURN GIRL   LIGHTNING BOY

*Top: Supergirl was designed by Al Plastino. Above: Plastino designed the costumes of the original three Legionnaires, which would only be seen in their first appearance. Superboy and the Legion of Super-Heroes TM and © DC Comics.*

remember doing it. I guess I did it. It's my work.

**TLC:** *Do you think you designed the costumes which the characters wore in that issue?*

**AP:** I don't know who designed those costumes. I just got something to do and I did it, I guess. I don't remember designing them.

**TLC:** *Would you say you're sure that you didn't come up with them?*

**AP:** I wouldn't swear to it. I don't know if [it was] the first one ever done...

**TLC:** *It was.*

**AP:** Then maybe I did. If it's the first one, I probably did.

**TLC:** *Back in those days when they would send you a script for a comic, if a character had not yet appeared, would it be up to you to design them?*

**AP:** Yeah, I think so. I had characters I had to make up. I'm looking at it now, and I probably did do it. I know the folds and the type of costume. It might have been mine, [but] it's so long ago.

**TLC:** *That was the only time that they wore those costumes. The next time that they appeared, they had on different outfits. If you had to guess, would that be a case of a lack of reference, or would they have changed it intentionally?*

**AP:** I really can't help you there. I remember when Nick [Cardy] followed my work on the wedding of Clark Kent and Lois Lane, I had a young kid and he made the character much older than what I did. I had him a young guy, and Nicky made him an old guy. I guess he didn't see my pages. I don't know what went wrong there, but he changed him entirely. I didn't understand that.

**TLC:** *When you would start a feature like "Legion" or "Supergirl" and it would go on to become a success, would you keep tabs on something like that?*

**AP:** I don't think I paid much attention to that. I don't want to sound too preoccupied, but I really didn't care. I did my job, and I never took comics that seriously. It was a job and I did it, and that was it. Some guys became really involved with

THIS STORY, PREPARED IN CLOSE COOPERATION WITH THE LATE **PRESIDENT KENNEDY**, WAS SCHEDULED FOR PUBLICATION IN **SUPERMAN** NO. 168, WHEN WORD OF HIS TRAGIC ASSASSINATION REACHED US. WE IMMEDIATELY TOOK IT OFF THE PRESS AND SUBSTITUTED OTHER MATERIAL. HOWEVER, WHITE HOUSE OFFICIALS HAVE SINCE INFORMED US THAT **PRESIDENT JOHNSON** WANTED IT PUBLISHED, AS A TRIBUTE TO HIS GREAT PREDECESSOR. AND SO WE DEDICATE THIS PLEA FOR HIS PHYSICAL FITNESS PROGRAM, TO WHICH HE WAS WHOLEHEARTEDLY DEVOTED DURING HIS LIFE...

"SUPERMAN'S MISSION for PRESIDENT KENNEDY!"

*Published after JFK was assassinated, the original art to the above piece now hangs in the Kennedy library. Courtesy of the artist.*
Superman TM and © DC Comics

their comics, which I never did. It was just a job. That's the only explanation I can give you on why I didn't follow up on most other things.

**TLC:** *When you were drawing "Superman," were you also looking for newspaper strips to draw?*

**AP:** Yeah, I had other stuff I was doing, too. I was drawing **Hap Hopper** for United Features. Jack Sparling, who I worked with, did **Hap Hopper** for the **Daily Mirror**, and he said to me, "You wanna do it? I'm leaving the strip." I said, "Yeah!" I did that for a while, then we changed it to **Barry Noble**. But I was doing so many things at once. I would paint murals. I don't want to sound like a big shot, but you name it, I was doing it. I did portraits of executives in the different publications, just everything. When I was a kid, that's all I remember doing. When I was going to grade school, just about to graduate, I used to go to the Metropolitan on Saturday

and copy Rembrandt, Renoir... you name it. Just copied them to learn how to paint. I did that for a while.

**TLC:** *Did you ever try to launch your own newspaper strip?*

**AP:** Oh, don't even mention it. It's a pain in the neck. We had one strip I was working with Jack on called **Justin Case**. It was [about] a small town lawyer, and I put my heart and soul into this thing. It didn't take off. In those days, what they did was they gave you a hundred and fifty dollars a week plus commissions on how many papers they sold. I had a couple of strips I [created]. What I used to do when I had a new character was I'd

mail it to myself.

**TLC:** *To keep the copyright.*

**AP:** Yeah, mail it to myself. Especially in stories. One time I invented a figure of Superman made out of paper. Kellogg's was interested in it. The cape folds back into his back and you shoot [it] up with a rubber band, and the cape opens up and he spins down. Kellogg's was interested in it, and like a damn fool they sent me to another agency, and they stole it. They made it outta plastic. So from then on, I learned my lesson the hard way. There are so many things I could tell ya. God...

**TLC:** *How did the syndicates treat you compared to the comic books?*

**AP:** Oh, the syndicate, that was a joy. What a difference! The guys were gentlemen. We got along great.

**TLC:** *And I bet they paid a lot better, too.*

**AP:** Yeah, it paid better, providing you kept up the newspapers. If you lost papers, you'd lose out.

**TLC:** *You basically stopped drawing comic books in the late Sixties...*

**AP:** No, no, no. It was beyond that. I stopped **Batman** [in] '84...

**TLC:** *The newspaper strip...*

**AP:** Yeah, and then I... let's see: [in] the

*An example of Plastino's **Batman** work, also featuring Superman.*
Superman, Batman and Robin TM and © DC Comics

*A previously unpublished **Peanuts** strip, scheduled for a Sunday newspaper. Courtesy of the artist.* Peanuts TM and © 2003 United Features Syndicate.

Seventies I quit "Superman," then I went to **Batman**. I did that for about eight years. I don't know the exact date, but I did the **Batman** strip. That was for Ledger Syndicate, and I got pretty good with that. I did some good stuff, dammit. Too bad I didn't get all of it. I got a lot of it, but I really worked like a dog on that. More like illustration than anything else. I remember doing **Batman**, I [used to draw] a head as big as my fingernail with a brush, and today I can't do that anymore. I gotta wear glasses and use a pen, which I never did. But it was fun. It was a different era. Did I tell you I did **Peanuts** once?

**TLC:** *I heard that you were going to do* **Peanuts***.*

**AP:** I did **Peanuts** when [Charles Schulz] had a heart bypass. I didn't get what he was getting, and I had to do everything original. It was never used, but they had it just in case something happened to him. 'Cause he was way ahead. He was months ahead, but they didn't think he was gonna make it, so being I worked there, I did some samples. They liked 'em, and I liked drawing it, too. It was fun drawing that damn thing.

I learned his technique. His gag was never the obvious. If you read his stuff, it wasn't the obvious punchline. I would do three punchlines, and I would work backwards. Get the gag and work backwards. I would show it to my wife and my kids, and they more or less picked the one I would

think, but most [people] would pick the obvious. I started to enjoy it, and then he recuperated, and that was it.

**TLC:** *There was a period there in the late Sixties when a lot of guys of your generation got out of comics.*

**AP:** I don't know if they got out of comics, but they just disappeared. I was not a snob, but I didn't associate with too many [artists]. The only fella I knew, [who] I'd see once in a while was Curt. Nick Cardy was a good friend of mine. He dropped out for a while. Nick was a good, fine artist. We used to go painting together when we were younger, and make watercolors together. He shoulda been born in the 15th Century with Michelangelo. He's a good sculptor, but kind of a laid back guy. I hired him when I was fading out from **Batman**, and I was going into **Ferd'nand**, which I loved to do. He was penciling for me for about maybe half a year.

**TLC:** *What's your take on the comic book*

*industry today?*

**AP:** They asked my opinion last year [about] the new stuff. One fella asked me, "Al, what's wrong?" and I said, "You guys are killing Superman with these muscles." The guy has super-powers. He doesn't need the muscles. I don't know if you look at the latest books...

**TLC:** *I've seen them.*

**AP:** Oh, they're so grotesque! My God! And the backgrounds! They're so confusing! The background guy is trying to outdo the guy that's doing the figures, and when you look at a page, you get so confused with all this [clutter]. We did nice, simple clean stuff that you pick it up, [and] it's easy to read. It may not have been as exciting as the ones today, but I think they overdo the muscles.

They make more money on the reprints, the old stuff, 'cause it was simple, it was to the point. The artwork wasn't especially great, but it was clean and clear. Now these guys are trying to outdo one another. The penciler, he's trying to outdo the inker, the inker's trying to outdo the penciler, the background men are trying to outdo everybody—'cause they got separate guys for everything—and it's like doing a painting and putting every little detail in the sky. The foreground, the figures... everything is the same value. It shouldn't be that way. You got a dominant figure in a panel [and] he's the action; the rest is just prop. Not the way you've got a guy in a window, [and] every bar in the window's drawn. What the hell do you need that for? That's what I objected to, and I told them the truth. I said, "I think you guys are overdoing it."

**TLC:** *Tell me a bit about working conditions back then.*

**AP:** My wife used to say, "Why do you talk to Mort that way?" and I'd say, "Hey, he's only an editor. He's not my boss!" If a man doesn't respect me, [or] what I'm doing, [if] he's gonna talk down to me, I'm not gonna take it. I never took it in commercial art, either. I used to play tennis up in

*Another unpublished **Peanuts** strip, this time for a daily newspaper. Courtesy of the artist.*
Peanuts TM and © 2003 United Features Syndicate.

Montclair for a big agency, and I did work for them. I'd go in Monday morning [and it went from] "Al" from when we were playing tennis to "Mr. Plastino." We'd come in on Monday morning and they'd let you wait in the outer office for fifteen minutes. So I got pissed off and said, "What am I waiting out there for?" "Well, Al, in our business you can't... you gotta..." and I said, "Horsesh*t." So I got outta that.

I remember waiting to go in to see them, and there was a big drawing when I went into the office. A full color drawing. Beautiful! Done in tempera. And the guy outside was crying. It was a big portfolio, and he was waiting to come in. The guy inside said, "Al, I want you to redo this for me. We don't like it." So I looked at him and I looked at the work, and I said, "I can't do better than that!" I was honest. I said, "How am I gonna do better than that?" "Well, we don't like it, Al. The hand's not right. This is not right..." So I said to myself, "They're gonna get me involved with this on a spec, and then turn it down? I'll stick to black-and-white."

One thing about me: I turned down a lot of jobs which I figured I couldn't do. I worked with Ernie Bushmiller on **Nancy**, and they wanted me to do a pop-up book. They were gonna give me four thousand dollars to do a pop-up book. I had to do all the engineering—how it'll work, how it's gonna pop up. I got half-way through the job and I said, "I can't do this." So I went in and I was very honest with them. I said, "Look, I'll give you whatever I have, but I can't finish it." There was no sense in me knocking my brains out, making a nervous wreck of myself when I know I can't do it in the specified time they wanted. And they were very nice. They said, "Okay." They gave me two thousand dollars. They gave me half-price. And they got another guy.

But I've always done that. When I worked with **Captain America**, inking, I got a little tired of that because [I was] working on somebody else's pencils. Jack Kirby was very loose, and I would have to tighten up the pencils and ink 'em. I was a young guy then. They liked my work, they really did. They said, "Al, you're doing a good job." I said, "Yeah, but I'm knockin' my brains out. I'm up to two, three in the morning. It doesn't make sense." I wasn't even married then, but still... [So] I said, "No, no, no." And there were a lot of incidents where guys would try to take advantage of you.

Jack Binder, one time I did a job for him when he was with Chesler, and I had the

work. He said, "I'll pay you next week." I said, "No, you're not. You're paying me right now." And one thing led to another, and I went in the corner room and I had the pages in my hand, and I said, "If you don't pay me, I'm gonna rip 'em up." "No, no, no, no! Don't rip 'em up!" And he got out and got me the money. That's the kind of business it was. It was a rat race, and [there was] jealousy amongst artists, which was ridiculous. There was a lot of crap going on. I don't know if it's still the same [today]—it might be—and if you weren't sure of yourself... I saw a couple of shaky guys that weren't sure, and they would take a lot of abuse. I mean, it was sad. It was a sad, sad thing. And I couldn't see it. I just said, "This is ridiculous." And that's when I made my demands. I said, "I'm workin' home. Whatever I send you, that's gonna be it, and if it's not good enough, fire me." And we got along fine.

**TLC:** *Is this your first interview?*

**AP:** [There was a] fella from Denmark [who interviewed me about **Ferd'nand**], and another guy was going to do a book on **Batman**, and he wanted some of my proofs, which I had a tough time getting back. I got proofs of all my work. I got all the daily proofs, and a lot of the Sundays, and he held on to them. He interviewed me on the phone, [and] he was gonna

write a book. So when I asked him to send me the proofs, he said, "Well, I'm gonna make copies." I said, "Look, send me the proofs. Send me back the proofs." I just don't trust anybody anymore. My daughter says, "Daddy, they're selling your work like crazy on the Internet." Where the hell they got my work, I don't know. I don't know how the hell they got it. Like a jackass, I didn't take it. A lot of guys would say, "Al, can I have that story?" when I'd get it back, and I'd say, "Yeah, here, take it," not realizing they'd be worth money some day. Crazy, isn't it?

**TLC:** *I thought that they didn't give the original artwork back in those days?*

**AP:** At the time, I didn't know the artwork was so valuable! I left 'em in the warehouse, and a lot of these guys grabbed that stuff and they're making a fortune on it now. It's one of those sad stories. When we were working, we didn't realize that someday they would be worth money. I have a few left. Not too many, just a few.

You know what drives me nuts? I got two or three guys that wanted to buy my work, and they said it's for their personal use. I've done that in the past and find out that they sell 'em. I'll sell 'em for like two, three hundred dollars a page, [and] they get a thousand! So I saw this one guy, and

*More examples of Plastino's **Ferd'nand** work, courtesy of the artist.*
Ferd'nand TM and © 2003 United Features Syndicate.

*The artist surrounded by some of his "associates." Courtesy of the artist.*
Superman, Batman and Robin TM and © DC Comics. Ferd'nand and Nancy TM and © 2003 United Features Syndicate.

for an appearance. I used to know all the Yankee ballplayers in Jersey. Yogi [Berra], [Phil] Rizzuto... I knew 'em all, and they wouldn't do anything unless they got paid. And here's an artist, and he doesn't get paid. I don't understand [it]. [This guy] says, "You can make money on the side. You know, sell your stuff." I said, "No, I'm not peddling my art." I got to a point where I got so fed up with being taken advantage of that I said, "The hell with it. I'm not doing it anymore." That's the way I feel about it. That's about it in a nutshell.

**TLC:** *Do you do any commissions other than recreations?*

**AP:** No, no, I haven't done too much of that. It's really tough. Believe me, it's tough, because you gotta do everything from scratch. You're doing the whole thing over again, and then if you don't get it exact... Like one guy, he says, "Oh, it's not [exact]." I said, "What the hell do you want?" I get as close as I can, but when you're recreating something, you gotta work from an old print of your stuff, and I tried blowin' 'em up, and that doesn't do any good, 'cause they were in color. So you gotta draw everything from scratch. So maybe you forget a little thing in the fold, or something, but the conception was there. Everything was there. Then I color with inks, getting the color just right and whatnot. It was fun for a while. [It's] a lot of work, though. It's not easy.

**TLC:** *Do you remember a period there in the early Seventies when Jack Kirby was*

he says, "Oh, Al, we bought that already." You bought it? I gave it personally to this guy as a favor, 'cause he bought a lot of my stuff. He said, "Oh, we bought that." So when these guys send me nice letters, and they say, "Oh, Mr. Plastino, blah blah blah... I'd love one of your things, but I can't afford the price," I say, "Look: I only have a few, and I have to hold onto them for my grandchildren." I know they're gonna sell 'em. I know.

I got stung so many times. They say, "Oh, no, no, no..." but it winds up they sell 'em, so I put a price on 'em. I said, "That's it. You want 'em, that's the price." I don't believe 'em. I don't believe 'em anymore. [Just] tell me the truth. Say, "I'd love to buy your stuff. I'm in the business of reselling them. Give me a fair price," and that's it. Be honest. But I guess they just don't [care]. So I just said, "The hell with everything." I just don't answer the letters anymore.

**TLC:** *How did you get into recreations?*

**AP:** I went to one of those conventions, which I hated. One of these cartoon conventions? I sat there and I was giving my sketch and my autograph for nothing. There's a guy getting twenty-five dollars a piece for [his] next to me. I said, "Hey, what the hell's going on here?" and he

said, "Al, you could get money..." I said, "I'm not here to make money on my signature." In those days, you weren't allowed to sign on stuff, but all these kids knew what I did. The way I drew my folds, the way I drew Lois... they knew exactly who [did what]. Now, everything is signed. They have about five signatures on the original works now. They got everything in there. But in those days, you weren't allowed to sign on your artwork.

But it was a rat race. I never went back to a convention. They wanna wine and dine you to go to a convention. One guy, he musta called me and said, "Without you, there won't be a convention." I said, "Well, I'm not coming if you're not gonna pay me." I said, "Look, I don't want to go. You want me to go, you gotta pay me." "Well, we don't pay." I said, "Well, forget it then."

You know what peeves me off? These guys that run 'em, they make a lot of money. I said [to them], "You're getting paid, and you want these top [artists to show up for nothing]." A stupid ballplayer gets all kinds of money

*The first appearance of the Legion Clubhouse, from* **Adventure Comics #247.** Superboy and the Legion of Super-Heroes TM and © DC Comics.

*working for DC and you were called in to redraw some of his faces?*

**AP:** Yeah, I would do that once in a while. I remember bringing it in. I said, "What the hell are they bringing me this [for]?" That's another pain in the neck. You gotta redo a face over a body. You have to paste a piece of paper over it, [and] redraw it. Yeah, I would do that from time to time.

**TLC:** *Who asked you to do that?*

**AP:** Carmine took over at that time. I was working with Carmine, and [he] started that crazy panel stuff... you know, big panel, lots of action? I worked with Carmine for a while. Maybe it was Carmine. I don't know. Carmine's a nice guy. I got along with [him]. He understood me. He would say, "Al, excuse me, but..." He would apologize first. [*laughs*] He'd say, "Could you do this for me?" and I'd say, "Sure."

A sample of the artist's illustration work, courtesy of Plastino.

You know, I'm the type of guy, if a guy treats me like a person, not like a piece of dirt, I'll do anything for them. But those bastards up at [DC]... they [didn't know] who the hell they were. The guys would be shaking in their boots. I mean, actually shaking. It's like, "God forbid I do something wrong. He's gonna fire me." And there was always somebody at your back who wanted your job. The guys would say, "Al, we got a guy here that will do the page for ten dollars less than yours." I said, "Well, hire him! Hire him! What are you telling me for?" "Well, we don't want to do that, Al, but, you know...." I said, "Hire the guy. What the hell do you want from me?"

[Gil] Kane? He used to hang around the studio when we had the studio on Lexington Avenue. He was a young kid when he used to come up. Yeah, he was a bloodsucker. He'd bloodsuck ya, he'd stab you in the back, 'cause he tried to get "Superman" from me at one time, they told me later on. I said, "Hey, hire him! What the hell do you want from me? If you think he can do a better job, hire him."

**TLC:** *When you look back at your career, is there any particular part of it that you're more proud of than others?*

**AP:** Yeah, Snoopy! [*laughs*] Oh, I enjoyed that. And, of course, **Ferd'nand**. I loved **Ferd'nand**. And then I worked [on **Nancy**]. I told you when Ernie was dying, I did the Sunday page. There's a story there... boy, they must regret it to this day. I was doing it in his style—which was tough. His stuff looks simple as hell, but he was a real German craftsman, and to draw Nancy's head, I used to hold my breath. Anyway, I got his style down pretty good. This guy was a tough guy [to follow]. They hired a guy up at United Features—a younger guy—to do it because they figured they were gonna change the style. And it laid an egg. It lasted a year and just died. And that was the only time I was ever fired from a job, [but] in a nice way.

I really enjoyed doing that, too, 'cause I knew Ernie very well, and then when he passed away, they hired these two editors, a woman and another guy at United Features [who were] real jerks. [They said,] "We gotta change the strip, modernize it." So they hired this guy from California, who could write pretty good, but would never draw Nancy and Sluggo in the full figure. It was always three quarters. And it was grotesque! I mean, **Nancy** was a style, like the old style [of] the old comics, which was successful. The guy made a fortune. And they changed it. I told 'em, "You know, it's none of my business, but you're gonna kill the strip." "Oh, no, no, no. We know what we're doing." I said, "Okay." And that was the only time I was let go, [but] in a nice way. And that was it. That was the only bad taste I had with the syndicate. Those people are not there anymore.

A watercolor by Al Plastino. Courtesy of the artist.
© 2003 Al Plastino.

United Features, I got along well with Jim Freeman up there. I really got along with them. In fact, I was instrumental in getting **Peanuts** started in United Features, 'cause they used to ask my opinion. They'd get new strips in, and it was called **Little People**. Jim Freeman called me and he said, "Al, we've got a strip here we're not sure of. I like it, but four of the other guys don't like it." So I looked at it, and I said, "Yeah, I think it's pretty cute. It's fresh, it's different." He said, "What do you think?" and I said, "Yeah, I think it's [good]." Boy, was that a decision they made! A big decision they made! They made a fortune on that. They're still making a fortune on the reruns.

**TLC:** *What are you doing now?*

**AP:** What I'm doing now is really painting. I exhibit out East. I sell some of my artwork. I like watercolors. I'm doing a watercolor right now looking out of my window at a snow scene. I also donate original drawings of Superman and Batman for auctions at golf outings and raise a lot of money for charities, churches, and cancer funds. That's what I'm doing now.

A recent self-portrait by the artist.
© 2003 Al Plastino.

**SIMMS LIBRARY**
**ALBUQUERQUE ACADEMY**

# Jerry Siegel

In lieu of an interview with Jerry Siegel himself, what follows is an article which attempts to cover all the aspects of his career, including those both Super and otherwise. Special thanks go out to Bob Hughes for providing a copy of Siegel's 1975 press release, and to Phil Yeh for giving further insight into the events surrounding Siegel's legal woes.

Jerome Siegel was born on October 17, 1914 in Cleveland, Ohio. One of six children, Siegel attended Glenville High School, where he met his best friend and Superman collaborator, Joe Shuster. Shuster and his family had moved to Cleveland from Canada years earlier, and the two met in 1931 while both were seventeen years old. They were drawn together by their love of the science-fiction genre, made popular by the pulp magazines and comic strips of the day.

At age fourteen Siegel had begun a science-fiction fanzine called **Cosmic Stories**. Although it was unsuccessful, it bears the distinction of being one of the earliest, if not the earliest, science-fiction fanzine. Later on, Siegel would launch another science-fiction fanzine, this time with Shuster as art editor, called simply **Science Fiction**. It was more of a success than its predecessor, and featured contributions by Forrest Ackerman in addition to the two teenagers.

But not everyone was convinced of the merits of the science-fiction genre. When a teacher at Siegel's high school noticed his literary talents, she encouraged him to write serious fiction, and not the juvenile fantasies which he had been engaged in writing. "Well, I like this kind of stuff, and that's why I write it," he responded, and continued to write to please himself.

Inspired by **Detective Dan**, one of the very first comic books, Siegel and Shuster sent a comic book featuring their creation to **Dan**'s publisher in Chicago. After the publisher rejected it, a distraught Shuster tore up the submission, leaving only the cover intact. "We had a great character," said Siegel, "and were determined it would be published."

One night in 1934, Siegel awoke with his mind filled with ideas for his character. Said Siegel, "...it was so hot that I had trouble falling asleep. I passed the time by trying to come up with the dramatic elements of the comic strip. One premise I had already conceived came back to me, but in sharper focus.

"The story would begin with [Superman] as a child on far-off planet Krypton. Like the others of that world, [he] had super-powers. [His] scientist-father was mocked and denounced by the Science Council. They did not believe his claim that Krypton would soon explode from internal stresses.

"Convinced that his prediction was valid, the boy's father had been constructing a model rocket ship. As the planet began to perish, the baby's parents knew its end was close. There was not space enough for three people in the small model craft. They put the baby into it. The mother chose to remain on the doomed planet with the man she loved, and die with him. Tearfully, hoping that their baby boy would survive, they launched the craft toward the planet Earth. Shortly, Krypton exploded and its millions of inhabitants were destroyed.

"On Earth, the super-tyke was found and adopted by a couple. They loved him and taught him to conceal his super-secret from the world. They told him that someday he must use his incredible abilities to aid those less gifted than he. And he would fight for justice, too!

"Very early the next morning, I didn't bother to eat. I ran all the way, twelve blocks, to Joe's apartment where he lived with his family. Joe read the script. Instant approval. He loved the new 'Superman' format... Filled with high inspiration, Joe sat down at his drawing board and began making pencil sketches."

But Superman was not created entirely out of whole cloth. "At the time that we became interested in the comics field," Siegel recalls, "the two outstanding adventure strips were **Buck Rogers** and **Tarzan**. I yearned to be another Edgar Rice Burroughs. His creations Tarzan and John Carter of Mars really got to me in those days long before the expression 'far out' came into existence. I read enormous quantities of eerie-hero oriented pulp magazines like **The Shadow**. Joe and I haunted movies, often cashing in milk bottles to finance getting past theater box-offices. Seated side-by-side in uncomfortable theater seats, we ate popcorn and absorbed 'B movies' galore along with 'A production' films. I was especially strongly impressed by the Warner Brothers movies with their social injustice messages."

It was those very messages which would become the theme of Superman's early adventures. Unlike other heroes who would follow, Superman preoccupied his time combating everyday villains—bank robbers, crooked sports figures, wealthy but indifferent members of society—and not the costumed villains which would make heroes such as Batman famous. Superman would also share a common trait with the heroes of Edgar Rice Burroughs, whom Siegel so admired: like Tarzan and John Carter before him, Superman was not of his world.

The pair then proceeded to attempt to sell their creation as a comic strip.

*Two names which will forever be linked together: Jerry Siegel (top) and Joe Shuster (above).*

Unfortunately for the duo, the established syndicates were not interested in what they had to offer. According to the Bell syndicate, "We are in the market only for strips likely to have the most extraordinary appeal, and we do not feel **Superman** gets into that category." United Features called it, "...an immature piece of work, attractive because of its freshness and naïveté, but this is likely to wear off after the feature runs for a while." Esquire Features cautioned, "Pay a little attention to actual drawing... Yours seems crude and hurried."

Undaunted, the pair continued to attempt to sell their creation. Then in 1933, a curious thing happened: the modern comic book was born. McClure syndicate employee M.C. Gaines published **Funnies On Parade**, a collection of reprinted newspaper strips which sold for a dime. Two years later, Major Malcolm Wheeler-Nicholson founded National Allied Publications, later to become National Periodical Publications. Forced out of necessity to produce original material since Gaines had tied up the reprint rights to all the major strips, Wheeler-Nicholson published **New Fun Comics**, a comedic anthology title which would feature all-new material. Nicholson would soon add another all-new title to his line, and would even hire Siegel and Shuster to produce features for him. Recounts Siegel, "The Major offered to publish 'Superman' in one of his comics magazines. We turned down his offer because we wanted to place our favorite brainchild with a better organization."

Mounting debts would soon force Nicholson to sell shares of National to Harry Donenfeld, the distributor of the company's products. The first title added to the line after Donenfeld became co-owner was **Detective Comics**, the magazine from which the company would eventually derive its name. Siegel and Shuster would collaborate on "Slam Bradley" on the title before their big break came in the form of **Action Comics** #1. Sheldon Mayer, an editor at the McClure Syndicate, loved the idea of Superman, and attempted to persuade his boss, M.C. Gaines, to publish it. Gaines refused, but in 1937 when National Periodical Publications was looking for features to fill a new magazine, they approached Gaines for material. At the urging of Mayer, Gaines sent over "Superman." Remembers Siegel, "Soon, **Detective**'s editor Vin Sullivan informed me that of all the new comics features I had submitted for consideration, they liked 'Superman' the best."

What happened next is the source of

legend. "Joe cut and pasted the four weeks of 'Superman' newspaper format daily strips onto 13 comic-book-sized pages. He and I added a promotional final panel on the last page. It's blurb read: 'And so begins the startling adventures of the most sensational strip character of all time: Superman!' Joe and I thoroughly believed that blurb."

It was then that Siegel's long-term problems began. Assured that they would be taken care of, Siegel and Shuster signed over the rights to Superman for $130.00. Almost immediately, tensions between the creators and the publisher ensued. Upon learning of "Superman's" success, Siegel inquired about an increase in page rate for both Shuster and himself. At the time they were both earning a combined ten dollars a page, and Siegel felt that they were worth more. Jack Liebowitz, Donenfeld's partner, replied, "Frankly, when I got through reading [your letter], it took my breath away. I did not anticipate that when I asked you to come to New York to discuss this matter of newspaper syndication, that you would want to take advantage of this visit and try to boost your price on 'Superman'." He went on to say, "...you are grossly exaggerating the importance of 'Superman.' Don't forget that there are 64 pages in the magazine and that there isn't any magazine being published today that can sell on the basis of any one feature, whether that feature is 'Popeye,' 'Mickey Mouse,' or any other top-notch strip, and if I thought for a moment that our magazine depended on your strip, I would certainly make every effort to avoid any such situation." In reference to a poll conducted within the pages of **Action Comics** in which readers were asked to identify their favorite feature, Liebowitz said, "...only 30% have designated 'Superman' as their favorite, the balance being scattered

A portrait of the Silver Age Legion of Super-Heroes by artist Jeffrey Moy. Courtesy of Kevin McConnell. Art © 2003 Jeff Moy; Legion of Super-Heroes TM and © DC Comics.

among the other features in the magazine, so come off your high horse."

But Liebowitz didn't stop there. He continued with, "Is it possible that because we treated you like a human being, you suddenly got a swelled head? It may also be that you are under the mistaken delusion that because you came into town to a large organization, which gave you time and showed you every courtesy which would be accorded to any big personage, you construed all these actions in the wrong light, that we were trying to get something from you. The case is distinctly the reverse. We were trying to give you, an inexperienced young man, the benefit of our experience and good will, in order that you get ahead in your ambition to become somebody in the comic field.

"Don't get the idea that everyone in New York is a 'gyp' and a 'highbinder' and because you are treated as a gentleman and an equal, not only by ourselves but by Mr. Gaines and the McClure people, that we are seeking to take advantage of you."

Siegel continued to work on "Superman" until he was drafted into the Army in July, 1943. Up until that point, the comic book

*The front cover to* Adventure Comics #498 *by Gil Kane. Courtesy of Miki Annamanthadoo.* Legion of Super-Heroes and the Challengers of the Unknown TM and © DC Comics.

adventures of Superman (including both the daily and the Sunday newspaper strips) had been produced by Siegel and Shuster's studio in Cleveland. Recalled Siegel, "I was under contract because I had signed a ten-year contract; this was one of the things that happened as time went by. While I was in the service, [National] started ghosting the 'Superman' scripts, because obviously I couldn't write them while I was away in the service. At the same time, they took over Joe's end of it. Joe and I had a studio in Cleveland; Joe had artists working for him. When I went into the service, Joe and his staff went to New York, or at least Joe and some of them did. I wasn't around, and eventually most of Joe's workers worked directly for National instead of for Joe. When I came out of the service, I wanted to set up our studio again and operate the way we had before. Incidentally, before I went into the service, I wrote that I hoped they wouldn't take advantage of [my absence] and try to take away the production of 'Superman' from Joe and me, and that's exactly what they did turn around and do, or attempt to do, because when I came out, I tried to get things as they were before, where all the material would come solely from Joe and me, and I encountered great resistance on that, and our troubles were on."

Siegel's problems didn't end there. "During the time I was in the Army overseas, and in no position to protect my interests, Detective Comics, Inc. published 'Superboy,' which I had earlier created and submitted to Detective Comics, Inc, the predecessor corporation of National. Detective and Liebowitz published

'Superboy' without any notification or compensation to me, thus precipitating the Westchester action."

Dissatisfied with their treatment by the company, Siegel and Shuster decided to sue. In 1947, Judge Addison Young ruled in their favor concerning Superboy, writing, "It is quite clear to me... that in publishing 'Superboy,' Detective Comics, Inc. acted illegally. I cannot accept defendant's view that Superboy was in reality Superman. I think Superboy was a separate and distinct entity. In having published Superboy without right, plaintiffs are entitled to an injunction preventing such publication and under the circumstances I believe the defendants should account as to the income received from such publication and that the plaintiffs should be given an opportunity to prove any damages they have sustained on account thereof."

Siegel and Shuster decided to appeal the decision, not because they disagreed with the court's ruling on Superboy, but because it failed to deliver to them the one thing which they really wanted—Superman. They both eventually settled out of court as mounting legal bills threatened to bankrupt them both. They received an undisclosed settlement, and DC retained full legal rights to Superman, Superboy, and all related characters. In 1948, with their contracts expired, Siegel and Shuster failed to secure further work from

Detective Comics, Inc., and their names were taken off the features which they had begun.

The pair would collaborate on another character, **Funnyman**, but it would fail to be a success. The creators of Superman then went their separate ways, with Siegel becoming an editor at Ziff-Davis (and later the comics director there) and Shuster attempting a career as a freelance artist. Neither job lasted very long, and as the 1950s replaced the 1940s, their descent into hardship began.

In 1958, unbeknownst to Siegel, his wife Joanne met with DC publisher Jack Liebowitz and petitioned him on behalf of her husband. Liebowitz was uninterested in providing further employment to the creator until Siegel's wife threatened to take her husband's plight public. "Do you really want to see in the newspaper, 'Creator of Superman Starves to Death?'" she asked. Fearing the negative publicity, Liebowitz agreed to allow Siegel to return as writer of the Man of Steel's adventures, although this time he would receive no by-line or noticeable credit. To those not in the know, it would still be as if he was no longer associated with the character.

*The front cover to* Adventure Comics #499 *by Gil Kane, featuring another previously unseen Challengers of the Unknown portion. From the collection of Miki Annamanthadoo.* Legion of Super-Heroes and the Challengers of the Unknown TM and © DC Comics.

Things had changed by the time Siegel returned to DC. For one thing, the Silver Age of comics had begun. Under the helm of editor Mort Weisinger, many of the elements of the Silver Age Superman had begun to appear, including the Fortress of Solitude, the Phantom Zone, and the Bizarros. Siegel would be employed writing various stories for the entire "Superman Family" of titles, including *Jimmy Olsen*, *Lois Lane*, *Superboy*, and the Man of Steel himself. He would also return to the *Superman* newspaper strip (both daily and weekend versions), and it was during this period that he wrote two of his most critically acclaimed Superman stories: the original "Death of Superman" in *Superman* #149 (Oct. 1961) and "Superman's Return to Krypton," which appeared in *Superman* #141, (Nov. 1960).

Shortly after his return to DC, Siegel also found himself writing a feature which had not existed during his previous incarnation with the company: "Tales of The Legion of Super-Heroes." The Legion first appeared in *Adventure Comics* #247 (April, 1958), and was launched by writer Otto Binder and artist Al Plastino. With its second appearance, Siegel immediately became its author. He would continue to write the adventures of the Legionnaires, barring runs by Edmond Hamilton and an occasional issue by Binder, until he left DC again, this time in 1966. Before his departure, he was responsible for the creation of no fewer than a dozen Legionnaires, including Ultra Boy, Brainiac 5, Phantom Girl, Colossal Boy, Invisible Kid, Chameleon Boy, Triplicate Girl, Shrinking Violet, and Sun Boy. Some of Siegel's creations, like Matter-Eater Lad and Bouncing Boy, reflected his interest in comedy, and were added to the Legion to provide an element of humor. Siegel would also write the adventures of Supergirl in *Action Comics*, another feature which had been launched by Binder and Plastino and which was derived from Siegel's continuity.

Siegel again sued National Comics in 1966, claiming that he had not signed away the copyright renewal rights to Superman which had recently become available. Under the existing copyright law, a creator was entitled to do so twenty-eight years after a property's creation, and Siegel felt that the out of court settlement which he had signed years earlier did not preempt his rights. The courts did not see it his way, however, and in 1968 they ruled against both himself and Shuster. The very act of filing the suit had put an end to his second career at DC, and with it he was forced to find work elsewhere. For a brief period he worked for MLJ Comics as part

*Chameleon Boy and Proty by former **Legion** inker Bob McLeod. From the collection of Kevin McConnell. Art © 2003 Bob McLeod; Chameleon Boy and Proty TM and © DC Comics.*

of the revival of their super-hero line, and was even credited with the creation of the *Mighty Crusaders*. But MLJ's return to super-heroics was short-lived, and Siegel was again forced to find work wherever he could get it.

Siegel and Shuster appealed the decision, and continued to appeal it until early 1975, at which point they stopped short of bringing it all the way to the Supreme Court. When asked why they abandoned legal action, Siegel responded, "We were induced to drop our case and not take it to the Supreme Court because National had indicated that if we would do that, that they would decide whether or not they could do something for Joe and I, and so we figured that after all we had been through, we would take a gamble and trust

to the generosity and good intentions of National. Many years have passed and we thought perhaps there might be a higher level of thinking up there..."

In October of '75, after more than seven months had passed since he had been led to believe that some sort of financial recompense may have been forthcoming, Siegel could maintain his silence no longer and issued a press release to the media chronicling both his and Shuster's plight. Motivated in part by the news that DC had been paid three million dollars for the film rights to Superman and that the movie itself had been budgeted at fifteen million dollars, Siegel revealed that, "Joe is partially blind. My health is not good. We are both 61 years old. Most of our lives, during Superman's great success, has been spent in want... As far as Joe and I are concerned, we have been victimized by evil men and a selfish, evil company which callously ruined us and appears to be willing to abandon us in our old age, though our creation Superman had made and continues to make millions for them." In his cover letter which accompanied the press release, Siegel stated, "I, Jerry Siegel, the co-originator of Superman, put a curse on the Superman movie! I hope it super-bombs. I hope loyal Superman fans stay away from it in droves. I hope the whole world, becoming aware of the stench that surrounds Superman, will avoid the movie like a plague.

"Why am I putting a curse on this movie based upon my creation Superman? Because cartoonist Joe Shuster and I, who co-originated Superman together, will not get one cent from the Superman super-movie deal."

Siegel took it a step further when he said, "The publishers of Superman comic books, National Periodical Publications, Inc., killed my days, murdered my nights, choked my happiness, strangled my career. I consider National's executives economic murderers, money-mad monsters. If they, and the executives of Warner Communications, which owns National,

had consciences, they would right the wrongs inflicted on Joe Shuster and me.

"A curse on the Superman movie!"

Reaction to Siegel's comments was not immediate. In fact, when Phil Yeh, publisher of the West Coast newspaper **Cobblestone** approached Siegel for an interview, he was surprised to find out that he was the only one who had responded to the release. Remembers Yeh, "I recall that he told me that he sent out 400 press releases and I was the only person who called him for the story. After we broke the story, the **LA Times** picked it up, and the rest, as they say is history... Jerry was very, very happy and grateful that we called to interview him and I recall that he was very clear when I asked him if other folks had called from the few hundred press releases that he sent to them. His response that not one single reporter called totally amazed me."

After the **LA Times** article, Siegel's fellow creators rallied to his defense, spearheaded by Jerry Robinson and Neal Adams. "[A]t that time," said Adams, "I was President of the Academy of Comic Book Arts. ...Essentially what I and the guys in my studio did was, we decided that

day that we would make an effort that these two guys would at least be treated reasonably at the end of whatever effort that might be. [It] turned out to be about three and a half months long and used up a tremendous amount of energy in the studio, but it worked out fine." Robinson, a past President of the National Cartoonist Society, said, "I took it immediately to the National Cartoonist Society. We wrote a resolution. We held a press conference. I took it to the Magazine Guild and got a resolution backed by them. I wrote organizations around the world. We really orchestrated a whole national campaign—international campaign, actually. I think without that we maybe wouldn't even have got the settlement that we did."

The settlement in question consisted of an annuity whose amount is reported to have initially been $20,000 a year for each creator, and which rose over the years to a reported six-figure sum by the time of Siegel's death in 1996. In addition, both creators were given health insurance for the rest of their lives, and their names were restored to the Superman legend in all media, not only that of comic books. In fact, when the **Superman** movie was released in 1978, both Siegel and Shuster were given screen credits as the creators of Superman.

In 1983, in a piece celebrating Superman's 45th anniversary, the wounds which Siegel mentioned earlier appeared to have been healed. He even went so far as to thank former enemies Liebowitz and Donenfeld, whose "...comic book publishing and distribution foresight and ability played a major role in boosting [Superman], after... years of languishing,

*The complete Silver Age Legion of Super-Heroes, as depicted by Neal Adams. Jerry Siegel co-created twelve Legionnaires, all of whom appear here. Courtesy of Richard Martines.* Characters TM and © DC Comics.

A panel from Siegel's *The Starling* by Val Mayerik.
The Starling TM and © 2003 the estate of Jerry Siegel.

life, according to Evanier, "Jerry was also receiving honors that meant a lot to him; at the time, a lovely letter from President Clinton and the issuance of a Superman postage stamp in Canada (Shuster was of Canadian origin). Jerry had the note and a prototype of the stamp framed side-by-side on a small table next to his favorite chair in the living room... and that's how I remember Jerry. He was sitting in an easy chair, without a trace of anger about him, looking at the framed items and smiling."

In the end, Siegel had made peace with his creation. After all that time, surely he deserved no less.

Superboy TM and © 2003 DC Comics.

into the bigtime." He again became active in the comic book community, attending conventions, writing letters to fanzines, and even applying for work with new up-and-coming companies. That same year saw Siegel's "The Starling," a story about a child fathered by an alien, published by Eclipse Comics. Said Eclipse publisher Dean Mullaney, "Jerry's one of the most enthusiastic people I've ever encountered. He's written the script for the first two issues of *The Starling*'s own book, and we don't even have the title on our schedule yet!" According to David Singer, then-publisher of Deluxe Comics, "The biggest thrill I've had so far was when I got a letter from Jerry Siegel, who co-created Superman, asking us if we could use his services. What I loved was the opening in his letter, which said that he was one of the co-creators of the character known as Superman, one of the best-selling characters in comic-book history. He wrote it in such a formal fashion, as if I was some 80-year-old publisher who didn't know that my company published comic books and that I wouldn't know who Jerry Siegel was and who Superman was. I had his letter framed over my desk. I just love that letter."

Siegel himself, in a letter to **David Anthony Kraft's Comics Interview**, said it best when he commented, "Writers, working in their lonely little room, are always interested in learning how other writers (and artists) manage to do their very best work. **Comics Interview** is always interesting and sends me charging back to the typewriter, all fired-up. Since I'm 70 years old, that's quite a compliment..."

What is perhaps most overlooked about Jerry Siegel's career, and is overshadowed

by all of the legal struggles which he had to endure throughout his lifetime, is the reason why those struggles came to be in the first place. Jerry Siegel was a writer, and throughout his career, even in those moments when he was not employed by DC Comics (and even before then), he would write. On occasion it would involve topic matter similar to that upon which he had made his reputation. On others, it may have involved something entirely different, such as when he was writing "Huey, Dewie, and Louie" stories for an Italian publisher. Throughout all of his legal battles and lean times, Siegel continued to write. The fact that he made a return to comics, however brief, in the 1980s shows that his imagination was still active, and that the desire to form whole worlds from said imagination was still there.

About a month before he died, Siegel was visited by comics historian Mark Evanier at his Los Angeles home. At that point in his

Flights of fancy: the Space Age kept pace with the developments of science-fiction writers such as Siegel. From the NASA archives.

# George Papp

*Superboy places Mon-El in the Phantom Zone in a pair of panels from **Superboy** #89.*
Superboy and Mon-El TM and © DC Comics.

George Papp was born on January 20, 1916, and began his career by drawing filler pages and cartoons in early issues of **Action Comics**. He was one of the first artists to work for DC (then National) Comics, and was perhaps best known for creating Green Arrow with newly-hired editor Mort Weisinger in 1941. With an exception for the war years, Papp would continue to draw the adventures of the emerald archer uninterrupted until 1958, at which point he would assume the regular penciling duties on **Superboy**.

Papp would also become the semi-regular artist on Superboy's appearances in **Adventure Comics**, and it was in that capacity that he got to draw some of the earliest appearances of the Legion of Super-Heroes. He was the second interior artist to ever portray the group, and the original three Legionnaires were first drawn in their traditional Silver Age costumes in his first Legion assignment, which was the group's second appearance. He would also pencil the first appearances of Star Boy, Mon-El, and Legion reservists Kid Psycho and Insect Queen, and was the artist of record on Insect Queen's induction into the Legion in **Adventure Comics** #355.

Throughout the course of the 1960s, Papp would return to the Legion on several occasions, including Jim Shooter's first Legion script (albeit third one published) in **Adventure Comics** #348, as well as the first appearance of Orion the Hunter in **Adventure Comics** #358. He would also continue to draw **Superboy** until 1968, for an impressive ten year run on the title. Solo stories featuring the Boy of Steel illustrated by Papp would also continue to appear in **Adventure Comics** for much of the decade until "Tales of the Legion of Super-Heroes" expanded to fill the entire book.

In 1968, Papp was one of many longtime DC freelancers who found it difficult to acquire work under the company's new editorial regime. He left comics entirely to pursue other venues, mainly those of commercial art. Although he was no longer producing new material for the industry, stories illustrated by Papp continued to be reprinted by DC well into the Eighties, and are still reprinted today as part of their DC Archives program. Ironically, it is his work on the "Legion of Super-Heroes" which has been reprinted the most, overlooking his substantial body of work on both "Green Arrow" and the solo stories of Superboy. George Papp died on August 8, 1989.

*Papp drew the Legion's second appearance in **Adventure Comics** #267, during which the traditional Silver Age costumes of the Legionnaires first appeared.*
Legion of Super-Heroes TM and © DC Comics.

# Jim Mooney

An industry veteran whose career has spanned over sixty years, Jim Mooney was one of the first people to be interviewed for this volume. Living up to his "Gentleman" nickname, he braved a poor phone connection and other technical difficulties to be interviewed from his Florida home on April 29, 2002. The following interview was conducted and transcribed by Glen Cadigan, and copyedited by Mooney.

**TLC:** *How old were you when you first started drawing comics?*

**JM:** I think I was about twenty-one. I had been working in Los Angeles, and I met Mort Weisinger through a friend of mine, Henry Kuttner, who was a sci-fi writer.

**TLC:** *You met Mort that early?*

**JM:** Uh-huh. He came out, and we showed him around. About that time I realized that the comic field looked as if it was getting pretty active. I had a good job, but I wanted to get into drawing. I decided to make the trek to New York, and I wasn't really ready for it [chuckles].

I knew Mort, and I had some pretty good contacts, but it was probably quite a few years later—I think it was four, five years later before I was working for DC. I tried all the different firms at that time. I worked for Eisner and Iger, and I worked for Fox, and then finally later on I worked for Fiction House, but about 1947 I realized that they were looking for somebody to do **Batman**, and I went up to the office and latched onto it. I showed them my samples. They weren't too impressed, but they gave me a script to try out with, and that worked out pretty well.

**TLC:** *Weren't you drawing funny animals for Marvel at that time?*

**JM:** Yes, around '42, '43 I worked for

Timely Comics, and from '47, '48 on I worked for DC almost exclusively. Then I switched over to Marvel about 1969.

**TLC:** *Somewhere along the way you ended up drawing "Robin."*

**JM:** Yup. Later on. That would be on **Star-Spangled** [**Comics**].

**TLC:** *And right about the time "Robin" wrapped up on **Star-Spangled**, you started drawing "Tommy Tomorrow."*

**JM:** Oh, that was [laughs] a filler. Yeah, I liked "Tommy Tomorrow" very, very much.

**TLC:** *Then back around '58, '59, they shipped "Tommy Tomorrow" over to **World's Finest**, and, of course, they replaced it with "Supergirl" in **Action Comics**.*

**JM:** That was—let's see, '59, I think, that I started "Supergirl." It was a nine-year stint.

**TLC:** *Do you remember the circumstances around that?*

**JM:** They just wanted to try me out on it. I was doing quite a few things for DC at that time. I was doing **House of Mystery** and quite a few different things, and Mort thought, "Maybe we'll give Jim a shot at this."

I had suggested doing something like that a long time before they actually came up with a "Supergirl" script. Unfortunately, the first one they gave me was the one that Al Plastino did, and I had to ape that at first, and I really didn't like it. At the same time I had a studio—an art service—in Hollywood,

California, and I was busy as hell at the time [laughs], but I didn't want to neglect doing it. Consequently, that first year and a half, two years, some of that was my work. I had other people working with me, so we projected a lot of it. It was a joint effort, and I think if you notice you'll go through some of that stuff, [and] it's not that great, that first archival edition. So I think it improved a lot through the years when I finally got on it myself totally.

**TLC:** *Do you know why they got Al Plastino to draw the first appearance of Supergirl?*

*Top: the artist in an undated photo, circa the '70s. Above: Still an active artist, Mooney often provides commissions for fans, including the one featured here. From the artist's collection.*

Art © 2003 Jim Mooney; Supergirl and the Legion of Super-Heroes TM and © DC Comics.

*Supergirl and Tommy Tomorrow, two features which Mooney illustrated for DC Comics. From the collection of Peter Hansen.* Art © 2003 Jim Mooney; Supergirl and Tommy Tomorrow TM and © DC Comics.

**JM:** Plastino was a house artist. He did Superman, he worked for them, and they wanted it to have that look. They never did like the way I did Superman, anyway. [*laughs*] When I started, Mort said that I made Superman look not quite "super" enough. Not masculine enough. [*laughs*] So occasionally they'd have somebody—Curt Swan or Al Plastino or whoever was in the bullpen at the time—work over my Superman faces.

**TLC:** *You spent a long time on* **Action Comics**. *As a matter of fact, that issue Plastino drew introducing Supergirl [#252] broke a streak of yours. You had been drawing it continuously since around issue 200, and you continued to draw it almost continuously right up until you left DC.*

**JM:** Yeah, I drew it for almost nine years, and I think it changed through the years. Hopefully it changed for the better. 'Cause I had the time. You see, when I came to New York I was drawing "Supergirl" at the time, and I gave up my studio in Hollywood. Mort's incentive was, "We'll give you more work," and that was when I did "The Legion of Super-Heroes." That was the extra work that I was given. Actually, it was more of an incentive to come back to New York to work more

closely with Mort. And that wasn't always [a pleasure.] [*laughs*]

**TLC:** *So before you were drawing "Supergirl," you were working from Hollywood?*

**JM:** Yeah, I had an art service right opposite from Grauman's Chinese theater, right on Hollywood Boulevard. So I handled just about everything that came in the door. [*laughs*]

**TLC:** *Wasn't that unusual in those days, to work from outside of New York?*

**JM:** Well, it was. Actually, I really didn't think that I would make it last that long. But I mentioned to Mort, I said "I'd really like to work out in Hollywood for a while. I'd like to visit my folks, and would it be all right if I took a couple of months and worked out there?" And he said "Yeah, sure. Just send the stuff in." [*laughs*] And it just dragged on and on and on. I mean, week after week, month after month, year after year. I was out there ten years—no, I shouldn't say that. I was out there, I guess eight or nine years before I made any trip to New York to make actual contact again with the others at the office. And it was just toward the very last year that I decided that I would take the offer to come to New York and work more closely with Mort, because at the time there were a lot of things going on. I was going through a divorce, so I was happy to get out of the area! [*laughs*]

**TLC:** *Getting back to the Legion, you could say that you started drawing it almost by accident.*

**JM:** Well, actually, no, he assigned it to me. But it wasn't something I asked for. He wanted to give me extra work and said, "You want to do the Legion?" and I said, "Fine. Great. I've seen it before. I'd like to do it."

**TLC:** *I'm referring to the first time that you drew it in "Supergirl," when they made a guest appearance there.*

**JM:** That was, I think, when she met the Legionnaires.

**TLC:** *I don't know if you're aware of this, but you drew the first appearance of a number of Legionnaires.*

**JM:** Yeah, I did.

**TLC:** *Did you design them? Their costumes and such?*

**JM:** I drew them. Of course.

**TLC:** *So you came up with their character designs?*

**JM:** Oh yeah, I did the character designs. The costumes and everything.

**TLC:** *Did you maintain an interest in any of the Legionnaires which you had designed after you stopped drawing the Legion?*

*A recreation of the first meeting between Supergirl and Brainiac 5, from the collection of Kevin McConnell.*
Art © 2003 Jim Mooney; Supergirl and Brainiac 5 TM and © DC Comics.

**JM:** Well, I didn't want to pursue it any further, or anything like that, but I enjoyed doing it. It wasn't a series that I disliked in any way. Unlike "Dial 'H' for Hero." [*laughs*]

**TLC:** *You didn't like that?*

**JM:** [*laughs*] It was a pain in the butt.

**TLC:** *How so?*

**JM:** Well, I had to create three or four new characters, costumes and all, every issue.

**TLC:** *I was going to ask you about that.*

**JM:** Yeah, it was a nuisance. It was time-consuming. I had to produce every month, and come up with all those different characters. So it was time-consuming. At first it was kind of fun, but after a while it got to be a real drag! [*laughs*]

**TLC:** *Who was your editor on "Dial 'H' for Hero"?*

**JM:** That was Jack Schiff.

**TLC:** *Yes, because the look of the comic was entirely different from your "Supergirl" work.*

**JM:** Yeah, that was Jack Schiff. Jack and I worked together. Jack could be a little irascible at times, but he was okay to work with. I worked with Murray Boltinoff occasionally, George Kashdan—[*laughs*] of course Mort Weisinger. I never worked with Julie. Julie and I were friendly, but we never worked together.

**TLC:** *How well did you know the other artists who were working for Mort in those days?*

**JM:** Well, I knew Curt [Swan] fairly well. Curt was a nice guy. Whom else would you be thinking of?

**TLC:** *How about George Papp?*

**JM:** Yeah, I knew George. George was a real nice guy. I'd meet him in the bullpen occasionally. And Al Plastino. We weren't necessarily all that friendly. It wasn't any animosity; it's just we didn't necessarily see each other that often.

The same thing with Marvel. I'm asked that so often. "Oh, God, that must have been wonderful working at Marvel. It must have been a party all the time." And they were nice people—I loved working at Marvel in contrast to DC—but it was no big party. They thought that we were all in there having a big time. Well, hell, I never met John Buscema, or Sal Buscema. I

never met Gene Colan. All these guys that were working at the same time, I never met them. They weren't there at the time that I went into the office. Stan gave that impression that we were having one hell of a big ball there, and it was fun working there, believe me. Sometimes the sessions with Stan were hilarious. [*laughs*] I enjoyed them very much, but it wasn't as if we all got together. Occasionally we'd go for a few drinks or something like that, but it wasn't that much of a party game.

**TLC:** *Getting back to Supergirl, you said that you made some suggestion to them that they should do a character like Supergirl.*

**JM:** Well, I didn't call her Supergirl. I said, "Wouldn't it be nice to do some sort of super female character other than Wonder Woman?" I guess that was the remark I made.

**TLC:** *How long after that did Supergirl appear?*

**JM:** Oh, I'd say probably when I was assigned to it, it was probably a year or two later, at least.

**TLC:** *There was that one story before Supergirl appeared which they put it in the Archive. They called it the prototype story. Do you remember anything about that?*

**JM:** No, I didn't have anything to do with that. I know there was a prototype before I got the first strip, or got the first assignment, and the first issue that Al Plastino did, which was supposed to be my model. I really didn't like it particularly. I had a bad time with it.

**TLC:** *I understand that Mort sort of pinned you in, in the sense that he cramped your artistic style.*

**JM:** Well, he did. He insisted that I pattern a lot of it after Plastino. But again, I didn't

Another pair of Mooney's features meet: Robby Reed dials 'L' for "Legion of Super-Heroes" in this picture provided by the artist.
Art © 2003 Jim Mooney; Dial 'H' for Hero and the Legion of Super-Heroes TM and © DC Comics.

like it, and I had a couple of girls working with me in the studio, and we used to project a lot of this stuff, and sometimes they'd do some of the inking, I'd do some of the inking, so about the first two years there that was really not totally my work. Later on, when I got into it a little bit more heavily and did more of an illustrative style, Mort called me in one day, and he said, "Jim, are you doing this stuff?" He said, "Are you trying to make a million bucks [*laughs*], hiring somebody to do it for you?" And I said, "No, I was just trying to do it a little differently." And he said, "Well, don't do it any differently! Do it the way you did it before!" [*laughs*] Which was amusing as hell, but he'd get a little tough sometimes—to say the least.

**TLC:** *The Superman titles were selling extremely well back in those days.*

**JM:** Yeah.

**TLC:** *I guess he was afraid to tinker with success.*

**JM:** Yeah, they were making money. I've had a lot of people say, "Geez, 'Supergirl.' How come they kept that on?" And I realized that whether I liked it or not, or whether I thought I was doing a good job on it, or whether a lot of people thought I was or wasn't, they would not have kept me on it if it hadn't been selling, and selling well. So that was my attitude. I mean, I put up with an awful lot of flak from Mort. And after a while, it got to the point that I was just about ready to quit anyway.

**TLC:** *Around when was this?*

**JM:** Well, let's see: I went over to Marvel in '69. That was when they were trying to go for a more illustrative style with Neal Adams and Carmine Infantino. I'd say it

was probably a couple to three years before that. I came into the office one day and I went in to see Mort, and he waved me out—"I'm busy! I'm busy!"—so I walked in and talked to Jack Schiff, and I saw all the guys in the editor's bullpen, and Mort came in, and he was just fuming. I thought he almost swallowed his own cigar.

He said, "You're supposed to see me first!" and I said, "Mort, I did come to see you first, but you were busy," and so on, and he said "Well, after this you come to see me first! Otherwise, you're not doing 'Supergirl!'" And I said, "Mort, I've got news for you. I'm not doing 'Supergirl' anymore." [*laughs*]

And he was stunned. So I figured, that's it. He walked out in a real [huff]. He was angry as hell. And I was pissed. I was

annoyed. It was embarrassing. All the editors were saying, "Oh Jim, we'll find work for you. Don't worry about it. You lost 'Supergirl,' but it's okay." And I just figured, look, all right, I'll do something else. And I came in a couple of weeks later, and Mort walks down the hall, and he hands me a script just as if nothing had ever happened, and he said, "Here's your 'Supergirl' script." [*laughs*]

**TLC:** [*laughs*]

**JM:** [*laughs*] And I figured, "What the hell." I'm not going to say I'm not going to take it. I needed the money, I liked the strip at that time fairly well, so that was the way that happened. I was there a couple of more years before I moved over to Marvel. It was getting a little too uptight at DC.

**TLC:** *And over at Marvel they had a totally different way of making comics.*

**JM:** Oh, wonderful. Yeah, I remember that so fondly. I thought, "Gee, this is the way it should be." Relaxing and fun. It wasn't a big party thing or anything like that. It was always pleasant. You came into the office, and everybody was nice.

**TLC:** *You could say that Mort had a more adversarial style of editing. He was the boss, and he wanted people to know it.*

Supergirl auditions for the Legion in a take on the cover of **Adventure Comics #247**, seen here in both the original penciled version and inked by Bob McLeod. From the collection of Miki Annamanthadoo. Art © 2003 Jim Mooney; Supergirl and Legion of Super-Heroes TM and © DC Comics.

**JM:** Yeah. He used to play that game sometimes. "Today I'm going to be the bad father." "Today I'm going to be the good father." And I thought, "Geez, who the hell needs you for a father?" [*laughs*] But I shut my mouth.

**TLC:** *You were responsible for a lot of Legion firsts.*

**JM:** Yeah, that's true.

**TLC:** *You drew the first appearance of a lot of characters. You drew the first story which showed a Legion couple being married. You drew the first story in which the Legionnaires used their flight rings, and back in the Seventies when they were reprinting the "Legion" shortly, the very first story in the first issue was one of yours. They chose that to lead it off. I guess you didn't realize that you were such an important Legion artist!*

**JM:** [*laughs*] Well, I certainly didn't have any delusions of grandeur. [*laughs*] To me it was a job.

**TLC:** *And of course, back in those days you guys didn't think that people would still remember your work decades later.*

**JM:** Well, no, and we didn't even want our originals back in those days. They were shredding them, for God's sake. It never occurred to us that they might be worth any money. The only time that I ever got one back was when I needed it for reference, or some neighborhood kid asked for an original drawing, and I'd give it one. [*laughs*] But that stuff was being shredded. I remember going down in the freight elevator one time, and there were stacks of this stuff, and I'd ask, "Where is this stuff going?" "Aw, we're taking it down to the shredder." They just cut it up.

**TLC:** *Did you ever think about all the things you could have bought with the money you could've made from that art?*

**JM:** Well, I think now about some of the stuff I sold early on that was returned to me for rather ridiculous prices. I made my own price when I went to conventions. I sold all of my John Romita **Spider-Man** stuff to a collector whom you probably know, and I sold everything—Gil Kane, John Romita, John Romita, Jr.—the whole shebang. And some of those John Romita pages are going for pretty big prices, as you're well aware. I remember when John Romita was giving those Sunday **Spider-Man** pages away at conventions. My God, as a gift.

**TLC:** *If only you knew then how much they'd be worth years later.*

**JM:** It's kind of ironic, isn't it?

**TLC:** *When you went over to Marvel, you basically did more inking than drawing.*

**JM:** Well, that was primarily because I wanted to move to Florida, and I got a contract from Marvel. To fulfill the terms of my contract I had to take on more inking—finalizing and inking—than I'd liked, so I didn't get a chance to do as much full penciling as I would have preferred doing. But in the meantime I had ten good years. I didn't make a helluva lot of money, but I had a check coming in every couple of weeks, I had insurance, I had a savings plan, a lot of things that a lot of freelancers never had. It was a compensatory thing.

**TLC:** *Still, up to that point you had pretty much exclusively been a penciler. You'd ink your own stuff...*

**JM:** Yeah, I preferred inking my own stuff, of course. I enjoyed a lot of the work that I did. I did the penciling on **Ms. Marvel**. I had the great inking in Joe Sinnott, who was a great inker. And Frank Giocoia inked some of my stuff on **Spectacular Spider-Man**. And I did some **Sub-Mariner** stuff. I did a lot of stuff where I did a lot of my own inking, and I did mostly penciling with damn good inkers. But the majority of the stuff that I had to do were rather sloppy layouts, and I had to finalize and ink them and get them out on time, so it wasn't that satisfactory from my point of view.

**TLC:** *You did a lot of work with Spider-Man.*

**JM:** Yeah, I did. I did [**Marvel**] **Team-Up**, and I did a monthly feature for the Electric Company magazine **Spidey Super-Stories**. I did that one weekend every month. I certainly did my stint on Spider-Man, that's for sure.

**TLC:** *Do you think it's fair to say that you've handled more Spider-Man pages*

*Mooney also spent a considerable number of years at Marvel illustrating **Spider-Man** during the 1970s. From the collection of Brian Tidwell. Art © 2003 Jim Mooney; Spider-Man TM and © 2003 Marvel Characters, Inc.*

*than "Supergirl" pages?*

**JM:** Maybe I did turn out more **Spider-Man** pages than "Supergirl" pages, because it started out as six, eight, and then finally twelve [pages], I believe. Whereas the **Spider-Man** stuff was eighteen, twenty-two [pages], something like that. So I probably did do more **Spider-Man** pages. [*laughs*]

**TLC:** *I'd like to lighten the mood a little bit and ask you a question about Comet and Streaky—the Super-Horse and the Super-Cat. Whose idea were they?*

**JM:** Usually the editor came up with the idea. I just designed them. So you've got a Super-Horse. You draw a pretty horse, and put a cape on him. [*laughs*] Streaky was my design. Totally. That was the little cat that got into the... whatever the hell it was. The kryptonite or something like that. I

*The Legion of Super-Pets, as illustrated by the co-creator of Comet and Streaky. From the collection of Scott Bierworth. Art © 2003 Jim Mooney; The Legion of Super-Pets TM and © DC Comics.*

designed him so he looked a little bit more like an animated cat. I fell in love with Streaky from the very beginning. I still draw him. I have a cat that looks just like him, a cat called Obie. [*laughs*] He's really Streaky III, I guess. I love cats anyway, and Obie is my favorite model.

**TLC:** *So the writers didn't come up with that. It was the editor?*

**JM:** You mean Streaky?

**TLC:** *Yeah.*

**JM:** I think the writer came up with that. But what I'm getting at is instead of telling me, "Make him look like this," or "Look like that," I pretty much drew him my own way. Most of that kind of stuff was whoever it was—[Jerry] Siegel, Edmond Hamilton—I don't remember who wrote most of the scripts. I didn't pay that much attention to it unless I liked them.

I do these commissions, and almost every one of the commissions for Supergirl has a Streaky in it. One guy wanted a little bit more erotic stuff. He wanted three of the DC superbabes in the DC super-babes locker room. And they're all dressing in their costumes, half undressed, or undressed, and so on, and Supergirl, Batgirl, and Wonder Woman [are there]. And when I did this thing, the guy said, "Why in the hell did you have to put

Streaky in it?" [*laughs*]

**TLC:** [*laughs*]

**JM:** I don't know... it was just fun. But it's amazing how many of the guys of that particular period have some sort of an erotic interest in Supergirl. It just amazed me. Every convention I go to—and some of my best customers for commission—they all want something slightly naughty with Supergirl. [*laughs*] It's kind of funny.

**TLC:** *I guess that never really crossed your mind at the time that you were drawing her.*

**JM:** No, it really didn't. Of course, I used to draw her in the nude, because I always drew my characters in the nude before I put costumes on them. To me, there was nothing particularly erotic about it, but evidently to some people [there was].

**TLC:** *Did you have much contact with the writers back then, or did you deal exclusively with the editor?*

**JM:** I dealt mainly with the editor. I met some of the writers, of course, at one time or another. I was very friendly with Henry Kuttner, and he knew most of those writers that were doing comics at that time. They had all worked for sci-fi—**Weird Tales** and so on. So I met quite a few of them that way, and we got along okay. There was no

big problem. We very seldom had much contact, though. The only editor I had much contact with was Chris Claremont, who wrote my **Ms. Marvel**. He used to call me up just about every couple of weeks to give me the outline of the story that I was supposed to draw before he wrote the script. [*laughs*]

**TLC:** *What about the artists who followed you on "Supergirl"? Kurt Schaffenberger took over right after you left, I think.*

**JM:** Yeah, he was good. I met Kurt in San Diego a few years ago, and we talked for quite a while. I said, "If anyone else was going to do 'Supergirl,' I'm glad that you did it."

**TLC:** *Could you see the writing on the wall back then, in terms of DC was shifting gears from one generation of artists to the new guys who were coming into the field?*

**JM:** Oh, I could tell right away. I was well aware of it. It's like, "We want people that draw very, very well, we want slick stuff, and we don't want George Papp, we don't want Wayne Boring, we don't want you [*laughs*] necessarily." I got the message after a while. I thought "Look, there's no sense in trying to hang around here and beg for scripts. Screw 'em." I just took off and went to Marvel and I said, "Do you have anything for me here?" I picked the right time 'cause Stan said, "Yeah. Boy, we really could use you right now." So that was it.

**TLC:** *You landed on your feet nicely at Marvel.*

**JM:** Yeah, it was good. It worked out well. With the situation toward the end there they made it quite evident they wanted everything to look real illustrative like Neal Adams. I think that they had a point, but I don't think that it increased their sales to that extent at that time. I don't have figures on it, but I don't think that it made them that much ahead of the game financially.

**TLC:** *Did many more artists make the move over to Marvel then?*

**JM:** I think I was probably the only major artist that went over there. A lot of the artists had worked off and on at DC, but I was... Good Lord, I was there almost twenty years.

**TLC:** *I know that Win Mortimer was over at Marvel, so that's one more artist who made the move.*

**JM:** I think that probably most of us went back and forth. A lot of the ones that were working for Marvel that were working for DC at the same time used a fake name. Mike Esposito and others.

**TLC:** *I was going to ask you if you ever used an alias.*

**JM:** No. About the only thing I ever used was a quarter moon and an 'E' [*chuckles*]. Noel Mooney I think I used once [**Note:** *Mooney's full name is James Noel Mooney —Ed*].

**TLC:** *Do you get many Legion commissions these days?*

**JM:** I've done quite a few, yeah.

**TLC:** *Back when you were working on the Legion, were you guys aware of how popular the feature was?*

**JM:** I guess I really didn't. I was working on the Legion after I moved from Hollywood, California, and I had a studio in Woodstock, New York. I think that was about 1965, and I rather enjoyed it, but I really didn't realize whether it was that popular or not. It just didn't enter into my mind at all. It wasn't a consideration. The idea was, "This is what we pay you a page." [*chuckles*]. And if I thought it was fair, and it was standard, that was okay with me. I didn't care what their sales were. It really didn't occur to me.

**TLC:** *There were a number of artists who didn't like drawing it because of the number of characters.*

**JM:** Well, I didn't like that particularly, either. It took me a little more time, but I wasn't going to be choosy at that time. I'd given up my studio on Hollywood Boulevard, and I gave up all my accounts there. I was making far more money there [than] when I moved back to the Northeast to do the "Legion" and some of those other strips. I did a lot of stuff, and one of the main reasons that I wanted to move was because I was going through a rather unpleasant time with a divorce and a lot of other things. I just wanted to get the hell out! [*laughs*]

**TLC:** *Does DC send you the archives which reprint your work?*

**JM:** They do do that. If they reprint [my work], I do get a check. That helps a little financially.

**TLC:** *So what do you think of the archives format?*

**JM:** I didn't like the thing they did on **Supergirl**. I happen to think Frank Miller is a damn good artist, but that drawing he did on the **Supergirl** cover really turned me off. I just thought there was no reason for it. It was like, "I don't give a damn. That's the way I'll draw her." I could have done it. They could have taken reprints, anything... any number of artists that are really good artists could have done that cover. And Frank, although he's good for what he does, he was not very capable in that particular respect.

**TLC:** *I think the polite word to use is "inappropriate."*

**JM:** Yeah, it was terribly inappropriate. The lady at Dark Horse...

**TLC:** *Diana Schutz.*

**JM:** Yeah. She was instrumental in getting that series going on the archives, and I do appreciate it, but I wish that she had not gotten her buddy Frank Miller to do the cover. [*laughs*] That was rather disappointing.

**TLC:** *At least they're reprinting them.*

**JM:** Yeah, I got a fairly nice check out of it. As you get older, the longer you live the less money you have! [*laughs*] Especially being a comic book artist. Very few of us put much away for our so-called "old age." I'm still working. I'm doing commissions. I've damn near sold all of my original art off. I'm still having fun drawing. Some of the stuff I really enjoy doing.

**TLC:** *So do you still draw everyday?*

**JM:** Nooo, not really. I draw two or three times [a week]. I probably put in maybe fifteen or twenty hours a week. Most of the time I go to the Y and I do my laps, and if I don't wear myself out too much I come back and do some drawing. [*laughs*] For a while I did **Soulsearchers** [**& Company**] inking on Dave Cockrum. And I did **Elvira**. I still do an **Elvira**. I probably do one or two **Elvira**s a year.

**TLC:** *When you were inking*

Dave Cockrum, did it cross your mind that you were one Legion artist inking another?

**JM:** It didn't really occur to me. I know I liked a lot of Dave's stuff. I enjoyed some of his work very much, but I hadn't remembered if he'd been a Legionnaire artist or not.

**TLC:** *Actually, he redesigned some of your characters.*

**JM:** Oh, did he? Well, that's typical of Dave. [*laughs*]

**TLC:** *I'm going to throw out a few names here, and ask you to make a few comments on them. First up: Otto Binder.*

**JM:** Great guy. Wonderful person.

**TLC:** *Did you know him well?*

**JM:** I didn't know him well. I had lunch with him a few times. I had a few drinks with him occasionally. I found him to be a very

*Outer space fun with Supergirl in this picture courtesy of the artist.* Art © 2003 Jim Mooney; Supergirl and related characters TM and © DC Comics.

*A retake on the cover of **Action Comics** #252, Supergirl's first appearance. Courtesy of the artist.* Art © 2003 Jim Mooney; Supergirl TM and © DC Comics.

congenial, a very nice person. One of the best.

**TLC:** *Jerry Siegel.*

**JM:** I met him only once, so we didn't really have much contact.

**TLC:** *Leo Dorfman.*

**JM:** Never met him.

**TLC:** *Never met him?*

**JM:** No.

**TLC:** *He wrote "Supergirl" for a while, though.*

**JM:** Yeah, I know, but I never [met him]. Like I mentioned before, people think, "Oh, you guys know each other," but our paths never crossed.

**TLC:** *Okay. Stan Lee.*

**JM:** [*chuckles*] Stan and I were very good friends. We're still good friends, but we had a lot more contact in the early days.

**TLC:** *Jim Shooter.*

**JM:** Ahhh.... You really want a comment, huh?

**TLC:** *Well...* [laughs]

**JM:** [*laughs*] I think Shooter was a very talented guy—still is—but he was a very difficult man to deal with.

**TLC:** *Would you say that he learned a lot of that from Mort?*

**JM:** No, I think it was just his natural nature. [*laughs*] I think the power went to his head a little bit, and he got a little too autocratic, a little too dictatorial.

**TLC:** *You drew one "Legion" story which he wrote. Do you remember that?*

**JM:** Yeah.

**TLC:** *The reason why I want to ask you about it is because he didn't write full scripts—he drew his scripts.*

**JM:** Yes, I thought he did very well. He was only about fourteen at the time. I was very pleased with the stuff he did. And when we first worked together at Marvel I tried to get along, but after a while I got to the point where I thought, "My God, nobody's going to get along with this guy. He's just gonna have to tell you to do it his way or else it isn't going to be done." He was the one that bumped me off of doing the finalizing on [***Amazing***] ***Spider-Man*** over John [Romita] Jr.

**TLC:** *I want to ask you about another writer now. Alan Moore.*

**JM:** Never met him. I like his stuff.

**TLC:** *How about the "Suprema" story?*

**JM:** I thought that it was fun. I liked his stuff very much.

**TLC:** *In the story that you drew, Suprema meets the League of Infinity, which was Alan's version of the Legion of Super-Heroes. It seems like the Legion just keeps following you around!*

**JM:** [*laughs*] That was coincidental, I guess, but it was kind of funny, wasn't it?

**TLC:** *Did you enjoy working from his scripts?*

**JM:** Yeah, I did. They paid me well. I think the first one that I did... who was it that did the layouts on it? On the first "Suprema" story?

**TLC:** *I couldn't tell you.* [**Note:** Mooney is referring to Rick Veitch. **—Ed.**]

**JM:** I can't think of the guy's name. But the second one, I did most of it myself.

**TLC:** *I've been saving one name for last: Mort Weisinger.*

**JM:** I knew Mort for years and years. When he first came out to Hollywood, I was just a kid and he was just a young editor. I showed him around, and when he was working at the studio doing the ***Batman*** series—working with Whitney Ellsworth—we used to go out occasionally. I'd take

*Supergirl lives on in the form of Suprema.* The League of Infinity and Suprema TM and © 2003 Awesome Entertainment.

him out to some of the clubs that I knew. We did a little bit of hobnobbing. Socially he wasn't a difficult person to get along with, but as far as playing editor sometimes, he would be a very, very difficult man. I would say that it was a fifty-fifty thing. As I said, he used to love that term, "Now I'm going to be the good father, now I'm the bad father." And my feeling was [laughs], "C'mon, you're not going to be my father at all." [laughs] Thank God. [laughs]

No, Mort was okay. I mean, Mort was a very talented guy. I'm not taking that away from him.

**TLC:** *Did you know that he said that you were his favorite "Supergirl" artist?*

**JM:** Well, he had good taste. [laughs]

**TLC:** *But I bet he never said it to your face!*

**JM:** No, he never did, but it was nice of him. He could have gotten by without saying anything, so that was a plus. As for the "Supergirl" strip, [if you] skip the first couple of years there, I think I developed it into a pretty interesting character. At least, I hope I did.

**TLC:** *I figure that we might as well wrap up the interview talking about her. Do you remember what you thought when you found out that DC Comics was going to kill her off?*

**JM:** I was a little aghast, I guess. That was... what was it? **Crisis on Infinite Earths**?

**TLC:** *That's it.*

**JM:** I had mixed feelings about it. I never got that much attached to any character that I ever drew that I would have been bereaved. But I was kind of shocked, let's say.

**TLC:** *Are you comfortable being associated with that one character, moreso than others?*

**JM:** Not really. I think a lot of the stories were pretty juvenile, and rather contrived, and pretty much the same thing over and over again. I got awful damn tired of it. Some of them were interesting, some of them more innovative, but if you're going to be associated with any character, I guess that Supergirl is just as good as any other. [laughs]

**TLC:** *It seemed like she always had a prob-*

The artist at work: Jim Mooney surrounded by old friends. Note the Legion of Super-Heroes in the foreground. Art © 2003 Jim Mooney; All characters are TM and © their respective owners.

*lem with that tree in which she kept her robot double. There was always something going on back there.*

**JM:** No, I wasn't terribly enthused about it, but it was a steady income for a while there, and toward the end I tried to do the best I could with it, and tried to give it as much pizazz as possible as far as the drawing was concerned. At times it was a little dull and a little boring; I'm thinking of the concept of it.

**TLC:** *Does the fact that a lot of people look back at it fondly and have fond memories of it offset the fact that maybe it wasn't your favorite assignment?*

**JM:** Well, it's pleasant. I'm always pleased. When I do conventions, people come up and mention, "Oh, I remember I was such-and-such when I first read 'Supergirl,'" and I guess probably the most touching of all was Diana's tribute. She was five years old when she read it in her father's dental office, and she's a really, really nice person. Sometimes those things are really gratifying.

The thing that to me is so... so...

astounding isn't the word... surprising... [is] so many of the guys in their forties and fifties [who] have a little bit of expendable income now, who want to buy all the erotic Supergirl [art] they can find. It's amazing.

**TLC:** *Well, it's a guarantee that they won't find it in the comics.*

**JM:** That's for sure. [laughs] And I'm not against the type of thing—it isn't that—but I just thought, this isn't something I guess I want to [laughs] spend my golden years doing. [laughs] Not that I feel it's reprehensible. I think that good pornography has its place, like anything else. [laughs] I just found it kind of amusing.

**TLC:** *You've had a career which has spanned over sixty years.*

**JM:** Yup. A long while.

**TLC:** *What's your secret?*

**JM:** I don't know. Probably good genes. [laughs] Good genes, perseverance, and a need for money. [laughs]

# John Forte

With its September, 1961 issue, **Adventure Comics** underwent a change. Due to overwhelming fan response, "Tales of the Legion of Super-Heroes" was introduced, replacing the "Tales of the Bizzaro World" feature which had previously been the back-up in the title. Rather than displace an artist, Mort Weisinger choose to keep John Forte as the penciler of the back-up, and in this fashion he became the first regular penciler of the "Legion of Super-Heroes." Throughout his four-year stint, Forte would draw many classic Legion tales, including "The Super-Moby Dick of Space" (**Adv.** #332), "The Super-Sacrifice of The Legionnaires," (**Adv.** #312), and the two-part "Starfinger" storyline (**Adv.** #'s 335-336). Also the artist who introduced such characters as Element Lad, Lightning Lass, and the entire Legion of Substitute Heroes, little was known of Forte until the following article, written by Peter Hansen in 2003. It is published here for the first time with Hansen's permission, and special thanks go out to the Forte family for their invaluable assistance in providing much of the following information. Mr. Hansen would like to dedicate the article to Diane, Bob, and Charles Forte, the artist's daughter, son, and brother, respectively.

John Forte (pronounced "Fort") was born on October 6, 1918, in Rockaway, Long Island, the oldest son of working class parents. He attended the local high school in Lawrence, and is described by friend Dave Kyle as a tall, gentle man with a good sense of humor and a hearty laugh, who was reserved and not terribly outgoing. Always artistic and not very athletic, he smoked a pipe, did not drink, and had a habit of wiggling his eyebrows. He was an Alex Raymond and Hal Foster fan for all of his life, and although he later married, he and Kyle would go out chasing girls together while still at art school, as well as later on when they shared an apartment together. According to Kyle, John's younger brother Charlie apparently inherited all of the family athleticism, and that's why John went to art school. Remembers Charlie, "He always had a pencil in his hand, and we knew he would become an artist."

Upon leaving high school, Forte attended the Art Career School (later called the Commercial Illustration Studio) on the top floor of the famed Flatiron building in New York. The art course lasted one year, and while in attendance Forte lived at home with his parents. Unlike his close friend Kyle, Forte was not drawn into the goings on in the emerging science-fiction scene, but was instead attracted to the budding comic book market.

The earliest known works of Forte are his spot illustrations for the sci-fi pulp magazine **Future Science**, published by Columbia Publications Inc. of Holyoke, MA. His earliest known comic book work was for Timely (then Marvel) Comics, where he drew and inked a 12-page story of "The Destroyer" called "The Demon's Deadly Secret" in **All Winners Summer Edition, 1942**. This popular second-string Timely character simultaneously appeared in **All Winners Comics** #2 and **Mystic Comics** #6 in the fall of 1941, and it is possible that Forte penciled some of these earlier appearances. Forte must have earned a living in either the sci-fi or comic book market between his graduation in 1937 and his first acknowledged appearance in the marketplace in 1941, and his friend Kyle commented that Forte's specialty in the early days was penciling and not inking, so identifying his earlier work can be difficult.

Like many others of his generation, after America's entry into WWII Forte joined the Armed Forces, specifically Patton's 3rd Army as an infantryman with the 359th infantry 90th Tank Division, where he served overseas until the end of the war. He took part in the D-Day landings in Normandy, and was moved from an infantryman to an artist for his company magazine **Carry On**, where he drew political cartoons, calendars, and propaganda for his unit. He frequently sent V-mail home covered with sketches from the war with very little writing in evidence. On his return to America after VE-Day in 1946, Forte began working for the Fiction House line of comics. In 1947 he moved into an apartment rented by his long time friend Dave Kyle in New York. Together they took time out that summer to go camping on Mohican Island in Lake George in upstate New York.

*. . . threw the projector beam over those at the gate . . .*

*Top: a picture of the artist provided by Charles Forte. Above: a sample of the artist's pulp work, courtesy of Peter Hansen.*

Forte was the artist who introduced and designed the *Legion of Substitute Heroes*. From *Adventure Comics* #306. The Legion of Substitute Heroes TM and © DC Comics.

While working for Fiction House, Forte drew such characters as Captain Fight, Glory Forbes, Hook Devlin, ZX5, and Stuart Taylor. During the time they lived together in New York, Kyle recounts an episode that took place while Forte was penciling a layout for an episode of "Sheena." "I looked at John's page and Sheena's boyfriend was manacled to a bunch of slaves, as I recall. He broke free when Sheena attacked his capturers and cut off the hands of the slaves with a machete to free himself. I redrew a severed hand in one panel to show the severed bone and blood dripping as the hand lay on the ground. John laughed and erased it saying it would never get past his editor."

Later Kyle would use Forte to illustrate the cover of Robert E. Howard's **Conan the Conqueror** book for his publication company, Gnome Press. It was also Kyle who introduced Forte to Robert W. Lowndes, the New York Editor of Columbia Publications' pulp division.

From his earliest known comic book work in 1942, Forte went on to draw for virtually every major company in the industry, producing work for ACG, Ajax, Avon, Better/Pines/Standard, Charlton, DC, Fox, Gilberton, Gleason, Fawcett, Fiction House, Marvel/Timely, Quality, St. John, and Superior. He displayed his versatility by working in several different genres, including western, sci-fi, humor, horror, adventure and romance. This versatility, along with connections to the early science-fiction marketplace (which also included Otto Binder, Edmond Hamilton and Mort Weisinger) probably kept him working steadily in an industry where other artists struggled throughout the 1950s. In addition to those connections, he was also known to be a good worker who consistently made his deadlines, and he devel-

oped a quick, efficient style which was well suited to the youthful audience for whom his work was intended.

Forte was a private man, and did not associate much with others in the comic book industry after he married. Occasionally would he take his family to visit Mort Weisinger at his home in Great Neck, Long Island. Without a doubt his greatest pleasure was his family, and although he was not necessarily religious, he would attend the Friday night pot luck dinner at the local Methodist church with them, where he would entertain the children by sketching illustrations with them gathered round. On one occasion he was even co-opted into repainting the church's three feet high nativity figures.

In his spare time, Forte would paint for his own enjoyment, usually landscapes, still life, or portraits of his children, who would frequently hang out in their father's studio, snatching away the scripts which had arrived that day to read before him. On occasion they would stay and watch as he transformed the script into pictures. On the nights that his wife was doing some private nursing, Forte would gather the children in the kitchen to cook dinner as he tried, with much hilarity, to recreate favorite recipes which he had enjoyed as a child.

While Forte worked in the comic book and science-fiction industry, he would also toil away on numerous commercial projects, including drawing fashion pieces for catalogs, including women's clothing, hats for men, and advertisements for gloves. He would also draw advertising pieces for Macy's, Sterns, and Norge Refrigerators, among others. He even drew and painted calendar pages in a Norman Rockwell

style, and sold many cartoons to humor magazines.

His first known work for DC Comics was a story called "My Angry Heart" in *Girls Romance* #26, April/May 1954. This was the beginning of a long-standing relationship with DC, for whom he worked on such features as *Jimmy Olsen*, *Lois Lane*, "Tales of the Bizarro World," and *Superman*. His ultimate achievement would be his artwork on the newly created "Tales of the Legion of Super-Heroes" feature which began in *Adventure Comics* #300, and which he drew until the time of his death. Characters such as Matter-Eater Lad, Lightning Lass, Element Lad and Dream Girl made their first appearances during Forte's run, as did the entire Legion of Substitute Heroes. What has not been known before now is the fact that Forte had been fighting a losing battle with colon cancer since late 1963. He was hospitalized for surgery on at least two occasions, the first being in late summer, 1964, which would coincide with him not drawing *Adventure Comics* from #328 until #332. His second and final surgery came in June, 1965, after which time, due to ill health, he never drew or painted again. He died on on May 2, 1966, at the age of 47.

Many years later, Forte's name would be incorporated into Legion continuity as the Science Police research facility on Forte Hill in *Legion* #1 (December, 2001), and the Forte District in *Legionnaires* #0 (October, 1994). Coming from a lifelong Legion fan, there is probably no greater tribute to a creator than to be remembered in this way.

When the Legion received its own feature in *Adventure Comics*, Forte was the artist who got the assignment. From *Adventure Comics* #300. The Legion of Super-Heroes © DC Comics.

# Edmond Hamilton

One of the benefits of being a former science-fiction pulp editor was that Mort Weisinger knew various pulp writers personally, and could recruit them for the comic book industry. One such writer was Edmond Hamilton. When he needed an author to script **Batman** during the 1940s, Weisinger hired Hamilton for the job. For his part, Hamilton was looking for more work given the decline in the science-fiction marketplace, and thus a new career was begun. Hamilton would eventually move on to the Superman family of characters, and with them, the Legion of Super-Heroes. Ideally suited for the strip given his sci-fi background, Hamilton would become the Legion's second regular writer, and would introduce characters such as Dream Girl, Lightning Lass, Element Lad, and the Legion of Substitute-Heroes. He would eventually leave the Legion in 1965 after three years as its author and in 1977, shortly before his death, he wrote the following article, aptly entitled, "Fifty Years of Heroes: A Career Retrospective." Unfortunately, he would not live to see it in print. Edmond Hamilton died on February 1, 1977. He was 72 years old.

*"I get enough of ordinary people in my everyday life... when I read fiction, I want to read about heroes!"*

I can't remember who said that, but I've always thoroughly agreed with it... not only as regards reading fiction, but also in writing it.

My first science-fiction story, a serial entitled, "Across Space," appeared in **Weird Tales** magazine in the summer of 1926. In it, evil Martians attempted to take over the Earth by means of a great machine on Easter Island. Their plans were defeated by a scientist who perished heroically in the struggle... and who was

memorialized as the man who saved the whole Earth.

The readers liked that story. So did I. Therefore, being a new and very young writer, I wrote basically the same story over and over again fourteen or fifteen times. In each tale, a scientist-hero saved Earth from a terrible menace.

The dooms that poured upon the hapless Earth from the Hamilton typewriter made the atom bomb puny by comparison. Colossal metal robots, directed by a malefic computer-brain, mucked about stamping the cities of America flat. Seal-like aliens from the depths of the ocean tried to drown the world by the simple expedient of pumping vast quantities of seawater to double the ocean depth. Menaces poured in on the hapless Earth from every quarter... from the depths of the ocean, from under the polar ice, from the other side of the moon, from the planet Saturn, from a subatomic universe. And in each case the Earth was saved by some noble-minded scientist-hero who outfoxed the hellish invaders at the last moment.

It is not surprising that I soon became known among the readers and fans as "World Saver Hamilton." In fact, in 1930 in one of the earliest issues of **Astounding Stories**, the letter section carried a long, not-too-serious poem of tribute to Hamilton the World Saver, written by a young reader named Mort Weisinger. Chuckling over that, I little dreamed that Mort and his young pal, Julius Schwartz, would in days to come be foremost among my editors.

I wound up the world-saving with a long story that appeared in **Weird Tales** as a four-part serial in late 1927. Its title was "The Time Raider," and this story, which has never been reprinted, was a wowser. The Raider of the title was a mysterious entity of mind and force that could travel into the past and future, and could drag people along with him from other ages.

Intent upon a total conquest of Earth, the Raider brought thousands of fighting men from past ages and penned them up, until he needed them, in a vast underground pit. This story really had five heroes instead of one... the young chap of our present-day era made fast friends with four other fighting men... a centurion of ancient Rome, a seventeenth-century

French musketeer, an Aztec warrior, and a noted English swordsman of the late eighteenth century.

At the climax of the tale, the five friends, by dint of heroic swordsmanship, held a stair that was the only exit from the pit, preventing the ravening hordes of the past from surging out to attack all Earth. There, I tell you, was a fight!

When the story was published, it troubled me a bit that I had unconsciously modeled some parts of it after the fantastic novels of A. Merritt, which I had always admired greatly. Several years later when I met A. Merritt, I earnestly apologized for this. But Merritt simply waved aside my apology and assured me that he had enjoyed my tale very much. He was a prince among men.

By this time I was getting tired of writing stories about the doom menacing Earth (and no doubt my readers were tiring of them, too). So in 1928 I struck out in a new line. My heroes were now officers of the Interstellar Patrol. These stories were laid in the far future, and postulated a galaxy ruled by the Federated Suns. The law-and-order arm of this vast federation

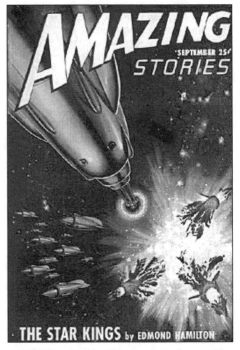

*A prolific pulp writer, Hamilton's novel **The Star Kings** originally appeared in **Amazing Stories** in September, 1947.*

was the Interstellar Patrol, the officers of which came from many different star-worlds. Only one of these officers was a human man of the future Earth. The others were nonhumans but intelligent aliens from many far stars... a metal-bodied chap from Antares, an insect-man from Procyon, a great furry, four-armed person from Betelgeuse, and so on. They were a colorfully variegated lot, with complete loyalty to each other and to the traditions of the great Patrol.

I wound up this series with a novel-length story of the Patrol entitled "Outside the Universe." In this long story, the heroes of the patrol ventured clear outside the galaxy to distant Andromeda galaxy to foil a cosmic plot against our own island-universe. In the finale, the starfleets of both galaxies had at each other in an epic fight.

I remember that I was so excited when I wrote the final space battle, and punched my little portable typewriter so hard, that the machine "walked" all over the surface of my old flat-topped desk—and I sort of followed it, banging away at it as I finished my climactic scene.

These wild tales were quite popular with the readers. And I was immensely pleased that my hero, A. Merritt, liked them and wrote in praise of them... not only to me but to *Weird Tales* magazine, where his letters were published. He even tried to get his own publisher, Horace Liveright, to publish them in book form, but Mr. Liveright did not think they would sell, and doubtless was quite right.

But eventually they were published in two paperback volumes. A young reader of the magazine, Donald Wollheim, was a great admirer of these tales, and when long years later he became editor of Ace Books, he published the old stories. Also Don, in his recent history of science-fiction, *The Universe Makers*, devoted a chapter to the Interstellar Patrol stories, saying that they were the first stories ever to visualize a future universe ruled by intelligence and law of many different life forms.

Another young reader who liked them was a lad in Cleveland who started writing to me early in 1930. He was instrumental, by his letters, in bringing together Jack Williamson and myself in a long friendship. He wrote me that he had an idea for hero stories himself, and that he and a friend were going to try to work up a new character. This youngster's name was Jerry

Siegel, and the hero character he and his friend eventually created was... Superman!

At that time in the early '30s I made the acquaintance of a lot of other science-fiction, adventure, and fantasy writers. The first I met, at the Chicago home of Farnsworth Wright, editor of *Weird Tales*, was E. Hoffman Price, a flamboyant and colorful writer of Oriental adventure and fantasy. I am glad to say he is still my friend and at least once a year comes zooming down from the San Francisco Bay area where he lives to spend a week here with us in the southern California desert where we stay in the winter, and to talk far into the night about the old days.

Jack Williamson and I pooled our resources in those Depression years to make some forays together... a long trip down the Mississippi River in a skiff, a winter on the beach at Key West, travels around his native New Mexico and Arizona. Jack was at the time just beginning his great "Legion of Space" adventure series.

And how we could talk in those days! I remember a wintry night in 1933 when Jack and I and Price went to the home of Otis Adelbert Kline for dinner. Harold Ward, who was then writing the "Dr. Death" series, was there, and Gordon Gurwit, and Wright and others. We talked stories, editors, publishers, and more stories. Mrs. Kline courteously bade us goodnight and retired, but when dawn came we were still sitting there at the table, talking away.

Kline was a big, hearty man, with shoulders like a professional wrestler, and a genial, friendly manner. He had sent me an inscribed copy of his first novel, and I met him in June, 1931, in Farnsworth Wright's Chicago apartment. He and E. Hoffman Price came in together... they had been combing rug merchants in search of treasures, Price, whom I also met then for the first time, being an Oriental rug collector.

Price waved triumphly to a rather grimy swatch of carpet which he declared would be of surpassing beauty when clean. "I'll just wash it out now in your bathtub," he said. Marjorie Wright, doubtless thinking of her spotless bathroom and what this grimy

*A visual interpretation of Edmond Hamilton's imagination by artist Alex Niño.*
© 1976 Alex Niño.

carpet would do, suggested, "It's too big for a bathtub, isn't it?" Price waved her objection aside. "Hell, I once washed a thirty foot runner in a bathtub," he retorted, and departed for the bathroom with a worried Marjorie trailing him.

Kline looked across at me and grinned, and I grinned back... and we were friends from that time on.

At about the same time I was meeting a good many of the writers based in New York. In 1934 Mort Weisinger, my one-time fan, was working for Standard Magazines' editorial department, and he and the editorial director, Leo Margulies—alas, it is now the late Leo Margulies—acquainted me with many of the great group in New York. Among them was Lester Dent, author of *Doc Savage*; Arthur Banks, "the king of the pulp magazines" as he was rightly called; Norvell Page; and many others, including Eando Binder ("Otto") and Henry Kuttner and his wife, C.L. Moore.

The NY sf scene in the later '30s and

*Hamilton wrote all but three of the **Captain Future** stories, an assignment originally given to him by Mort Weisinger.*

early '40s was a yeasty and exciting one. New magazines were appearing, new writers popping up, and we were all fascinated by the field. Every Friday an unofficial meeting of sf writers was held at Steuben's Tavern in mid-Manhattan, and when I was in town I enjoyed it very much. Henry Kuttner, Alfred Bester, Manly Wade Wellman, Otto Binder and many others were regulars. We had great discussions and hot arguments about new developments in sf. Julie, Mort and David V. Reed were also regulars. Lester Dent did not attend these... I met him at the old Tale Twisters group of pulp writers who foregathered at the Algonquin. Lester was a heck of a nice guy... big, genial and friends with everyone. I remember a period when he got a consuming interest in photography, and would rather use a camera than a typewriter. Others at the Tale Twisters gatherings were many of the old **Black Mask** writers... Carrol John Daly, Theodore Tinsley, Steve Fisher, Frank Gruber. They were all old friends and welcomed an infrequent out of town writer like myself in the friendliest fashion. Leo Margulies and Mort got me into the group.

All through the '30s I kept trying my hand at various different kinds of fiction... mystery and detective stories, supernatural stories, and also science-fiction of a more serious sort. One such sf story that I wrote in 1934 was a grim, realistic account of one of the first expeditions to Mars. It was so harrowing that no magazine would publish it then, and not until the mid-1950s was it published, under the title of "What's It Like Out There?"

But adventure science-fiction was still my chief interest, and I wrote a lot of it for Leo Margulies and Mort Weisinger, especially after Standard Magazine started **Thrilling Wonder Stories** and **Startling Stories**. In 1938 I wrote for the latter magazine a novel entitled "The Three

Planteers," about a trio of comrades—an Earthman, a Venusian, and a Mercurian—who adventured across the solar system. This novel led them to ask me to do a series for a science-fiction hero magazine they planned to begin publishing the following year.

Their first title for it was "Mr. Future, Wizard of Science." The chief character was to be a small man with a big head and brain. Leo decided that was too freakish a lead character, and so he became Captain Future, a red-haired scientific adventurer. They sent me their ideas about the series and I went to New York and talked it out at length.

Their original prospectus—I still have it—outlined three comrades Captain Future would have. One was Simon Wright, an elderly man who was a sort of living memory—that is, he could remember every scientific fact in existence but could do nothing else; Otho, a warrior from Ganymede, who was to be a living jewel set in a ring worn by Captain Future; and the third, an automaton—not an intelligent robot, but a sort of manlike machine.

I convinced Leo and Mort that these three characters would be very hard to use in a story, and suggested changes in them. Simon Wright became an aged scientist who, about to die, had his living brain transferred into an artificial serum-case, and was known as the Brain. (At first, he could not move around at all, but after doing a few of the novels I found this was too hampering a restriction, and gave him powers of movement.) Otho became an android, a living man of synthetic flesh created in their moon laboratory by the Brain and Captain Future's father. And the

automaton became Grag, the intelligent robot, who was not very brilliant but was immensely strong and very faithful.

There were seventeen of the **Captain Future** novels in all, before the wartime paper shortage killed the magazine. Of these, I wrote fourteen; "Worlds to Come" and "Days of Creation" were written by William Morrison and "The Solar Invasion" by Manly Wade Wellman. What happened was this: I wrote all the **Captain Future** novels until Pearl Harbor in December 1941. As I was then a bachelor and figured I'd soon be in the army, I notified Leo I wouldn't be able to write any more, so he got two other writers and changed the authorship of the magazine to the pseudonym "Brett Sterling." But in 1942 the army ruled they would not accept men over thirty-eight years old, so, on the verge of being inducted, I was ruled out, and went back to writing Captain Future again. Some of my stories then appeared under the "Brett Sterling" byline, and others under my own name; but aside from the three I've listed, I wrote them all.

*Curt Swan's recreation of the Hamilton-penned "Super-Sacrifice of the Legionnaires" from Adventure Comics #312.* Art © 2003 Estate of Curt Swan; Superboy and the Legion of Super-Heroes TM & © DC Comics

*Another Niño piece, this one of Captain Future and his loyal companion Grag.* Art © 1976 Alex Niño.

One story about the **Captain Future** novels remains in my mind. In the winter of 1943 I lived for a few months in Monterrey, in old Mexico. I wrote there the **Captain Future** novel called "Magic Moon." When I returned into the States, the wartime customs inspection of all papers and written material was very strict. Now, I always did the two "departments" of the **Captain Future** magazine... one called "Worlds of Tomorrow," with a map of the planet on which the action took place. The Customs men seized with it the whole manuscript of the novel and sent them to Washington for closer examination. It was months before I got them back, and in the meantime I had to write another **Captain Future** novel in a great hurry to fill the schedule.

Years later, in the 1950s, **Thrilling Wonder Stories** revived the old **Captain Future** stories as a series of ten-thousand-word novelettes. I did all these stories, and in them I was able to take a more subtle approach to the Futuremen. At that time Sam Merwin was the editor, one of the best science-fiction editors I ever worked for, and he gave me a freer hand with the stories than I had had before.

About this time, in 1946, I heard again from Mort Weisinger. He had returned from his war service to take up his job again at National Comics Publications, as DC Comics were known at the time. He and Jack Schiff had left Standard Magazines in 1941 to work in the comics field, and later on Julie Schwartz had joined them at DC.

We were old friends by then. Julie and I in 1941 had driven out to California and spent a summer there, living in a rented bungalow which we made into a sort of hospitality center for the whole Los Angeles science-fiction gang. (The kid who sold newspapers on our corner there, and who had ambitions to be a science-fiction writer, was Ray Bradbury. He would come often to our cottage after selling papers. Julie would read his stories in mss and give helpful criticism.)

Mort wanted me to write comic strips for DC magazines, to start with Batman. I had some doubts at first, as the format was quite different from fiction stories. But in those days after the war, the pulp magazine market was very poor, and so I decided to try it. I went up to New York and had long conferences with the boys. They were very helpful, realizing that this was a new form of writing for me, but even so, I had to write a few very poor scripts before I began to catch on to the ways of comic writing.

But once I started, I found that it wasn't really too different from fiction writing. In fact, comic scripts are very much like movie screenplays. I never had anything to do with the films myself, but my new wife, Leigh Brackett, had done a lot of screenplays, from Humphrey Bogart and John Wayne movies on, and looking at her scripts I discovered a great similarity.

For the first year or two, all my scripts for DC were **Batman** stories. As I learned the ropes, they became fun to do. But anyone who thinks comic scripts are just dashed off any old way is totally wrong. Mort and Jack Schiff were the nicest guys in the world to work for, but they took their work seriously, and if I made a stupid error or scuffed over anything, they told me so at once, and loudly.

It was fun to think up new wrinkles for the character. Most of them Mort thought up himself, but I did have some ideas which were used. If I remember rightly—

and it's hard to be sure after all this time—I thought up some things like Batwoman, the Batman of the future, and so on. But Batman was a valuable character and no quick, off-the-top-of-my-mind ideas were taken. I would say that generally, Mort was more gag-minded on the stories and that Jack was more logical-minded. Together, they made a great editorial team.

After a year or two I started to do **Superman** stories also. Here I was, working on this immortal character dreamed up by my young fan-reader who had written me back in 1930! I think I did better on **Superman** than on **Batman**, simply because it was more science-fictional. But on the other hand, Superman could present some knotty problems in plotting.

Recently, somebody—I think it was Julie Schwartz—said that kryptonite, the substance which makes Superman vulnerable, was just a crutch for the writer. This is absolutely true. On the other hand, the writer needs such a crutch. It's difficult to make up a suspenseful story about Superman, who's invulnerable to ordinary harm, unless he's vulnerable to *something*. And green kryptonite is a great help, as is the fact that Superman loses his powers when he is under the rays of a red sun.

In fact, my favorite of all the scripts I wrote was one entitled "Superman Under the Red Sun." [**Action Comics #300 — Ed.**] In that story, Superman traveled into time by using his super-speed to "burst the time barrier." But unwittingly he went too far, into a time when Earth's sun had become old and *red*. The result was that he had no super-powers—and couldn't get back. Earth was dead, and he was condemned to wander alone upon it. Mort objected to the fact that, being alone on

*Hamilton at home with wife Leigh Brackett. Courtesy of Bertil Falk.*

Night Girl by Steve Lightle, from the collection of Kevin McConnell. Art © 2003 Steve Lightle; Night Girl TM and © DC Comics

Earth, Superman wouldn't have any companions to talk to, and the pictures, always an important element, would be dull. I got around this by having Superman, in his loneliness, constructing robots who were doubles of Lois Lane, Perry White, Jimmy Olsen, and his other pals.

Another I liked was "When Superman Was Superbaby"—I believe the first of the Superbaby yarns. I always remember that as the only script I ever wrote in one day, the reason being that, as a baby, he couldn't talk very well... he could just say things like, "Pretty... bright ..." "Bad mans!" and so on. This made dialogue writing a breeze.

I have to admit that the villains of the **Batman** and **Superman** stories interested me more than the heroes themselves. The Joker was my favorite Batman villain... he had a flair for zany crime that I liked. I also was fond of Catwoman, but I never did too many scripts with her as a villainess. In the Superman characters, Luthor the evil scientist was a favorite... I suppose, again, because he was more science-fictional. The Superman villain I hated to write about was the zany Mr. Mxyzptlk... not only because I could never spell his name right, but also because it was hard to think up tricks to make the imp spell his name

backwards... that being the only method of sending him back to his own dimension.

I also did some of the "Superboy" stories, although someone else did most of those. Later on, when Mort launched the "Legion of Super-Heroes" series, I did a lot of those. Superboy was one of them, but all the super-heroes had some terrific super-power or other. One of them was a girl, Shrinking Violet, who could make herself tiny at will. That wasn't so hard to use. But one character I found it the devil and all to use: the girl called Triplicate Girl. Her power was that she could split herself into three different girls, all exactly alike. You think that's easy to use in a story? Triplicate Girl was one character who consistently baffled me.

Julius Schwartz first edited the science-fiction magazines at DC—**Strange Adventures**, **Mystery in Space**, and so on. I did a good many sf stories for those, and when I started doing them I thought, "This will be a breeze... writing for an old pal like Julie will be no trouble." I was wrong! Friendship cut no ice when Julie read a story, and he was as strict with me as with anyone else. I guess that's why he became one of the greatest editors in the business.

I didn't like to live in New York, as most of the writers for the comics did. So I worked at home in our little 150-year-old farmhouse in rural Ohio, which is still our home for half the year. Mort and I worked out our plots on the phone. But for the first year or two we lived there, we couldn't get a private phone line. There were nine different parties on that country line! Not only did that make it hard getting through, but also some nice old ladies on our line who happened to overhear our conversations really got an earful. Mort would say, "Then we tie this fellow hand and foot and lock him in a safe and drop it in the ocean..." and so on, detailing a plot sequence he wanted. I would hear one of the old ladies on the line say, "Ulp!" I sort of got some queer looks around the village in those days. But after we got a private phone line, my reputation improved.

I wrote for DC Comics from 1946 to 1966. During that time, I was still writing science-fiction and produced a good many sf books and magazine stories. Working on both projects sometimes kept me hopping. When I resigned from comic work in 1966, it was only because Leigh and I were about to go on some long-deferred world travels—to Egypt, India, and so on—and I would not be able to fill my schedules. But I always enjoyed working for the hero comics, particularly for such a great bunch of guys.

In recent years, there has been much talk of "serious" science-fiction, and adventure stories have been decried. I dissent from this absolutely. To my mind, the core of science-fiction is the great theme of the coming conquest of space. And, as I have asked before, if that is not adventure, what is? Armstrong and Aldrin taking the first steps upon the surface of the moon, the crew of Apollo XIII fighting to get back to Earth with their crippled rocket—these are stories more adventurous than any we science-fiction writers ever dreamed.

No, I remain convinced of the value of hero stories. I could cite Thomas Caryle's great essay "On Heroes and Hero-Worship" to support that belief. But I think the best defense of the great adventure stories was that given by G.K. Chesterton, the famous English critic of a generation ago. When someone sniffed at "blood-and-thunder stories," Chesterton roared, "I *like* blood-and-thunder stories... for they are about the blood of man and the thunder of God!" And he added, "Mankind still drives its dark trade in heroes, in many little-known publications, and I hope it always will."

So do I.

Hamilton at his California home, circa 1974. Courtesy of Bertil Falk.

# Curt Swan

The quintessential Silver Age Legion of Super-Heroes artist, Curt Swan is best remembered for his 30 year run on Superman. Just as his approach to Superman defined the look of the character for generations, so too did his approach to the Legion define that title for its fans. In 1983 Neil Hansen interviewed Swan for the short-lived **Comics Collector** magazine (#1), and in 1992 he interviewed him again for a **Comics Values Monthly Special** also known as its **Superman Memorial** Issue. What follows is an edited version of both interviews, combined in chronological order. The first interview is copyright Krause Publications, and the second is copyright Attic Books.

**TLC:** *Do you remember the first time that you saw a comic book?*

**CS:** The first time I saw a comic book was in London, England. I was on **Stars & Stripes**, around '41 or '42. Then, when I was assigned to the Paris office, France Herron was one of the writer/editors. He worked on the feature section in **Stars & Stripes**. I did illustrations, maps, anything. That's when I got introduced to Mort Weisinger and Whitney Ellsworth. That was about '45.

**TLC:** *Did you have any formal art training?*

**CS:** Outside of what you can get in junior high and high school, it's pretty much self-taught. I went to [the] Pratt [Institute for a few months, after getting out of the army], and the schooling I was getting at the time I thought was redundant.

**TLC:** *Who were some of your artistic influences?*

**CS:** I was fascinated by the illustrators in **Collier's** and **The Saturday Evening Post**. I dreamed of one day becoming an illustrator, but that would have taken three to four years' worth of art school. However, I was grateful when I got into the comic book business because I was desperate for work. The influence there would have to be the first person who inked my work, Steve Brodie. I was doing **Boy Commandos**, and I had to copy [Jack] Kirby's style to some degree. Impossible, of course.

But you're better off going with your own style. I tried to make the costume and characters as illustrative as possible, rather than going to a cartoony area. That was a mistake on my part for the short run. It meant hours more work, and it slowed things down. But for the long run, it was a good income.

**TLC:** *How did you begin your association with Superman?*

**CS:** Wayne Boring was doing it at the time. I'd done two or three stories when Wayne Boring was overloaded. We got into the 3-D stuff—everyone would work on the book—and Mort Weisinger liked what I turned out, so I got more and more work. But, of course, I was doing **Superboy** and **Jimmy Olsen** when the book first came out.

**TLC:** *You're well-known for your time on "The Legion of Super-Heroes." How would you describe that assignment?*

**CS:** Horrendous! Too many characters involved. The writers, bless 'em, they don't understand. It was painstaking and boring work.

**TLC:** *You did return to the Legion to do an issue of **DC Comics Presents** [#43 —**Ed.**].*

*Top: Curt Swan in 1979. Above: Swan working at home, circa 1969, courtesy of Eddy Zeno.*

**CS:** It wasn't so bad, because I learned so much since those early days, so I could filter the script and eliminate redundancies, concentrate on the thread of the story. But I told them [it] would be a one-shot.

**TLC:** *Would you ever consider doing the **Legion** on a regular basis again?*

**CS:** Please, I don't want to get in that box again. You're going to lose me rapidly.

**TLC:** *Does cinema influence your story-telling?*

**CS:** I do watch the camera angles, how a director treats a story, backgrounds, *et cetera*. It's useful, very useful.

**TLC:** *You've worked with many different writers during your career. Overall, how well do they consider the artist when writing their scripts?*

**CS:** There are some writers working together. They're in the same area. Myself, I've always lived some distance from the

*A sample of Swan's cartoon work, from **Cartoonist Profiles**, courtesy of Eddy Zeno.*

Superman TM and © DC Comics

writers. The only time I'd see them would be in the office. I've had occasion to sit and talk to writers and tell them my problems.

Cary Bates is good. He's not an artist, but he has picture sense. He understands the problems of the artist, so he doesn't load each panel and then expect the artist to be an editor in that sense and eliminate the unnecessary things. Some writers go rattling along. Consider the artist! The writer, writing a script, has to put the words down on paper to show the scene, present the scene, and the emotions for his own sake. But all the artist needs is to know what's happening.

**TLC:** *You've been drawing **Superman** for a long time. How do you keep it fresh?*

**CS:** I don't know whether I keep a fresh look to him. Many times in a given day I'll draw Superman like it's drawn with my left hand because it doesn't look like Superman. I'll erase, redraw, redraw, redraw. Other times, the mind tells me what to do.

**TLC:** *Do you feel that your pencils are intimidating for an inker to follow?*

**CS:** I'm conscious of the other guys who are inking. I suspect they look at it and say, "How do I treat this? There's no definite line." I don't think they are scared or intimidated. I have seen pencils other artists have done, and I can see where the inkers would be more comfortable with their work. So with my pencils it's all there, except the definite line. I hate to be critical of any inker. With Neal Adams, Giordano can handle it. Another inker, I suspect, would be intimidated.

**TLC:** *Every artist has certain things which they enjoy penciling. What are some of yours?*

**CS:** The most fun is when Superman goes to another planet, another society. I'm not talking monsters or strange creatures. Assuming the people are similar to our own, it gives you a lot of latitude, so you don't have to go through the scrap file. If you see some of the stories, you see I

have fun with certain costumes.

**TLC:** *Do you draw for a particular audience?*

**CS:** I'm not drawing just for ten-to-twelve-year-olds. There are college kids, fathers, and grandfathers reading **Superman**.

**TLC:** *Who are your favorite characters to draw?*

**CS:** I like Perry White, who goes into a more illustrative area. I can do things with his face I can't do with Clark Kent or Superman. Jimmy Olsen I'm comfortable with. Lois Lane and Lana Lang from time to time I can get expressive with.

**TLC:** *You've said that each artist who has drawn Superman has influenced the character. Would you care to elaborate?*

**CS:** [Joe] Shuster's Superman was, for its time, very good. But if you look at comic strips—the hero strips, the adventure strips—at that time, the treatments, with the exception of Alex Raymond, were quite similar. Shuster studied those strips at that time—the short figure, almost cartoony.

Boring's touch was that he made Superman a dynamic figure, which today is the best, much better than mine. Stan Kaye inked Boring at the time. When Superman looked lantern-jawed, I suspect Kaye put in some of his own style in the inking. Then we softened the face a little bit, and tried to make the figure a little more like real life. I think it lost something in the transition. We should go back to that style. Maybe I'll sneak it in, because it is so good.

**TLC:** *How long do you*

anticipate drawing Superman?

**CS:** I don't know. Into the sunset. [*laughs*] I expect to go as long as they'll have me. I don't want to stop, maybe ease off a bit in three or four years hence.

**TLC:** *Why do you think Superman is still going strong after all these years?*

**CS:** That I don't know. I'm just happy he keeps on growing and growing. Where other heroes fall by the wayside, Superman will always be there. What is beautiful is that ofttimes, when you least expect it, someone mentions him. I saw an old movie the other night, Monty Wooley in **The Man Who Came To Dinner**. There's a line in there where somebody says, "Who do you think you are? Superman?"

[**Note:** *The remainder of the interview was conducted in 1992.* —**Ed**]

**TLC:** *Dan Jurgens asked me to ask you*

*A recreation of probably the most popular Legion scene ever, the cover to* **Adventure Comics #247.** *Courtesy of Steven Weill.*
Art © 2003 Estate of Curt Swan; Superboy and the Legion of Super-Heroes TM and © DC Comics.

Above: A scene showing Swan's ability to convey emotion, from **Adventure Comics #350**. Below: Swan kept busy in the 1990s illustrating commissions for fans, as in this scene featuring Colossal Boy and Validus courtesy of Mike Napolitano. Art © 2003 Estate of Curt Swan; Superboy, Validus & Legion of Super-Heroes TM & © DC Comics

---

what you think of all this "Death of Superman" business.

**CS:** I'll put it this way: they had to get themselves out of a hole, a deep, deep hole going back many years. I told Mort Weisinger this some time ago. I saw it in the cards. I said, "Superman is so invulnerable that you're going to run out of story ideas." Soon after that, they came out with that stupid kryptonite stuff—green kryptonite, yellow, red, and so forth—and I thought, what a lousy crummy crutch that was. Something drastic had to be done. This is it. Kill the guy off and come back with a new version of Superman, much more vulnerable. I don't know how they want to treat it, but I think they're on the right track.

**TLC:** I was reading in one of your old interviews that you discovered comics while you were stationed in London in 1941 when you worked for **Stars & Stripes**.

**CS:** Yeah, that's right, at London Red Cross-Eagle Club in the theater section of London. As I said to [Dick] Wingert, "Look at this! This is not going to last," [laughs], "no way." I said, "Who the hell would ever want to get into this business?" In another couple of years, it'll be fifty years in this business. [laughs] So, I didn't see the handwriting on the wall. Had I seen the handwriting on the wall, I think I would have gone into another field.

**TLC:** Your first job with DC was the **Boy Commandos**, right? With somebody named Steve Brodie?

**CS:** Yeah.

**TLC:** I guess while doing it, you had to learn to change your work habits.

**CS:** Yeah, because I was putting everything into each panel. There were five characters in the Commandos, plus the hero, Rip [Carter]. They were involved in some action throughout the two or three pages. I'd put in every damned one of those characters in panel after panel. Now, Steve Brodie was going nuts inking this stuff, and he got me aside one day and said, "Let's sit down here and I'll give you a little friendly advice that will help you and help me, and make everyone happy." He explained, occasionally throw in a head shot or a knuckle or a finger or whatever. The reader knows that it's that character. You don't need to repeat full figures.

**TLC:** I know that magazine illustration was your major influence for getting in the business. You were looking at people like Harold Von Schimidt and John Clymer. What did you get out of that when you transferred from magazine illustration to comic book work?

**CS:** I was so enthralled by the art that I saw in the periodicals at that time and reading the stories. If the illustrations were good, you wanted to read that story. That was the key to the whole thing. I found it very exciting to see how the artist treated the illustration, how he illustrated a particular scene, which I would read over and over again and refer to the illustration. I fooled around with illustrating stories prior to that when I was a kid at school, but I think that's where I got into trouble. I carried that over into the comic books. The writer was being a bit too descriptive and long-winded in each and every panel at the time, because apparently the amount of verbiage on a page enhanced the editor's position. This filters down the line. The people who really got ticked off at the time were the letterers [laughs], and the inkers who had to slave over those lousy pencils.

The Legion of Substitute Heroes take center stage in this page from **Adventure Comics #351**. The Legions of Super and Substitute Heroes TM and © DC Comics

**TLC:** *I know you did some **Gangbusters** stuff and other things, and eventually, **Superboy** and **Jimmy Olsen**...*

**CS:** ...and a thing called "Tommy Tomorrow." [*laughs*] That was a peach that they dumped on me. John Fusetti, a political cartoonist, was hitting on me—he was in between newspapers, editorially speaking—he asked what it would be like for him to ink some book. I said, "I don't know." [*laughs*] But, he went into it and ended up inking my pencils. Maybe he asked for it, I don't know. [*laughs*] He asked for trouble. He had, at the time, a splash page showing the public library in New York City. Hell, I had just about the whole building—I had lions, I had people, cars—and he went out of his skull! I apologized and said, "If I had known you were going to get it, I wouldn't have done it." [*laughs*] But I have a literal mind. I just can't help myself. What was the question?

**TLC:** *You ended up on **Jimmy Olsen** and **Superboy** before doing **Superman**. These were your first introductions before your long association with the character. Was it just another job at the time?*

**CS:** Yeah, it was just another job at the time. In the break-in period, I helped

Wayne Boring and pulled in someone else at the time to do a **3-D Superman**. Prior to that, I had done one or two Superman stories, but that was the first time I really got involved with the Superman character. I wasn't aware of it at the time, but apparently Wayne Boring was disenchanted with his association with Weisinger and was going to move to the Southwest and start a new life, new career or something. Eventually, they put the **Superman** syndicated strip on me that Boring had been doing. There was another young fella that was working also. He did the **Superman** dailies for a while, a Canadian fella who was very good...

**TLC:** *Win Mortimer?*

**CS:** You got it. [He was] a nice fella, too. He was doing the **Superman** dailies and some of the comic book stories, too, and doing very nicely I thought. But, I think Weisinger was the primary person to bring me in. We had our verbal battles, but he respected me and liked me...

**TLC:** *Was he difficult to work for?*

**CS:** Yes, somewhat, because I was primarily locked into the product itself, the comic book format, and talking to all the various writers, editors and looking at all the different titles. They all seemed to be the same, whether it was a super-hero or the way they dealt with the characters, the story, the content, etc., all seemed pretty much the same. I think the main thing with **Superman** [was that] Weisinger and I, in a way, respected each other. I respected him as a editor, not a writer so much as an editor. I believe he respected me for my ability to meet a deadline.

**TLC:** *I see you also were thrown on "The Legion of Super-Heroes" for a while. That was one of your favorites, wasn't it?*

**CS:** Sure. You see, there was this kid from Cleveland, you know who he is, and he moved up rapidly. He would send in the pencils; he penciled the storyboards themselves. That's the way he wrote

his script.

**TLC:** *You're talking about Jim Shooter...*

**CS:** Yeah, Jim Shooter. Weisinger was very impressed with the young fellow. As time went on, he brought the kid in for an interview, so Weisinger reached out to me to do the pencils on the Legion. Boy, oh, boy! [*laughs*] That made me think back to the Boy Commandos—five or six main characters.

**TLC:** *With the Legion, you had about thirty...*

**CS:** Legion, oh my God, it multiplied. I handled it for a while and survived, but the Superman thing was the best bit.

**TLC:** *Speaking of writers, do you find that most of them understand the rudiments of visual storytelling?*

**CS:** No, not at all. Some of them have the knack for it, but the ones that don't will include things in the dialogue that the

Dream Girl dreams up trouble for Superboy in this commission courtesy of Mike Napolitano. Art © 2003 Estate of Curt Swan; Dream Girl and Superboy TM and © DC Comics

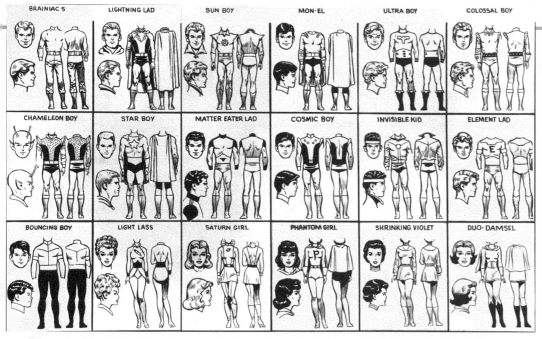

Above: you can't tell the players without a scorecard. Curt Swan's Legion model sheet, courtesy of Steven Weill. Below: Superman in action from a reproduction of Swan's pencils courtesy of Neil Hansen. Superman and the Legion of Super-Heroes TM and © DC Comics

illustration shows. Even then, they wouldn't catch it because they would give a description of what was to appear in the panel, and in that description, they would repeat that description again. Then I am illustrating it. I thought, my God, there's such redundancy here and a lot of wasted effort and work. The reader doesn't require this. If it's in the illustration, you don't need it in the caption or the lines, or vice versa. That's it. I got my point all right.

**TLC:** *Regarding inkers, who did the job of inking your pencils effectively?*

**CS:** Well, in the early days that was an inker that worked on the **Gangbusters**...

**TLC:** *Ruben Moriera?*

**CS:** It may have been. I know he did beautiful work, but he was a good artist as well. Most of the good inkers are good artists on their own. I could never figure it out, and then I realized one day that they didn't want to go through all that sweat, transcribing the script to illustration—transposing, I should say. This was their way of getting out from under that and still keep their hand in illustrating work.

**TLC:** *How about Al Williamson?*

**CS:** Williamson? Oh, that guy's so good. And of course, [Dick] Giordano is very good. He has a way with a line that's probably better than anybody.

**TLC:** *Murphy Anderson?*

**CS:** His art/drawing is very similar to

mine, and maybe that's why it's not terribly complementary in the art sense. I insist that any inker put his own identity into his work. I didn't like it when somebody tried to follow my pencil because it just lost its expression. If they put in a little bit of their personality into the inking over the pencils, it usually strengthened it.

**TLC:** *How about Bob Oksner?*

**CS:** His style didn't suit mine. It wasn't suitable to my style of drawing. He was very good on his own.

**TLC:** *Jerry Ordway?*

**CS:** Oh, he's very good, very good.

**TLC:** *When you were doing **Superman** in the 1960s, you drew a number of bizarre stories—things with Beppo the Super-Monkey and Bizarros running around square planets. Was it fun doing these ridiculous stories?*

**CS:** Oh, yeah, sure... it was a relief to get away from the realism, and also it kind of moved into the direction of cartoons. Now I can do cartoons, but it's something I never really nailed down. I wanted to come up with a syndicated strip at one time—the cartoon strip—but I didn't have the faculty to come up with the gags on a day-to-day basis. Back with **Stars & Stripes**, I did panels, cartoon panels, and they did demand that I have one in each weekly issue.

**TLC:** *How about the '70s when it started going back to realism?*

*How did you feel during that time?*

**CS:** I was comfortable with it.

**TLC:** *In the early '70s, there were a lot of regular stories that dealt with social issues...*

**CS:** Yes, we went through that, and that was a good thing to do. The one that did well on that was **Green Lantern** and the team that worked on it [Denny O'Neil and Neal Adams] did a nice job, but Superman, somehow, didn't fit it so well. There again, there was this man, all powerful, and it was ridiculous! I used to joke with Weisinger. I said, "Good God! Here you have the catastrophe. The city is leveled and Superman rebuilds the city." I stretched it a little bit [laughs], but that's what they would do. Think of the thousands of men that were put out of work because of this idiot rebuilding the city! We laughed about it, but he saw the injustice, so to speak, on the social side of that. It was ridiculous, but the whole concept was ridiculous.

**TLC:** *You drew **Superman** regularly until about 1985 and then you left the book. What feelings did you have when you left because you were associated with it for so long?*

**CS:** Do you mean in the sense of doing other titles?

**TLC:** *Yeah.*

**CS:** I felt good about that, and I insisted that they didn't throw at me the thing that bothered me in the early days, the **Legion**. I said, "Don't involve me in that, I'll quit first." [laughs]

It was a nice change. Just as now I maintain, and I think it's true, I have a burnout. I've been at it too damn long as I've been just stumbling along.

**TLC:** *You have more of a relaxed schedule now?*

MUST YOU DO THAT?

*Another Swan cartoon from* Cartoonist Profiles, *courtesy of Eddy Zeno.*

**CS:** Relaxed [*laughs*], just long enough to put bread on the table and a roof over my head. That's it.

**TLC:** *What do you do now, about a page a day of pencils?*

**CS:** Sometimes, not that. I should do two or three pages a day.

**TLC:** *Well, at one time, you were doing three or four...*

**CS:** Yeah, long days...

**TLC:** *Were they ten or eleven hour days?*

**CS:** Yeah, seven days a week. That wasn't greed. That was to pay the mortgage on the house. The business, itself, pays pretty good now, but even today, with the value of the dollar, it's ridiculous. There's not much money there. You have to work so damn hard to make a decent living.

**TLC:** *Even with the royalties happening now? People are coming out with books more for the money than anything else.*

**CS:** The whole industry is going through a phase, but that, too, will lessen, and there will be something else, I'm sure. Just as with the killing off of Superman, they had to do something. I'm sure the sales of that particular issue will be just tremendous. I know I'm not involved, but it should be money in the bank for several of the people involved. They had to do something, no question about it.

**TLC:** *What artist did you specifically look at to get your feel for the Superman character? Did you look at Shuster and Boring?*

**CS:** No, no. Boring's work I looked at only for the way he handled the figure. It was kind of cartoony, but I thought it was very good. I think it was the best. As to the fea-

tures, I didn't really look at anyone's work in particular. I modified that and toned it down and with Weisinger's blessings. He wanted that, and he asked me to do that.

**TLC:** *So, Weisinger wanted a total change from what had gone before?*

**CS:** He didn't want the "lantern jaw." Wayne Boring had developed a style—maybe that's the best word to use—that suited him and made it easy for him to produce that character, and even people on the street, the supporting characters, started looking like one another. It was becoming a cartoon. Weisinger wanted to turn it around and get it back to more illustrative—do my thing on it.

**TLC:** *Did you use George Reeves because you drew Superman while the television show was on?*

**CS:** No, as a matter of fact, I didn't watch the show much, only for two or three episodes.

**TLC:** *Are you still doing watercolors these days?*

**CS:** No, I haven't touched watercolors for a while. I lay awake nights thinking about doing things. I have some nice visuals in my head. No, I haven't touched them. I should.

**TLC:** *Finally, to end it off, what do you feel is the appeal of Superman and why is everyone going crazy finding out he's about to buy the big one?*

**CS:** In a sense, he was the first, wasn't he? He was really the first super-hero. The original conception was good, and they should have kept it there, not fooled around with it. I think Siegel and Shuster were on the right track. There was a vulnerability to Superman, and he was

more appealing in those days. Even so, the early versions of the animated Superman...

**TLC:** *The Fleischer Studios in the 1940s?*

**CS:** They did a beautiful job. My, the work that must have gone into that. How they handled it. The story was so well done. Some of the early television **Superman** was also quite good.

**TLC:** *The first season. It became a kiddie show after that.*

**CS:** It goes back to what I've said before, the writers have put themselves into a box. They have no way of getting out. They were trapped once they got into that format.

*The cover to* **The Legion Outpost #9,** *courtesy of Harry Broertjes.* Superboy and the Legion of Super-Heroes TM and © 2003 DC Comics

# E. Nelson Bridwell

Originally hired to be Mort Weisinger's assistant editor, E. Nelson Bridwell outlasted his boss at DC, eventually becoming an editor in his own right. His contributions to the Legion legend include various fill-in issues during the Sixties, as well as the first post-Weisinger Legion story in **Superboy** #172. Considered to be a walking encyclopedia and the resident expert on topics as diverse as Superman, Shakespeare and the Bible, Bridwell was a valuable member of the DC staff right up until the time of his death in January, 1987. The following interview was conducted by John G. Pierce and originally appeared in his Captain Marvel fanzine **The Whiz Kids** #2, 1981. It is reprinted here with his permission.

**TLC:** *How did you get hired at DC?*

**ENB:** I'd been trying to break into the comic book field for several years. I did some writing for **Mad**. I continually read, obtained back issues, and wrote letters. However, I was living in Oklahoma at the time, so my prospects didn't look too bright. Then, in December 1963, I got a letter from Mort Weisinger at DC, offering me a job as his assistant.

**TLC:** *Which task do you prefer: writing stories, editing, selecting reprints, creating text pages, or compiling letters columns?*

**ENB:** Writing.

**TLC:** *You have been regarded as a very well informed individual. You are an expert in mythology, history, literature, and in DC's mid-'70s adaptation of Bible stories you are listed as the "Resident Biblical Scholar." What is your academic background?*

**ENB:** I never went to college. But I read a lot.

**TLC:** *If you could work on any comic book character(s), from any company, old or new, alive or defunct, other than any of those that you have already written, who would they be?*

**ENB:** Well, I dropped the names of a couple of them in **Super Friends** #5: Larry Davis (Funnyman) and Linda Turner (Black Cat). I just liked them.

**TLC:** *I understand you knew Gardner Fox.*

**ENB:** Gardner was one of my boyhood heroes and later he became a good friend of mine. He was tops in his day, along with John Broome, Ed Herron, and others.

**TLC:** *Whose artistic version of Superman is your favorite?*

**ENB:** Swan's.

**TLC:** *What do you think of the Marvel Comics style of writing?*

**ENB:** I've tried doing the panel-by-panel breakdown, and then dialoguing the pencils... it worked fine. But having the artist break down a brief plot line could bring headaches, though some are doing it successfully.

**TLC:** *Which is the easiest feature which you've written?*

**ENB:** Probably "Captain Marvel."

**TLC:** *Other than the DC and Fawcett lines, what were some of your other favorites during your childhood?*

**ENB:** Kid Eternity, Black Cat, Sheena, Popeye, Dick Tracy, Flash Gordon, Tarzan, Buck Rogers, and later Funnyman.

**TLC:** *What about your favorite comics artists?*

**ENB:** Swan, Adams, Giordano, Schaffenberger, Williamson, Mayer, Davis, Drucker, Frazetta, Eisner, Cole, Evans, Kubert, Beck, Severin, Wood, Crandall, Kirby, Oksner, Caniff...

I could go on and on!

**TLC:** *How about Carl Barks?*

**ENB:** Yes, I love Barks' stuff. I still cherish the original edition of "Christmas on Bear Mountain," which introduced Uncle Scrooge. I bought it when it first came out.

**TLC:** *Other than comics, what do you like to read? Favorite authors?*

**ENB:** My literary tastes are very broad. A few of my many favorites include Shakespeare, Lewis Carroll, Bradbury, Poe, Gilbert & Sullivan, H. Rider Haggard, Twain, Baum, Ogden Nash, Kipling, Damon Runyon, Stevenson, and on and on...

**TLC:** *Do you miss the task of selecting reprints regularly?*

**ENB:** Not particularly. I did it for so many years; it did indeed become a bit of a job.

**TLC:** *Are you pessimistic about the future of comics?*

**ENB:** No, I just think we need new ideas... but we'll get it!

Top: Bridwell at work, presumably in the 1960s. Above: the identities of Sir Prize and Miss Terious are revealed in the Bridwell-penned **Adventure Comics #351.** The Legion of Super-Heroes TM and © 2003 DC Comics

# Jim Shooter

A child protegé at the age of thirteen, Jim Shooter would go on to become a regular writer for Mort Weisinger's Superman family of comics during the latter half of the 1960s. After leaving the industry in 1970, he returned to comics in 1975 to once again write the adventures of the Legion of Super-Heroes. Then after more than a decade as Editor-in-Chief of Marvel Comics he left the industry again, this time to return with his own company, Voyager Communications, publishers of Valiant Comics. After behind the scenes struggles led to his departure, Shooter launched a new company, Defiant, which was sued by Marvel Comics before it could even publish its first title. He later followed Defiant with Broadway Comics, but by that point the general unhealthiness of the comic book industry proved to be an insurmountable obstacle, and Broadway closed its doors.

What follows is an interview conducted with Shooter on Jan. 25, 2003. It provides new insights into multiple comic book eras, not the least of which is the one during which his career began. From his days working with Mort Weisinger to his reign at Marvel, Shooter takes us behind the scenes of key events in comic book history. Both Part One and Two of the interview were conducted by Glen Cadigan, and both were copyedited by Shooter.

**TLC:** *Let's go back to the very beginning of your career. When you were thirteen years old, what made you think that you could write comics?*

**JS:** I read comics when I was a little kid. In those days, almost everybody read comics. The comics I read were **Donald Duck**, **Superman**, **World's Finest**, and stuff like that. I got bored with 'em when

I was about eight years old because they were all the same. It was all the same stuff again and again... Lois Lane always trying to discover who Superman was and all that. So when I was twelve I came across these Marvel Comics, and they were way better. I was like, "Whoa! Look at that!" I actually went and checked to see if **Superman** had gotten good, too, but they were the same. They were exactly the same as when I left them. So it occurred to me if I could learn to write like this Stan Lee guy, I could sell stuff to these other people, 'cause Lord, they needed help. That was my plan.

I spent a while acquiring Marvel comics—this would be [the] middle Sixties, I guess; '64 or '65—and when I thought I was ready, I wrote a script for "The Legion of Super-Heroes." Why did I pick them? Because I thought that was the lamest comic book on Earth. The ones I

*Top: A very young Jim Shooter, taken from his high school yearbook. Above: a page of layouts for an issue of Adventure Comics by Shooter.* The Legion of Super-Heroes TM and © 2003 DC Comics

had been reading around the time I created this were those old John Forte comics. He was a very nice man and everything, but the drawing was kinda stiff and wonky. The covers were always great, and the stories never lived up to them. So I thought, "I'll do one for 'The Legion of Super-Heroes.' That way I'll show what a difference I can make." I didn't know what a script looked like, so I actually drew little panels and balloons and made it look as much like a comic book as I could. I couldn't draw very well, but enough so that they could understand that's Superboy, and that's Lighting Lad, and all that. I sent it in and got back a letter. The letter said, this is very good, and someday maybe I could quote "draw" features for DC. It was signed by editor Mort Weisinger, and he invited me to send more like I'd sent.

I was all inspired and everything, so I wrote this elaborate two-parter, which was rare. That was kind of a mistake in a way, because they usually didn't do two-parters in those days. In the first one I'd made a great attempt to try to make sure I didn't put any red flags in it. Too many people who send submissions into Marvel Comics, they kill Aunt May in their first story. So I didn't want to make any radical changes or anything, 'cause that would be a red flag. But anyway, the second one I did—the two-parter—I sent it in, and then I got a call from the editor, Mort Weisinger. That would be February 10, 1966, to be precise. He said he wanted to buy the second two stories that I'd sent, and he wanted me to write a "Supergirl" story. Later he called back and he said he wanted to buy the first one, too. Then after that I just kept working regularly. He kept me busy every minute. I sold everything I ever wrote. "The Legion" was sort of my regular

*Above and right: more Shooter layouts, plus a Ferro Lad commission by Curt Swan courtesy of Mike Napolitano.* Ferro Lad art © 2003 Estate of Curt Swan; Superboy and the Legion of Super-Heroes TM and © DC Comics

title, but I also did **Superman**, **Superboy**, the whole Superman family except **Lois Lane**. I never wrote a **Lois Lane**. I did it for about five years, [and] in that five years, there were, I think, four stories that were not written by me. Mort and Nelson Bridwell had cooked them up, so he let Nelson write them, which was fine. They kept me busy anyway. I was doing **Superman** or something that month. So that's the story.

TLC: *Do you think you would've gotten noticed if you hadn't drawn your submission?*

JS: No, I don't, because I wasn't that great a writer. Mort told me one of the reasons they were interested was because of the visual thinking. That was a problem that they had with writers. Writers tended to do talking heads, but I was very much influenced by Steve Ditko and Jack Kirby, the Marvel comics I read, so I was really trying to tell a story like they did, and trying to go for great visuals. He said that the combination of my visual thinking, and at least some basic writing ability, was good enough. Then he spent the next five years beating me up regularly, teaching me what I needed to know.

TLC: *Did he know right away that you were a teenager?*

JS: As I recall, no, he didn't. I remember that after we'd done a few stories and he was convinced that I was worth training, [we had] a conversation in the spring where he said, "I want you to come on up to New York and spend a couple of days in the office. Sit down with editors and artists and people and learn some things." Because I still had never seen a comic book script. [*laughs*] So he said, "When can you come?" I had the feeling that he thought I was a college student. He knew I wasn't over twenty-one, but I think he thought I was a college student. So I kind of waffled a bit, and then he said, "How old are you?" I said, "Ummm... I just

turned fourteen," [*laughs*] and he said, "Put your mother on the phone." So I put my mother on the phone, and actually what happened was after school got out that year, which would have been early June, I went on my first business trip to New York and I had to take my mother with me. It was kind of embarrassing to have to take your mother on a business trip, but that was great. We spent three days there, and then after that I actually went to New York by myself quite frequently, and went to the office and met people, and each time I would sort of get a lesson. Mort was really trying to... I mean, he was a tough guy. He was mean. He was mean as a snake, but he really did a lot for me. He was trying to teach me not only writing, but the whole business. So they taught me to color. They taught me at least enough so I knew about production. Mort spent a long time explaining to me licensing and merchandising and the business end of it. I think he thought some day that I might get a job there and be his little protegé successor or something. But anyway, I really got the overview of the whole business—inking and storytelling and drawing and writing. I would periodically bop up to New York and spend the day there, [or] a couple days there, and then get my occasional dose of comic book lessons.

TLC: *What did your parents think of your job?*

JS: They thought it was fine. They were very happy. The reason I got the job was because my family needed money. I didn't just decide one day, "Oh, this will be fun." If you're thirteen years old and

"your family's in a desperate financial situation, what do you do? They won't give you a job in a steel mill. [*laughs*] You can't get a job. Your only hope is to make something and sell it. Yeah, I could deliver newspapers and make five bucks a week. So what could I make? I wasn't gonna weave any baskets. I had no idea, and then I saw these comics, and I thought, "Oh, that's an idea!" It was like an act of desperation, and the money that I brought in kept us going. It kept the wolves from the door. So my mother thought it was great. My father wasn't the talkative type. He didn't say a whole lot about it, but I'm sure he was happy that I was doing something and it was going well. I had nothing but support.

TLC: *What would a typical day in the life of Jim Shooter have been like back then?*

Ferro Lad TM and © DC Comics

**JS:** Well, I'd get up in the morning [and] go to high school. See, I never thought I was gonna be in the comic book business. I never wanted to be in the comic book business. I loved comics. I loved creative stuff, but I was gonna be a scientist, so my high school day was a long day. In four years of high school, including summer school and one special advanced class, I took six years of science, and then I took a special after school science course for four years. I took six years of math. I took every advanced course that I could take, and graduated pretty high in my class. I don't remember exactly [where]. So I had a long school day with lots of work [laughs], and then I'd come home and either sit on the left-hand corner of the couch [laughs], or I'd go up and sit on my bed with a lap-board and sit there and write and draw. I'd go to bed, I guess, at a normal time. That was my day. I did that pretty much every day, and every once in a while I'd have to take a break and be a kid. I'd go play basketball with the guys or something.

But there were deadlines. I mean [chuckles], you did not want to miss a deadline for Mort Weisinger. They didn't have any Federal Express back then. The best you could do was Air Mail Special Delivery, but that was pretty good. It would often get it there the next day, and it was sixty cents, which I thought was outrageous. But there were times where I would have to finish something, throw it in the envelope, run to the streetcar stop, take a streetcar to downtown Pittsburgh, go to the main post office (which was open twenty-four hours a day), mail that package Air Mail Special Delivery, because if I didn't do that [chuckles], and it was late, I would get my head handed to me. There were even times where, back in those days, you could fly student standby to New York, and the round trip airfare was twenty-six dollars, so even though money was an issue in my house, there were times I actually caught the first flight out in the morning—which I guess was 7:00 am— took the bus from Newark into the city, which cost fifty-five cents—which I thought was outrageous—went to DC's office, [and] snuck in, because I knew if he saw me [laughs] I wasn't gonna get away without a lecture. So [I] snuck in, handed the package to the receptionist, beat it the hell out of there, went back to the airport and flew home. I did that more times than is reasonable, because as I went on in high school, it just got harder and harder. [If] you work your way through high school, sometime around the fourth year you start getting tired. So I kept being late, and having to do these heroics to get the script delivered on time. So that was a little hard.

**TLC:** *If you were in Mort Weisinger's shoes back then, would you have hired you?*

**JS:** Yeah, I think so. The thing is, the timing was right. It's not that I'm so great. The fact is, comics had been in severe decline for a long time. Comics kinda hit their peak in '50-'51, and then throughout the Fifties, especially after the Kefauver commission, the hearings, the introduction of the Comics Code and stuff like that, comics kinda got a bad reputation, and they were fading out. Toward the end of the Fifties, sales were lower and lower, [and] there were fewer and fewer published. So okay, what does that mean? That means that all during the Fifties, you didn't have to develop any new cartoonists because there were plenty of unemployed people walking around. [If] you needed a cartoonist, you just called up one of the guys that you know is not working. So very few names that you recognize came into comics in the Fifties. Vince Colletta, John

Superboy and the Legion of Super-Heroes TM and
© DC Comics

*A sketch of Timber Wolf and Bouncing Boy by Neal Adams. From the collection of Steven Weill.* Timber Wolf & Bouncing Boy TM and © DC Comics

Buscema, [and] one or two others. It wasn't a big time for new talent, and most of the writers at DC were these old science-fiction guys, guys who were middle-of-the-road science-fiction writers, and some of them did some great stuff—I mean, Otto Binder, Edmond Hamilton...—but they were kinda getting long in the tooth. And that was just it. There hadn't been a whole lot of new people come into the business for years, and so Mort was looking for new talent.

All of a sudden, all of these guys who used to be unemployed and hanging around weren't around anymore. They either retired, or they'd gotten something else to do. There was kind of a shortage of talent, and then right around that time, Marvel was starting to take off, and so they were sucking up some of the loose talent. So he needed help. The idea of getting in young guys and developing them was, I thought, a smart thing to do. I tried to do that myself when I was Editor-in-Chief at Marvel. So Mort brought in this young fan, Roy Thomas [*laughs*], who put up with Mort for about two weeks, and then quit and went to Marvel. He just couldn't take Mort. Mort was a handful. Like I say, he could be nasty. I guess I was more tolerant. But then he brought in this other fan, a fairly young guy—a good bit older than me—named E. Nelson Bridwell, and then me, and then about the same time Archie Goodwin and Denny O'Neil came in. A little bit later Neal Adams [arrived]. One of Neal Adams first jobs was doing covers from my sketches. I did sketches, he did the covers. We were a great team [*chuckles*]. So anyway, this little new wave started, and then finally Cary Bates, and then years later there was Len Wein, Marv Wolfman... but that was when the new wave of talent started. So yes, if I were in that situation, and somebody looked like they might have some talent, I'd hire 'em. Especially young people.

When I was at Marvel, I did the same thing. We had an intern program called Romita's Raiders. There's a lot of busy work in comics—ruled lines in the background, and stuff like that—so we offered aspiring artists [the opportunity to] come in, and they could be John Romita's assistant and do all the little sh*t work. [*laughs*] We paid them some tiny amount of money—minimum wage or something—but the advantage was then you're sitting there in the office and Walt Simonson comes by and you can show him your stuff, and he'll give you advice, not to mention Romita teaching you and all the other people that you encounter there. Of course, we tried to encourage the interns and to get them to learn skills, and then we gave them freelance work so they could make extra money so [that] they didn't have to live in the fifth floor cold water flat. We really put on a bunch of programs, and some of the people that came out of those programs, like Kyle Baker, Jim Owsley (who's Christopher Priest now), Kenny Lopez—who turned into a fantastic letterer—and more I can't remember right now, but lots and lots of good guys came out of that, and it was really worthwhile. So I learned that from Mort. Find young talent and develop it.

**TLC:** *Am I correct in assuming that Karate Kid was a favorite character of yours?*

**JS:** Yeah. The first issue that they actually bought, which was the second issue that I actually wrote, introduced four new characters, and Karate Kid was in there

because I'd seen some book about karate. I did a book report on some book about karate when I was in fifth grade or something, and I thought the Legion of Super-Heroes had far too many people who would just point their fingers and things [would] happen. I thought we needed somebody who did some more active things for the sake of the visuals. And so [I thought] "Super-Karate! Yeah, that's it!" So him and a couple others [were added]. Anyway, the thing is, he was kind of a favorite of mine. I liked him. I also tried to give him a personality that was [non-derivative]. Every Asian character you'd ever seen up until then was inscrutable, y'know? A cliché-ridden stereotype. I said, "This guy is brash." [*laughs*] "[There's] nothin' inscrutable about him."

In my crummy drawings he was half-Asian, but Curt, I guess, couldn't figure that out. Actually, it wasn't Curt. It was Shelly Moldoff. When Shelly drew him, he made him like an American. Which is a shame. I kept trying to [add diversity to the Legion]. I wanted Ferro Lad to be the first black Legionnaire, and Mort said "No, we'll lose our distribution in the South." So I said, "Whatever. He has a mask on.

Who'll care?" [*laughs*] But couldn't do it. I said, "How is it that you can have orange people from other planets and green people from other planets, and you can't have a guy from China, or a black character?" But those were the rules back in those days. That's another reason why Marvel appealed to me, because they were trompling all over the rules. They were daring to do things that DC wouldn't do.

**TLC:** *How did the Adult Legion story come about?*

**JS:** That was Mort's idea. He had done stories with adult Legionnaires before, but usually, I think, in the **Superboy** magazine. They'd done a couple where they'd shown them as grown-ups briefly. I think only the three of them—Saturn Girl, Lightning Lad, and Cosmic Boy. So he said, "Why don't we do a story set in the future farther and they're all adults now, [so] we can see what happens to them?" And I thought that was the worst idea I'd ever heard, because I said, "Well, then, there goes your suspense, doesn't it? You know who's gonna live, you know who's gonna die." But after I thought about it for a while, I thought, "Hey, you know, that's kinda cool. What if you know one of these guys is gonna die and you don't know when? What

*Karate Kid in action versus Nemesis Kid, courtesy of Mike Napolitano.*
Art © 2003 Estate of Curt Swan; Karate Kid and Nemesis Kid TM and © DC Comics

*The Shooter-introduced Shadow Lass, courtesy of Kevin McConnell. Art © 2003 Steve Lightle; Shadow Lass TM and © DC Comics*

if you know this romance that's happening is gonna come to a tragic end? I mean, it's kinda cool! Yeah, I could go with it." So I worked out this elaborate plan for what would happen to all these people, and I liked my plan, but then Mort's assistant was E. Nelson Bridwell, and I'm not sure whether this was official or whether Nelson was kinda jerkin' me around here, [but] Nelson was a big fan, and he just had his ideas about what should happen to these characters. So he called me up, and I had to assume that he was speaking for Mort, and he just sort of dictated to me, "These two get married, those two get married..." He made sure that everything he wanted [laughs], all the little relationships that he cherished as a fan [came true]. Like I said, I guess I took it that it was coming from Mort, although later thinking about it, that's absurd. Mort wouldn't do that. Mort was not fannish that way. He would have rathered I'd come up with some really interesting twists and good stories. So then I was kinda saddled with some of that. Everything turns out just the way you'd expect, right?

So I threw a few wrinkles into it. I said,

"All right, well, fine. I can't kill the person I want to kill, so what I'm gonna do is I'm gonna kill somebody who isn't in the Legion yet, and then an issue or two from now, I'm gonna introduce her." [*evil laugh*] So I did that. You see a statue of a fallen Legionnaire, and it's Shadow Lass. Well, there's no Shadow Lass in the Legion, but a couple of issues later there was. When I introduced her a couple of issues later, there was a collective gasp. "Ahh! That's her!" It was cool. So I did some stuff there that was cool, and I don't know if they still do, but even for years after I left, they were still following that story as the blueprint. Writers of the Legion were still using stuff that I'd set up in that story and fulfilling it. So it worked out really well. And then over at Marvel, when Chris [Claremont] came to me and he wanted to do "Days of Future Past," I said, "Okay, but do it well. Remember, you have to live with this stuff." I think it was a good thing, and we actually did something like it at Marvel, [but] it was Chris's idea, not mine. In retrospect, I think it was a good thing. I wish I'd been able to do it the way I'd originally planned.

**TLC:** *When you started to introduce those characters, how long did you intend to keep them around before you killed them off?*

**JS:** Shadow Lass was the one I was planning on killing, and I planned to keep her around for a good long time. Ferro Lad I killed because my plan was that he was a black guy, and Mort said no. Then I said, "Well, let's see. I've got this idea for a story, someone needs to die... Ah-ha! Him!" [*laughs*] So basically, I killed him off because it annoyed me that I couldn't do with him what I wanted. And Mort didn't care. If I wanted to kill one of the originals, Cosmic Boy or something, I think he would have said no. But it was a character which I created, so who cares? Go!

**TLC:** *Did DC ever give you a sense of where the Legion was in their hierarchy at the time?*

**JS:** You read the sales figures which were published in the books, and when I started writing "The Legion of Super-Heroes," it was selling about 500,000 copies a month. Five years later when I stopped writing it, the last issue also had a statement of ownership in it, and it was selling about 500,000 copies a month. During that time, *Superman* went from something like a million and a quarter down to around five hundred, six hundred [thousand]. Practically every other book that DC published fell dramatically, so by holding my own, I was actually doing very well. At the same time, Marvel was sort of taking off and taking market share away from DC. DC was just living in the past. They were still doing comics for eight-year-olds, and Marvel had sort of seized the initiative there. In the hierarchy of DC, the Superman family of titles was the cream of the crop, and number one was *Superman*, number two was *Action Comics*, and then, I believe, by the end of my run, I believe *Adventure Comics* with "The Legion of Super-Heroes" was easily number three,

*Some more samples of Shooter's layouts, courtesy of Harry Broertjes.*
The Legion of Super-Heroes TM and © DC Comics

maybe number two.

**TLC:** *You've been given credit with bringing characterization to the Legion. Do you think your plots have been overlooked?*

**JS:** When I was a kid, I made more mistakes... [*laughs*] Sometimes I look at those stories, and I just wince. Sometimes when I'm in a more charitable mood I'll look at them and say, "Well, that wasn't bad for a fourteen-year-old kid." But I would make mistakes and stuff, so there were one or two good stories in there with some good plots and stuff like that. Now I'm sort of known as Captain Construction. I'm good at plots and structure and so forth, which is what Mort was trying to teach me, but back then I was just starting out. I made my share of mistakes. The thing that I do think that I was able to bring at that stage was a little more character, because I saw what Stan was doing. I said, "Oh, I see. Okay. That's what you do." And originally I was trying to give these guys personalities, so the idea was I looked around at my schoolmates, and swiped their personalities and assigned them to different Legionnaires. I thought I was cheating. I thought, "Boy, I hope nobody ever finds out," 'cause I thought, "Real writers make characters up. I'm a fake writer." No! Everybody does that. Well, I didn't know that. I was a kid. But that's what I was doing.

For instance, there was a guy in my class whose name was Tom Kalaski. Tom wasn't terribly athletic. He's a really nice guy. He was a little bit nerdy. His way of being accepted was he was funny. He told jokes. Everybody loved being around him. He made you laugh. He made you feel good. A lot of it was self-effacing humor. He was this great guy. So here I am, I'm writing the "Legion of Super-Heroes," [and] I got a character called Bouncing Boy. Before I came along, this guy took himself seriously, and the other people took him seriously. Come on! [*laughs*] He bounces! He's fat! So anyway, I started playing him as Tom Kalaski. I had him say he was the self-appointed morale officer. He looked at himself as kind of ridiculous, and he played it. Finally, he became one of my favorite characters, because he wasn't powerful and he knew it. Yet he ended up, by his wit and his intelligence—and also just by holding the rest together sometimes—he ended up making a difference. I thought that was unique. I'd never seen anything exactly like that before, and I had a couple other characters that I really spent some time developing, going into their personalities. I had "manic-depres-

sive" Ultra Boy. [*laughs*] But I did try to [give them personalities]. I think I succeeded in that even before I was an accomplished plotter.

**TLC:** *You're responsible for a lot of the Legion's villains. I'm going to list off some names here, and I want you to give me your thoughts on them. Let's start with the Fatal Five.*

**JS:** The story there was that there was a movie coming out right around that time called **The Dirty Dozen**. I don't know if you remember the early Legion stuff, but Mort would often tell a writer, "Let's do **Moby Dick**, only with the Legion of Super-Heroes." So they did "The Moby Dick of Space." Or he would take some classic tale and tell the writer to do the Legion version of that. He would also, occasionally, when a movie or something like that came out, tell a writer, "Take that idea and do a story." So he called me up, and he says, "There's a movie coming out called **The Dirty Dozen**. Go see it and then write a story like that for the Legion." And I said, "Oh. Okay." To me, that was like cheating. I said, "I can't do that." So what I did was I looked at the ad for the movie, and you could pretty much tell all you needed to know looking at the ad. They get these twelve criminals to go on this suicide mission. Okay, well, who needs to see the movie? Then I approached it logically. I thought, "Well, why on Earth would the Legion of Super-Heroes need help from bad guys? Unless they check everywhere else first!" [*laughs*] "Unless there's no one else who can help them." And so I had to have them go through that, and then they finally do recruit the bad guys. Then after that, everything's sort of natural. Of course, the bad guys are treacherous, and blah blah blah, [but] it actually came out pretty well. You gotta remember the context of the times. In those days, we

The unpublished cover to **Demand Classics #2** by Ross Andru. **Demand Classics** was a title cancelled by the DC Implosion before a single issue saw print. From the collection of Steven Weill. Superboy and the Legion of Super-Heroes TM and © DC Comics

weren't as sophisticated, but I thought the Persuader and Tharok were kinda cool at the time, especially compared to some of the other Legion villains, who were kinda dorky. Anyway, that's the story of them.

**TLC:** *How about Universo?*

**JS:** I think I just wanted to do a time travel story. I was kinda a history buff, so I had the Legionnaires go to the various time periods I was particularly interested in: Napoleonic France and ancient Egypt. Like I said, I was a little academic head. I was kinda a nut for stuff like that. It just seemed like an idea, and he was just created as a vehicle to accomplish that. The science fair winner kid [*Rond Vidar* —**Ed.**], that was shortly after I had won the Buhl Planetarium Science Fair [*laughs*], so I put a little version of me in there. So [it] was just a combination of those elements.

**TLC:** *Your first story had Dr. Regulus in it.*

**JS:** Right. That's the first one I wrote.

**TLC:** *I guess you didn't know that they had already created an arch-nemesis for Sun Boy.*

**JS:** I guess not.

**TLC:** *There was Sun Emperor in the Legion of Super-Villains.*

**JS:** I didn't know that.

**TLC:** *He was a direct rip-off of Sun Boy, but that's another story. How about the Dark Circle?*

**JS:** Mort hated that. I don't really remember much about it, except that he said that it was the worst cover ever designed—I designed that cover—and the sales were terrible, and he never wanted to see anything like that again. I said, "Oh, okay." [*laughs*] I don't really remember much about that, except that he hated it.

**TLC:** *And last but not least: Mordru.*

**JS:** Mordru, of course, [was] influenced by *Lord of the Rings*. I wanted to do the evil sorcerer, and also I liked the idea of implying that there was history of the Legion that you didn't know, that they'd had this arch-nemesis they didn't even talk about, that's how scary he was. So I did the story as if it were the sequel [*laughs*], and Roger Stern, one of my buddies, [who] I think [is] the most underrated writer in the history of comics, he, as a fan, read that story and kept looking to buy the issue that Mordru had appeared in before. He thought that there was one. I remember that was one of the covers that I think Neal did, and aw, man, he did some great covers off of my sketches. [It'd] be like he'd read my mind. I'd do a crummy sketch, and then he'd say, "Oh, I know what he means." Neal once went to Mort and said, "Why are you wasting this guy as a writer? I think he could draw if we trained him." [*laughs*] I said, "That's nice." Neal told me that.

But anyway, [what] I was trying to do [was] influenced by *Lord of the Rings*, and I wanted to do something that gave the Legion a sense of history, and also I guess I got a little typecast there. Mort said, "Maybe they can flee into the past?" "Uhm-mm. Did that. But how about if they go to Smallville?" 'Cause I was also writing *Superboy*, and felt comfortable with Smallville. I don't remember much else about it, except I can guarantee that put-

ting Insect Queen in it was not my idea. I never liked a lady that turns into half a bug. Give me a break.

**TLC:** *You also created entire alien races for the Legion. You're the one who came up with the Khunds and the Dominion... you even came up with the Controllers. Were you planning for those races to have important roles later on?*

**JS:** Yeah. I always figured if it worked at all, then you could later develop it. Here's the thing about the Legion of Super-Heroes that was really cool, two things that I don't think people immediately grasp: one is, it's probably the only time in the history of comics where the writer, the characters, and the audience were all the same age, and we all grew up together. The other thing about the Legion is that DC had no continuity. You could read *Superman* stories in any order. It didn't matter. But there was only one series that was set in the future, and so I owned the future. I could keep the continuity. It was the only DC book, really, until later on [when] they started trying to do that with the other books—not so much Mort's books, but *Green Lantern* and everything—so I owned the future, and I was able to keep the continuity. Therefore if I did introduce something and I liked it, I could bring it back later and logically develop it, whereas if I wrote a *Superman* story with, say, the Parasite [*Another Shooter creation.* —**Ed.**], the next time the Parasite was written it might be written by Cary Bates, and who knows what he's gonna do? Also, there was no attempt made in the other stories to keep the continuity tight or to develop anything long term. Mr. Mxyztplk was always Mr. Mxyztplk. He never got

married or had kids, you know? And so I had this unique opportunity there to actually do things like that, to bring something on board, some alien race or something like that, and then have them come back, or develop them. For DC, that was unique.

**TLC:** *When did you start to feel comfortable as a writer?*

**JS:** I think my second year at Marvel I got the feeling like I was starting to get the drift. It had always been a struggle 'til then. Sometimes I'd feel like I'd done something okay, and sometimes I thought, "Gosh, it sucks, and I don't know why." Finally, what did it for me is my first job at Marvel, I was the line editor. I think my title was associate editor, but basically, I was the one who edited the script—plots and scripts. So every day I'm sitting there and I'm reading everyone else's stuff, and I could see easily the mistakes in their stuff. So then I said, "I get it," and I

*Shooter's original character designs for Tharok and Validus, courtesy of Harry Broertjes.* Tharok and Validus © DC Comics

The Legion of Super-Pets, as depicted by Bob McLeod. From the collection of Scott Bierworth. Art © 2003 Bob McLeod; the Legion of Super-Pets TM and © DC Comics.

started being able to see them in my own. It's the hardest thing in the world. See, the thing is, when you think of an idea and you're trying to write a story, you've got a movie running in your head. It might make perfect sense to you [laughs], and then later somebody says, "Why'd they do that?" [and] you're thinking, "Did you see the movie?" [laughs] No, they didn't. So when you get to the point where you can switch back and forth between the movie in your head and an objective view, then you start getting comfortable. At least for me, it's always been a process of analysis and synthesis. I keep switching my point of view from inside my head to disinterested third party, and then I can see the errors or see the construction. Actually, my friends tell me I've ruined movies for them now because I'll go with them to a movie, and they'll say, "Ah! Did you see that?" and I'll say, "Yeah, well, he should've done this, and he screwed that up, and this wasn't established," so now my friends J.J. and Joe, they don't like to go to the movies with me anymore. [laughs] "Aw, you'll just spoil it. We just want to like it. We don't want to know what's wrong with it!" [laughs] Of course, if it works, it works. There are no rules.

**TLC:** Do you think you made it possible for other young writers to break into comics after you?

**JS:** Oh, I know I did.

**TLC:** Did any of them come up to you and say that you inspired them?

**JS:** Gerry Conway did. Gerry Conway started when he was fourteen, and it always sort of pissed him off. Actually, he heard about me, and he was trying to beat the record. He was submitting stuff, trying to get in before he turned fourteen at least, and he ended up selling his first work when he was fourteen. That always annoyed him.

Little known fact: the number one record holder in the history of comics is Joe Kubert. Kubert did his first professional work when he was twelve. It was really funny. Joe [is] the nicest man in the world. He's such a nice guy. One time we were talking, or I think he was giving a lecture or something like that, and somebody asked him how old he was when he started, and he said twelve. I was in the audience, and I went, "Whoa-ho! Look at that!" So I ran into him later, and said, "I used to think I was the record holder, but it looks like you are." He said—and I love Joe. He's such a nice guy—he said, "Yeah. The difference is, you were good." [laughs] Give me a break! But that was the nicest thing. He's such a nice guy.

**TLC:** When you were working for DC, how often did Mort suggest ideas?

**JS:** Often. The thing is, sometimes he'd say, "Send me a plot," and sometimes he'd say, "Go see this movie and rip it off," and sometimes he'd say, "Hey, here's an idea. How about they go back in time?" He often had ideas, and was not shy about them. Sometimes there were things that I just didn't want to do, but it wasn't my choice. For instance, I never really wanted to do Super-pet stories. You're talking to a man who's written dialogue for Krypto the Super-Dog and Streaky the Super-Cat, and I always sort of bristled at that. I ended up having to write a couple of them, because here's another little known secret behind the comics: Mort thought that a comic book audience turned over every two years, and so [he] kept a record of all the

covers for each magazine—he kept two years worth of covers up on the wall—and he kept the sales figures posted beside them. If a cover had sold well, then what he wanted you to do was another version of that cover, another version of that story two years later. What he would do was each two years there'd be a couple he'd experiment with, but mostly he was just recycling the ideas that had worked. And then, of course, he'd start weeding them out if one of them wasn't working very well anymore, or if one of the experimental ideas turned out to work, then that would get into the rotation. So every two years they would do the Legionnaires become super-babies, because that cover, the cover with the Legionnaires as super-babies, always had sold well for him. Now, they'd do a different version of the cover, but essentially he would say, "Okay, this is the month we're gonna do the super-babies story, and we'll need a new cover designed for it."

I actually managed to escape the super-babies story. I was supposed to do one, and then he wanted me to do something else for **Superman** or something, and I couldn't do it all, so they let Nelson Bridwell write the super-babies story, thank God. But I did end up having to do a couple of Super-pets. Also, one of his favorite covers was the revolt of the girl Legionnaires. These were recycled ideas. They did these every two or three years, and when I was asked to do that, I always

The second issue of Shooter's Adult Legion storyline, with art by Curt Swan.
© DC Comics

*A page from* Adventure Comics #355, *showing Karate Kid and Cosmic Boy in action. From the collection of Mike Napolitano.*
Cosmic Boy and Karate Kid TM and © DC Comics.

felt, "I gotta do something different. I can't regurgitate the same story." Other writers, I think, said, "Oh, great!" 'cause it was easy money. Just dig out the old story, change a couple of things, and there you go. I always tried to do something more interesting, but I did find it kind of a chore writing dialogue for Streaky.

**TLC:** *How would you define your relationship with Mort?*

**JS:** He treated me like dirt. Basically, since I lived four hundred miles away, we had a phone date every Thursday night right after the **Batman** TV show, and he wanted me to watch the **Batman** TV show. "You must watch the **Batman** TV show!" "Okay, fine." I don't know why; he [must've] thought we were a Nielson home or something. He would ask me questions to make sure I'd watched the TV show, and we'd have these conversations, sort of like our scheduled talk every Thursday night, and he'd go over whatever was pending. If I'd sent him a script, he'd go over the script. If I sent him

plots, we'd talk about the plots. Now, these conversations were ugly. The first couple we had, he was fairly civil. But I remember the time he told me, "You're fourteen, but I'm not cutting you any slack. I'm treating you just like everybody else." I said, "Fine." What I didn't know that meant was that he was gonna treat me like dirt. These conversations, he'd call me up, and he's screaming at me, "You f*cking retard! You can't even spell this!" and I'm like, "Umm, I'm fourteen." [*laughs*] But no, that didn't cut any ice. He says, "You're doing these sketches, this thing looks like a carrot, not a gun!" I [thought], "It's just a scribble sketch. C'mon!" I didn't say anything to him. Oh, you didn't dare say anything to him. But P.S., my family needed the money, so I needed the job. This wasn't a lark, or I would've quit a million times. I did quit. At the end of each conversation, it got to the point where I'd say, "I guess I just can't do this, and you gotta get somebody else," and he'd say, "Nah! I'll give you one more chance." So it was bad. He was nasty. That was his way of keeping people under his thumb, to keep you from asking for a raise. So that was a little tough. When you're fourteen, fifteen years old, and the big important man from New York, the executive vice-president and head editor calls you up and tells you you're a retard, you think you're stupid. You believe him, and you think, "God, I'm dumb. I just got lucky."

Anyway, the end of the punchline of that story is that I ended up leaving DC the end of '69, I think, [maybe] '70, worked for Marvel briefly, then finally I got into advertising and other stuff, so sometime like '73, '74, I got a call from somebody who worked at Marvel Comics, and they were saying, "Why don't you come back? We need writers!" So they encouraged me to come up and visit Marvel. So I came up, and they offered me some stuff, and at that time I wasn't doing anything terribly

important. I was making a living doing occasional advertising stuff and working in a department store or something. So I went up and they offered me a job, and I went, "Well, okay." But this was interesting: they offered me stuff, and one of them said, "You ought to go over to DC, too, and see what they have." Now, in my day, you did not cross that street. You worked one place or the other, and if they caught you, you'd be fired from both. But they were encouraging me. "Go see if you can pick up something from DC." I said, "Okay! Sure!" Actually, first I said "No, I don't want to go there because Mort's there," and they said, "Oh, he retired. Go ahead!"

So I went over, and the thing is, "Well, if Mort isn't here, who do I know?" Then I said, "Well, Nelson's probably still here." So I asked for Nelson, and he came out and [said], "Jim! Oh God!" and took me in, and before you know it, I was writing **Superman** and the **Legion of Super-Heroes** again. Now the punchline is, I'm talking to Nelson and Mort comes up—Mort was abusive to Nelson, too—and he said, "Boy, you just don't know. Mort used to brag about you. He'd tell everybody about how great he was to have discovered this young genius. He said he could ask you to write anything and you'd give him stuff that was usable right away, first time, no rewrites." I said, "The son of a bitch!" [*laughs*] "Why doesn't he tell me that?" And then I ran into Cary Bates, who was another guy who was working for Mort. He was in college when he started working for Mort. The first thing Cary Bates ever got published was he sent in a cover design, and then Mort asked me to write the story to go with it. Then later he let Cary write his own stories. But I ran into Cary, and he introduced himself, and he said, "God, I used to hate you!" I said, "Why?" and he said, "Because every time I turned in a story, Mort said, 'Why can't you write like Shooter? How come you do this crap?'" I said, "Cary! He said the same thing to me! He said, 'Cary Bates doesn't make these mistakes!'" [*laughs*] I said, "That son of a bitch!"

Anyway, that's history. But he was tough to work with. There's an apocryphal story about Mort's funeral. It's said that they couldn't get anybody to do a eulogy, and finally a guy who was supposed to be his friend—one of his only friends—stood up and said, "Well, his brother was worse." [*laughs*] But he was a tough guy. I'm grateful for all the things he taught me, but he was a mean guy.

**TLC:** *In all your years at Marvel as Editor-in-Chief, did you ever say to people, "Hey, I used to work for Mort Weisinger. I know what a tough boss really is!"*

**JS:** Yeah, exactly. The thing is, Marvel was anarchy when I arrived. No one ever told anybody anything, so when I'm telling people, "You know, you really have to mention the characters' names somewhere in the story," and things like that, no one had ever given them an order before, so they were all bristling. It was almost like, "God! I'm the nicest guy in the world! I know better than to be like Mort! You people don't appreciate [what you have]." [*laughs*] Yeah, the legend of my tyranny at Marvel, to me it's nonsense, because I said "Yes" a lot more than I said "No." I went along with the damnest things, and I let people make fun of me in the letters pages and the credits. They used to make fun of Artie Simek, the letterer, and that's not right to be making fun of the letterer, so if anybody wanted to do a joke in the credits, I let them do it with me. Really, from Mort I learned what to do. I also learned what not to do, and I tried to live up to it. The trouble is, when you're dealing with creative people, they don't like hearing the word "No" ever, and if you ever say, "No, you can't do that," they never walk away saying, "Well, he's a wise man, and I'm sure there's a good reason for this decision." They walk away cursing you, and then they go to the fanzines and tell everybody what an asshole you are [*chuckles*]. It never occurs to them that you might be right.

I had one guy who wanted to do a story where Spider-Man fathers an illegitimate child. I said, "Bill, picture the president of Union Underwear: it's a slow newsday. News of your story gets into the paper. The guy who makes Spider-Man Underoos opens up the paper and discovers that Spider-Man is screwing around and fathering illegitimate children. Imagine the president [of Marvel], Jim Galton's phone ringing while the president of Union Underwear calls him and demands the money back for the license." I said, "We can't do that. I'm sorry. Part of my job here is to protect the franchise, and I don't care whether you think it should be commercial or not, it is. You just can't go crazy like that." And so he goes to the fanzines and does an interview about how I'm denying him his creative freedom. [*laughs*] What do you mean creative freedom? I told him, "Do the same story, just do it for Epic Comics. Call him the Arachnid or some-

thing and everybody'll secretly know it's Spider-Man, but it's an adult story. Don't do it in **Peter Parker**." So when they say, "Oh, he was a monster!", well, that's the kinda monster I am, I guess.

**TLC:** *Did you ever get to speak with Mort before he died?*

**JS:** The last time I ever spoke to Mort was in 1969. I had left DC—I quit—and I went to Stan at Marvel, and Stan, after some initial reluctance, after we talked a while, thought maybe I could do what he needed, and so he hired me. But the trick was I had to work in the office, which was a little difficult since I lived in Pittsburgh. So I had to suddenly move to New York, which, when you're eighteen, that's an adventure. So I remember sitting in my desk the first day, the phone rings, [and] it's Mort. He's just screaming at me. "After all I've done for you!" And I said, "Look what you're doing now! That's what you did to me." [*laughs*] So that was the last conversation, with him screaming at me, as usual.

By the time I got to be eighteen, I started realizing, "You know what? If I'm that bad, there's no way they'd keep sending me these checks. If I suck that bad, there's no way that I would still be working here. No way. There's too many other people they could get." So I sorta toughed it out, that this is just Mort's way of dealing with people, and then later it was proven to me. Because like I said, I had those conversations with Cary and Nelson, and I thought, "You know, I must have something to offer here. I must be pretty good." And then that's why, finally, I got sick of that crap and tried it at Marvel. I didn't last at Marvel very long, because I just couldn't get [it together]. I was eighteen, I had no money, I'm trying to live in New York City, [I] didn't have a place to stay, didn't have any friends up here, [and] after a couple of weeks of soup and crackers and not being able to find a place to stay, and things like that, I finally said, "You know what? I can't do it now. I'll have to try it again later." Which I did. I went back a couple

of years later, a little older and wiser, a couple more bucks in my pocket, and it worked out.

**TLC:** *Tell me about your correspondence with Curt Swan.*

**JS:** Curt was one of the nicest human beings on the planet. Of course, I did these little layouts [for him]. One of the first correspondences we had was, in those days, original artwork [was kept by] the companies. What they would do was they would give it away to fans, or kids who came through on tours. So I remember one time I was up in the office, and Mort says, "Hey, would you like one of your stories? Here!" and he hands me this pile of Curt Swan pages, I think inked by Jack Abel, and it was really cool. I thought, "Wow!" So I took 'em and I went home, and I'm thinking, "This isn't right!" [*laughs*] "What am I doing with these? This isn't fair!" So I wrote a letter to Curt, and I said, "Look, Mort gave me this, but it's really yours. I don't want to have this if it's somebody else's. I don't understand why he would give it to me." Curt sent me a letter back, and he said, "Jim, I'd just throw it away. Go ahead. If you want it, keep it. I have no use for this stuff. I wouldn't have any place to put it." Which was generally the

*Another Swan commission, also from the collection of Mike Napolitano.*

Art © 2003 Estate of Curt Swan; the Persuader and Ultra Boy TM and © DC Comics

attitude of artists in those days. This fuss over original art and stuff, that was a thing that came later, 'cause back in those days, nobody cared. People started to care when they found out that you could sell it for money. And that sort of opened the correspondence.

Then once in a while—not often, but once in a while—Curt'd send me a letter, and it was usually drawn. It was usually on a big sheet of vellum, and it was all hand-lettered in comic book style, and on it there'd be lots of little sketches. What he would do is he'd give me little pointers about the layouts, like how I could do this or do that better, and it was neat! I'm getting art lessons from Curt Swan! [It was] long distance, but it was very nice. He was the nicest man in the world. And then, years later when I actually met him—'cause I hadn't met him—[he] was just the sweetest man. He just couldn't have been better. I think he's a much under-appreciated talent. He was one of the most amazing draftsman ever to be in comics, and he could just draw like crazy. He drew in a style that was required by DC Comics, which was a little calmer than the Kirby/Marvel stuff, but Curt was no less an artist then the best. Anybody you could name, Curt was certainly no [worse]. There was nobody you could name that, to me, was really any more talented.

**TLC:** *Were you disappointed when he left?*

**JS:** Yeah, a little bit. The thing is, he'd been doing it a long time, and he liked doing **Superman**, he liked doing the single character stuff. Of course, I was doing these ambitious epics with hundreds of characters, and it was a little hard on him. I understood. That was fine. It was no offense to me. He wanted to do easier work [*laughs*], and I was making him jump through too many hoops. Actually, the first time that any message came to me about Curt was relayed by Mort. Mort said, "Curt likes your stories, and he likes the layouts, but he wants fewer characters, so no more than seven Legionnaires from now on." And from that point on, all my stories had seven or fewer Legionnaires, 'cause Curt didn't want to draw armies. [*laughs*] Who

The Legion gets topical with comic's first drug storyline, "The Forbidden Fruit," in Action Comics #378.
© DC Comics

can blame him?

**TLC:** *What do you remember about the Legion's move from **Adventure Comics** to **Action Comics**?*

**JS:** I tell this to people, and they look at me like I'm crazy, but as I told you, if you check the statement of ownership in the very first issue I wrote, it's about 500,000 circulation. If you check it in the last issue I wrote, it's about 500,000 circulation, at a time when everything else was plunging. Mort had done a couple of experiments to try to figure out what the impact of Superboy and Supergirl on the Legion of Super-Heroes sales were. And, as you might expect, on those issues where he didn't have Superboy or Supergirl on the cover, the sales went down. Mort's conclusion was that this was really just another Superboy book, and that the Legion was not a successful property on its own. Now, **Superboy**, the magazine itself, sales had been plummeting. Mort's conclusion was that the Legion of Super-Heroes was draining away sales from **Superboy**, and that the property really wasn't good enough to hold its own. So he decided

that the Legion of Super-Heroes without Superboy was a back-up story, and that if he put "Supergirl" in **Adventure Comics**, that the sales would hold, still have a half a million, and that **Superboy**'s sales would rise, since it was no longer being diluted. Well, that was wrong. I mean, they put "Supergirl" in **Adventure Comics** and the sales just nosedived instantly. They put "The Legion of Super-Heroes" in the back of **Action Comics**—I don't know if it helped **Action Comics** or not (probably not)—and **Superboy** sales did not pick up, so the whole thing was [a] disastrous miscalculation, like the Edsel. They had a winner, and they eviscerated it.

**TLC:** *Did that help influence your decision to leave?*

**JS:** No. Like I said, they filled every waking minute they could. They demanded more and more work from me, and I was doing everything I could. It wasn't like I needed work. Also, Mort had come to me and said, "We still want you to have a regular book that you do every month, and for the moment that's gonna be **Jimmy Olsen**." Okay, I'd written some **Jimmy Olsen**s. It was all right. But around that time, I'd kinda had it with Mort, and tried to work at Marvel, and like I said, having to work in the office made that difficult, so I ended up getting out of comics for a while. But after I didn't take **Jimmy Olsen**, they gave it to Kirby. [*laughs*] So Kirby pinch-hit for me.

**TLC:** *You did manage to sneak in a couple of socially relevant stories during the **Action Comics** run.*

**JS:** Yeah. The very first drug story in comics was written by me. It was called, "The Lotus Fruit," [**Action Comics #378** — Ed.] and the code rejected it. Mort wielded great influence, [and] I had to write a couple of additional panels where, at the end, the guy is redeemed and renounces drugs. I had to write a couple of panels to shut up the code, which we did, and it ran, and didn't get any publicity or attention. Then substantially later, when Stan did the **Spider-Man** drug thing and ran without the code, then he got tons of publicity.

**TLC:** *Is that the sort of thing which we would have seen more of had you stayed?*

**JS:** Oh, sure. Like I said, we all grew up together. You read the stories I wrote when I was thirteen, fourteen, [and] the

# Win Mortimer

James Winslow Mortimer was born on May 23, 1919, in Hamilton, Ontario, and attended the Art Students League of New York after high school, where he studied anatomy in the same class as Stan Drake. Upon the onset of World War II, Mortimer enlisted in the Canadian Army, where he served until his discharge in 1943. Once the war was over, Mortimer found work difficult to attain, and so he moved to New York City, where he joined DC Comics in their bullpen.

A former romance artist, Win Mortimer became the new Legion artist when Curt Swan stepped down. From *Action Comics #378*. © DC Comics

Originally a **Batman** artist, Mortimer also illustrated **Superman** and **Superboy** stories in his early days with the company before going on to become their most prolific cover artist, producing covers for titles as varied as **Superman**, **Batman**, **Star-Spangled Comics**, **Real Fact Comics**, and **Mr. District Attorney**, among others. In 1950 he became the artist of the **Superman** daily strip, a position which he held until 1955 when he would leave DC Comics entirely to draw **David Crane** for the Prentice-Hall Syndicate. Mortimer followed **Crane** in 1960 with **Lance Bannon** for the Toronto Star Syndicate, which he worked on until 1966, at which point he returned to DC.

From 1968-1970, Mortimer was the regular artist on the "Tales of the Legion of Super-Heroes" feature which ran in **Adventure Comics**, and then **Action Comics**. He also illustrated the lead "Supergirl" feature in **Adventure Comics** following the Legion's departure from the

title, but worked less and less for the publisher as the Seventies wore on. Instead, Mortimer moved over to Marvel, where he was the regular artist on **Spidey Super-Stories**, as well as a sporadic penciler on Marvel's black-and-white horror magazines, such as **Dracula Lives!** and **Tales of the Zombie**. Mortimer also worked for Gold Key Comics, an association which began in 1965 with back-ups in **Dr. Solar, Man of the Atom**, and which continued throughout the 1970s with stories in **Boris Karloff's Tales of Mystery**, **Ripley's Believe It or Not**, and **The Twilight Zone**, to name just a few.

In 1983 Mortimer joined Neal Adam's Continuity Associates, where he worked mostly as a commercial artist. He did not abandon the comics field entirely, and had returned to DC earlier in the decade to once again draw "Supergirl," this time in **Superman Family**. He continued his association with the Superman universe in 1988 when he illustrated the **World of**

**Metropolis** mini-series written by John Byrne, and he would also return to his Legion roots that same year as the artist of various entries in **Who's Who in the Legion of Super-Heroes**, including the Taurus Gang and the Tornado Twins, characters whose first appearances he also drew.

In 1987 Mortimer returned to work at Continuity after undergoing a heart bypass operation, and continued to draw a weekly editorial cartoon for the Putnam County Courier, as well as a five-page religious comic book called **Faith and Stuff** on top of his regular duties. The latter was a throwback to his DC days when he would also illustrate public service announcements for the publisher, covering an array of topics from racism to littering with many more in between. Win Mortimer would continue to draw right up until the time of his death on January 11, 1998. He was 78 years old.

Continued from page 60

Legionnaires seemed to be thirteen, fourteen, and the stories were a little more childish. And then as I grew up—and this was the Sixties, don't forget—I was really trying to make these characters real and relevant. Like I said, I always wanted to have a Legionnaire who was African-American, and years later, when they did that, they did it in the worst way possible. Sorry, Cary Bates, but instead of just incidentally having a character who happens to be black, then never mentioning it, they

made a big fuss about it. He's a racial separatist. Give me a break! Why is it every time you introduce a black character, the story's got to be about him being black? Come on! So I just found it pathetic and appalling. What I wanted to do was just break new ground and tromple all the clichés and try to have some meaning in the stories, 'cause I think that makes them better stories. That's one of the things that Stan did. He's a cliché buster.

[But] he made some of the same mistakes. I mean, his first black character had the unfortunate name of the Black Panther—c'mon, Stan. Geez!—but he's a pioneer, [and] pioneers make mistakes. And I wanted to do that, too.

# Mort Weisinger

Probably the single most important contributor to the Legion of Super-Heroes in its early days was the man with whom the idea of such an organization began. Originally conceived of as a throwaway story, the Legion of Super-Heroes was brought back again and again, each time to increasing reader demand, until Mort Weisinger decided to give it its own regular feature in the pages of **Adventure Comics**. Over time the Legion legend would grow, resulting in it becoming one of the earliest features to become a fan favorite. Eventually Weisinger would even incorporate ideas from fans in the form of new characters, and he even instituted the first Legion leadership election in which readers were able to vote. Weisinger also recruited future professionals from fandom, including E. Nelson Bridwell, Roy Thomas, and a very young Jim Shooter.

The following interview was conducted in 1974 by Matt Lage, and it is truly a rarity. In it, Weisinger covers the entirety of his comics career and answers the claims of his critics. It originally appeared in **The Legion Outpost** #9, 1975, and appears here with the permission of Harry Broertjes, former editor of the **Outpost**.

**TLC:** *The base questions first. In your years as comic editor and writer, what contributions did you make to comics? This also including series which you were instrumental in creating.*

**MW:** Green Arrow, Vigilante, Air Wave, Aquaman, TNT and Dan the Dyna-Mite, Tommy Tomorrow and numerous others that I can't recall. I originated such characters as Bizarro, Krypto, Supergirl, Superbaby, et cetera, and assigned them to various writers for scripting. I also invented the Bottle of Kandor, the Phantom Zone, the "LL" running gag—Lois Lane, Lana Lang, Lori Lemaris, et al., the proper-

ties of the various forms of kryptonite—with the exception of Green K, which was the invention of Robert Maxwell, producer of the radio series which featured Superman; Maxwell also introduced Jimmy Olsen there. I think the innovation I'm proudest of was the use of the "imaginary story" to present stories that weren't otherwise possible. And I also created the series, "Tales of Krypton."

**TLC:** *In your 30 years in comics, what companies did you work for, the first feature and when?*

**MW:** In comics, I've always worked for DC. My first assignment was to dream up some new characters for **Adventure** and **Action**. My first week on the job produced the first Green Arrow, Vigilante, and Aquaman, in 1941.

**TLC:** *When you were Mort Weisinger, writer, which DC editor did you produce your best work for?*

**MW:** My best work was for Whitney Ellsworth, who originally hired me in 1941. He never interfered with me—let me do as I pleased. Then he summoned me to Hollywood to serve as story editor for the **Superman** TV series. Here again he let me operate without interference. There I built a team of **Superman** TV writers. I am proud to say I discovered Jackson Gillis, who went on to write many of the **Colombo** scripts; Peggy Chantler, who later wrote the pilots for **Hazel** and **Dennis the Menace**, and several others who made good in a big way.

**TLC:** *Superman is the ultimate Weisinger character. In what way did you fashion the character?*

**MW:** I think my greatest contribution to

Superman was to give him a "mythology" which covered all bases, from the history of Krypton to his relationship with the people of Atlantis, the survival of Kandor, the inhabitation of the Phantom Zone by various Kryptonian villains, et cetera. All this makes Superman credible. I also went to lengths to elaborate on the "Superman family," and cross-pollinated these relationships by simultaneously interweaving their causes and effects in magazines appearing during one month.

**TLC:** *In your years as Superman's editor, probably more so in the Sixties, did you try to make Superman relevant to the reading audience?*

**MW:** During World War II, I wrote stories for the magazine in which Superman aided the war effort, got the readers to buy war bonds, save scrap metal. Also did stories to promote safety, conservation, fire prevention, et cetera, tying up with the Red Cross, Boy Scouts, et cetera. Many of the TV stories were pleas for tolerance. One film in particular George Reeves and I were proud of was a story in which Superman

BUT IT **IS** ME, PUNYMAN... THE **COMPOSITE SUPERMAN**, WHO POSSESSES **ALL** THE POWERS OF THE **LEGION OF SUPER-HEROES** OF THE 30TH CENTURY... EVEN THOUGH I'D NEVER BEEN TO THEIR ERA! *

*THE **COMPOSITE SUPER MAN** BATTLED **SUPERMAN** AND **BATMAN** IN **WORLD'S FINEST** NO.'S 142 AND 168.-Ed

*Top: Weisinger in the '70s. Above: An example of Weisinger's "cross-pollination" at work: the Composite Superman addresses the real Superman in a story by Curt Swan and Jack Abel.*
Superman and the Composite-Superman TM and © DC Comics

*From left to right, starting with the back row: Jack Williamson, L. Sprague deCamp, John D. Clark, Frank Belknap Long, Mort Weisinger, Edmond Hamilton, and Otis Alderbert Klein. Front row: Otto Binder, Manly Wade Wellman, and Julius Schwartz in a photo taken in 1937. Provided by Peter Hansen.*

asked the public to give rehabilitated ex-convicts a second chance. This was done dramatically.

**TLC:** *Many people find that the Fifties were a bad time for the comics, with all of the poor sci-fi stories floating around. Especially so with the case of World's Finest...*

**MW:** I'll cop out on this one. When **WF** went wild with alien creatures, it was not under my helm. This was the doing of Jack Schiff. His bug-eyed monsters almost ruined the property. It was taken away from him and restored to me. I junked his policy, put **WF** back on the beam, and the circulation improved healthily immediately afterward.

**TLC:** *Superman's sales are pretty bad when you match them up against his old circulation. But the story is the same all over and no company is an exception to the rule. Why is this happening? Don't people want fantasy anymore? Some people claim that it's because the reading audience of today is brighter than that of yesteryear, and that today's technology makes some of the stories believable anyway...*

**MW:** I think poor stories, lack of originality, the willingness of the editors to accept "market conditions" as the cause of poor sales, *is* the cause of poor sales. Why does **TV Guide** continue to soar upward in circulation, despite numerous attempts by rivals to gain a foothold in the field? Why did **Cosmopolitan** suddenly come to life as a winner? Because the old editor was fired and the new one, Helen Gurley Brown, knew her stuff. There are no poor market conditions, only poor hack editors.

**TLC:** *Every artist, writer and editor considers some of his colleagues as his favorites, professionally. Otto Binder cited C.C. Beck as artist, Bill Woolfolk and Ed*

Herron as writers, and Herron and Wen Crowley as editors. Could you give us some of yours?

**MW:** For Krypton stories: Wayne Boring. For "Supergirl": Jim Mooney. For **Lois Lane**: Kurt Schaffenberger. For **World's Finest**: Curt Swan. Best script writer, light years ahead of the pack: Edmond Hamilton and Jerry Siegel. Siegel was the best emotional writer of them all—as in the unforgettable "Death of Luthor." Also, John Forte was tops in the "Bizarro" series and George Papp in the "Legion" series.

**TLC:** *Otto Binder wrote the first Legion tale. Was the story created for a purpose, or was it just another story to fill space? And did Binder write any of the Legion stories after the first?*

**MW:** The first Legion story was a spontaneous idea—no thought that the readers would flip over it and demand a spate of sequels. However, the credit for the introduction of Bouncing Boy and the others should go to Jerry Siegel. He revitalized the series after Binder went stale with it.

**TLC:** *Was it hard leaving the comic book industry after 30 years in it? Did you ever have a time when you wished you'd stayed?*

**MW:** No regrets. In all my years at DC I wrote articles for all the major magazines, about 300, for national publications such as the **Saturday Evening Post, Colliers, Reader's Digest, Cosmopolitan, True, Redbook, Argosy, Holiday, Esquire,** and many others. Also wrote a Bantam Book paperback, **1001 Valuable Things You Can Get Free**, which has sold over three million copies, a new edition coming out every two years—ninth edition coming out this fall. Also wrote a novel, **The Contest**, which was a best-seller and sold to the

movies for $125,000. Quit my job at DC so that I could write my second novel in prime time, instead of moonlighting. It will be an exposé of astrology. I quit **Superman** because it was too much of a burden to write in my free time and do my job competently. I've always preferred to write. But I haven't really abandoned the Man of Steel; I speak at colleges all over the country on "The Superman Mystique," and get paid handsomely for each and every spiel.

**TLC:** *When you left DC, did you give any recommendations to Carmine Infantino as to what editor should get which title? And if you did, who did you suggest get what?*

**MW:** I suggested to Infantino that all my books be given to one editor, instead of being fragmented. Result, from what my audiences tell me when I lecture, is that there are inconsistencies in the various books, due to the right hand not knowing what the left is doing. I think Infantino made a big mistake in not heeding my advice.

**TLC:** *Yet another base question which I ask in every interview I do with a writer or editor: When doing your stories or directing other writers, did you ever use a set formula?*

*The Legion of Super-Pets by sometime Legion artist George Tuska. Courtesy of Scott Bierworth. Art © 2003 George Tuska; the Legion of Super-Pets TM and © DC Comics*

Saturn Girl by Bob McLeod, from the collection of Kevin McConnell. Art © 2003 Bob McLeod; Saturn Girl TM and © DC Comics.

**MW:** My formula was simply: Be original. Be clever. Have suspense. A good picture sequence in every story. A surprise ending. Or a twist, whenever possible.

[**Note:** *In The Legion Outpost #8, Dave Sim wrote a letter containing the following criticisms of Weisinger:*

Mort Weisinger puts me away. Every time that guy writes a letter, he sticks his typewriter in his mouth. To hear him tell the story, DC was a vast wasteland of nothing until he came along. He keeps trying to get people interested in the Bizarros, since it was one of the few things he ever created. It's taken people like Len Wein and Denny O'Neil a number of years to undo all the damage he inflicted on the Superman comics (which, unfortunately, includes the Legion of Super-Heroes) line. You'd be hard pressed to find any artist or writer with anything nice to say about Weisinger and the way he handled the Superman line.

*TLO #8 also featured comments about Weisinger from Jim Shooter, said comments being similar in nature to those made in Shooter's new interview which appears elsewhere in this volume. To both comments, Weisinger had the following response. —Ed.*]

**Q:** *What have you to say regarding Dave Sim's comments in your last issue: "You'd* be hard pressed to find any artist or writer with anything nice to say about Weisinger and the way he handled the Superman line."... "To hear him tell the story, DC was a vast wasteland of nothing until he came along."*

**A:** Let's look at the record. I wrote and created the pilot scripts for "The Green Arrow," "The Vigilante," "Aquaman" and many other series which had long runs during the "Golden Age." I developed and stimulated the entire Superman mythology, which included the introduction of kryptonite and Jimmy Olsen on the original **Superman** radio show, then was later transplanted to the magazines. I created red kryptonite, as well as some other forms. I innovated the "LL" running theme. I innovated the "imaginary stories" series. The first **Superman Annual**, which depended on a theme, rather than simply a collection of old reprints, was solely my concept. It sold 750,000 copies overnight.

If writers didn't like me, why did such top science-fiction writers who wrote for me when I was editor of **Thrilling Wonder Stories** leave the pulps and come over to DC to write for me? I'm referring to Otto Binder, Edmond Hamilton, Manly Wade Wellman and Alfred Bester.

It was I who innovated the letter pages in the **Superman** magazine, which fostered reader participation that eventually spun off into the fanzines. (Incidentally, it was Julie Schwartz and myself who originated the *very first* fanzine in America, **The Time Traveler**, in 1931).

It was yours truly who started the trend at DC in combing the slush pile to discover new talent. I discovered Cary Bates. I discovered Jim Shooter. I gave both of them the credit and publicity they well deserved. (Incidentally, Shooter may not know it, but it was I who had **This Week** magazine do a profile on him, for the simple reason that I was a contributing editor to that magazine at the time). I discovered Nelson Bridwell in the fan-letter piles, and paid his expenses to come to New York so that I could hire him.

I discovered Dick Lederer, a modest but excellent writer who wrote many fine stories for me when I was editor of **Batman**. Lederer is now vice-president in charge of publicity for Warner Brothers. And speaking of Hollywood, when I was story editor of the **Superman** TV series, I discovered Jackson Gillis, who went on to become associate producer of the **Perry Mason** shows, then later wrote many of the Peter Falk **Colombo** shows, as well as serving as its story editor last season. I saw him in Hollywood the other month and he is now story editor of the new NBC series, **Petrocelli**. I bought Peggy Chantler's first script; she went on to create the block-

## MEET MORT WEISINGER: THE MAN BEHIND SUPERMAN

The Superman legend will live forever, so contends MORT WEISINGER, the super alter-ego behind the legend, who was for thirty years, the first editor of Superman and Batman, and the story editor of the Superman TV shows and comic books. After all, is there a true American who hasn't read Superman in the funny books, seen him in the movies or on TV? Of course not. Superman was part of everybody's childhood, as it still remains today in many cities around the country, where the shows are still being seen, not only by youngsters and college youths, but by adults as well.

Mr. Weisinger's lecture on the "Superman Mystique" is illustrated by a graphic film depicting the origin of Superman on the planet Krypton, his super-powers on Earth and his "Daily Planet" newspaper job. He then recalls for his audiences old nostalgic inside stories about the character who was able to leap tall buildings at a bound, break into solid steel vaults, turn up at all emergencies and save Lois Lane. He also reveals stories involving Presidents Kennedy and Eisenhower, Emperor Hirohito, Kruschev, Albert Einstein with Superman.

Mort Weisinger, a writer who has had more than 300 articles published in such varied magazines as The Saturday Evening Post, Today's Health, The Reader's Digest, Pageant, Parade, Family Weekly, Cosmopolitan and Redbook, among others, came into the headlines again, at the publishing of his novel, "THE CONTEST", a frank expose of the beauty pageant business, which sold over 800,000 paperback copies, and is now being made into a film by Columbia Pictures. His first book, "1001 Valuable Things You Can Get Free", is now in its 8th edition. His most recent project, an anthology of white lies, "THE COMPLETE ALIBI BOOK", tells the reader how to lie to his wife, his neighbor, his friends and boss.

A former Air Force Technical Sergeant in World War II, where he wrote the Air Force show "I Sustain the Wings" for Captain Glenn Miller, the noted band leader, Mr. Weisinger is now working on still another show-stopper, a novel about a flamboyant astrologer, "The Great Aquarius," who becomes a consultant to the President of the United States. The novel debunks the astrology racket and is based on three years of pioneering research. As Mr. Weisinger puts it: "It is a block-buster and it is going to do to astrology what the "Snake-pit" did to psychiatry."

*A Mort Weisinger promotional flyer, used to advertise Weisinger for public speaking engagements. Courtesy of Harry Broertjes.*

*More artwork by Bob McLeod, courtesy of Kevin McConnell.*
Art © 2003 Bob McLeod; Fire Lad and Chameleon Boy TM and © DC Comics.

buster TV series **Hazel** and **Dennis the Menace**. Why didn't smearer-Sim check with these people as to my abilities and contributions? And let's not forget Mann Rubin, who was discovered by me, and wrote for Julie Schwartz and myself when we co-edited **Strange Adventures**. Mann is one of TV's top writers today; he writes **Mannix**, **The Rookies**, and many 90-minute ABC movies. All these pros are still my friends, and whenever I am in Hollywood they roll out the carpet for me and my wife.

As for Shooter sounding off that I gave him a hard time, perhaps. But don't forget I was under tremendous pressure all those years. I was the sole editor of the *entire* family of **Superman** magazines; they weren't fragmented in those days among other editors, as they are today. It was a Herculean job. I had production responsibilities, and when Shooter missed a deadline, or his airmail delivery of a script was late, or he failed to provide material for a cover, *I* was the one who had to climb the walls. And, at the risk of bruising his ego, let me disclose now that when I *did* use cover ideas he suggested, against my better instinct, they bombed in sales.

Shooter neglected telling of the times I phoned him from my home, late at night, and at my own expense, to give him ideas or to help him thrash out his plots. I still think the kid is a genius. But if I'm the heavy he made me out to be, how come he couldn't survive more than a few weeks at Stan Lee's? Methinks the lad is a bit paranoid!

Has anyone ever pointed out that the **Superman** magazines enjoyed their greatest circulations under my helmsmanship,

and has dramatically declined, both in sales volume and frequency of issues, since I left? Has anyone ever mentioned that I was given a $10,000-a-year salary raise *one month* before I resigned? And that Infantino got our management to give me a year's stock options if I would not take a vacation due me and build up an inventory for him before I left, which I did? And has it ever been made known that in addition to my magazine duties, I was also vice-president in charge of public relations for DC? It was *I* who got Macy's to use a Superman blimp in their annual Thanksgiving parade for five years. It was *I* who got George Reeves to play a feature role in an *I Love Lucy* episode, as well as getting stories on Superman and Batman placed in such magazines as **Life** and **Look**.

And if all this makes me sound like an egomaniac, let's review what I've done so far this year of 1974. I had nine cover stories published in **Parade** magazine, which has the largest circulation in America—20 million. Several more are slated to be published in coming weeks: an exposé of losers in Las Vegas; the story of America's 107 lottery "instant millionaires," and an inside preview of the new J. Edgar Hoover FBI building. This November, Bantam will publish the ninth edition of my paperback, **1,001 Valuable Things You Can Get Free**, which has already sold over four million copies, and has earned me almost half a million dollars. The most successful magazine in America, **Reader's Digest**, will publish a "drama in real life" about my son, Hank, in January or February, 1975, entitled "Moscow Doesn't Answer." I have also sold a stream of articles to **Seventeen**, **True**, and other leading magazines.

This year I received four-figure fees for lecturing at the University of Kansas, University of Alabama, University of Minnesota, as well as several other colleges. I am program chairman of the Society of Magazine Writers, whose members include the top writers in the book and magazine field, and was their vice-president for the last two years. I also am finishing my second novel, **The President's Astrologer**, for David McKay, and already have sold paperback rights and have a movie option on it. Articles I wrote last year have been read into the **Congressional Record**, been reprinted in the **Encyclopedia Britannica**, and in college textbooks. In addition, I teach classes in creative writing at NYU. And, if you'll permit some more name-dropping, I am listed in **Who's Who in the East** and next year will be in their national edition. I also do voluntary public relations (at no fee) for the National Multiple Sclerosis Society and have helped them raise millions of dollars by directing their charity campaigns.

Next March my wife and I will be living in England, so that I can research material for a book I have contracted for on Lloyd's of London.

This is a hell of a lot better than taking sh*t from Shooter or Sim, wouldn't you say?

Finally, why don't you give credit to the one guy who *really* brought the Legion of Super-Heroes to life—Jerry Siegel (with an assist from Otto Binder). Jerry, whom I consider the most competent of all the Superman writers, established the foundation for the series. What his successors did was just embroidery, including my own contributions.

*Mort Weisinger as a young man, presumably from his pre-comics days.*

# Murray Boltinoff

When Mort Weisinger retired from DC Comics in 1970, the "Superman Family" of titles was divided up amongst the remaining DC editors. As a long-time editor at the company, Murray Boltinoff received **Action Comics** and **Superboy**. Deciding that the "Legion of Super-Heroes" back-up feature in **Action** was more suited to Superboy's younger audience, Boltinoff moved the feature for the second time in three years, then proceeded to publish it only periodically. Upset with the Legion's demotion, Legion fans began writing in demanding that it be returned to a regular schedule, if not its own title. In fact, it was one of the of the main goals of **The Legion Outpost** fanzine, and the primary reason why the Legion Fan Club was formed.

In 1973, DC heard their call and promoted the Legion to equal billing with Superboy in his own title. What follows is an article written by Boltinoff announcing that move. Originally published in **The Legion Outpost** #4, Summer, 1973, it answers many questions as to what went on behind the scenes concerning the Legion during the early Seventies, and is reprinted here with the permission of Harry Broertjes, former editor of the **Outpost**.

When Harry Broertjes, who guides this publication from his control center in Evanston, Illinois requested some remarks from the hot seat otherwise known as the Editor's Chair, how could I spurn the guru of the Legion?

I had backed into the assignment of handling **Superboy and the Legion of Super-Heroes**. Superboy had been one of the staples at National Periodicals, and when an unprecedented hue and cry was raised for the return of the Legion, who was I to ignore the call? We tested the feature with some pardonable timidity. The response was overwhelming. In all the years that I've clutched an editor's blue pencil, never have my ears resounded with such a din. Obviously, the Legion's readership was, in a word, legion.

So we amputated some of the Superboy sagas and replaced the pages with the LSH. We followed that pattern for several issues with Superboy as the lead feature and the Legion as the back-up. Until...

Until the tail began to wag the dog. Sales indicated that the "Legion" was waxing stronger and stronger. Heady with success, the office released a tome of "LSH" reprints. The first issue scored a resounding bull's-eye, and the office promptly put a second into the works. And on the heels of what may one day be hailed as a monumental meeting, it was decided to step up the Legion to equal status with Superboy.

In #197, the Legion makes its first major appearance in a 13-page chronicle called, "Timber Wolf, Dead Hero: Live Executioner," and Superboy slams through a swiftly-paced story, "The Slay-Away Plan," both from the steaming typewriter of Cary Bates.

Parenthetically, Cary has just returned from powwows in London with the movie

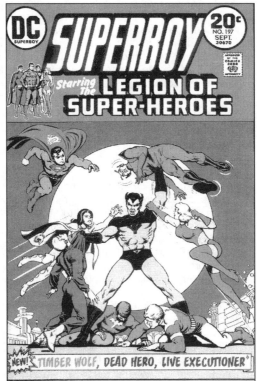

*The Legion gained respectability again with the publication of* Superboy and the Legion of Super-Heroes *#197, Sept. 1973.*
Superboy and the Legion of Super-Heroes TM and © DC Comics

potentates who produce the James Bond movies. As noted in a recent issue of **Superboy**, Cary is negotiating to do the screen play for a new Bond bombshell.

LSH aficionados should be heartened by the tidings that their motley membership of 26 miniature super-heroes will appear in a full-size, book-length lalapalooza titled "The Fatal Five Who Twisted Time" in #198. And by the way of replying to the fevered fans who batter us with the same question, "What about #200?", we can only reveal that plans have been made, which must be kept secret for the time being but will be disclosed all in good time.

The notion of handling a mag with a clutch of super-kids would faze any editor, but in my opinion I am aided and abetted by two of the best in the business. Dave Cockrum is Instant Genius, and Cary Bates can handle the twists and turns of a plot like few writers. I couldn't think of anyone else I'd rather have on my team than Demonic Dave and Canny Cary, as Mike Flynn, the Bard of the Bronx, labels them. I've been carried up, up and away on their wave of enthusiasm.

Dave has gone so far as to prepare a guide book for our Color Department. It should prove to be of such immeasurable value that one day it may find its way into the Library of Congress. Dave has already introduced some changes in the attire of some of the Legionnaires, but from here on in these will be kept to a minimum. None of us wants to make changes simply for the sake of changing unless something superior results.

Villains? We're going to give you some of the old ones and develop some new ones. On the whole, we're going to keep the LSH roster the same, but don't be surprised if we lop off a Legionnaire here and there, now and then, and replace him (or her) with another member of sterling quality.

From here on in, the Legion of Super-Heroes will contain a bit of the old, a bit of the new. There'll be nothing static about it. With their names on the cover of the mag, the Legion will be a whole new ball game! And we hope that all of you have a super-good time reading about them.

# Cary Bates

The following interview with then-Legion scripter Cary Bates was conducted in February, 1973 by then-Legion Fan Club member Mike Valero. It originally appeared in **The Legion Outpost** #4, Summer, 1973, and unlike interviews conducted today, it provides an interesting snapshot into was going on in the mind of the then-Legion author while the series was still appearing as a back-up feature in **Superboy**. Like all material reprinted from **The Legion Outpost** in this volume, the following interview is the property of **TLO** editor Harry Broertjes, and is used with his permission.

**TLC:** *First off, Cary, could you give us a quick rundown of how you broke into comics, which companies you have worked for, and what features you've worked on.*

**CB:** Mort Weisinger bought my first story in late 1966, when I was a freshman in college. I worked almost exclusively for him until he left National three years later. Since then, I've worked with every editor at National, with the exception of Jack Kirby. National is the only comics company I'm associated with. I've sold several cover ideas to **Mad** magazine over the past two years.

As for the features, I've done every book and character in the Superman Family, Flash, Elongated Man, El Diablo, Wonder Woman, Rose and Thorn, Vigilante, Legion of Super-Heroes, and an occasional mystery and romance story.

**TLC:** *Which feature or features have you enjoyed working on the most and why?*

**CB:** Superman, because he's a very versatile and rich character, full of countless possibilities, the best-developed secret identity and secondary characters in comics, in my opinion, and with so many super-powers you can have him do just about *anything* if you're clever enough at it.

El Diablo, because of Neal Adams' work in the earlier stories, and the great potential of this supernatural ghost-rider. Also, the strip gives me a chance to do what I

call my "Italian Western Schtick," as I'm an avid follower of Sergio Leone movies.

Flash, because of all the heroes in comics, you can do the most outlandish and absurd things with him imaginable. To see what I mean, just think about some of the things Flash has been turned into, not just in my stories, but Fox's and Broome's. And, of course, there are all those great villains.

**TLC:** *Does writing the **Legion** feature present any special problems?*

**CB:** You'd better believe it. The total number of characters is over double that of the next biggest super-group... the task of working a sizable number of them into an eight- to thirteen-page story is appallingly difficult... following another writer's footsteps, Jim Shooter, is no picnic, especially with so many characterizations involved. The strip cannot really be done right unless it's the whole book. In a shorter-length story, characterization must give way to plot and action. That's the nature of the business.

**TLC:** *Do you plan to add any members to the Legion roster?*

**CB:** Hell no. Thank God for Nelson's story, which set the legal limit at twenty-five. If any new members do join—and at least one will in the near future—it will only be after a current member is dropped.

**TLC:** *Where do you get your ideas for your stories?*

**CB:** From anything and everything. That sounds like a brush-off

answer, but I really can't be more specific. If you've got the imagination, you'll know what I mean.

**TLC:** *If you wrote a **Legion** tale wherein a Legionnaire was killed off or expelled from the Legion, could it simply be printed or would you have to "get permission" from the editor and/or publisher?*

**CB:** I wouldn't directly consult Carmine, but certainly Murray would have to OK such a development. But your question omitted Dave Cockrum, who would be the person I'd consult first.

**TLC:** *I think the biggest question in everybody's mind is if the new **Legion** mag does print new stories will you be writing them?*

**CB:** As of this date, yes. Frankly, no other

*A convention sketch of Colossal Boy by Dave Cockrum. Courtesy of Kevin McConnell. Art © 2003 Dave Cockrum; Colossal Boy TM and © DC Comics.*

established writer at DC has the background or particularly wants the job, as far as I know. Nelson may still do an occasional piece, and I'd like to see Dave try his hand at writing one as well as draw it.

*Mike Grell's very first Tyroc sketch, from the collection of Steven Weill.*
Tyroc TM and © DC Comics

**TLC:** *The Legion has a long and illustrious past. What new events can we look forward to in the future?*

**CB:** As I hinted before, one member will be leaving—you'll have to wait to find out who and why. More classic villains will be returning, as well as some new ones which Dave has already sketched on his drawing board.

**TLC:** *A lot of people seem to think that the super-hero is on his way out, giving the spotlight to the adventure hero—Tarzan, Conan, Kamandi, Ka-Zar, and so on. What's your opinion?*

**CB:** Yes and no. Yes, they seem to be in a slump now, but comic books show how cyclical the business is; not only have super-heroes had peaks and slumps, but the same applies for westerns, sci-fi, horror, etc.

**TLC:** *Getting back to the new Legion book: if—and when—it does go into new stories, will Dave Cockrum continue to illustrate it? I heard he wasn't.*

**CB:** You heard wrong. As the saying goes up here, the *Legion* is Dave's baby.

**TLC:** *What was going on with the Who-wants-to-be-editor-of-the-Legion-mag? game DC has been playing? Rovin-to-Asherman-to-Bridwell tends to leave the reader a trifle confused.*

**CB:** I suppose so, but the switch-overs have been made for various reasons I can't go into. Since the job mainly consists of choosing which stories to reprint, the effects of the changes aren't catastrophic. All the new stuff is and will remain Murray's.

**TLC:** *What new and different things can we expect from Cary Bates?*

**CB:** In a few weeks I'll be going to Denmark for a sex-transplant. Seriously, I can't answer that because even I usually don't know what I'm going to do next. A lot of the time I'm really amazed, or disappointed, as the case may be, by what comes out of my head.

**TLC:** *What are some of your hobbies outside of writing?*

**CB:** Cars, music, and writing outside the comics field.

**TLC:** *What advice do you give to our young, future comic-writers out there in fandom?*

**CB:** Don't give up. It took me four years to sell my first story, and the Weisinger-***Superman*** market was tougher to crack than any editorial office is today. Back in '66, Shooter was the only other "boy wonder" working professionally, so the precedent for hiring any writer under 45 wasn't set yet. I don't need to list all the writers my age and younger who have entered the field since then.

But I'm not saying it'll be any easier today, either,

because the competition is much tougher than it was seven years ago. When you're first starting out, your best bet is to make sure your ideas are terrific, at least as good and hopefully better than what's being published. The mechanics and technique of comics writing can only be mastered after working with the professional editors here; and if your story ideas are good enough, an editor may be swayed to break in a new writer. And believe me, it's a big, time-consuming task.

**TLC:** *Finally, Cary, I'm sure you have some words of wisdom that you'd like to pass on to our readers.*

**CB:** No, I don't. But I do want the readers out there to keep passing along their words of wisdom to me, Dave, and Murray. Your club and the rest of the Legion fan following have been a great help and boost to us, and we hope it continues to be.

*The cover to **The Legion Outpost** #8, Summer, 1974, by Dave Cockrum.*
Art © 1974 Dave Cockrum; Validus and the Legion of Super-Heroes TM and © DC Comics

# Dave Cockrum

After revitalizing the Legion of Super-Heroes in the early Seventies, Dave Cockrum went over to Marvel Comics where he changed the **X-Men** into what would eventually become the company's best-selling title. After launching his own creation, **The Futurians**, in the 1980s, he wrote and penciled a mini-series featuring his favorite X-Man, **Nightcrawler**, shortly thereafter. Responsible for co-creating the Starjammers, the Imperial Guard, and the entire Shi'ar Empire, Cockrum was interviewed by phone on November 18, 2002, and he copyedited the final transcript.

**TLC:** *Let's begin with an obvious question. How did you get the* **Legion** *assignment?*

**DC:** I was working as Murphy Anderson's background inker, and I'd been nudging around for some kind of series. I actually had done three sample pages of **Legion** stuff. The problem with the **Legion** was that it was slowly dying. Nobody really wanted it. George Tuska was the last penciler, and I guess either he was too busy or he didn't want it, either. Murphy Anderson alerted me to the fact that, "Hey! There's this series! You might be able to get it!" [So] bang, zoom! I was on my way to Murray Boltinoff's office. I got it on the premise that since I worked for Murphy, he would oversee it and make sure that I didn't do any crummy work. So Murphy was kinda like quality control for the strip.

**TLC:** *How familiar were you with the* **Legion** *at that time?*

**DC:** Fairly familiar. I'd read a lot of the **Legion** stuff.

**TLC:** *Was it the science-fiction aspect of the strip which appealed to you?*

**DC:** Oh, yeah. The combination of the

two—science-fiction and super-heroes. That's probably ideal for me. [They're] the two things I like best. It gave me an opportunity to really show off.

**TLC:** *How closely did you work with Cary Bates?*

**DC:** We'd sit down and we'd plot together. The first two or three stories, no. Murray handed me plots, because Cary was a known quantity and I wasn't. So he was writing on his own, but after we did several [issues] and we were getting favorable reviews, Cary and I started putting our heads together about stories.

**TLC:** *Did you have any interest in writing your own* **Legion** *stories?*

**DC:** I had several **Legion** ideas, and put some of them forward. They all got "No, no, no, no." One of them was a **Legion** story that involved the Blackhawks. Blackhawk relics, really. Murray said, "Blackhawks are dead. Nobody cares about them." And I had an idea that I wanted to do [on] multiple time levels [which would feature] the Legion in the 30th Century, the Teen Titans in the late 20th Century, and I don't know what you would call the group, but it would have Superboy (he wouldn't be hanging out with the Legion in the Legion end of it), Bruce Wayne in his Flying Fox identity, Diana (Wonder Girl), and maybe even a young Oliver Queen fooling around with bows and arrows years before he became Green Arrow, all fighting the Time Trapper. I don't remember whether there was any reaction to that one at all, but nothing happened. And I had an idea about wanting to get some of the Legionnaires involved in trying to break up a galactic slave trade [by] getting some of the girls sold into slavery, and working undercover. They weren't interested in that one, either. I was interested in doing more serious science-fiction than what they were actually doing in the **Legion**. I guess they weren't interested in that.

**TLC:** *How many people were involved in what went into the* **Legion** *back then?*

**DC:** Cary wrote 'em, and I penciled them. Actually, I inked them in those days. I don't know who lettered them. Tatjana Wood, I believe, colored them. And, of course,

there was Murray Boltinoff as editor, and whatever other production people, etc.

**TLC:** *Was E. Nelson Bridwell still involved with it then, behind the scenes?*

**DC:** I don't remember if he was actually involved, but I talked to Nelson a lot. I liked Nelson, and whenever I was in the office I'd stop by and say hello, so he probably influenced me one way or another.

**TLC:** *What kind of a guy was Murray?*

COSTUME DARK BLUE EXCEPT FOR WHITE GLOVES, WHITE ON INNER PART OF LEGS, & YELLOW LIGHTNING BOLTS.

*Top: Cockrum in the Seventies. Above: an original costume design of Lighting Lad by the artist.* Lightning Lad TM and © DC Comics

*Another original costume design by Cockrum.* Phantom Girl TM and © DC Comics

Solid white except for silver belt, & cutouts where skin shows.

**DC:** [*laughs*] Well, the thing that I like to say about Murray is that he was a conservative old fart. I liked him, but he was frustrating as hell because he was so damn conservative. He didn't want to do anything that was going to upset the fans. That's why Nightcrawler didn't make it in. He was too funny looking. That's why there was no black guy in it for such a long time. He didn't want to offend the readers.

**TLC:** *Right from the get-go you started to redesign their costumes...*

**DC:** Well, not quite from the get-go. It was my fifth story, I think. Let's face it: the guys' costumes were all bad imitations of Superboy's costume, except for Matter-Eater Lad's, which was [*laughs*] like out of a comic opera or something. The fact is, I kind of liked Matter-Eater Lad's. So, yeah, I wanted to do something with them. Make them more interesting. I also wanted to change the names of some of them; get rid of the 'Lads' and 'Boys' and that stuff, and no chance on that.

**TLC:** *How much resistance did you get on changing the costumes?*

**DC:** Not really much at all, at first. I guess I had to nudge [Murray] about it a little,

but he said, "All right. Go ahead and try some." It was "The War [Between] the Nights and Days," [*Superboy #193* —**Ed.**] I think, where I gave Chameleon Boy, Shrinking Violet, and Karate Kid new costumes. Duo Damsel got a new costume, but it wasn't my design. One of the fans designed it, and I don't remember if we ever gave him credit [*They did. Nick Pascale, then of Brooklyn, NY.* —**Ed.**].

That was fairly easy, and so for the next several stories I just started introducing new costumes. Then finally, I think it was the Timber Wolf story [*SLSH #197* —**Ed.**], Murray got very conservative and said, "I don't think we should change any more costumes." So I had to sneak in costumes. I hadn't yet changed Lightning Lad, for instance, and I definitely wanted to do his costume. So I had to sneak in the rest of 'em, and make sure that the colorist got the information. I don't know whether Murray ever took notice or not. He never said anything.

**TLC:** *You didn't just change Timber Wolf's costume—you changed his whole look. Did you have a back-story in mind for that?*

**DC:** Not really. I just wanted to make him more interesting. I did start that Timber Wolf story that I was plotting by doing art. I got five pages into it, and then got distracted and never went any further with it. But he was sporting that new look in that.

**TLC:** *Did that predate his new look in the comic?*

**DC:** I really don't remember. It's possible, but then again, I may have done that after I introduced him. 'Cause I liked to become the character. I thought it would be fun to do something with him. Cary didn't seem to be leaning in

the direction of writing Timber Wolf stories, so I worked on that one. I was gonna come up with a total plot and present it and say, "Hey! Let's do it!" I figured if I was showing them outline art, if I'd done that much work, they might've gone along with it.

**TLC:** *Why didn't you keep your original redesign of Colossal Boy's costume?*

**DC:** Once I saw it in print, I hated it.

**TLC:** *Just before you took over the strip, they'd already begun to introduce costumes designed by fans. Do you remember if they tried to get you to continue along that path?*

**DC:** They didn't try and make me do that, no. Light Lass' new costume was sent in by a fan [*Carol Strickland* —**Ed.**]. I got it in

*The redesigned Timber Wolf makes his first appearance. From the collection of Mike Napolitano.* Superboy and the Legion of Super-Heroes TM and © DC Comics.

## A NEW TALE OF THE LEGION of SUPER-HEROES

WELCOME TO THE 30TH CENTURY...AND TO THE FABULOUS HEADQUARTERS OF THE LEGIONNAIRES-- WHERE THE SUPER-POWERED TEENS HAVE JUST FORMALLY SWORN IN A *NEW MEMBER* TO THEIR RANKS--A GALLANT HERO CALLED ERG-1...

NOW THAT I'M ONE OF YOU, I RESPECTFULLY HAVE A REQUEST--I WANT TO BE CALLED BY A *NEW* NAME!

HE'S EMBLAZONING LETTERS IN MID-AIR WITH A SIZZLING ENERGY BEAM!

LOOK AT *THAT!*

THEY SPELL... *WILDFIRE!*

*ERG-1 is rechristened Wildfire. From the collection of Mike Napolitano. The Legion of Super-Heroes is TM and © DC Comics*

a letter. I liked it, I used it, and I turned the letter over to editorial, but I don't think she ever got credit.

**TLC:** *One of the things you're best known for is creating characters. What was the story behind Wildfire?*

**DC:** When I first came up with him, I wanted to call him Starfire. We all know that there are other Starfires, but I pointed out, "Yeah, you've got a half-dozen Starfires, why can't I have a Starfire, too?" I think [they were] just coming up with Starfire from the **Teen Titans**, and they wanted her to be a major player, so I couldn't have the name. In lieu of anything else, I don't know whether it was Cary or Murray, but somebody slapped ERG-1 on him, Energy Reserve Generator or some such nonsense. I said, "No! No! No!" but it was too late to change it by the time I found out, so when we actually did bring him back again, I said, "All right, if I can't have Starfire, I want Wildfire."

I had him writing his name backwards in fire on that splash page [*"Wrath of the Devil-Fish," SLSH #202 —Ed.*]. I showed the pencils of that to Mark Hanerfeld, and he said, "Wildfirf? What's Wildfirf?" I said, "What!" I grabbed it and looked at it, and sure enough, W-I-L-D-F-I-R-F. I changed it real fast. I've always wondered how far it would've gone if he hadn't spotted it.

**TLC:** *Do you prefer the name Wildfire over Starfire now?*

**DC:** Actually, yeah, I think I like Wildfire better. I can't really give you a reason, but I'm comfortable with it.

**TLC:** *Didn't Cary Bates also slip in the Manphibian in your last story without telling you about it?*

**DC:** I had tried selling Manphibian at both companies, and I had sold it to Marvel, finally. Marv Wolfman and I were working on a Manphibian strip, so I was really kind of horrified to get my next **Legion** plot and discover that Manphibian was in that, too. I scrambled over to DC and got with Cary and told him, "Listen, you can't use that! I just sold it to Marvel!" So we changed the name and I changed the visual, and Devilfish made out better. I mean, he got a sequel, which Manphibian never did.

**TLC:** *Were you disappointed by that?*

**DC:** I sort of saw it as a series. We set it up as a series, but nobody showed any interest in doing any more of it, and I think maybe that even included me. [*laughs*]

**TLC:** *You didn't get a chance to draw your own covers while you were on the **Legion**.*

**DC:** No. The only cover I got to draw was the one with Superboy with Tyr's gun on his hand [*SLSH #199 —Ed.*].

**TLC:** *Was that a sticking point with you?*

**DC:** Yeah. I said, "Let me draw some covers," and they let me draw that one. Then they had Nick Cardy redo Superboy, because my Superboy didn't fit the cover version of Superboy.

**TLC:** *At what point did you become aware that **Legion** fans were watching your every move?*

**DC:** I was getting letters from them. Mercy Van Vlack and Harry Broertjes and I don't know who all were writing me from **The Legion Outpost**, sending me copies. I thought it was kinda neat.

**TLC:** *Did you take fandom seriously because you had done some work in fanzines yourself?*

**DC:** Yeah. I knew that the editors didn't take fandom seriously, but I did because hell, yes! I came up from their ranks [*laughs*], and I figured they ought to have an influence.

**TLC:** *When you took over the **Legion**, did you have any contact with any of the artists who drew it before you?*

**DC:** No. Sometime later I met Curt Swan, but it was way later.

**TLC:** *How about the guys who came after you?*

*Colossal Boy's "blue" costume by Cockrum. Courtesy of the artist. The Legion of Super-Heroes is TM and © DC Comics*

FACE ALWAYS IN HEAVY SHADOW-- AN EFFECT HE CREATES HIMSELF.

NIGHTCRAWLER
DAVE COCKRUM

*Nightcrawler's original design, courtesy of the artist.* Nightcrawler TM and © 2003 Marvel Characters, Inc.

*Did any of them make contact with you?*

**DC:** Well, I met Mike Grell and Jim Sherman somewhere along the way, and just recently I met Steve Lightle, but I think that's pretty much it. Of course, Jim Starlin drew it, and I knew Starlin.

**TLC:** *You came up with a lot of new characters while you were on the title, but the only one that made it into the group was Wildfire. Did it disappoint you that you couldn't get more characters in?*

**DC:** Yeah, especially Nightcrawler. [*laughs*]

**TLC:** *Do you think that worked out for the best?*

**DC:** I suppose so. I mean, if Nightcrawler'd gone into the Legion, I suspect that I wouldn't have left quite as easily as I did, and who knows? They may have been making **Legion** movies instead of **X-Men** movies.

**TLC:** *Let's talk about some of the other characters which you intended to go into the book but never got seen. How about that group of villains which you designed?*

**DC:** They never had a name at the time. I've recently started calling them the Strangers. Tyr was in the group. He was the only one that made the cut. The others [included] Wolverine and his twin sister Belladonna. Over in the **X-Men** interview I just did, Roy [Thomas] said to remind everybody that I showed him that art before he told Len Wein to think up a Canadian Wolverine. So [*laughs*] in a way, I guess I'm responsible for Wolverine at Marvel.

**TLC:** *You sort of came in at the beginning and at the end of Wolverine's creation. Your Wolverine started the chain of events, and when you took over the X-Men, you were the first person to draw him out of costume...*

**DC:** Yeah, I gave him his face...

**TLC:** *Which is all they use now, since they've gotten rid of his old costume.*

**DC:** Well, the face is more interesting than the mask was, anyhow. [*laughs*] I also had him dressed in Western gear—jean-jacket and boots, and occasionally the cowboy hat, but the trouble with wearing a cowboy hat was you couldn't see his hair.

**TLC:** *What would you have done with that group of villains?*

**DC:** I don't know. I never really had a chance to think about them. It was pie in the sky. I showed them to Murray and Cary, and they weren't willing to take the whole group. They only just took the one character, and that was a disappointment. But I think it would have gotten real interesting, especially the brother-sister dynamic between Wolverine and Belladonna.

Manta was sort of a humanoid manta with a biological jet engine. He could fly. And that would have been interesting to work with. Sidewinder was a reptile, so it was a real mixed group. I think it would've been fun to work with, but I didn't have any real plans worked out yet.

**TLC:** *Do you think that there'll ever be a **Legion Elseworlds** story with them in it someday?*

**DC:** If I get to do one, that's what I want to do. Aside from trying to borrow Nightcrawler. If I couldn't [do that], I would come up with a character similar to Nightcrawler. I wanted to use the other Legionnaires that didn't make it in, and pit them against the Strangers. I think that would've been a real hoot.

**TLC:** *What else would you have done with the Outsiders?*

*A group shot of the Strangers, featuring Tyr, Belladonna, the original Wolverine, Sidewinder and Manta.*
Art © 2003 Dave Cockrum; all characters © 2003 Dave Cockrum except Tyr, who is TM and © DC Comics

**DC:** I don't know. A couple of those guys, Reflecto and Power Boy, were seen at some point in the future as dead Legionnaires, so at some point they would have become Legionnaires. Maybe the whole group would have. I don't know. I saw them as a supporting group more than anything else. Either irritants to the Legion, or people who wanted to help the Legion, or needed to help the Legion, or something. But I never had specific plans on any of them.

**TLC:** *That reminds me of something else: in the very first issue after you left, they killed off Invisible Kid. Was that in the works while you were still there?*

**DC:** No. I didn't have anything against him. [*laughs*]

**TLC:** *Were you surprised when you saw the Tyr toy?*

**DC:** Yes, I was. I was even more surprised [when] not only did they give me some of

them, but they actually paid me some money for it.

**TLC:** *That worked out well.*

**DC:** Yeah. Marvel wouldn't have done anything like that.

**TLC:** *We've now arrived at the True or False section of the interview. True or False: you and Jim Shooter used to be roommates.*

**DC:** Yes. True.

**TLC:** *I find that hard to believe.*

**DC:** [*laughs*] So do I. My first wife and I broke up, and I had this nice, three-bedroom apartment in Queens. Shooter was looking for an apartment, and I said, "Well, I've got one." And he wound up moving in. We lived together for a year, and actually got along pretty good together, most of the time.

**TLC:** *How did you meet him?*

**DC:** Probably because somebody told me he was looking for an apartment. [*laughs*] I don't remember.

**TLC:** *True or False: He was working on the Grimbor story while you two were living together.*

**DC:** Yes. The fans were agitating for me to do the artwork on that, and I really kind of wanted to, because I had a visual in mind for Charma. I wanted to use the face of an actress from the '30s named Helen Mack, and I thought, "Oh boy! I can see some great stuff with her." My **X-Men** schedule just wound up not allowing me to do that. But it would've been fun.

**TLC:** *Did you actually do any drawings?*

**DC:** Yeah, I had a drawing of Charma somewhere. I don't think I did a drawing of Grimbor.

*Proposal for the Outsiders, featuring Power Boy, Reflecto, Nightcrawler, Trio, Quetzal and Typhoon. Art © 2003 Dave Cockrum; all characters © 2003 Dave Cockrum, except Nightcrawler (TM and © 2003 Marvel Characters, Inc.) and Reflecto (TM and © DC Comics).*

**TLC:** *True or False: your design of Colossus was originally intended to be used as Ferro Lad's twin brother.*

**DC:** No. False.

**TLC:** *Yet another Internet rumor dies.*

**DC:** [*laughs*]

**TLC:** *True or False: Marvel and DC had planned for an unofficial crossover between the Legion and the X-Men.*

**DC:** Ummm... Sort of. When I did the Imperial Guard, I had shown the character designs to Paul Levitz, and he said, "Hey! Maybe we can do something reciprocal in the **Legion**," and I said, "Yeah! That'd be great!" But then they didn't. I suppose there was just no time, or I don't know what. But there was also originally going to be a **Legion/X-Men** crossover, and I was to draw it. Then they decided, "No, we'll make it a **Teen Titans/X-Men** crossover," and that's the one that Walt Simonson drew. They figured that the Teen Titans

LEGS, CHEST, SKULL-CAP & ARMS RED. SHOULDERS, GLOVES & BOOTS RED-PURPLE.

*An original costume design of Chameleon Boy, originally published in **The Legion Outpost #3**. Chameleon Boy TM and © DC Comics*

*The picture which created the X-Men. On the original art it reads, "Return art to Murray."
From the collection of Steven Weill.* The Legion of Super-Heroes and all related characters TM and © DC Comics.

were more commercial.

**TLC:** *Was the Imperial Guard your way of getting the Legion out of your system?*

**DC:** I don't know if I was getting it out of my system so much as I was having fun with, "Let's do the Legion in the **X-Men**." That's exactly what I did. Chris [Claremont] went right along with it. He thought it was great fun. It would've been great if DC had actually done a reciprocal story. Too bad they didn't.

**TLC:** *Did you have any concern that you might get in trouble over it?*

**DC:** Not really. As I said, I showed the designs to Paul Levitz, and he didn't say, "You can't do that." If anything, he said, "Geez, these costumes are better than the ones the Legionnaires are wearing." [*laughs*] No, I don't think we ever once thought that we were going to get in trouble over it.

**TLC:** *How many of the characters which you designed at Marvel when you were on the **X-Men** would have ended up in the **Legion** universe?*

**DC:** Storm, for instance, was an amalgam of characters. She was a little bit Quetzal and a little bit Typhoon, both of whom I'd proposed as Legionnaires, along with a Black Cat who wasn't the one that wound up in **Spider-Man**, which I'd proposed as

an X-person, if that makes any sense. But I don't know. I do tend to hang on to ideas and use them. Colossus in the X-Men was based upon a character that I came up with in college called Mr. Steel. They hang around until they get used, or versions of same.

**TLC:** *You're responsible for a couple of points of Legion controversy. You drew a scene which showed Dream Girl in bed, and next to her was Star Boy ["The Silent Death," **SLSH** #201 —**Ed.**]. Did you think that they were going to take that out later on?*

**DC:** That's why I did it so sneakily, because I didn't want anybody to notice except the fans. They didn't notice it in editorial.

**TLC:** *You also drew a Martian at the back of the wedding scene of Bouncing Boy and Duo Damsel. A lot of people took that literally and said, "There's J'onn J'onzz! J'onn J'onzz is going to live for a thousand years!"*

**DC:** Well, I drew two Martians. Tars Tarkas from Edgar Rice Burroughs' Martian series is in there, too.

**TLC:** *Does the fact that a lot of people didn't get the joke make it even funnier?*

**DC:** [*laughs*] I suppose.

**TLC:** *Of course, the real controversy over*

*that scene was the fact that they wouldn't give you your artwork back. Why don't you tell the story behind that?*

**DC:** At the time, DC was not giving art back. Marvel was. I asked for the wedding scene back. I never asked for any of the rest of it back, just the wedding scene. When I came in—I don't know how much truth there is to this—Murray Boltinoff said, "I was gonna give it to you. I had it laying on my desk, and Carmine [Infantino] came in and said, 'What's this?' and I told him, and he said,

*He's not Tars Tarkas, but he is a Martian from Edgar Rice Burroughs' **John Carter of Mars** series. From **The Dave Cockrum Treasury.** Art © 2003 Dave Cockrum.*

*Shrinking Violet's new costume, from* **The Legion Outpost #3.**
Shrinking Violet TM and © DC Comics.

'You can't give him that back.'" And that was the end of it. I said, "If I can't have it back, I'm quitting." And that's the way it went.

**TLC:** *Do you ever wonder where Marvel would be today if you had gotten that art back?*

**DC:** A number of people have brought that up lately. The **X-Men** would've been totally different, if they'd revived it at all. Like I said, they might have been making **Legion** movies instead of **X-Men** movies.

**TLC:** *It appears as if DC was its own worse enemy back then.*

**DC:** Yeah, they did a lot of stupid stuff. At one point, at about the period that I left, DC had managed to piss off just about every major artist that they had, at least of the newer crowd. They were all shifting over to Marvel, and that's why Grell got his pick of work, damn near, because he was just coming in. Everybody else was jumping ship.

**TLC:** *Did you get the sense that DC was grooming you for bigger and better things?*

**DC:** Carmine Infantino told me outright that they were grooming me to do **Superman** when Curt Swan retired. And I'm going, "But I don't want to draw **Superman**! It's boring!" [*laughs*] Not the proper response. I should've taken it and turned it into something that wasn't boring, is what I should've done.

**TLC:** *How long do you think you would've stayed on the* **Legion** *if you hadn't left it when you did?*

**DC:** I don't know. I liked the **Legion**. It depends on a lot of things. If they had headed towards more interesting stories, that would've helped. I got my fill of the stuff like Matter-Eater Lad having eaten a thought-transmitter for breakfast because his jealous brother wanted him to transmit treasonous thoughts. I could've seen me staying on for a long time, although if something like **Green Lantern** or **Flash** or **Hawkman** had become available, and I had the opportunity, I'd have certainly jumped ship real quick.

**TLC:** *Do you feel like you've still got unfinished business with the* **Legion**?

**DC:** There's stuff I'd still like to do. I'd still like to go back and do that Blackhawk-related story as an **Elseworlds**, and I'd like to see if I could borrow Nightcrawler from Marvel and have him as part of the cast.

**TLC:** *Do you think Marvel would go for that?*

**DC:** Probably not. But it couldn't hurt to ask.

**TLC:** *A lot of people think that your stay on the* **Legion** *was a lot longer than it actually was. I believe you only did twelve issues.*

**DC:** It was stretched out because a lot of it was back-up episodes in **Superboy**, and they weren't running every month. It did stretch out a ways.

**TLC:** *You could say that makes your impact on the title all the more impressive.*

**DC:** You could also say that it seems like I was there longer than I actually was because I bored the sh*t out of you. [*laughs*] I'd still love to do some **Legion**. All of the books that I would like to do are still at DC. **Green Lantern**, **Flash**, **Hawkman**, maybe a revival of **Blackhawk**, **Captain Marvel**.

**TLC:** *Have you given serious thought toward approaching DC to do an* **Elseworlds** *story?*

**DC:** Yeah. I e-mailed the **Legion** editor and asked him about it, and he said, "Sorry, we're not doing many Elseworlds stories anymore, and I'm full up on other stuff." Meanwhile, I've got two or three threads on the [DC **Legion**] board of fans who are demanding that I be returned to the **Legion**.

**TLC:** *Were you satisfied with the archive which reprinted your work?*

**DC:** For the most part. Somebody was telling me there were problems with the color, but I didn't really see it. But yeah, I was happy with it. It was nice to have all of my stuff in one volume.

**TLC:** *And they used your artwork on the cover of the next volume, too.*

*The X-Men fight the Legion in the form of the Imperial Guard in a recent commission by the artist.* Art © 2003 Dave Cockrum; X-Men, Imperial Guard TM and © 2003 Marvel Characters, Inc.

*Some back of the page silliness by Cockrum.*
Chameleon Boy TM and © DC Comics, Nightcrawler TM and © 2003 Marvel Characters, Inc., and Spock TM and © 2003 Paramount Pictures and Viacom.

**DC:** Oh, yeah. I was kind of annoyed that they went cheap on those covers. Rather than have me do a cover, they just assembled them from my color guide.

**TLC:** *You had some pictures which showed up in* **The Legion Outpost** *which looked like they were original character designs for your new costumes. Do you remember that?*

**DC:** I've seen some of those. Somebody showed some of them to me recently, and I don't know where they came from. They look like color guide stuff, but they're different from what was used on the cover. I don't know. I must have done more than one drawing of some of the costumes.

**TLC:** *You've returned to the* **Legion** *on a handful of occasions since you left. When you do* **Legion** *stories, does it feel like returning home?*

**DC:** Yeah, although I was never really happy with those stories. I guess the one I was happiest with was the Phantom Girl **Secret Origins** [#42], but even that leaves me looking at stuff, saying, "I wish I hadn't done that." There's one of the stories [where] I did Lightning Lad versus Lightning Lord [**LSH** Vol. 3, #45 —**Ed.**], and

I wasn't very happy with the outcome of that. It was all hard, harsh, ugly stuff.

**TLC:** *Do you think the fans see that, though?*

**DC:** Maybe not. I tend to be pretty critical of my own stuff. There's not many of my pieces that I like seeing again, what, ten years later? Or even a month later. [*laughs*] There are a few, but not a lot.

**TLC:** *Looking back at it now, do you regret leaving the* **Legion** *when you did?*

**DC:** Yeah. There was so much else I could do with it. You never know. I might still be on it. Let's face it: it was perfectly designed for me. I love super-heroes. I love science-fiction. All this opportunity to draw fancy costumes and fancy spaceships, weird futuristic machines, buildings, and civilizations... yeah, I'd have had a blast if I'd stayed on it.

**TLC:** *Did you follow the* **Legion** *after you left?*

**DC:** For a while. Then I kinda drifted away.

**TLC:** *When was the last time that you read a* **Legion of Super-Heroes** *comic?*

**DC:** Some of the ones that Adam Hughes did. The one that comes to mind is the one where some of them were at an underwater resort, and he had Bette Midler as a mermaid. [**Legionnaires** #7 —**Ed.**]

**TLC:** *That had a Devilfish in it, too.*

**DC:** Yes, it did. Although I remember Bette Midler better than the Devilfish.

[*laughs*]

**TLC:** *So you haven't read the rebooted* **Legion of Super-Heroes**?

**DC:** Actually, yes. Just a couple days ago I bought a stack of the new books and sat down and read them. Unfortunately, the earliest one I could find was #10, so I felt like I was coming into the middle of a movie or something. But I liked the art very much, and the stories were very good, too. Good enough to keep me coming back for more and to try to find the earlier issues. Lots of questions, though, like, "Where the hell did Legion World come from?"

**TLC:** *Do you have any thoughts on the concept behind it? The idea of starting over from scratch?*

**DC:** I don't know what the problem is with the **Legion**, or the people creating it, but it

*Published here for the first time: Page 1 of Cockrum's three page Legion tryout story. Courtesy of the artist.*
Art © 2003 Dave Cockrum; the Legion of Super-Heroes TM and © DC Comics

THE LEGION GALS!

HI THERE! I'M VI -- SHRINK-ING VIOLET, THAT IS -- WITH MY NEW COSTUME.

THE OTHER LEGION GALS ARE HERE TOO -- WITH THEIR OWN NEW OUTFITS...

SHADY HERE -- WEARING A MODIFICATION OF MY ORIGINAL SHADOW LASS COSTUME!

NOW, TAKE A GANDER BELOW, AT JECKY!

NEW COSTUMES DESIGNED FOR THE LEGION OF SUPERHEROES BY DAVE COCKRUM

NOT MUCH RESEMBLANCE TO THE OLD PRINCESS PROJECTRA, EH?

KEEP LOOKING -- THERE'S MORE TO COME!

INCIDENTALLY, THE CORONET EMBLEM ON MY BOOTS IS REPEATED ON MY CAPE!

*More character designs by Cockrum, courtesy of the artist.*
Art © 2003 Dave Cockrum; Shrinking Violet, Shadow Lass, and Princess Projectra TM and © DC Comics

seems like every couple of years they toss out everything and start over. Why?

**TLC:** *A lot of the character designs which you introduced are still being used today in one form or another. Do you get a sense of pride from the fact that things which you made thirty years ago are still resonating with fans today?*

**DC:** Yeah. I'm really pleased about that. I wish the editors would see it that way. [laughs] That's probably going to be one of the few things that I leave that has a lasting impression: costume designs and that sort of thing.

**TLC:** *Have you given serious thought to publishing your own work?*

**DC:** A lot. Mostly, I can't afford it. That's the problem. I have a strip that I've penciled the first issue of. A lot of it's inked, too, and some of it's written. It's a real departure from super-hero stuff, but a friend of mine, Cliff Methe, who owns Aardwolf Press, has been talking about possibly publishing this new series idea of mine. The first issue, at least. Actually, it's

**DC:** Trying to find work and collecting a lot of "Nos" and unanswered phone messages. If it weren't for commissions and eBay sales, I'd be up the proverbial creek.

**TLC:** *The comic book industry has changed a lot since you broke in. Compare and contrast the industry today with what it was like then.*

**DC:** When I came in, I was [part of] probably the first incoming class of wannabe artists who were fans of the books. The guys previous to us, they just found it as a job. That's what it was to them. There was a whole gang of guys that I call the Class of '70. Berni Wrightson kind of preceded us by a little bit, and then so did

got to be a three-issue story arc to introduce these guys, and I think I'd probably have to finish the other issues before we went to press with it, but that's the trouble. I'm not being paid for it while I'm doing the work, and that's kinda tough. And, of course, I also have the **Futurians**, my own group. I'm still looking for a publisher for new stories with them.

**TLC:** *So what are you doing now?*

Marv Wolfman and Len Wein, but Mike Kaluta, Bruce Jones, and even Vaughn Bodé was part of that group. It was a whole gang of guys. We came in, [and] we actually sort of hung out together for a while, but we were the first fans who became pros. We got work, a lot of us, because in those days you could go up to the company and hang around. They actually had places where freelancers, or prospective freelancers, could come in and hang around.

I got my first work at DC because I was just there one day. Julie Schwartz was looking for somebody to draw this awful story, "Tales of Krypton." Marv Wolfman wrote it, and it was about mutant Kryptonian kids with big heads and no thumbs, and the Kryptonians abandoned them in the wilderness. These kids survived the atomic war which wiped out everybody else, and they became the source of the later-on existing Kryptonian civilization. Julie stuck his head out the

*Page 2 of Cockrum's three page tryout, courtesy of the artist.*
Art © 2003 Dave Cockrum; the Legion of Super-Heroes TM and © DC Comics

Then at last they are ushered into a nearby briefing room to confront their new identities:

HARRY ROBBINS IS TERRAYNE, THE EARTHMOVER.

WALTER BONNER IS BLACKMANE.

ANDREW PENDRAGON HAS BECOME AVATAR.

MATTHEW BLACKFEATHER IS WEREHAWK.

DANA MORGAN IS MOSQUITO.

TRACY WINTERS IS SILKIE.

JOHNATHAN DARKNYT IS SILVER SHADOW.

*Cockrum's own group, The Futurians.* Futurians TM and © 2003 Dave Cockrum.

door and said, "Hey! Who's here?" and I said, "I'm here!" He said, "You're here. Yeah. Uh-Huh." He said, "All right! Come here!" So I went in, and he said, "I'm going to give you your chance. Here's the story." Neither Marv nor I was very proud of the end result, but it was my first color job at DC.

**TLC:** *And from humble beginnings....*

**DC:** Yes. [*laughs*] But that was the great thing about those days. Both companies had places you could come in and hang around. You could compare notes, you could talk to the pros, you could get advice. Previous to that story, I had done six jobs for Warren, over at ***Creepy*** and ***Eerie***. Neal Adams kind of got me those by telling me, "Okay, go over and tell Jim Warren that I said to give you work." And in those days, if Jim Warren heard Neal's name, he'd go, "Salaam!" So I would get these jobs, and I would bring 'em in to Neal first and show him, and he'd say, "Well, fix this, and fix this, and fix this," and I'd fix 'em and take 'em over to Warren. [He] would say, "Neal Adams is telling you what to fix, isn't he?" and I'd say, "What? I don't know what you're talking about."

That sort of thing just isn't possible anymore. The companies are big business. You can't do that sort of thing.

**TLC:** *How important is it to you to keep in contact with your fans?*

**DC:** Pretty important. Frankly, the main reason that I go to shows is that I get

some feedback. I think that knowing that somebody out there likes my stuff is part of the reason why I do it. I'm doing it also to please me, but it tickles the hell out of me when it pleases other people, and to hear it from them, that's great.

**TLC:** *When you look back at your career, you're responsible for a lot of different characters at a lot of different companies. In the case of Marvel, you're partly responsible for basically the foundation of the company, that being the X-Men. How frustrating is it when you look at the wealth which your characters have generated...*

**DC:** [*chuckles*]

**TLC:** *I think you know where I'm going with this one.*

**DC:** Yeah. It's very frustrating. I hate what they do with a lot of the characters. I absolutely hate that they've killed Colossus. I still consider those guys my characters. I realize they're not.

Unfortunately, I couldn't keep ownership of them. That was the way the game was played in those days. Nightcrawler especially. He's me. He was me in the X-Men. Seeing him becoming a priest with no possible time allowed to have gone to divinity school or anything like that, and all kinds of sh*t, I mean, I hate that. I think they just consider me an opinionated nobody. I tell ya, if I ever won the lottery, I'd buy Marvel, fire the lot of 'em and start it over.

**TLC:** *Do you feel any sense of kinship with creators like Siegel and Shuster when you look at what's happened to their creation and what's happened to yours?*

**DC:** Oh, yeah. It's maybe not quite the same, but let's face it: the X-Men have made Marvel millions and millions and millions of dollars, and I don't get sh*t. I resent the hell out of that. I resent the hell out of the video games and the toys

I·AM·TYREX—— I·KILL!

*The third and final page of Cockrum's three page tryout, never before published until now. Courtesy of the artist.*
Art © 2003 Dave Cockrum; the Legion of Super-Heroes TM and © DC Comics

A *Futurians* promotional ad, circa 1983.
Futurians TM and © 2003 Dave Cockrum.

Nightcrawler, Storm and Colossus TM and © 2003 Marvel Characters, Inc. Blackmane and Avatar TM and © 2003 Dave Cockrum.

**TLC:** *You're one of only a handful of creators who actually enjoyed his time on the* **Legion**. *What's wrong with you?*

**DC:** I'm probably screwed up in the head. I don't know. Did George Pérez ever do the **Legion**?

**TLC:** *George said in the past that he had always wanted to do the* **Legion**, *but that he didn't get the chance, and at that point, the Legion had changed so much it wasn't the same Legion anymore.*

**DC:** George would have had a good time with it, too. Paty [Cockrum] says, "George Pérez has a cluttered mind!" because he likes to draw all that detail. George and I were a lot alike in those days. I think he'd of enjoyed it. I enjoyed it. I liked drawing lots of characters. I was frustrated by the fact that Cary Bates only liked to work with four or five of them at a time. He didn't like to have to write groups. I kept on going, "Come on! Let's have a big group scene or something." He always resisted it. I mean, even in the wedding, the villain steals half the bride, there's fifty-odd super-powered guests there, and they pick four people to go after him. I'm sorry, I think they'd have risen up en masse and squashed him like a bug.

**TLC:** *You've got a great memory when it comes to the stories.*

**DC:** Yeah, I remember a lot. There's some I don't remember, but if I liked it, I remember it as a rule. Or if it annoyed me, like [*laughs*] sending four people after the villain. I remember that. [*laughs*]

and the TV shows and the movies, and I suppose it makes me sound like sour grapes, but I feel like Marvel owes me something. Marvel would disagree.

**TLC:** *Does the fact that you've made so many fans happy throughout the years take a bit of the edge off of that?*

**DC:** Well, that has always pleased me. Even when we were doing the books, we used to get some great letters. There was a couple that I got from people who were severely handicapped, who were looking at Nightcrawler as a role model. Actually, I've never felt that Nightcrawler was handicapped in any way, but if they could see that, and they could take hope and inspiration from it, that was great. I know a lady who went through a lot of terrible health problems and used Phoenix as her inspiration to help her get through it. That sort of thing is great, that my work has affected people that positively. I really love that.

*The artist and some of his creations. From* **The Dave Cockrum Treasury**.

# Unpublished Timberwolf
## by Dave Cockrum

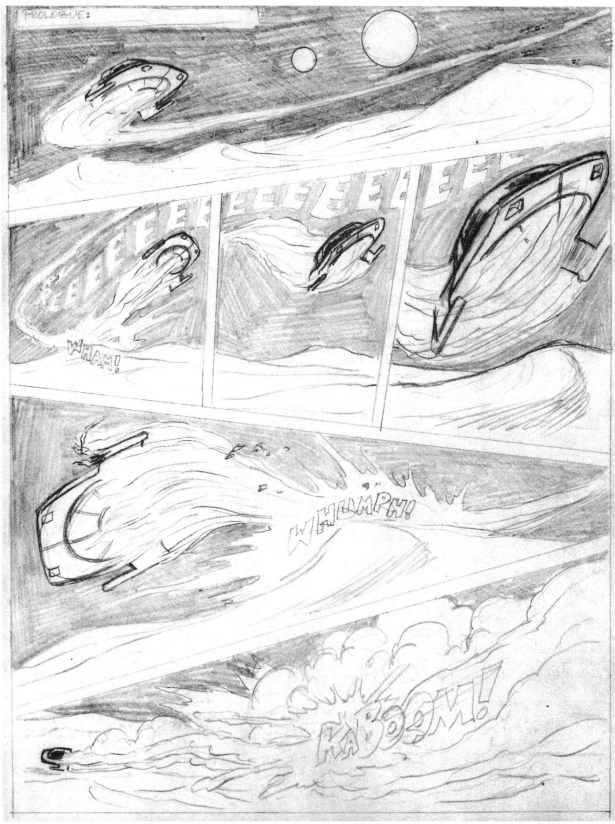

Timberwolf TM and © DC Comics.

Timberwolf TM and © DC Comics.

③

Timberwolf TM and © DC Comics.

Timberwolf TM and © DC Comics.

WHAMMM!

Timberwolf TM and © DC Comics.

# Dave Cockrum Gallery

TRIO

VIXEN

SPITFIRE

HELLION

COCKRUM '73

ERG

DEC

*Dave = Let me have sketch back for colorist. — WB*

QUETZAL
Dave Cockrum

STANDING AT RIGHT — SOME CRUDER, HARD OF QUALITIES SO WHERE DON'T SCAN OR DESIGN.

NIGHTCRAWLER:

DEL

Alien, from a parallel dimension. Real name Baalshazzar. His race is the basis for the legends of demons & other supernatural beings; in ages past, when Earth sorcerers & wizards called up demons, their spells opened gateways to Nightcrawler's dimension & the demons that appeared were merely aliens.

Powers: Fast, strong. Sees in the dark. Disappears in shadow, even the smallest of shadows. Likes darkness, digs Shadow Lass because she can cast shadows. Always lurking in corners. Sometimes runs on all fours, cat-like. Can run up walls & across ceilings. Bays at the moon, & when fighting or stalking, howls like some unearthly beast. Very animal-like in nature; can be very savage, very sneaky & underhanded. He is a paradox, as he has the attitudes & personality of a really rotten villain-type, but chooses to aid the law. Can appear & disappear in a burst of fire & brimstone, demon-like, but doesn't do it often. Uses too much energy. Has very sardonic sense of humor; would think a truckload of dead babies was hilarious. *"Hisses" his "S's" when he sspeakssss..*

STARFIRE:

Real name Drake Burroughs, comes from Earth. Was involved in experiments with ~~antigravity~~ antimatter propulsion, caught in an explosion which converted his body into an antimatter generator. A quick-thinking scientist got him into a protective 'neutral flux' suit before he blew up the whole place, later designed his Starfire costume, which absorbs the generated antimatter energy & channels it into useful energy. The duraglas faceplate on his helmet ~~isxx~~ contains a series of prisms that allow him to fire antimatter blasts, & he can control the strength & range of the blasts mentally. The folded-down glove-and boot-tops contain other outlets by which he can release energy; he can fire a blast from his arms, and by prolonged blasting from the leg outlets he can use them as rocket propulsion for flying.

If we could see into the costume, we would see that he has no real, solid form; he is almost pure, antimatter energy. Were he to take off the helmet, or accidentally tear his costume, the results could be catastrophic. Tends to be very gloomy & resentful; broods a lot about the accident that made him Starfire.

YR2, HIGHLIGHTS OF YR

Y

YR3B2

YR3

ORION II

YR3B2

TYR

DEC

85

Trio and Quetzal TM and © 2003 Dave Cockrum; Nightcrawler TM and © 2003
Marvel Characters, Inc.; Wildfire, Tyr, and Orion TM and © DC Comics

## QUETZAL

No one knows who she is or where she came
from, not even her real name. The name
Quetzal ~~Flamingo~~ was given her by Typhoon & Starfire.
She can't speak, can only chirp and warble
like a bird, but somehow manages to make
herself understood nonetheless. There is
some element in the sound of her voice that
conveys meanings, and she even has a certain
amount of mental control or some related
force, because the proper tone of voice can
cause people to go into a trance or do her bidding. She can
fly, of course; she is very tall and slender, as tall as any of
the male legionnaires, & hollow boned.

Even Saturn Girl can't communicate with her satisfactorily; her
mind seems to work on a different wavelength than humans. The
only thing that comes across in mental communication is a general
impression--satisfaction, or questioning, or fear, or joy, but
nothing much else. ~~Flamingo~~ Quetzal does, however, understand English
when spoken to.

Very cheerful personality, generally. Sings a lot, & her song
can have a subtle influence on others--cheering up gloomy spirits,
or invoking defeated people to greater effort, etc.

COLOR DETAIL OF "ERG'S" VISOR

(DEEP, HIGHLY REFLECTIVE PURPLE-BLACK, LIKE WEAPON CONTROL RADOME ON MOST MODERN JET AIRCRAFT)

## STARFIRE!
Dave Cockrum

THIS WAS MY ORIGINAL PROPOSAL SKETCH FOR WILDFIRE.
—Dave

TYPHOON!
Dave Cockrum

NOW--FEEL THE POWER OF... TYPHOON!

NOT A MEMBER

NOT A MEMBER

R, Y, & B1

B2

MOLECULAR MASTER
PRIMARY COLORS OVERLAP ON EMBLEM.

SKIN WHITE EXCEPT FOR B3 COSMETICS ON FACE. LIPS RB.

LIZ: THESE COLOR PATTERNS WERE THROWN ON AT RANDOM. DON'T BOTHER TRYING TO KEEP THE PATTERN THE SAME FROM ONE PANEL TO THE NEXT.

INFECTIOUS LASS

TYPHOON:

Real name Bryn Alban, comes from a planet called Zarathustra. His
family migrated there with the earliest colonies, formerly of Earth.
Comes from a long line of 'secret people' on Earth--elementals,
witches, warlocks, etc., with certain interbreeding with elves &
sprites, & other supposedly mythical beings. Bryn himself is a
super-elemental, the only one in existence. With a gesture he can
call down typhoon-force winds, rain, & lightning--or can conjure a
gentle breeze to cool a hot summer day. He can use these powers
locally, or on a planet-wide scale (note--this doesn't mean total
weather control--primarily just wind & associated phenomena). Once
he's loosed his gale force winds he can 'launch' himself on them
and fly, riding the wind.

Typhoon is an outgoing, overconfident, cocky type, & a real
wiseass.

Quetzal and Typhoon TM and © 2003 Dave Cockrum
Wildfire, Molecular Master and Infectious Lass TM and © DC Comics

# Mike Grell

After coming out of nowhere to take the comics field by storm, Mike Grell worked on such titles as **Superboy featuring the Legion of Super-Heroes**, **Green Lantern/Green Arrow**, and the **Warlord** during the 1970s. In the Eighties he helped to launch the creator-owned revolution with **Starslayer** and **Jon Sable, Freelance**, and in the Nineties he continued to work on his own properties in the form of **Shaman's Tears** and **Maggie the Cat**. Most recently the writer of **Iron Man** for Marvel Comics, Grell was interviewed by Glen Cadigan on December 19, 2002, and he copyedited the following transcript.

**TLC:** *Why don't we begin with the story of how you broke into comics?*

**MG:** I used a jackhammer and a crowbar. [*laughs*] Breaking into comics at DC was a fortuitous circumstance for me. I had gone off to New York in the summer of '73 to attend the Comic-con, and I had with me a portfolio containing a comic strip that I was trying to sell. When I got there, I found out that nobody was buying action/adventure comic strips at all. In fact, I couldn't even get an appointment to get in to see editors from the syndicate. But while I was at the Comic-con I met two guys from DC Comics. One was Alan Asherman, who was Joe Kubert's assistant at the time, and the other was a gentleman who introduced himself only as "Irv." I didn't find out until later on that it was Irv Novick, who was doing **Batman** at the time. They looked at my portfolio, and Irv told me in no uncertain terms that I should get my carcass up to Julie Schwartz's office and show him. Which I did, actually, about two months later. I had to fly back to Chicago [first]. I walked into Julie's office and showed him my portfolio. I started my encyclopedia salesman speech that goes, "Good afternoon, Mr. Schwartz. Can I interest you in this deluxe thirty-seven volume of blah blah blah," and if you get interrupted anywhere along the line, you have to go all the way back to, "Good afternoon, Mr. Schwartz."

Well, I got as far as, "Good afternoon, Mr. Schwartz," and he said, "What the hell makes you think you can draw comics?" I unzipped my portfolio, tossed it on the desk, and said, "Take a look and you tell me." And he did. He called Joe Orlando in from the office next door, they looked at my stuff, and somewhere in all that Joe decided that I had enough talent to take a chance. Joe assigned me a seven-page "Aquaman" story. It was my first job, [and it appeared] in **Adventure Comics** #435. I turned it in early the following week, and they gave me another assignment.

I went home with that second assignment, and as soon as I got there, Joe called up and asked me if I was interested in taking on a monthly assignment. I said, "Sure!" He said, "Here's what's happening: Murray Boltinoff, who edits the **Legion of Super-Heroes**, is on vacation, and he

Jon Sable TM and © 2003 Mike Grell.

doesn't know it yet, but when he comes back, he's going to be minus an artist." He asked if I would mind if he recommended me for the job. Would I mind! This was job security! So I met with Murray, and he looked over my stuff and gave me a tryout on the book inking one of Dave [Cockrum]'s stories—a short story that Dave had already penciled. Then he called me in and gave me the good news and the bad news. He said, "The good news is that you've got the job. The bad news is that you can expect to get hate mail." I said, "Why is that?" and he said, "Well, for starters, you're replacing the most popular artist we ever had on the book, and just to top things off, we're killing off one of their favorite characters." And he was right. But somewhere along the line, they seem to have forgiven me.

**TLC:** *What was Murray like?*

**MG:** I found Murray to be a really great guy to work with. He wasn't as artistic as Joe Orlando, of course, but had a great deal of experience in the business. I used to joke around with him because Murray always took everything so very, very, very seriously. I liked to occasionally pull his leg. I think the best example of that was one day when we were going over a story that I had drawn featuring Supergirl. There was a

Invisible Kid TM and © DC Comics.

A recent (2003) commission of the Legion of Super-Heroes versus the Fatal Five, courtesy of Miki Annamanthadoo. Art © 2003 Mike Grell; the Legion of Super-Heroes and the Fatal Five TM and © DC Comics.

line of dialogue in the story that said, basically, "I'm looking for the girl in the red and blue costume." I turned to Murray and said, "Murray, why don't we just change this line to, 'I'm looking for the girl with a big ass.'?" [*laughs*] He took me seriously, and he said, "Well, let me think. Do you think that fits better?" "Murray, Murray, it's a joke."

**TLC:** *At what point did you realize that the* **Legion** *wasn't a standard assignment?*

**MG:** The first time I had to draw those twenty-six characters! If it hadn't been for Dave Cockrum having created a wonderful pile of sketchbook [drawings]—all the costumes, and everything else—I would have been lost. I thanked him for it on more than one occasion, but it was years later before he confessed to me that even he couldn't remember what the damn costumes looked like. [*laughs*] He used to have the same sketchbook of reference sitting alongside his desk.

**TLC:** *How closely did you work with Cary Bates?*

**MG:** Cary and I had a really good relationship, probably as close as any artist and writer team could work. If you're asking if we collaborated on story ideas, no, but there was never any need for that with Cary because he was a terrific storyteller. I

mean, one of the best visual storytellers in the industry, and by that I mean Cary knew how to write a script to evoke the images in the artist's imagination so that he could translate it onto the page. If there was anything that was absolutely called for in the script, Cary would put it in there. He went so far as to do camera angles, which some artists might have found a bit annoying, but believe me, when you're dealing with twenty-six characters, not always all of them in the same panel or on the same page even, but certainly in any given story we usually had five or six of the key characters appearing, you had very crowded panels, lots of things happening, lots of people had to be there, and Cary would tell you where the camera should be, and what should be happening. It took away that much extra worry and thinking that you had when you were planning the layout of the page.

**TLC:** *Not too long after you took over, Jim Shooter returned to the* **Legion**. *What was his approach to storytelling like compared to Cary's?*

**MG:** Jim's approach to storytelling was the opposite of Cary's. Jim put every tiny little detail into the script,

whether it was pertinent to what was going on in that particular panel or not. I think in many cases he was thinking four or five steps ahead, and that came out on the page when he wrote the script. A typical Jim Shooter script for a twenty-two page or a twenty-four page comic book would run about sixty pages. A typical Cary Bates page would run between a page and a page-and-a-half per page of comic art. To put that in contrast, Denny O'Neil on [**Green Lantern**/] **Green Arrow** would write between a half-a-page and sometimes a page [per page of comic art], but very rarely a page.

**TLC:** *Did you know that Shooter used to draw his scripts?*

**MG:** I had heard that. In fact, in a couple of instances, Jim would include doodles or sketches of something that he had in mind—bits of equipment or stuff like that.

**TLC:** *Would that have made it easier to draw from?*

**MG:** Well, my way of thinking is that if you've got somebody drawing the script, what do you need another artist for?

Another commission by Grell. Like the headshots on the preceding page, it comes courtesy of Scott Kress at Catskill Comics (www.catskillcomics.com). Art © 2003 Mike Grell.

[*laughs*]

**TLC:** *Just before you took over, a lot of characters had their costumes redesigned by Dave Cockrum, but you still managed to slip in a couple of your own designs.*

**MG:** Yeah, and most of the fans have still never forgiven me for the Cosmic Boy costume.

**TLC:** *I was going to ask you how that costume worked.*

**MG:** It's very complex. It involves me drawing a human figure, and then drawing the costume on it.

**TLC:** [*laughs*] *You also co-created two Legionnaires.*

**MG:** I only remember one, and that was Dawnstar.

**TLC:** *Did you give her her name?*

**MG:** That's a darn good question. I honest-to-God don't remember. I think it was probably Paul Levitz. I came up with the visuals for her, and the concept of her having wings and being an American Indian. That was about it. Paul came up with her super-power, and I'm pretty sure he came up with her name.

**TLC:** *How about Tyroc? Do you remember him?*

**MG:** [*laughs*] Yes. One of the most embarrassing super-heroes in the history of comics, I think.

**TLC:** *What was your part in his creation?*

**MG:** I gave him a silly costume. It was somewhere between Elvis' Las Vegas costume and something you would imagine a pimp on the street corner wearing. Tyroc was sort of a sore spot with me because I had drawn a story featuring a character that I drew as black, and when I turned it in, the editor was not really happy with it because this character was drawn as a black man. I said, "We have every other color under the sun in the ***Legion of Super-Heroes***, but there aren't any black people." I just figured that this was a decent time to put somebody in who was black. It was "Soljer," or something like that [*"Soljer's Private War," **SLSH** #210.* —**Ed.**]. It was about a young man who's one of the Space Troopers who comes into a conflicting situation. He has to make a choice. Like a lot of us, he makes a couple of mistakes, but then he turns out all right. He does the right thing in the end. I saw that as a very positive thing.

Murray explained to me, "You can't do that because we've never had a black person in the ***Legion of Super-Heroes***, and now you're gonna have one in there who's not perfect. We can't do that. Besides, we're working on creating a black super-hero, and he's gonna be featured in the Legion." I said, "Okay, fine." So I changed a couple of things about Soljer, but left enough of them the same so that it was really obvious to anybody who looked at the artwork on the book that basically he had been a black man who had been colored pink. And most of my black friends spotted that and gave me hell for it over the years, but when I told them the story, they pretty much understood.

So months went by. Months and months

Dawnstar by Grell. Courtesy of Scott Kress at Catskill Comics. Art © 2003 Mike Grell; Dawnstar TM and © DC Comics.

Grell's '80s creation, **Jon Sable**, ran for 56 issues before it was relaunched as **Sable** in 1988. Jon Sable TM and © 2003 Mike Grell.

Like other Grell commissions within these pages, this one was originally in color, but holds its own in black-and-white. Courtesy of Tom Fleming at **www.fanfare-se.com**. Art © 2003 Mike Grell; Emerald Empress TM and © DC Comics.

Above: a splash page introducing Tyroc from Superboy and the Legion of Super-Heroes #216. Below: the cover to the same issue, plus Legion headshots by Grell. Splash page courtesy of Alan Bahr at Heroes Comics; cover and headshots courtesy of Steven Weill.
Superboy and the Legion of Super-Heroes TM and © DC Comics.

went by, and I kept asking Murray, "When are we gonna do this black super-hero?" I kept getting stalled off and stalled off, and finally comes Tyroc. They might as well have named him Tyrone. Their explanation for why there were no black people ever featured in the **Legion of Super-Heroes** up until this point was that all the black people had gone to live on an island. I was dumfounded. It's possibly the most racist concept I've ever heard in my life. [*laughs*] I mean, it's a segregationist's dream, right? So they named him Tyroc, and gave him the world's stupidest super-power. By screaming really loudly and making different noises, he could cause different things to happen. I modeled him somewhat after Fred "The Hammer" Williamson, who was a movie star at the time [and] a football player, and gave him this "Elvis Presley goes to Las Vegas" kind of a costume, and that's pretty much it. That was the extent of my contribution to Tyroc.

**TLC:** *Do you remember redesigning the costumes of the Subs?*

**MG:** Vaguely.

**TLC:** *How about the new villains who were introduced?*

**MG:** Again, vaguely. Are you talking about specific villains?

**TLC:** *Grimbor, for example.*

**MG:** Big sort of a strapping guy, kind of stocky with flat-top haircut, wore leather, hung around with a chick in a bra and panties by the name of Charma?

**TLC:** *That's the guy.*

**MG:** Don't remember him at all.

**TLC:** [*laughs*] *I have to admit to a certain fondness for Pulsar Stargrave. Do you remember him?*

**MG:** Nope.

**TLC:** *He was green...*

**MG:** [*laughs*] That describes several characters in the **Legion of Super-Heroes**! Brainiac 5, for instance. Who was Pulsar Stargrave?

**TLC:** *He was a guy who pretended to be Brainiac 5's father.*

**MG:** Oh, well, being green then probably was an advantage for him. [*laughs*]

**TLC:** *Sales on the **Legion** went up after you became the regular artist. Did they tell you that at the time?*

**MG:** No. They didn't necessarily tell

everybody what the sales results were, but through some poking and prodding I discovered that was the case.

**TLC:** *Did that make it harder to leave the title when you did?*

**MG:** No, not at all.

**TLC:** *What is it about the **Legion** that makes artists drop the title?*

**MG:** [*laughs*] O-kay. Twenty-six characters, twenty-six costumes, super-futuristic settings... Eventually you get tired of drawing thirty or forty characters on a page. It's a simple matter of time involved more than anything else. I can't speak for the difficulty of telling a particular story, but I can tell you that it takes a certain amount of time to draw a human figure, and if you have to multiply that by five because there's five times as many characters, or ten or twenty-six, then it takes you five or ten or twenty-six times as long to draw that page.

**TLC:** *Was there a point where you were hoping that something would happen so that you could get off the title?*

**MG:** There was not so much a point where I was hoping that something would happen. I got off the title because the **Warlord** had just been made monthly, and I

STARSLAYER
ISSUE #1

PC
"For the NEW Era in Comics"

$1.00 US
$1.25 Canada

STARSLAYER
the Log of the Jolly Roger

A CELTIC BARBARIAN IN THE FAR FLUNG FUTURE

ORIGIN ISSUE

*Grell helped launch the creator-owned revolution with Starslayer in 1982.*
Starslayer TM and © 2003 Mike Grell.

was also doing **Green Lantern/Green Arrow** at the time. Given the choice between one or the other, since **Green Lantern/Green Arrow**, at that particular moment, was my favorite title—Green Arrow was always my favorite comic book character—it was a really simple choice to make.

**TLC:** *You stayed on as cover artist after you left. Was that your idea or theirs?*

**MG:** I'm not particularly sure, although covers were something that I could do fairly easily. Back in those days, I don't seem to recall a particular mandate that the interior artist be also the artist who did the cover. In fact, if anything, the opposite was kinda the case. If you did the interiors, you kinda had to push to do the covers yourself.

**TLC:** *Was it understood when you left that you would come back and do more work later on?*

**MG:** Nope.

**TLC:** *So were you chosen to do the wedding special then based upon your previous experience with the title?*

**MG:** You know, I'm not sure what the timing was of that, whether that was a story that happened sometime shortly after, or a long time after. I couldn't tell you if it was two months after I had left the book or two years.

**TLC:** *Do you remember doing a follow up story to that for an anniversary issue [**LSH** Vol. 3, #45. —Ed.]?*

**MG:** Yeah. I only did about four pages of it, and I only agreed to it because they told me they'd get Dick Giordano to ink it.

**TLC:** *What was it like returning to the series, even if it was only for a few pages?*

**MG:** It was weird, because all of it came back to me. To this day, I can draw a lot of the characters from memory.

**TLC:** *Did your time on the **Legion** prepare you to do more science-fiction later on in your career?*

**MG:** Not particularly. Any kind of a story that I've ever done has always been a reflection of my own interests, generally either an ongoing interest or an interest that I had at the time. The **Starslayer** concept, [for example], had absolutely nothing whatsoever to do with the **Legion of Super-Heroes**.

**TLC:** *You never did draw another team book again.*

**MG:** That is one influence that the **Legion of Super-Heroes** has had on me over the years. Although it's not one hundred percent correct. When I did **Shaman's Tears** I created a group of genetically combined human/animal individuals called Bar Sinister, and they are definitely a team. They appeared in the early issues of **Shaman's Tears**, and went on into their own title. So that's a team book.

**TLC:** *But they didn't have twenty-six members!*

**MG:** [*laughs*] No! I learned *something* along the way!

**TLC:** *A lot of artists have risen to prominence drawing the **Legion**. Do you have any theories as to why it's such a great launching pad for careers?*

**MG:** I've got two answers for you: one is flip and the other is serious. Let me give you the flip one first. They give the **Legion** to the young artists starting out because we're so grateful to get the work that we'll take anything, and it takes us a while to get smart enough to realize that we've just been given the hardest book in the business to draw. That's the flip answer. The serious answer is that I strongly believe that the reason that the **Legion** has been at least partially instrumental in launching so many careers is that in the world of comics, there are no fans as loyal and devoted as **Legion** fans. If they take you into their hearts, they're going to keep reminding you of the work that you did. They never forget, they always come back, and they follow you on. They become interested and involved with creative people who are working on the book, and they follow your career from that point on as long as you don't disappoint them and let them down. They're great.

*Another Grell creation, **Shaman's Tears**, courtesy of Scott Kress at **www.catskillcomics.com**. Scott helps arrange Grell commissions for fans, and is ready to help readers get their very own piece of Mike Grell artwork.*
Shaman's Tears TM and © 2003 Mike Grell.

Above: Dream Girl, courtesy of Miki Annamanthadoo. Below: Night Girl, courtesy of Tom Fleming. Art © 2003 Mike Grell; Dream Girl and Night Girl TM and © DC Comics.

**TLC:** *Are you critical of your early work when you look back on it now?*

**MG:** [laughs] I'm critical of the work that I did last month. To me, that's a good sign. I have almost never finished a project, sent it in, and then seen it in print without thinking, "Oh my God, what was I thinking when I did that?" It's just one of those things. It took a long time before I could just let go and move on to the next [one]. I always agonized about what people were going to think about it when they saw it, and this is at the moment when I was sending it off in the mail. Typically, what would happen with DC was that there'd be a gap of anywhere from two months to maybe even four or five months before I would see it in print, and in the meantime I would have forgotten how awful the stuff was. When I would see it in print, I would just want to go slash my wrists.

**TLC:** *You were a rarity among hot artists in the Seventies in the sense that you didn't work for Marvel. Did they ever try to get you to go over there?*

**MG:** It was purely coincidence. I was always busy, always had more than my share of stuff to do, and

there was no particular reason [that I didn't work for Marvel].

**TLC:** *What did you think of the* **Legion Archive** *which reprinted your work?*

**MG:** It's a terrific book, and it's really nice to have all of that stuff in a collected volume like that. It's no less embarrassing to look back on it, and kinda be amused by it. However, I will say that it's far less embarrassing to look at drawing errors on the page right now because I stop and think back. This was, by and large, my first year or two in the business. I was a kid just learning the ropes, and you can forgive a lot. It's interesting to see where I came from, what I was doing back then, and also to get a refresher course on some of the stuff that I worked on.

**TLC:** *Have they approached you about doing a cover for one of those books?*

**MG:** No.

**TLC:** *I understand that you do commissions. What percentage would you say are* **Legion**-*related?*

**MG:** I would say twenty-five or thirty percent.

**TLC:** *That's pretty high.*

**MG:** It actually is. It's much higher than I would have expected. Recently I got a commission for Brainiac 5. I'm not saying anything against Brainiac 5, but he's not necessarily the most fun character in the book—during my tenure, at any rate—but very, very popular. I've had more requests, oddly enough, in the last year or so for Shadow Lass.

**TLC:** *Do you get a lot of* **Legion** *requests at conventions?*

**MG:** Not too many.

Grell's first **Legion** cover, courtesy of Fred L. deBoom. Superboy and the Legion of Super-Heroes TM and © DC Comics.

**TLC:** *Do you have any fondness for that time, given that it was your first regular assignment?*

**MG:** Oh, yeah. At the time that I got the assignment, I was grateful as hell for the work. I was also grateful as hell the day that I didn't have to draw it anymore, just because of the sheer volume. But those days were really great. You'd go in on a

Unpublished Grell headshots, circa 1975. From the collection of Steven Weill.
The Legion of Super-Heroes TM and © DC Comics.

was known as the guy who drew Aquaman on the toilet.

**TLC:** *When you're working on commissions, does it stir up old memories?*

**MG:** Oh, yeah. Sometimes it's really interesting, because I've always had a very strong visual memory, and on occasion someone will ask me to do a character from the **Legion of Super-Heroes**, and my first instinct is, "Oh my God, how am I supposed to remember that?" And then you go, "No, wait a minute. I remember exactly what this person looked like." I can even do a fairly accurate representation of the fancy doo-dads on the front of Shrinking Violet's costume, and that's going some. That's going some.

I could probably still draw... let's see: Element Lad is a snap. Lightning Lad is easy, Light Lass... all the major characters are pretty much easy to do. Interestingly, I had someone request Saturn Girl and I had to look to see exactly how the back of her costume went around, but other than that, not much of a problem.

**TLC:** *Were those your favorite characters to draw back when you were on the title?*

**MG:** Probably my favorite character to draw was Lightning Lad. I just thought that his power was really cool, and the costume was really classy. Anybody who can generate enough electricity to knock a bad guy on his ass from fifty feet... you've gotta like that.

**TLC:** *I'll ask you the opposite question now: which ones did you hate to draw?*

**MG:** Superboy was a little on the boring side. I can't really think of

any that I particularly hated to draw. I hated like hell to have to draw them all in the same panel. I could probably boil that down and say the ones that I really hated to draw were probably the fifth or sixth character that I had to draw in that panel. By the time you get to half-a-dozen of them, you're just going, "Aw, man..."

**TLC:** *Would you ever draw a **Legion** story again?*

**MG:** Sure.

**TLC:** *Just as long as it wasn't on a regular basis.*

**MG:** You know, in this day and age, work is work, my friend. If somebody came and said, "You want to take over the **Legion of Super-Heroes**?" I would internally groan, but my outside voice would be saying "Yes."

---

*Jon Sable in action, courtesy of Scott Kress at www.catskillcomics.com.*
Jon Sable TM and © 2003 Mike Grell.

Monday and collect a script, rip your brains off the next solid week—sometimes more—bring it in sometime the following week and go over it with the editor. Occasionally there'd be a problem or two. One of my fondest memories was when I would really horribly screw up on the art [and] Joe Orlando would take me under his wing, call me aside, sit down and give me a drawing lesson. I think it was the second "Aquaman" story that I did. I had him sitting on the throne, but I had him sitting a bit too low on the throne [*laughs*], a bit to the point where he looked like he was sitting on a toilet! [*laughs*] For quite a while, I

*Saturn Girl, courtesy of Tom Fleming at www.fanfare-se.com.*
Art © 2003 Mike Grell; Saturn Girl TM and © DC Comics.

# Jim Shooter
## Part Two

In Part Two of our interview with Jim Shooter, he discusses his return to comics in the 1970s and the necessary adjustments he had to make upon his return. Also discussed are the Marvel years, including a look at the **JLA/Avengers** crossover and his attempt to buy Marvel Comics. As with Part One, the following interview was conducted by Glen Cadigan, and was copyedited by Shooter.

**TLC:** *When you returned to the* **Legion** *in the Seventies, how difficult or easy was it to settle back in on the title?*

**JS:** It was incredibly difficult. It was almost impossible. I had an editor named Murray Boltinoff, and Murray was sort of the last dinosaur of the old-fashioned, 1950s kind of editors. He wasn't mean like Mort, but he had a million rules. It'd have to be this. It can't be that. All these formulas. He also insisted on having more than one writer. He didn't want continuity. So Cary Bates wrote his stories, and I wrote mine, and there was a vague continuity, because I'd set something up and later I'd find out that Cary had either ignored it, forgotten it, or trompled it to death. And I'm sure I screwed up his stuff, too, 'cause I didn't know all the things he was going for, but it was just a very bad situation. Also, Murray was into that old thing where there'd have to be three stories an issue, or two stories an issue. If you're trying to write these eight page stories and ten-page stories, that was confining. It's good discipline to be able to do that, but it was a little confining.

Also, Murray, God bless him... in some ways, I learned some stuff from Murray. He was very fierce on the plotting side. You'd tell him a plot, and there'd be something in it, and he'd say, "That's no good. That's not original. Give me something original." For instance, I had a scene where I needed to establish Superboy—this is an eight-page story. I don't have a lot of time to fool around here—I was gonna have him rescue somebody in a couple of panels in a super-powered way to set up something else, and so I just had him rescue somebody who had fallen in front of the monorail. Murray says, "Monorail's been done. Do something else." "Murray, come on! It's just a throwaway bit for Superboy to come in." He said, "I want something original." So I had to invent magnetic canals. I had to come up with something. And he did that. He forced you to innovate, which

was good, and he was pretty good with the plots.

Now, forgive me for saying this, but Murray was an older fellow, and he had some memory loss. It was difficult working with him because he would forget [things]. He would forget the character's powers. I remember one story he sent back to me, and he rejected it on the grounds that, "How could they possibly see Phantom Girl when she's a phantom?" I kept having to explain to Murray what the characters could do. Also, he would forget the story from panel to panel as he was editing it. And he *edited*. I mean, Mort never touched my stuff. This guy would cross things out and rewrite things, and because he would forget what the story was about, sometimes he'd cross out the wrong things. "Well, we don't need this!" Scritch, scritch, scritch, there goes the explanation for everything that's going on. And other things. He would also forget how many pages were in the book. I remember many times he'd tell me, "Write a fourteen-page story," I'd write one, and I'd find out he'd cut two pages out of it because he'd forgotten that he'd also commissioned a ten-page story, and he only had twenty-two pages to use. Stuff like that. So it was a nightmare working with him.

The funny story that I can tell you is the way he liked to work was he wanted me to send him springboards—little snippets of ideas—and then we would talk. I'd have to go to New York, sit there in his office and plot the stories, then come back to Pittsburgh and write them. Which was expensive and time-consuming. I thought, "Why am I doing this? I'm not making any money here." But I thought it was a learning curve. When I got back into it, [I thought], "Maybe I'm just rusty. Maybe I don't know what I'm doing." So one time, Murray—we'd done some plots—he said, "Send me some springboards." So I sent him some springboards, and I get a letter back from him, rejecting the springboards because he asked for plots, and "these aren't plots." No, he didn't. He asked for springboards. So I thought about it, and I called him up, and I

*Princess Projectra by Mike Grell, courtesy of Tom Fleming.* Art © 2003 Mike Grell; Princess Projectra TM and © DC Comics.

said, "Murray! I'm glad you liked these springboards!" "Oh? Oh, well, yeah! Refresh me!" So I told him what they were, and I said, "Which one do you want me to write first?" "Oh, well do the one..." And I ended up writing all three, because he forgot. Once I realized, "This guy is losing it, and I've gotta protect myself." I was writing eighty-page scripts for ten page stories, because in each panel I had to recap the story [laughs] so that Murray wouldn't forget. Like I say, in some ways he was very lovable, and in some ways I learned things from him, but boy, that was a nightmare.

**TLC:** *Is that why you eventually left?*

**JS:** That and the fact that I would've quit anyway. I had kinda come to the end of that. Once I realized, "This isn't me, this is Murray." 'Cause like I said, at first I thought, "Maybe it's me. I'm rusty. Maybe I'm not really any good. I don't know," and then after a while, I said, "Nah. This is him. It's not me." So I probably would have quit anyway, but

*Members of the Pittsburgh Comics Club dressed as their favorite Legionnaires. From left to right, starting with the back row: Todd Clark (Brainiac 5), Ben Pondexter (Ferro Lad), Jim Shooter, Ron Kienzle (Ultra Boy), Kurt Chebatoria (Chameleon Boy), Mercy Van Vlack (Phantom Girl), Charlie Hawse (Bouncing Boy), Mark Gaudio (Cosmic Boy), and Keith Mateson (Element Lad). Picture provided by Peter Hansen.*

right around that time I got a call from Marvel, and they wanted to hire me as an editor, and I said, "I can do that." So I did move to New York again, and I became an editor at Marvel. I was the second-in-command. There was the Editor-in-Chief, and then there was me. I ended up staying at Marvel for twelve years.

**TLC:** *Is that when you moved in with Dave Cockrum?*

**JS:** Actually, when I first moved up here, for the first couple of months I was staying at the Y because it was cheap and I was looking for an apartment. So I was staying in the cheapest place I could find, and then Cockrum had split up with his wife, and they had this monstrous, beautiful three bedroom apartment out in Queens, and he couldn't afford it without her salary. So he was looking for a roommate, and I thought, "Well, it's gotta be better than the Y." So I went out there, and I stayed with him for about eight months until I found a suitable place of my own. By that time he had developed a live-in girlfriend, so it all worked out. That was actually good, because I think in some ways I was useful to Dave, and he's a brilliant guy. Really a great talent. I really enjoyed being around him.

**TLC:** *When you left the* **Legion,** *you left partway through a storyline which you were setting up with Pulsar Stargrave. How would you have resolved that storyline had you stayed?*

**JS:** We had a great plan. I can't remember what it was, but I remember running it past Roger Stern, telling him what I had in mind, and he just thought it was brilliant, and I value Roger's opinion. I think Gerry Conway or somebody did the ending, and to me, it was just... I'm sorry, it was bad. It was just tossed off. "Well, let's just get this out of the way. They all die." I don't remember exactly what I had in mind, but I think it was pretty good.

**TLC:** *Do you think you were going to stick with him as Brainiac 5's father?*

**JS:** I might have. I don't recall.

You know, it's kinda cool, because I was sharing that apartment

with Dave, and of course, he had worked on the **Legion,** too. He was groovin' on all the stuff I was doing, and he almost was enticed to go and do some more **Legion** stuff. I wrote this one story, and he said, "I gotta draw this!" So he actually waffled around [it]. But I think the thing was, DC couldn't pay him enough. That was the Charma and Grimbor one. He just wanted to draw that. I worked with Mike Grell over there, and we kind of never [were in synch]. We got along fine, but we weren't in synch very much as far as the story-telling was concerned.

**TLC:** *When you went over to Marvel, did your experience with the Legion get you the job on the* **Avengers?**

**JS:** No. [laughs] The way that worked, I had actually done a couple of freelance jobs for Marvel. I'd written an **Iron Man** and a **Super-Villain Team-Up** or something, [and] I'd done a couple of freelance jobs for them before that. Marvel in those days... everything was late, everything was chaos, and it was, "Oh my God, we need this written overnight! Who can we get?" I remember one time I was actually gonna take a trip back to Pittsburgh for the weekend, and they came to me and they said, "We heard that you know how to color." I said, "Well, yeah." "Did you ever color anything?" "Well, no." I mean, I did rough color for covers, and Tatjana Wood or somebody would color it. And they said, "Can you color this book over the weekend?" "Ah, no." [laughs] "I'm going home, see."

Anyway, there was no one else, and so being a trouper, I said, "Oh, okay," and I spent the whole weekend sitting there with my Dr. Martin's watercolor dyes, twenty-two pages of story, and did a job. But that's how it was. Everything was a nightmare,

*Shrinking Violet by Grell, courtesy of Tom Fleming at Fanfare Sports and Entertainment Art © 2003 Mike Grell; Shrinking Violet © DC Comics.*

The infamous "Soljer" story, as mentioned in Mike Grell's interview. From Alan Bahr at Heroes Comics (www.heroescomicbooks.com). Superboy and the Legion of Super-Heroes TM and © DC Comics.

and so the reason I got the **Avengers** was Steve Englehart failed to deliver issue 150, and at the last minute—I think the editor was Gerry Conway—he said, "Jim, I need a script overnight. I can't do it, I've got too much to do. There's no one else. Can you do it?" I said, "Sure." So overnight, I wrote an entire issue. It took me all night. It wasn't bad, but then, a couple days later, Englehart's script came in, finally. And Gerry waffled about it. It was like, "It would serve him right if I used the one that was already half-lettered," but he didn't want to lose Englehart. So he came to me and he said, "I'm gonna use Englehart's." And I read Englehart's, and it wasn't as good as mine. I said, "Okay." I mean, it's Englehart's. It's perfectly professional. But I really [did] some nice stuff for overnight, so later, other people'd read [it], and they thought, "Hey, he could do the **Avengers**." So when it came around— Gerry did it for a while, and he only lasted a month or two, and then he went off to DC—they needed an **Avengers** writer. I think Archie [Goodwin] was the Editor-in-Chief then, and he asked me if I could do it, and I said, "Sure." I was writing **Avengers**, **Ghost Rider**, and **Daredevil**.

**TLC:** *Which do you think you're best remembered for today: the* **Legion** *or the* **Avengers**?

**JS:** [*laughs*] I think I'm best remembered for being Attila the Hun reborn. Vlad the Impaler, maybe. I really have no idea. No clue.

**TLC:** *Did being an editor yourself give you a new perspective on some of your older editors?*

**JS:** Oh, yeah. The thing was, the time was different. See, when I started out, there had been this generation gap. There were these new guys who had just come into the business, like me and Cary Bates, and then later Len [Wein] and Marv [Wolfman], and even though E. Nelson Bridwell and Archie and Roy [Thomas] were a little bit older, they were still a part of our historical generation. So there was us, the new guys, [in our] twenties and thirties, and then everyone else was fifty-five and sixty. There was this big generation gap, because [in] the Fifties, not many people came in.

So where am I going with this? The thing is, when I started out, it was all adults and me [*laughs*], and the adults were very professional and very well-behaved, and the editors ruled with an iron hand, and it was very business-like and civil, and maybe that's why it wasn't as creative as it ought to have been, but you didn't have people bad-mouthing the editors in the fanzines. You didn't have that kind of chaotic behavior, so when I became editor at Marvel, it was like running a kindergarten. It was like, "This one's catterwauling, and that one's throwing a tantrum," and they hated it if you told them the simplest things. Like, "Look, we really have to introduce the characters." "Rarrh! Nobody tells me anything!" Stuff like that. It had become normal to be a prima donna, and so I'm trying to find that happy medium where there's as much freedom as there can be, because I think that helps people to be creative, but you teach them the fundamentals so that they're not just doing this unreadable crap.

When I first started as Editor-in-Chief, I sat down with a couple of guys, and we're looking at all the covers up on the wall, and so we talked about each book one at a time. We judged that there were four of them that you could read. Four that you could read. Not that were good—four that you could read out of forty-five. And why couldn't you read them? Because this one makes no sense, this one is a tangled mess—no one can follow it—this one is stupid and simple—like **Spidey Super-Stories**—and the things going on. Len Wein was writing **Spider-Man**, and I don't know whether it was intentional or not, but we were also reprinting the old **Spider-Man**s in **Marvel Tales**, and Len's stuff had fallen into a pattern where his stories were almost exactly what was being reprinted in **Marvel Tales**. Like if **Marvel Tales** had Doctor Octopus on the cover, Len has Doctor Octopus on the cover. [*laughs*] "Len!" But I don't think he planned that. I don't know how it happened, but we were doing everything wrong. Just everything.

You'd talk to a writer about, "You should introduce the characters, and there should be sense in this story, there should be conflict. We need to have a climax. We need to have some reason for people to come back next month." And they'd blink at you with their big cow eyes, and they'd say, "No, I just do whatever I want." Well, now what do I say? [*laughs*] So kicking and

Shooter and some of his friends, from a cartoon by Fred Hembeck. Marvel characters TM and © 2003 Marvel Characters, Inc.

screaming, I dragged them toward doing more better stuff. I enforced things like, "No, you really do have to mention the character's names somewhere in the story. And Chris, if you have sixteen different names for Storm, pick one and use that the most. 'Windrider,' 'Ororo,' 'Storm'... I mean, what is her name?" [laughs]

Of course, they all bristled and everything like that, but then the books started to sell *like crazy*, and we were just marching from victory to victory. There was a while there when I wasn't Vlad the Impaler, where everybody was making so much money, 'cause we'd introduced royalties and stuff, and they kinda grudgingly thought, "Well, maybe he's not so bad." Because it was working. What I told 'em would work, worked. And they were making money and doing well, and they would all gripe and complain. Chris [Claremont] one time wanted to have this scene where Professor Xavier was captured by the Morlocks and dressed up in transvestite bondage gear, and I said, "Nah. I don't think so." [laughs] He was furious. "Well, that's what the Morlocks do!" "Well, they don't do it in a comic book that goes on a rack that says, 'Hey, Kids! Comics!'" So he'd storm off and he'd fix it, and that's the kind of thing [that went on]. But you know what? Arguing about the stories is what you're supposed to do. Stabbing each other in the back, that's not good. Years later, Chris actually came to me and said, "Oh, well, you know... you were okay." [laughs] And I said, "Well, you're pretty okay, too."

Anyway, the thing is, it was this nightmare. Walking into the middle of anarchy. Everybody'd been his own writer/editor, and I come in and try to save the company. Because we were going out of business. We were dying. Sales were in the tank, and things were bad, so the only weapons I had to fight with were creativity. We gotta get better creatively. We gotta do better stories. We gotta tell them better. They gotta be readable. We gotta get

The missing page from SLSH #212, recently restored in **The Legion of Super-Heroes Archives** Volume 11. © DC Comics.

people interested in these characters. And the fact is, all these guys are talented. They're all good. Like I say, they don't like being told what to do, but once I got them on the track, then it was really funny hearing Chris at a convention lecturing people using things I told him [laughs], pontificating about storytelling and things like that. Not that he was a stranger to it before I showed up, but it was funny to hear him using some of my phrases. It took a while, but we built a good thing.

**TLC:** *Do you remember talks of a Legion/X-Men crossover?*

**JS:** Oh, sure, yeah.

**TLC:** *What happened to that?*

**JS:** Well, after I became Editor-in-Chief, Jenette Kahn was still fairly new as publisher of DC, and I'd been to her house a couple of times. She had a party once,

and every once in a while we had an industry poker game, and it would alternate. Sometimes it'd be at Paul Levitz's house, sometimes at Jenette's house, occasionally at my house. So I'd been there to play poker, and I'd gotten to know her. Anyway, she calls me up and says, "Let's go to lunch." I said, "Okay." So we go to lunch, and we're sitting there talking about the industry and stuff we can do, and she says that she just found out that there had once been a *Superman/Spider-Man* book, and I said, "Yeah." She says, "Well, whatever happened to that? Why aren't there more?" And I said, "Well, it was a one-shot." I think at the time it was considered very radical and daring. And she says, "Well, can we do it again?" and I said, "We could do it more than that. We could do *Batman* and the *Hulk*, and *Avengers* and *Justice League*, and whatever you want."

So we made a deal right there on the spot. Of course, I had to go back and get it approved by the president of the company—which he was happy to do—but we made a deal, and agreed that we would do one a year in perpetuity. So I went back, pitched it to the president, told him how much money we'd make, [and] it was fine with him. I ended up writing the first one (*Superman/Spider-Man*), and then there was *Batman/The Hulk*, I think written by Len, and then there was *X-Men/Titans*. I think the next one was supposed to be *Avengers/JLA*, and by that time, Marvel was 70% of the market. We were just trouncing DC [and] everybody else, and there was a lot of hostility and enmity had developed between the companies. It used to be like we were buddies. The guys from DC would come over to Marvel and hang out after work, and stuff like that. That kind of ended when we moved downtown and it was too far to come, and for that and a lot of other reasons, there'd been a lot of ill feelings.

I think there were some people that didn't like me, and they went over to DC, and some people at DC who ended up at

Marvel at that point. I think we had just about everybody that we wanted, with the possible exception of George Pérez and [José Luis] Garcia Lopez. I mean, it was Who's Who. You looked around and there's [Bill] Sienkiewicz, there's [Frank] Miller, there's Paul Smith, there's Art Adams. We had everybody. It was great. Why? Because they made more money with us. Because no Marvel book did not make royalties. No Marvel book was below the 100,000 threshold. Only a couple of DC books were over that threshold. **Warlord**, the Mike Grell book, [**The New Teen**] **Titans**, and I think **Legion**. **Superman** was selling about 98,000 copies. **Dazzler** was selling 140,000. Go figure. So anyway, we were kicking their butts [*laughs*], and Ed Shukin, our circulation guy, used to say to me all the time, "You know, these guys out promote us, their production is better, they advertise, they do everything right. The stuff looks sharp, they just outpromote us like hell in comic book shops. The only place we beat 'em is between the covers." And I said, "Yeah, that's right."

So anyway, now and then I'd have guys coming to me, saying, "Well, you know this guy has friends at DC, and maybe you shouldn't have him in this meeting because they'll find out what we're planning." I said, "You know what? Invite 'em all in. They could listen to everything we say. I could tell them everything, and they still couldn't do it. What's the difference? We got the crew here. We're the A-team. I don't care if they know. Fine, let 'em know." But it did get kinda ugly. There was a lot of hostility. So then we're doing this **Avengers/JLA** thing, and I kept calling 'em up and saying— because it was their turn— "Where's the plot?" 'Cause they were doing the work, and we were going to approve. We alternated. So I kept calling up, "Where's the plot? Where's the plot? It's late. It's four months late. Where's the plot?" Couldn't get Dick Giordano on the phone. I mean, I'd call and call and call, and leave message [after] message. Nothing. I'm thinking, "Hey, come on, pal. We're in this together. Answer the phone." So finally I sent him a telegram, and then finally I got a call. I said, "Dick,

where's the plot?" and he said, "Well, umm, I thought you already approved it." I said, "I haven't seen a plot." "Uh, well, I didn't know we were supposed to show you one." I said, "Read the contract." "Well, we've already drawn twenty-two pages." I said, "Well, why don't you send me photocopies of the twenty-two pages, *and* the plot?" So he sent it to me.

Man, it was awful. It was terrible. I let other people read it. They're laughing and rolling on the floor. I'm kidding you not. You ask Roger Stern. They couldn't believe it. They thought it was a *parody*. And the thing was, even if you don't like my story judgement, okay, fine. The fact is, he had the characters wrong. He had characters in the Avengers that weren't there anymore. He had characters that were dead in the Avengers. Basically, Gerry hadn't read an **Avengers** book since the last one he wrote, and so all that had happened in the **Avengers** between then and current day, he was unaware of it. So he was writing the Avengers like where he left them

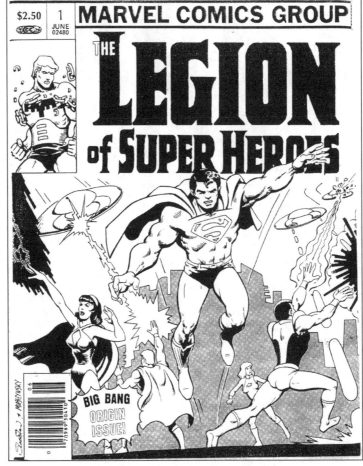

*What if Marvel published the* **Legion**? *From a Shooter sketch, with finishes by Andy Mushynsky. Originally published in* **The Legion Outpost** #10, Spring, 1981. The Legion of Super-Heroes TM and © DC Comics.

[*laughs*] with the Justice League. I guess he knew what the **Justice League** was about. But it didn't make any sense at all. There were so many mistakes. And on top of that lunacy you can't believe, there's a scene where Superman is in Galactus' ship, and he sees up on the board, like at McDonald's, there's a menu of the planets that he intends to eat, and the first one— this is in the past, now—the first one on the list is Krypton. So Superman changed it so Krypton is farther down the list. He put somebody else's planet first. *Excuse me?* I mean, look: I can understand that you might have trouble with Marvel characters, but if you don't know your own damn characters... Superman doesn't do that. I wrote him for years. He doesn't put somebody else's planet in harm's way.

So the book was terrible. The thing is, George Pérez, with the art...[it] looked great. [*laughs*] It was fine. But the plot was all screwed up. So I rejected it. So they get into just a hissy fit, and they're writing fanzine articles, and they're doing interviews, and they're writing in their Bullpen Bulletins page what assholes we are, and stuff like that. I finally had to reply. I wrote one column, saying, "This is what happened," 'cause that was the only question I ever got asked at conventions. And they were all up in arms. They kept saying, "It's *fait acompli*." Dick took me to lunch, and he said, "What's the difference? Who gives a sh*t? Just put a bunch of characters in it, they fight, it'll sell like crazy. We'll all make money." He said, "None of these books are any good." I said, "Excuse me, I wrote one, and it's not bad, and it could be good, and at least it should be faithful to the characters." I mean, I didn't think that the **Batman** one was great, but at least it didn't violate the characters badly. Anyway, I was just appalled by their attitude, and I went to Galton. I went to the president of the company, because DC threatened to cancel the thing, and I said, "Well, if they cancel this, it's a hundred and fifty grand off the bottom line for us. You tell me what to do. That's too big a call for me." And he said, "Stand your ground." I said, "Okay."

So finally, at the last minute, Roy Thomas, who I think at that time was working for DC, went to Dick, and he said, "Let me look at those pages. Maybe I can fix them." 'Cause Gerry had quit by that point. So Dick gave him the pages, and Roy called me up and said—at that time I don't think Roy liked me very well, so I don't know if we were... whatever. I think he was one of the people who left Marvel to go to DC who was kinda mad at me—but he called me up and he said, "Well, I don't know how you feel about it, but if it's okay with you, I'll take a crack at this." I said, "Roy, if there's a man on Earth who can fix that, it's you. Go ahead." So Roy took the existing art, wrote a plot that was faithful to the characters, that made sense, that was good, and it only required one or two little panels to be changed. I am, to this day, dazzled that he took this pile of unrelated pictures and turned them into something. Unbelievable. I said, "This is great. This is fine. We approve this. Okay, good." At that time, George Pérez said, "Well, f*ck you, I'm not doing it." And then Dick Giordano called me up and said, "Let's just forget it." I said, "Okay," and so each company lost probably $150,000 minimum, all because of big egos and crap, and them not playing by the rules. Of course, it all gets blamed on me. "Aw, that evil Shooter. He ruined the crossovers." Yeah, well, whatever. I'd do it again.

**TLC:** *When you're a writer on a comic and you leave it, do you still find ideas for it coming to you years after you've left?*

**JS:** Oh, sure. Absolutely. For instance, the **Legion**. I love the Legion. I once called Paul Levitz a few years ago [when] I needed some work. I called Paul, and I said, "I have an offer for you. I got one more **Legion** story left in me. Here's what I'll do: we'll set it back in time during the era of the Legion that I wrote. In other words, it'll be an untold tale. I will make sure that I don't screw up anything that's in future continuity, and it'll be this epic **Legion** story, and you publish it in eight issues, ten issues, whatever—and then bind it into one of those hardbacks," 'cause the only thing DC was, and probably is making money on, is the hardbacks. So they like things that they can bind into a hardback. "It'll be Jim Shooter's last **Legion** story. It'll be promotable. Some people will buy it just because of that." And he said, "I love it. I can't wait to read it. The only thing I wish is that Curt Swan was still alive to draw it." He said, "Think about what artists you want, make a list of

Another great Grell piece provided by Scott Kress at *www.catskillcomics.com*.
Art © 2003 Mike Grell; Timber Wolf TM and © DC Comics.

what reference you need, call me Friday, we'll talk, we'll work out the details. It's a go." I said, "Paul, there's some guys who work for you who don't like me, and that could be a problem." He said, "Aw, don't worry about that. They'll sulk for a while. They'll be all right." I said, "Okay." So I didn't hear from him Friday. I called him up Monday, and I said, "What's the story?" He said, "Well, apparently the scars are deeper than I thought. Some people here had just immense objections to you ever crossing our threshold. I think the whole thing'd be more grief than you need, and more grief than I need, so let's not do it." I said, "All right." Well, I still have that **Legion** story cookin' around [*laughs*], and maybe someday it'll see the light of day. Who knows?

**TLC:** *Did you write it up as a proposal?*

**JS:** I never wrote the plot. I have my notes to myself, but I never wrote the plot. Do I have an idea? Of course. I recently was asked to do an **Avengers** thing. That also didn't work out, but I had an idea for it. Every once in a while I think of something I

could do with Superman, or the Marvel characters. The Marvel characters, I didn't get as attached to any of them except the Avengers as I did with the Legion, but I did some **Daredevil**s and some **Ghost Rider**s, and along the course of the way, I probably did one of each [title], at least. [I] always had lots of ideas for **Iron Man**.

**TLC:** *How much of who does what in the comic book industry is based upon merit and how much is based upon politics?*

**JS:** Years ago, I would say it was mostly merit. These days, I would say it's 96% politics. To use a phrase that was bandied around back in the Eighties, it's quote "Who you know and who you blow." I just think that cronyism is absurd. It started happening even when I was there. You'd look around and you'd see editors hiring their buddies to do stuff, and superior talent sitting there with no work. I think that's one of the great downfalls of the comic book industry. There's still a lot of talent around, by the way, but I think management has gone to hell, and the in-house editorial is sort of uniformly lame.

**TLC:** *When was the last time you read a* **Legion of Super-Heroes** *story?*

**JS:** A couple of years ago.

**TLC:** *So you're familiar with the new* **Legion**?

**JS:** I wouldn't say I'm familiar with it. [*chuckles*]

**TLC:** *But you're aware that it's been rebooted?*

**JS:** Yeah, I know that.

**TLC:** *What's your opinion on that?*

**JS:** I don't know. I really don't have an opinion about it. I would go along with anything that was done well. At Marvel, I tried not to say no. I tried to think, "Well, if somebody has some crazy idea, [and] if they did that really well... Hmmm... Maybe it'd be good." So I went along with some crazy ideas, and later people said, "What could you have been thinking?" Well, I was thinking, "We're Marvel Comics! If we can't experiment, then who the hell can?" [*laughs*] So [we] did some crazy stuff, which, to this day, I'm proud of. [That] **New Mutants** stuff? It's wild, it's weird! Nothing like that was ever done before. Or **Elektra: Assassin**, for that matter. I mean, do some crazy stuff, and every once in a while, something works. And you fail a lot. But what I'm seeing now is every idea that comes along, just because people have an idea they think it's a good idea. No! The **Spider-Man** clone thing? Oh, come on! At the same time they're doing Tony Stark is really a Life Model Decoy. First of all, Life Model Decoys, I mean, that's 1960s. If Murray were running the joint, he would say, "No, think of something new." It's so derivative. Everything is so derivative. Every idea somebody has, no one thinks it through. They do it no matter how stupid it is. It's not a case of experimenting, it's a case of just floundering. I just find a lot of it's back to anarchy. There's nobody at the helm anymore. All right, Joe Quesada's trying. I don't think he has nearly the power that I had to cause things to happen. I think it's a whole different organization. It's not even about the comics anymore.

**TLC:** *You haven't written a **Legion** story since 1976, and yet you're still closely identified with the Legion today. Why do you think that is?*

**JS:** I think because I wrote it for a long time. I think if you gather them all together, there's probably at least six years' worth of stuff. Since I owned the future, I was the first one to really do continuity and advance the characters, and develop things and stuff. I built up this world which I think people have mined, and in some cases, strip-mined. And some of that's good, 'cause you want the familiarity of the world to continue. You want that world to continue to grow, and that means you bring back the Dark Circle, or you bring back things like that. That's fine, but as I was just saying, there's an awful lot of derivative crap going on these days where you keep having to add things, you keep

*Shooter at Marvel during the '70s.*

having to come up with something new, be original, you know? Bring new light to it. I'm not seeing a lot of that. In both of those cases, what it means is a lot of the stuff that I developed or built or used, a lot [of it] keeps showing up, and so therefore I think my name comes up a lot.

**TLC:** *Does it knock you out that you're getting royalty checks today for comics which you wrote while you were still in your teens?*

**JS:** Yeah, actually. And considering how times have changed, sometimes the royalties are bigger than what I got paid for the stories back in the old days. When I first started out, my first story was a twenty-three page story, for which I received one hundred dollars. What's that? That's four dollars and change a page. When I first heard this story, I didn't believe it, but it was confirmed to me by Nelson Bridwell. The first couple stories I did, I was getting four dollars a page, basically. Which we needed the money. I don't care. A hundred bucks, that's good. In 1966, that was money. Then mysteriously one day, my rate [was] at eight dollars a page. Never discussed, never mentioned. I didn't ask, I was just happy to get it. And then it seemed like a month later, or two months later, my rate is twelve dollars a page. And then it wasn't too long after that my rate was fourteen dollars a page. So years later, I was talking to Nelson, and he said, "The man you replaced on the Legion, Edmond Hamilton, he found out somehow that they were paying you way substandard money. He went into Mort in a rage, and he said, 'It's bad enough you're using child labor! Do you have to rip him off?'" So basically, he shamed Mort into paying me a reasonable amount of money for the work that I was doing. I thought that's cool. P.S., I was required to do a cover design for each one, in color, and never got paid for that. Never was paid anything for the layouts, but hey, that was all right. Fourteen bucks a page was life or death in those days.

So I thought that was great. I assume that's true. Nelson wouldn't make that up and lie to me. What a great story [*laughs*], 'cause I basically replaced the guy. I think

*The Emerald Empress by Steve Lightle, courtesy of Dylan Clearbrook.* Art © 2003 Steve Lightle; the Emerald Empress TM and © DC Comics.

he probably had enough work anyway, and he was an older guy. He was probably going to retire, anyway.

**TLC:** *Actually, he left to travel the world.*

**JS:** Yeah, something like that. But what a nice thing to do for someone...

**TLC:** *Who didn't even know you.*

**JS:** Yeah, you never met, or whatever.

**TLC:** *Are you happy those stories are being reprinted and shown to a new audience?*

**JS:** Like I say, I look at them sometimes and they make my face hurt. I look at them and [think], "Oh God, I was dumb." And then sometimes I look at them and I think, "Well, they're not so bad," considering how old I was when I wrote them. Some of the art's real nice. You know, you got the Curt Swan art, and some of the Win Mortimer stuff isn't bad. Win would cheat, though. I'd call for a long shot and he'd give me a big head [*laughs*], because he just didn't want to do that much work. When Curt did it, he would give me everything I'd ask for, and then more besides.

But some of the art's really pretty, some of the stuff that Jack Abel inked really looks great, some of the Neal Adams covers [look great]. Some of the packages are pretty good.

Now also, the thing is, these days, most comics, you really can't give them to little kids. I'm not talking about moral issues here. They can't follow them. They can't understand them. Number one, a lot of them are like Swedish movies with no sub-titles; you can't figure them out. I've been reading comics a long time, [and] some of these I'm reading, I can't tell who the good guys are or who the bad guys are or what the problem is. I don't know what's going on here! So some of them are confusing, and of course a lot of them got a lot of T&A and stuff like that that some parents would find objectionable for kids. So these old stories, which were written for younger kids, let's face it, they're pretty mild compared to the other stuff that's coming out today. So yeah, [they're] probably the only comics around that younger kids can really get into.

My kid loves them. I showed him the books, and he's like, "Ho-hum," and then Paul Levitz sent me some toys, some Legion of Super-Heroes toys, and I gave those to my kid, and then when he saw the toys, then he got it. He said, "Oh, I see," and he saw that the characters that were in these stories looked the same as the toys. Well, now he's groovin' 'em. He just loves 'em. He will read the stories—he's only six, but he reads pretty well—or his mother will read to him, then he'll act out the stories with the characters, and it's kinda cool. It's like, "Hey! I wrote that!" [laughs]

**TLC:** *Do you think a lot of kids get their hands on those archives?*

**JS:** Like I said, it's the only thing DC's making money on. They're selling some of them. I know they're expensive, but they're getting out there. I assume if they sell enough copies, somebody must be reading them. Certainly I've given away a bunch of them, and I know my kid likes 'em.

**TLC:** *You know, I'd say that you're probably the best-selling **Legion** author of all time.*

**JS:** Yeah, that's not hard if you did it in the Sixties.

**TLC:** *Do you miss working in comics today?*

**JS:** The thing is, even when I haven't been in comics, I've been in comics one way or

another. I told you I went and did advertising? Well, the way I got advertising work is I had gotten some good publicity in the Pittsburgh area. I was sort of known as the kid who does comics, and so advertising agencies, out of the blue, called me up, and they said, "We want to do a comic-style ad." And so they would hire me to do these comic-style, cartoon-style ads and various things. The thing is, it was spotty. It paid fantastically well, but you'd go for a while and you wouldn't have any work, and then you'd get another job, kinda on and off. But in the course of time, I did a bunch of ads for U.S. Steel, for some local companies in Pittsburgh, for Levi's jeans, [and] for a couple of other big companies, so even when I wasn't in comics, I was doing comics. And recently, what I've been doing is I've been working with a fellow on web-based entertainment. He has this plan for an Internet operation that has an entertainment component, and it's basically comics. It's this combination of visuals and words, and that's been keeping me busy, and I've been asked to do some commercial and advertising custom comics stuff. I've been doing some film development, too. So I always feel like I still have my hand in. I'm still working on comics, it's just not the mainstream super-hero stuff.

**TLC:** *How's your book coming along?*

**JS:** I haven't actually worked on it much. I've had too much else to do, and it was kind of preempted by that **Comic Wars** book. A lot of the same information was in my book, and I feel sort of preempted. It'll probably have to morph into a slightly different book. It's probably going to be more like this interview—recollections—than it is about the adventures of Marvel, Perelman, and Icahn. You know, I was the one who bid against Perelman for Marvel. I came in second.

**TLC:** *What do you think would have happened if you came in first?*

**JS:** Oh, well, the best laid plans... You just never know. Our plan was magnificent. First of all, at that time, Marvel was either making very little, or losing money. I knew that the reason that it was losing money was because of a bunch of really stupid businesses that the president of the company [had started]. The president never believed in comics. Even when I was making them eighteen million bucks a year pre-tax profit—publishing only—he was always con-

vinced that comics was some kinda fluke, or fad or... he just didn't see any future in it. He'd come out of the book publishing business, and he didn't want to be in the comics business. So he told me, early on, when I was hired as Editor-in-Chief, "You're gonna preside over the demise of the comics, 'cause they're gonna die. You can do anything you want, as long as it doesn't cost money. Try to lose money slowly. Try to keep us afloat until I can get us into other businesses." And I said, "What other businesses?" "Children's books."

Okay, you want to be a mass-market children's book publisher, you need a hundred million dollar ante to sit down at that table, 'cause you're competing with Random House, and, in those days, Western Publishing. I don't think so. Not on a shoe-string. So they were losing six million dollars a year in this idiot book publishing thing, and another thing he wanted to get into was animation, and they started a studio. They're losing some millions of dollars a year with this studio. They're busy as hell. It's all work-for-hire. They got no back end, and most animation loses money on the production. Just

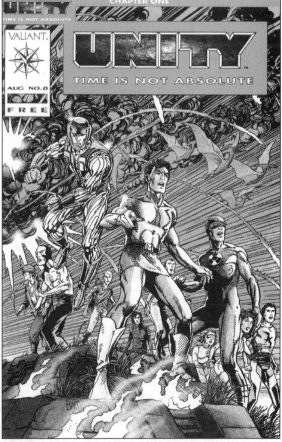

*Shooter revitalized characters such as Magnus and Solar at Valiant during the early '90s before his departure from the company.* © 2003 Acclaim Entertainment.

moronic stuff, you know? And if you'd ask the guy, "What do you do?" he'd say, "Well, I publish children's books, we do animation, and [clears throat, lowers voice] comics." He was embarrassed by the comics.

So, anyway, my plan was to get rid of the books, liquidate the books, and get rid of the studio, or turn it into a small, executive production facility like a Sunbow or something like that. You concentrate on your core business. Six to ten million dollars drops the bottom line, you're instantly profitable, you can service your debt, and you have wherewithal. You now can do all the things that I always thought should have been done. I was gonna bring [Jack] Kirby and [Steve] Ditko and all the other old-timers back into the fold. Create something where they started getting the same kind of participations which people get now, but they would get them for the characters that they had created in the past. Try to bring them back on board, and bring them home. I thought that Marvel could be turned into as big as Disney, which, strangely enough, Perelman brought in all his marketing guys, and he did make it a several billion dollar company like a Disney. 'Course it was mostly illusionary. It was all marketing driven. It was all eighteen collectable versions of the same damn comic book. Speculator frenzy, you know? Or to use Greenspan's term, "irrational exuberance." We had plans to really turn the place around, and focus on the publishing, and get better production, and build the distribution, and make Marvel what it ought to have been. The fact that the comics thrived at a time when the people upstairs had no interest in them, and wouldn't support them.... Everything I did had to be self-liquidating. I couldn't spend any money. Every time I did something, I had to prove to them that they would make money quickly and a lot if they went along with some crazy scheme of mine.

Like the royalties. I mean, that was a tough sell. See, DC announced royalties. Guess what? None of their books would pay royalties, so they could announce that program [with] the big, cheesy grin on their face knowing that unless their sales skyrocketed, it wouldn't cost them a penny. To match that program would have taken a million and a half bucks off of my bottom line, because all of my books would have been paying royalties. Try selling that to the

board of directors. "Yeah, this is gonna cost us a million and a half bucks." So the way I pitched it was, "If we do this, we'll keep the good people that I've acquired, number one. Number two, I believe that these incented people will do better. Number three, I will make sure they do better, and the sales will go up, and I guarantee we will not lose money because we'll make it up in higher sales." I sold that to them! They bought it! [laughs] So they went along with it, we did the royalties, and we made more money. We didn't lose any. We made *way* more money, because the sales skyrocketed. We were happy to pay these people hundreds and hundreds and hundreds of thousands of dollars in royalties because we were making so much more. So, that trick worked.

Also, I introduced other plans. First of all, I told you that I was forced to do cover sketches and stuff for free? Well, my mantra was nobody works for free. Everybody gets paid for whatever you do. Nobody works for free. I also said, "All right, it's work-for-hire. I can't change that. There's no way I'm winning that fight. But why does work-for-hire have to be bad? Let's pay 'em real well, let's give 'em royalties, and if it's work-for-hire, we buy all the materials. Every pen nib, every eraser, every [little thing]." You know, you can't ask people, "Bring the leather," and then you own the shoes. I introduced the standard insurance program for everybody, which came in real handy for Gene Day's widow. I wanted to make it a choice. You can do work-for-hire on **Spider-Man** and you *know* you're gonna make a damn good living, and you're gonna have all these benefits, and you never have to worry about buying your paper and stuff like that, or you could work at Epic Comics, and okay, you're betting on yourself. You're taking a little bit of a risk, but a lot of these guys, they want to do something [which] they own, so you have that choice. Work-for-hire is guaranteed you're gonna do really well, and the creator-owned is creator-owned. You own it, but then you rise or fall, depending on how good you are. I thought we had a nice balance going there for a while.

But my point is, if we had taken over Marvel, there would have

been a lot more of that, a lot more programs introduced. We would have brought the old creators back in the fold. I don't know if I could have paid them back from the Sixties, but we could certainly start that day, 'cause we had developed creator incentives. If you created a book, you got one percent of that book forever. If you created characters, you got points on that character forever, including all licensing. So basically, what if I went to Kirby and Ditko and those guys and said, "Look, I can't do it retroactively, but as of today, you guys get a piece of everything that's done with the characters you've created and you'll get a check every month, every time we publish one of those books." It still wouldn't have been a vast fortune, but then a guy like Jack Kirby or Steve Ditko or someone like that, they'd have an income from Marvel, a hundred, two hundred grand, and they'd be living like they oughta live. Then if we continued to succeed, if we did well, who knows? We might even have done better. We had grand schemes. Of course, anything can go wrong, but we had some big plans. We were gonna revolutionize the world.

**TLC:** *Are you happy with where you are today?*

**JS:** Yeah. It's okay. I'm doing creative work. I get paid okay. Are there other things I'd like to do? Sure, but I'm really enjoying the work I'm doing. I got plenty of it, and I'm late on everything. [laughs]

*Shadow Lass courtesy of Tom Fleming at www.fanfare-se.com.*
Art © 2003 Mike Grell; Shadow Lass TM and © DC Comics.

# Michael Netzer

A regular fill-in and back-up artist on **Superboy and the Legion of Super-Heroes** during the 1970s, Michael Netzer's run spanned two writers, three editors, and seven issues. Now living in Israel, Netzer ran his own commercial studio until recently, and still maintains links with the comic book industry. The following interview was conducted by Glen Cadigan on December 16, 2002, and was updated by Netzer the following spring.

**TLC:** *Where are you from originally?*

**MN:** I was born in Detroit. At the age of three, my family moved to Lebanon and returned to the States about eight years later. After a few years in comics and other endeavors, I came to Israel by way of Lebanon, and I've been here since.

**TLC:** *Did you know any of the other pros from Detroit before you moved to New York?*

**MN:** A few. My closest acquaintance was Greg Theakston, who went on to chronicle some of comics' history under the Pure Imagination imprint. We spent a lot of time together, and he was my first mentor in the craft. I also knew Arvell Jones and Keith Pollard, who invited me to join them on one of their sojourns to New York, a trip which launched my comics career. I didn't personally know Rich Buckler, Al Milgrom, Jim Starlin, Walt Simonson, or a host of other talent who came from Detroit, and was surprised to find out that there was such a heavy concentration of Michiganers in comics. I do remember that I delivered a newspaper, the **Brightmoore Journal**, to Rick Buckler's house soon after he took off to New York. His mother was on my list of customers, and we talked a few times about Rich's infatuation with comics and his progress on breaking into the industry. Those few conversations helped cement in me the desire to do the same, and I followed him about a year later.

**TLC:** *Around when was this?*

**MN:** November 1975.

**TLC:** *What comics did you read growing up?*

**MN:** A wide range, from **Archie** and **Classics Illustrated** to **Batman** and the **Fantastic Four**. I was into the drawing,

which led to a greater interest in visually dynamic and unique comics. Many of the books at DC that Neal Adams had a hand in were among the things that I'd collect more fervently, although I'd often be disappointed because he'd do a lot of covers, and I'd buy the comics from a vending machine hoping to see his art inside, and it wasn't always there. I spent a lot of time reading and studying Jack Kirby's work, basking in the pure energy his pages screamed with. I was also in awe of [Jim] Steranko's run on **S.H.I.E.L.D.** and **Captain America**. In my later teens, a new generation of artists were making some breakthroughs which began to catch my eye. Alan Weiss, Berni Wrightson, Mike Kaluta, Jim Starlin, Barry Smith, Jeff Jones, and Walt Simonson, to name a few, were among the talent which beckoned [me to] jump into the fray and become a part of the industry.

**TLC:** *At what age did you think you had what it took to become a professional comic book artist?*

**MN:** I thought I was ready at fourteen or so. From around the age of six I came into a large supply of blank paper through an uncle in Lebanon who had a printing house and knew that I liked to draw. I spent a great deal of the rest of my childhood drawing from everything in sight: comics translated into Arabic (including some of Neal's early work), photos of art and sculpture in encyclopedias, books and magazines, as well as images from the rich natural environment of Lebanon. Horses, donkeys, birds and lizards were common sketching subjects for me. By the time I was in my early junior high school years in the U.S., I thought I was ready to take on professional comics.

**TLC:** *Do you remember your first professional job?*

**MN:** [It was a] "Tales of the Great Disaster" back-up for **Kamandi** [#45 —**Ed.**]. It was a script offered by

Jack Harris on the day I landed in New York. I visited Continuity Studios, [which was] Neal Adams' base of operations, after an invite by Neal when I'd met him at the Triple Fan Fair convention in Detroit a year earlier. Neal welcomed me and said, "I won't have much work for you at first, but here are some phone numbers. Call up a few people and see if they'll give you a script. You're welcome to grab a drawing table and work from here." Jack Harris was on the list, and he invited me for an interview. He saw my work, and gave me the **Kamandi** back-up as a try-out. It was an lucky thing to have happened. That afternoon I became acquainted with a few artists at Continuity that'd been trying to get a script from one of the Big Two for some time, [artists] like Joe Rubinstein, Carl Potts, Joe Barney, John Fuller, Joe Brozowski (J.J. Birch), and a few others. I never had that benefit of a training period

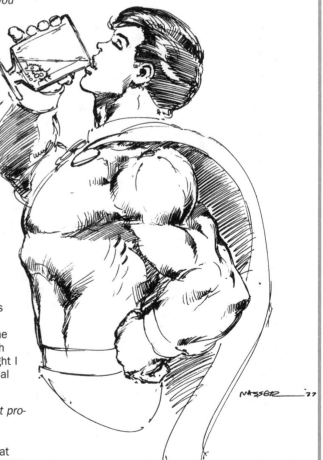

*Mon-El drinking his anti-lead serum by Netzer. Courtesy of Kevin Gould.*
Art © 1977 Michael Netzer; Mon-El TM and © DC Comics.

THEN, THE BACKDROP OF THE COSMOS FADES AWAY AS PROJECTRA LEAPS INTO HER LOVER'S ARMS!

BUT EVEN AS THEY *EMBRACE*, AND THE DREAM BECOMES COMPLETE ONCE MORE--IT IS *BROKEN*!

KARATE KID *DISSOLVES* INTO DREAMSTUFF -- AND PROJECTRA IS *ALONE* ONCE MORE.

I *WON'T* LOSE YOU-- NOT NOW!

*Princess Projectra in a scene from* **Superboy and the Legion of Super-Heroes** *#233.*
© DC Comics.

where I could've gained a little more experience before taking on a professional comic book. I was into the fray from day one, but I was confident that it would all work out.

[Continuity] became my base of operations [right away]. I was there through that entire stint in comics until September, 1981. The latter years, however, from November of '77 [on], I'd spend the winters in California, not doing comics at all, and then head back to Continuity for the summers, working on a strange mix of occasional comics work and another endeavor which had some expression in the comics industry, but was directed at a much wider audience. It was no secret to most of the industry folk, [and] **Star*Reach** #12 and **Hot Stuff** #6 had some work related to it.

**TLC:** *Were you one of the Crusty Bunkers?*

**MN:** Not officially. I did work on Crusty Bunkers jobs, but I came in at the tail end of the Crusty Bunkers. None of the well known stories credited to them had my work. The Crusty Bunkers work I did was on later, little known books such as the Charlton black-and-white magazine format books, [like] **Space 1999, Emergency,** and the **Six Million Dollar Man**.

**TLC:** *What was the atmosphere like at Continuity in those days?*

**MN:** It was pretty magical. I can't describe it any other way. For me, at least, it was a good time and a good spirit. Neal was a very strong driving force. He'd basically provide an environment that people could come in and feel comfortable and work. He had his own way of doing things, and that kind of affected everybody. For me, I had everything I could ask for at that time

of my career: a steady influx of work from DC and Marvel, Neal's professional tutoring (along with that of a host of other friends and professionals who frequented the studio), and the family-like environment that the studio, and the comics industry, provided. It was a virtual paradise for those early years, and I still cherish every moment. Certainly, no other period in my life has been comparable to the youthful exuberance and naïveté that was within me then.

**TLC:** *How long was it after you moved to New York that you started drawing the **Legion**?*

**MN:** It was the next job after the **Kamandi** back-ups, early 1976. I still cringe at the sight of that first story [*"Death of a Legend," **SLSH** #222* —Ed.]. It was a story about a hero that was a staged phony, not brave or heroic at all. After that there was a short break in **Legion** work and I was given other assignments—**Kobra, Isis, Wonder Woman,** "Supergirl," "Green Arrow," and "Black Canary" [*The last two appeared in **World's Finest**. —Ed.*]. By that time, I suppose that my work had improved to satisfy the special standards of the **Legion** book. Paul Levitz was writing some issues, and we started working together then. That was the period that Jim Sherman and I collaborated on the main features while I did some additional back-ups. They were all very good stories, and something about the youthful heroism worked well with the way I saw the world then.

**TLC:** *Who hired you for your first **Legion** job?*

**MN:** The then-editor. I believe it was also Jack Harris, but you might check that. [**Actually, Harris was the Legion's assis-**

tant editor at the time. —Ed.]

**TLC:** *You did a lot of back-ups and fill-ins for the **Legion**. Why did you stop?*

**MN:** I never stopped doing the **Legion** specifically, I just stopped doing comics. I didn't navigate a career or pick my books, as my colleagues did. I just accepted everything that DC offered and never asked for a personal preference. I continued doing the **Legion** until the day I left comics. Most of the non-**Legion** work I did were sporadic one-shots or short series. The **Legion** was the title I'd worked on most, so maybe that's why it seems like I stopped doing it.

I never had a reason to quit the **Legion**. Just the opposite; it was one of my favorite books. Working with Paul was a great experience. He was a very good writer/plotter, and we had some great times throwing a lot of ideas around while we did those books.

**TLC:** *You were actually given credit for the plot of one of the stories which you drew.* [*"The Final Illusion," **SLSH** #233. —Ed.*]

**MN:** I'm credited as having that plot, but I'll tell you how that worked out. I discussed a very vague idea of Princess Projectra's illusions coming back at her and menacing her within the illusionary world that she drifts into. Paul put that together into a very nice, concrete story. I saw comic stories as big, vague ideas then, and enjoyed the all-encompassing concepts, the kind that take you around all the way to the outer edge of an idea and bring you back to its beginning. There were, perhaps, other such ideas discussed from time to time that never became finished stories, but this one found its way into print. I wasn't very [involved] as to the story content, perhaps because I hadn't yet understood that I could or should be. I'm certainly more sensitive to the story content of everything I do today. I wasn't yet ready for that kind of involvement then, maybe not very cognitive of the full scope of the work. I was mainly concentrating on the art and trying to bring across the spirit of the story, while the actual nuts and bolts of it were secondary to me. Paul understood this in me, and reached for those wider concepts, one of which was this Projectra back-up.

**TLC:** *Did you ever hope that the **Legion** would turn into a more regular assignment?*

**MN:** I wasn't looking for a regular assignment. I wasn't shunning away from it, but I

wasn't really looking for it. I wasn't looking to grab a title and turn it into my own. I was just doing the work as it came along, trying to get better at it. I was too young and had other aspirations that weren't yet clear to me then, so I wasn't navigating a career or looking for any regularity in the comics work. By the latter end of 1977, I was offered the **John Carter** [**Warlord of Mars**] series at Marvel, [and] that would've been the most serious commitment I would've ventured into. But it wasn't meant to be. I called Marv [Wolfman] and told him that I wouldn't be doing the book. I'd sensed that comics wouldn't be a final landing spot for me, and that may have stopped me from going full force and seeking a regular title to work on.

**TLC:** *You had a few different inkers during your run. Did you have any preferences?*

**MN:** Jack Abel did the bulk of the inking of my **Legion** work. I know I didn't appreciate his work back then [like] I do now. I was more entrenched in the Neal Adams/Dick Giordano line in which Joe Rubinstein inked. Looking back at those books, I like [the work] that Jack did, and he probably stands up as being identifiable more with the **Legion** work for me than anything else. He's probably one of my favorites. Bob Wiacek also inked some stories which I enjoyed greatly. Joe Rubinstein was the definitive inker of the bulk of my work for DC, and he knew how to clean up my pencil line. He was my first choice on most of the assignments I had at DC. Strange thing about printing, that one guy does the pencils and one inks it. Today I work on a computer. I produce comic book pages on a computer, so I pencil, ink, color and do everything together. I don't draw on paper anymore. No more paper.

**TLC:** *I guess that hurts original art sales.*

**MN:** It hurts original art sales, [but] we're not in the business of original art sales, we're in the business of producing good comic book art. Whatever it takes to make the work better is more important than the additional income from the sale of originals. I know it's a controversial issue with many of my colleagues, but I stand at the opposite end of this debate [more] than most. The computer is a far more versatile and powerful drawing tool than pencil, ink and paper. The difficulty we have in adapting to the digital art tools is similar to the difficulty that a caveman would've had if he'd been exposed to a canvas and oil paint, which would've given him far richer results than stone carvings on cave walls.

**TLC:** *Were you aware of the organized*

*Legion fandom which was around back then?*

**MN:** Sure. *Legion* fandom was coming into its own around then and it was cultivating a vociferous following. I wasn't absorbed into it as some of the other artists and writers, but there were quite a few Legion fans who looked for me at conventions and sought my originals from that run. Dave Cockrum and Mike Grell rode the crest of that wave perhaps more than others, and Jim Sherman had a good spot there next to them. I was more on the fringe of comics fandom, and apparently was never around long enough to become an active part of it.

Discovering comics fandom—and its implications to an emerging artist growing in popularity—was a phenomenon for me. Sure, I was aware of its presence from the few conventions I'd attended prior to getting into the business, but I wasn't ready to relate to it with any intent at that age. I was mostly overwhelmed with the audience, their love for the work, and their desire to meet and get to know the creators. By the time I began realizing that I had an audience for my work, I began to question what it was that I was saying with my art. This was one of the factors, albeit a minor one, which led to my stepping out of the industry when I did.

**TLC:** *I know that a lot of artists didn't like drawing the* **Legion**. *What was your take on it?*

**MN:** It was certainly a little more work than a **Batman** story. There were far more characters, and there was a lot of interaction, but I liked the multiplicity of the team mentality and the look of an action/adventure team, so I guess that made up for it. Legion fandom's positive response also made the extra work a little more tolerable.

**TLC:** *Everyone's got a favorite Legionnaire. Did you have any preferences when it came to drawing?*

**MN:** I was always attracted to Brainiac 5, but didn't get to draw him very much. I enjoyed the Bouncing Boy story I did [*"The Day Bouncing Boy Bounced Back,"* **SLSH**

*A sample of Netzer's work at Continuity, courtesy of Spencer Beck.* Metalith TM and © 2003 Continuity Studios.

*#230.* —**Ed.**], where he was half-Bouncing Boy, half-regular chubby guy. It gave him an added dimension I hadn't thought of earlier. I liked drawing the girls, even though they didn't always come out too feminine. Drawing Superboy was nice as it almost felt like doing a Superman story, and brought me closer to exploring the look and feel of the father of all super-heroes. Shadow Lass was also a special one for me. I can't, however, single out any one of these characters as an absolute favorite.

**TLC:** *Were you aware that the* **Legion** *was one of DC's best-sellers back then?*

**MN:** Not really. It almost felt to me like the kind of book that DC didn't pay much attention to. There seemed to be a lot of hoopla about other books and new projects within [the] industry, but not the **Legion**. I think that **Superman** was a topseller, and **Batman** was close up there, and then from there everything was downward. The Legion was somewhere in the middle. That's the way that it felt from the way it was related [to] me. I can't remember having a feeling that this was a runaway sales book.

**TLC:** *When you look back at those days now, what are your impressions of them?*

**MN:** I think what made it so magical was maybe the naïveté of the generation that I emerged into. This is the generation that followed the Wrightson, Simonson, Kaluta era. A lot of good, smart young talent began emerging and merging into the established community of creators, seeking to improve our lot within the industry and to make some considerable creative breakthroughs together. There was a feeling that doors were opening up and things were about to change in a big way, which they actually did in the early Eighties. That change, however, came at the expense of what made the late Seventies so magical: the bond that held the community of comic book makers together.

Besides Continuity there was also the studio which Wrightson, Kaluta, Jones and Smith had put together. Most everyone who was active in making comics lived in New York back then, and we had our share of social occasions, from First Friday parties at the beginning of every month to the weekly volleyball games on Sunday mornings in Central Park. A month wouldn't go by without knowing that you'd see just about everyone who was working in the industry at one of these gatherings. The

*Shadow Lass and the Emerald Empress in a convention sketch by Netzer. Courtesy of Kevin Gould.* Art © 2003 Michael Netzer; Shadow Lass, Emerald Empress TM and © DC Comics.

camaraderie I shared with Alan Weiss, Marshall Rogers, Joe Barney, Cary Bates, Joe Brozowski, John Fuller, Tony Dispoto and Chris Goldberg—to name a few—was a twenty-four hour thing, and when we weren't working on comics together, we'd [hang out] together. Good Seventies concerts at Madison Square Garden and tooling around Manhattan till the early morning hours was how we looked forward to taking our break from making comic books. It was an era very different than today's electronically connected generation. Fond remembrances of that time are amongst the more deeply embedded memories I hold today.

**TLC:** *Do you still keep in contact with anyone from back then?*

**MN:** Sure, I talk with Alan Weiss regularly and Joe Rubinstein visited me here in Israel several times. When I returned for a brief stint in '91-'93, I saw most everyone I'd worked with then, especially the close circle of friends. Jim Sherman and I hooked up and had a good time remembering those days.

Until recently, I was highly active in an e-mail forum for comic book professionals. A lot of people from back then are on the list, including Marv Wolfman, Len Wein, and Steve Leialoha, plus a whole bunch of pros which have emerged since those days. This forum of creators has been connected for a few years and has a lot of members from all over the world, including many of the Brits. We'd embarked on publishing an anthology of new work that would be the fruit of—and perhaps express the interconnectivity we had—on the forum. [It was] maybe the closest thing to the feeling of a community that we had in the Seventies. I've since had to step out of it as I've embarked on another endeavor which doesn't allow me continued access to a computer, but last I heard, the project is still on, and the forum members plan on publication sometime this summer.

**TLC:** *What are you working on today?*

**MN:** I operated a studio in Jerusalem until recently. My partner, Sophia Federov, and I did a lot of commercial advertising including corporate imaging, packaging design, illustration, and animation work. We produced animation openings of TV shows, multimedia presentations, designed web sites, and succeeded in proliferating a little more comics work into the Israeli culture. We'd

*The opening page of a Caspar coloring book, designed specifically for an Israeli audience. Courtesy of Spencer Beck at* **www.theartistschoice.com.** Caspar TM and © 2003 Harvey Entertainment.

recently finished a comic book format advertising campaign for a major promotional company in Tel-Aviv. Alongside this I was looking forward to the anthology project on the email forum. Interestingly, Kurt Busiek, also being a forum member, talked to me about doing a run of the *Legion* with him sometime soon. I agreed enthusiastically and he discussed it with the editors at DC. Last I heard, they were looking for a spot to fit it into their *Legion* plans.

**TLC:** *When was this being discussed?*

**MN:** January this year. [2002 —Ed.]

**TLC:** *That's very interesting.*

**MN:** It is very interesting, and I was looking forward to the prospect, but much has changed since and I'm not sure I'd be up for it even if it were to come through today. The Israeli economy is suffering a slow and steady collapse in light of the security situation in the Middle East. Our studio has ceased to be a viable business, and with no hope of an economic resurgence anytime soon, we had to shut it down this last March. I myself have been at a crossroads for some time, and this development pushed me into a very definitive direction, an endeavor that's a sequel and continuation of the same crossroads I was at in 1977 when I stepped out of comics. Suffice it to say, I don't see myself doing another comic book project for some time. I do foresee, however, that the fruits of this endeavor will soon reach the ears of the comic book industry, as well as those of the world at large.

# Paul Levitz

## Part One

In the long history of the **Legion of Super-Heroes**, no author has written more issues starring the team than Paul Levitz. From his days as an assistant editor to his current status as President and Publisher of DC Comics, probably no name is more closely identified with the super-heroes from the future than his. After over 120 issues and nine years as **Legion** writer (including an uninterrupted streak of seven years during his last stint on the title), Levitz stepped down from the series on which he established his reputation to focus on other areas. Kept busy with publishing concerns today, Levitz was interviewed by Glen Cadigan on March 13, 2003, and he copyedited the following transcript.

**TLC:** *When did you first start reading the Legion of Super-Heroes?*

**PL:** I think it was a coverless copy of **Adventure** [**Comics** #] 310 at a barber's office in Barryville, New York one summer.

**TLC:** *What was it about the comic that made you keep coming back?*

**PL:** That was a cool issue. That was the story in which all of the Legionnaires were apparently killed one by one [in] a kind of Agatha Christie routine, and then you finally found out it was Mr. Mxyztplk's descendent [who was behind it]. I guess it was just imaginative enough, [with] all the heroes, [that] the combined magic of it said, "This is pretty cool stuff!" At least to my seven-year-old imagination.

**TLC:** *So how long was it before it became your favorite title?*

**PL:** That's an interesting question. It clearly was by about [#] 330, 'cause by then I had shifted the one subscription I had conned my parents into getting me over from **Action** [**Comics**] to **Adventure**. So I guess that by the time I was nine, maybe, or a little younger.

**TLC:** *You were involved in comics fandom before you became a pro. How did you get your start there?*

**PL:** Being born in New York helped a lot. There was a fairly active and energetic fandom around New York. I became aware of fandom probably originally through a friend showing me Mark Hanerfeld's version of **The Comic Reader**. I think that was the first real fanzine I saw. I did some little kid, pretty horrible carbon paper, then xerox, fanzines alone and with friends. New York's comics convention was July 4th, and I wasn't able to attend that the first few years that I knew about it, because one of the peculiarities of New York in those years was that much of the Italian and Jewish working-class population would decamp the city for the surrounding mountains in the years before air-conditioning. Even stores in my neighborhood would close down for the two months of the summer and open up in the Catskills. So I always had the frustration of leaving the city about a week before the convention.

When I was fourteen, Don and Maggie Thompson announced a year in advance that they were gonna close down **Newfangles**, which was really the only news-oriented fanzine out there at the time. My friend Paul Kupperberg and I were sitting around reading this, bemoaning this, and with the naïveté of our ages—Paul is a year older than I am, so he would have been

around 15—said, "Well, why don't we do it?" So we scraped together sixteen bucks and we started a fanzine. And [it's been] all downhill from there.

**TLC:** *At what point did you give serious consideration into turning comics into a career?*

**PL:** Probably several years after I had. I started working freelance for DC when I was in high school. I was working here a couple of days a week as an assistant

*Before "The Great Darkness Saga," there was "Earthwar." From the collection of Mike Napolitano.* Superboy and the Legion of Super-Heroes TM and © DC Comics.

editor *per diem*, doing a little free-lance writing in addition to paying my way through school, figuring I'd get honest work [later on]. Then in early '76 Jenette Kahn arrived here, and was kind of a breath of hope and fresh air, because she was the first young person in an executive job in the business in many, many years. It was roughly the same time Jim Gaulton had come in at Marvel, and although he wasn't nearly as young, he was certainly energetic and professional, and I started to feel like there was some hope that maybe comics will be around a while. "I like this, I'm starting to make a few bucks at it, maybe I should do this instead of selling widgets for IBM." And I said, "The hell with it. Let me give this a try for a couple of years. I have enough money to go back and finish my degree if it turns out I need it," and I dropped out and gave it a shot for a while.

**TLC:** *Do you remember what your first published story was?*

**PL:** "The Witches' Way," in **Weird Mystery Tales** [#] 14 or 15. Something like that.

**TLC:** *How old were you then?*

**PL:** I think I probably wrote it in '74, so I would have been seventeen.

**TLC:** *So you started early.*

**PL:** Again, it's being a city kid. I knew everyone in the field from [editing] **The Comic Reader**. The comic business was very small in those days. There were maybe two hundred working professionals in the entire business, so by doing a fanzine, you literally knew everybody in a way that isn't physically possible now. Virtually all of those people were living in the New York metro area, 'cause you couldn't get work in the business otherwise.

Comics were going through a generational shift. The original generation that had really built the field [was] aging out, and, in some cases, being pushed out due to a variety of circumstances. At the same time, more work was being created than had been the case for a number of years, so there was a really solid opportunity for anybody hanging around the edges of the place wanting to get in. Most of New York fandom that had any real interest in doing it and anything resembling skills at least

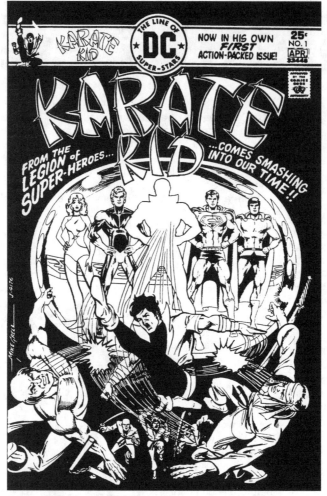

*Levitz's* **Legion** *career began on* **Karate Kid** *#1.* Karate Kid and the Legion of Super-Heroes TM and © DC Comics.

got a try working for one or another of the comics publishers in those years. Some of us lasted, some of us didn't. Some of us decided that we really didn't like knowing what was inside the sausage, but it wasn't a hard time to make it in.

**TLC:** *Was it known around the office that you were a fan of the* **Legion**?

**PL:** Certainly by the younger guys. The older editors who were still driving the business at the time were fairly cynical about the concept of being a fan. Julie Schwartz came out of science-fiction fandom, [and] Joe Orlando was, as a kid artist, passionate about the artists who had preceeded him who had influenced him, but the organized, "This is someone who knows everything about what happened in the **Legion** 'cause he's indexed it and documented it," the grown-ups didn't really give much of a damn about.

**TLC:** *So how did you end up on* **Karate Kid**?

**PL:** One of the peculiarities of that period

at DC was the line changed fairly dramaticly in reaction to business conditions. People thought comics were selling better, so all of a sudden we'd add eight or nine new books. People thought comics would do better in thicker formats, [so] we'd suddenly change a half-dozen books to hundred pagers. But in one of those bursts, when martial arts seemed to be a trend—and this is the period when the standing joke about DC was when we started putting out something matching a trend, you could be absolutely sure the trend was over—the company made a decision to add a couple of martial arts-influenced books, [and] assigned one to Joe Orlando as editor. I was Joe's assistant, and having liked the Karate Kid character from his **Legion** days, being a big fan of Jim [Shooter]'s period on the book, I said, "Why don't we try this?" and Joe was inclined. Murray Boltinoff, who was editing the **Legion**, didn't scream that loudly. He had no enormous attachments to any one of the Legionnaires at that point, [and] wasn't producing that much **Legion** material, so we got to try it.

**TLC:** *Did you have any long-term plans for that title as a writer?*

**PL:** If I did, they're long lost.

**TLC:** *So why was your stay so short?* [**Note:** *Levitz was only credited with* **Karate Kid** *#1. —*Ed.]

**PL:** Fairly shortly after I started that, my writing career hit a wall 'cause Carmine Infantino, who was company President and really still hands-on in charge of the editorial area at the time, was starting to read some of my material that was coming out and felt I was in over my head. [He thought that I was] still a little fresh as a writer to be carrying the kinds of work I had, and wanted me pulled off the major assignments I was on at the time. In retrospect, I think it was probably a pretty reasonable decision. My skills were not where they ought to have been at that time. So off I went back to my assistant editor's desk to play and polish for a little while, and by the time I came back, I was doing better.

**TLC:** *What were the circumstances around you getting the* **Legion** *assignment?*

**PL:** Murray had retired from full-time

Dawnstar was co-created by Mike Grell and Paul Levitz. From the collection of Greg Huneryager. Art © 2003 Mike Grell; Dawnstar TM and © DC Comics.

work—I guess that's in '76—and Denny O'Neil was inheriting the book as editor. Jim Shooter had just resigned the assignment effective pretty much at the end of Murray's run because Jim was going on staff as an assistant editor at Marvel and couldn't continue freelancing for us and I probably would have killed anyone else who got it. All of this is where the proximity of being there in place makes an enormous difference in getting a shot at it. I probably wasn't ready to be handling the **Legion** at that time. I certainly did that whole first run at a period when I had over-committed myself tremendously, causing a bunch of fill-in issues and other problems, but boy, I wanted it.

**TLC:** *I don't think you had to beat out too many other people for it, did you?*

**PL:** There weren't too many of the quote unquote "major writers" of the business who were desperate to do the **Legion**. But it's a monthly book. That's a solid paying assignment. Cary Bates never loved the **Legion** as his particular favorite assignment, but I'm sure he would have been happy to have another monthly at some point in there. He knew the characters reasonably well from his work with Murray, and there were probably at least a half dozen young writers with as good credentials as I had at that point in my career who would've loved to have taken it on.

**TLC:** *Was it understood when you took over that Mike Grell would no longer be there?*

**PL:** No, 'cause Dawnstar was created by

Mike and me for Mike to draw. It was, "Mike what would you enjoy doing if you're gonna stay on the **Legion**? What would be fun?" and he came up with the sketch, and I built the character around that.

**TLC:** *Did you have many conversations about what the two of you would do?*

**PL:** Probably not, in the tenor of the time.

**TLC:** *Did you have anything to do with Jim Sherman getting the job?*

**PL:** I'd be surprised if I had anything to do with it. Between Joe Orlando and Vinnie Colletta, who was art director at that time, and Denny O'Neil, who was editing it, all of them were more knowledgeable about art and artists than I was. Jim was hanging out at Continuity Studios in those years, so I would suspect that Neal [Adams] had sent him up, which probably works for the tone of the times. It's probably the time at which Neal was doing a batch of covers for us again, and was hanging out with Jenette socially. So it more likely came out of that than anything else.

**TLC:** *Did you feel like the two of you were in synch as far as writers and artists go?*

**PL:** I had a lot of fun working with Jim. I thought he was very much a modern evolution of a Curt Swan. Like Curt, he drew incredibly well as an illustrator—people's faces, expressions, understanding anatomy—and he did some really imaginative stuff on some of the jobs. It was hard for him to work with the schedule of the amount of material needed for the **Legion**, but he was a lot of fun to work with. [He] did some beautiful stuff. Mike Nasser, as well, who was doing the back-ups, and eventually alternated with Jim.

**TLC:** *You didn't waste much time before you addressed the Adult Legion story. I think it was in your third or fourth issue that you killed off Chemical King.*

**PL:** Yeah, something like that.

**TLC:** *Was there any particular reason why you got to that so fast?*

A recent picture of Sun Boy by George Pérez. Courtesy of Spencer Beck at www.theartistschoice.com. Art © 2003 George Pérez; Sun Boy TM and © DC Comics.

**PL:** I can't swear that it was my thinking at the time, but it's consistent with the way I later thought as a writer that the virtue of a book like **Legion** was that you could show real world consequences. One of the burdens when you're writing something like **Superman** is how you establish the drama when the reader is convinced that you're not gonna kill Superman off in the story. The **Legion** had the tremendous advantage that you could run that risk. In #312 of **Adventure**, the return of Lighting Lad/death of Proty story had been one of my early favorites, so probably in all of those influences [which] I would've gone through I said, "This guy's doomed to die in theory anyway. His powers don't make sense to most of the writers, much less to the readers. He doesn't have much of a personality at this point, [so] let's sacrifice him to fate to show that anybody can get screwed with in this book."

**TLC:** *How much of a burden was the Legion's change to giant-sized status to you?*

**PL:** I probably had something to do with getting it changed to it, so although it was a major contributor to my screwing up on the schedule, I don't think I viewed it as a burden as much as an opportunity to do longer length stories or solo back-ups and some fun like that.

**TLC:** *You were relieved a few times by Gerry Conway that year. How busy were you?*

**PL:** Way busier than anybody with a brain ought to be. I think I peaked somewhere in that year with a month where I wrote about a hundred and forty pages of comics on top of having a full-time job.

**TLC:** *That's a lot of work.*

**PL:** I'm a fairly fast writer today, and have been through most of my career, but for the level of skill I had at the time, that's just loads more than anybody ought to be doing. You're whatever I was at the time—twenty years old, twenty-one—[and] you can pull a fair number of all-nighters and work late into the night on other nights, and devote more of your life to something and put more energy in, but clearly I was overcommitted.

**TLC:** *When was the decision made to marry Lightning Lad and Saturn Girl?*

**PL:** Probably when they decided to do more original tabloids. Once we decided to do a *Legion* tabloid, to try and do something that would make it an event, that was

The original cover rough to *SLSH* #237 by Walt Simonson. Courtesy of Al Milgrom. Superboy and the Legion of Super-Heroes TM and © DC Comics.

the most logical first major event in the Legion, [to] come back to fulfilling the beginnings of where the book came from.

**TLC:** *So how did the **Legion** get consideration for a tabloid?*

**PL:** You have to remember, once you get to '76 or so, part of my job was at least to be in the room in all of those discussions, and over time it evolved into more and more of my responsibility, so whether it was the double-sized format or going monthly or getting a tabloid, the *Legion* had a pretty good advocate in the room. The book was doing fairly well at that time, so it wasn't unreasonable to argue for it, but it also had somebody there really with a definite interest in promoting it.

**TLC:** *How long did you intend on writing those two out of the title?*

**PL:** Oh, I have no idea. My practice in writing the book was I usually had probably six or seven issues ahead identified as what their likely storylines would be, and how the subplots would play out at any given time. Most of that was kinda written in chalk and tended to get revised as the issues went by, but I rarely made any plans beyond that stage.

**TLC:** *You had some big name fill-in artists during that year. You had Walt Simonson and Jim Starlin and Howard Chaykin fill-in on the title.*

**PL:** We had Al Milgrom editing it at that point, who was an artist himself, and a very good buddy of a lot of those guys. He had roomed with Walt, and had shared studio space with one of the other guys at one time or another. [He] was a good buddy of Starlin, for example, who was another one of the major artists who dropped by, so that was really Al being able to say, "Hey! C'mon, guys, come pitch in and do something here."

**TLC:** *Was it a kick getting to work with different artists?*

**PL:** Oh, it's been one of the

thrills of my career. From being able to work with a Curt Swan, who I grew up on, to work with the guys of my generation like Jim Sherman or Walt, to discovering the new folks and how to play with them.

**TLC:** *That Jim Starlin story got a sequel. [**SLSH** #'s 250-251. —**Ed.**] What do you remember about that, and how it was originally supposed to come out?*

**PL:** That was originally bought for a sixty-four-page spectacular, and Jim had plotted it and penciled it. I had, I guess, stopped writing the book regularly at that time. I had just given it up. The spectacular got cancelled in the Implosion cutbacks—we dropped that line—and maybe Jack Harris, as he was inheriting the *Legion*, asked me if I could take those pages and make 'em work for a couple of issues for the regular book. I played essentially fifty-two card pickup with it. I recreated the story, we threw out a few pages, we had Joe Staton do a new splash for the second part, [and] ran it in entirely different order with a somewhat different plot than what Jim intended—somewhat to his frustration, if memory serves—and kinda incorporated it

A convention sketch by George Pérez, courtesy of Kevin Gould.
Art © 2003 George Pérez; Lightning Lad and Saturn Girl TM and © DC Comics.

*The cover rough for SLSH #243 by Al Milgrom, courtesy of the artist.* Superboy and the Legion of Super-Heroes TM and © DC Comics.

into the storyline a little more smoothly, I hope.

**TLC:** *Did DC ever keep copies of those missing pages?*

**PL:** Possibly, but I'm sure they didn't survive this long.

**TLC:** *So if they ever turned up, would there be any possibility of DC republishing that story the way it was originally intended?*

**PL:** Anything's possible if the stuff survives. When we did the last volume of the *Legion Archives* about a year ago, for whatever set of reasons we managed to remember that we had dropped a page out of one of Murray's later issues of the *Legion* during one of the advertising changes, and had run the page in [*The*] *Amazing World* [*of DC Comics*], so it survived there. So we ran the page in the archive edition, but comics have traditionally run themselves as a disposable sort of medium. We don't archive an awful lot of stuff within the business. The odds of anything like that surviving in coherent form are pretty low.

**TLC:** *Your first big multi-part storyline was "Earthwar." Did you originally intend for that to be a big, important story?*

**PL:** I hoped it would be. I mean, the idea of doing a five-parter for DC was pretty audacious. It was originally intended to be sort of a major work for Jim. We had bought some time in the previous couple of issues with fill-ins in the hope that he'd be able to do all five of the leads, and then that didn't work itself out, unfortunately.

**TLC:** *Were you disappointed that he didn't do the whole story?*

**PL:** Yeah. I mean, I love Joe Staton. He's one of my best friends of the artists I've collaborated with over the years, and I think a very smooth storyteller. I always wrote Joe's [stuff] more quickly than any other artist. But whenever you're changing horses in midstream, something suffers, and Joe was never particularly fond of doing the *Legion*, so I think it damaged what that could have been as a storyline. The story structure was set up as a sort of matrioshka doll—the Russian one-doll-inside-the-other-doll routine—stolen off the structure that E.E. "Doc" Smith had used for the *Lensman* novels, which I had read in the year or two previous to that, and been fond of. I thought it was a good shot, but the combination of my limitations and changing artists midway—and changing inkers, if I recall correctly, about three times, because I think Murphy [Anderson] inked one, Joe Giella inked one, I forget who else inked one [*Jack Abel* —**Ed.**]—a fairly significant number of things went wrong in a short period of time.

**TLC:** *In that storyline, you brought in the reserves, you brought in the Substitute Heroes, you used every Legionnaire except one—Tyroc. What did you have against him?*

**PL:** I always thought he was just such a stupid character. The idea of using a sound-based character is, I think, intrinsically futile in a silent medium. He just never worked for me, so I did my best to

dodge him over the years.

**TLC:** *You didn't last too long yourself after that storyline.*

**PL:** That was the end of my regular run. I think I had plotted the next couple of stories, but that was when the Implosion happened, and we juggled all of our assignments around. I gave up *Legion* 'cause I couldn't hold on to that large a body of work with so many people having to take reduced workloads. It wouldn't have been fair, and since I'd been, in my view, screwing up the *Legion* pretty badly with the fill-ins, given the choice between staying on *All-Star* [*Comics*], which I was not screwing up because of its lesser frequency, or staying on *Legion*, which was a bigger commitment than I apparently was able to handle, I chose to give up *Legion*.

**TLC:** *So it wasn't a case of preferring the Justice Society to the Legion?*

**PL:** I loved both. I felt I was writing "Justice Society" a helluva lot better than I was writing *Legion*.

*Another recent picture by George Pérez, courtesy of Spencer Beck and Michael Lieb.*
Art © 2003 George Pérez; Star Boy TM and © DC Comics.

# James Sherman

A commercial artist by trade, James Sherman brought new levels of realism to the **Superboy and the Legion of Super-Heroes** before he left partway through the "Earthwar" saga two years later. On January 9, 2003, he was interviewed by Glen Cadigan via phone, and he copyedited the following transcript.

**TLC:** *First things first: where have you been all of these years?*

**JS:** Working in other fields of the graphic industry, applying what I learned in comic books to it. I came from publishing and graphic design prior to comics, which is responsible for all the realism that's in the cartooniness. I finally landed a job after five years of trying to get into comics, got it, and then got requests to work in other areas which paid a helluva lot more, but were less satisfying. Although now I've been doing movies for the past ten years.

**TLC:** *When did you become interested in comic books?*

**JS:** I was a big fan of comics in college. I hadn't read comics since I was a little kid, since my mom discovered my collection from the girl next door. I had to read them flashlight-under-the-blankets in the dark late at night when everybody else was asleep, 'cause I wasn't allowed to have any. But when I got into college, it was like, "Wow! Freedom!" It was great. I was blown away by the level of art in comics, specifically the art of Mike Kaluta and Bernie Wrightson and Robert Crumb.

**TLC:** *What titles were you reading then?*

**TLC:** *Anything which people would recognize?*

**JS:** *Men In Black*, *Lost World*, *Hercules* (the animated Disney movie), but a whole slew of stuff that's never made it to screen.

**TLC:** *Are you just doing storyboards for those movies?*

**JS:** Storyboards, art direction, production design, costume design, props. For **Men in Black**, I just did aliens, weapons and the vehicles.

**TLC:** *How did you get into that industry?*

**JS:** Simply because the phone rang and somebody asked me if I could handle it, and I said yes. The first job I ever did out of college was for a movie. I don't believe it ever got made, 'cause they had tie-ins to theme parks and all this other stuff that never happened. The money wasn't there.

*One of the films which Sherman has worked on is **Men In Black**. Men In Black TM and © 2003 Marvel Characters, Inc. and Lowell Cunningham.*

**JS:** All the super-hero stuff, mostly DC. **Flash**, **Green Lantern**... most of the side stuff. "Tommy Tomorrow"... "Adam Strange" was one of my favorites. **Challengers of the Unknown** were my absolute top favorite, but when I got into comics they had been cancelled. I said, "Can we bring them back?" and they said, "Okay." So we did three issues of the **Challengers**, and they yanked me off of that to do **Legion**. I said, "I don't want to do the **Legion**. The **Legion**'s the dumbest book in the universe." [*laughs*] "It's just the trash barrel for all the characters you can't otherwise publish." And then I finally read it—'cause it was ridiculed among my fellow comic book readers in college [and] I hadn't actually read it—and I said, "Wait a minute: this is amazing, this is better than **Star Trek**! This is cool!" So I got into the first gig, and didn't want to give it up for the next two years. But I had other jobs outside comics coming at me at the same time, so it was a constant deadline conflict, and I finally had to give up comics, because that stuff paid the bills [and] comics didn't. Comics were just fun.

**TLC:** *Was it a hard choice to make?*

**JS:** Yeah. I really didn't want to give up

*A convention sketch by Sherman from 1977. From the collection of Steven Weill. Art © 2003 James Sherman; Legion of Super-Heroes TM and © DC Comics.*

comics. *Really* did not want to, but I just couldn't pay the bills on comic book money.

**TLC:** *How exactly did you become a professional comic book artist?*

**JS:** I would take my portfolio and, once or twice a year, get an appointment, polish the portfolio up, go in and show the stuff. After five years of rejections by Herb Trimpe, Johnny Romita, Sol Harrison, Mort Weisinger, Joe Kubert, Carmine Infantino, and Dick Giordano, I made an appointment for Marvel and DC on the same day 'cause I just didn't want to draw out the agony. I figured, "This is my last shot. If I don't get it now, that's it." So I went to see Joe Orlando at DC and Archie Goodwin at Marvel around mid-December of '75 and they gave me a script for the Blackhawks and the "White Tiger" on the same day. I was stunned and suddenly I had twenty pages of **Blackhawk** and twenty-five pages of "White Tiger" to do in a month. That was my break-in.

**TLC:** *Trial by fire?*

**JS:** Trial by electric jumper cables pinching each end of my spine. I did it, but wow! Yeah, that almost killed me right there. [*laughs*] No sleep that month, and nobody to help me out. Both editors complained about the fact that some of the panels weren't finished pencils. There was just enough there for somebody to ink, but they didn't have all the tone values and stuff they expected from the other panels on the pages and samples shown in the portfolio that I had presented. Tone values were of absolutely no use in comics because they couldn't reproduce graded tones. The technology existed but they weren't using it. They only wanted tone values in there so the inkers could 'feather' the shadows, but I thought the feathering looked horrible, so I eventually stopped doing graded tones. But on that job, I just didn't do tone values because there wasn't time. I just did the outlines, got most of the details, but that was it.

**TLC:** *When did you join Upstart Studios?*

**JS:** Good question. I think it was sometime in '79.

**TLC:** *So it was after you were working on the **Legion**?*

**JS:** Yes. In fact, I was practically forced out of comics by that point in order to meet my deadlines on the bigger projects. I had hopes we'd all jam on the various issues, because each one of the guys in the studio had done a fill-in for me so that the

book would stay on deadline, even if I couldn't work on it. I thought more of that might continue so I could stay in comics, but we ended up all working on our own projects, and never really getting the chance to jam on a project. But that was the idea behind the studio.

**TLC:** *Who else was working there?*

**JS:** Jim Starlin, Walt Simonson, Howard Chaykin, Val Mayerik, and later, Frank Miller.

**TLC:** *That's a pretty A-list group of people.*

**JS:** No sh*t. I was so starstruck. I [thought], "Geez! These guys are letting me in with them? This is great!"

**TLC:** *What was the atmosphere like in the studio?*

**JS:** Really down to business. It was funny. Somebody interviewed us and we said, "Well, the atmosphere is we hardly ever talk, nobody plays any music, 'cause nobody wants to interfere with anybody." Outside of comics, when you're not at the drawing board, [when] you're at a convention, it's all talk about story ideas and jamming on ideas and it was great! But in the studio, where you expected that to be [the case] nine-to-five every day, it just didn't happen. Everybody was just too busy getting their job done. Because of the nature of comics, you're always in fantasy. Real world stuff disappears. You're playing in fantasy all the time, trying to put all the pieces together to make the story work, so you're just too busy to talk.

**TLC:** *Did you leave the studio, or did the studio split up?*

**JS:** I was the last one in the studio. Everybody got [big] jobs. Val Mayerik went back to Cleveland to work out of there, and now he's in Portland, Oregon, doing

*Drawn at the same convention as the picture on the preceding page, the Legion springs into action by James Sherman, again courtesy of Stephen Weill. Art © 2003 James Sherman; Legion of Super-Heroes TM and © DC Comics.*

great, doing advertising and movies and concepts. Jim Starlin landed **Dreadstar**, bought a house upstate, built a studio there, and started working out of that. Frank Miller did **Daredevil** here, and got his big **Ronin** gig for DC, and I'm sure other stuff, but he got some gig out West and went to California. I think that's when he started working on **Robocop**. Howard Chaykin got a job with the **Flash** [TV show], but I think he was already out of the studio by then. He'd gone to Hollywood to sell his own scripts. Last I heard he was working for Paramount doing projects. But he was always freelance, as far as I know. Walt and his wife, Louise, bought a house, built a studio there, and now work out of their house.

**TLC:** *Did new guys come in to take their place?*

**JS:** No. Well, Walt and I brought one guy in named Gary Hallgren, who's done a lot of stuff for the entertainment and humor magazines—**New Yorker**, **National Lampoon**, **Mad**, **Crazy** and stuff like that. Brilliant guy, but he also did the same thing: got a house, [and] built a studio at

*A Dark Circle sketch done at the 1980 San Diego Comic-con, courtesy of Steven Weill.* Art © 2003 James Sherman; Legion of Super-Heroes TM and © DC Comics.

his place out on Long Island. Besides, I needed the space. I was working on big projects and started building big tables, so little by little I took over the studio. I'm still here.

**TLC:** *Have you kept in contact with any of those guys?*

**JS:** We've talked on the phone occasionally, sent some Christmas cards here and there. We're all friends, but everybody's too scattered. Frank's back in town. We've talked. We've gone out to dinner and gallery stuff.

**TLC:** *How did you end up on the Legion?*

**JS:** I'm not sure. Like I said, I was doing **Challengers**, which was my number one love, and suddenly they said, "The next script,"—the fourth script—"is not available yet. In the meantime, will you do me a fill-in?" This is Paul Levitz [speaking]. So I said, "Gee, I'm not gonna have time to do a fill-in if we're waiting for the next **Challengers**. I have other things I can do until the **Challengers** script comes in," and he says, "No, that's gonna take too long. It'll probably be another month. Do this **Legion** thing." Okay, that was it. That's how

I got on.

**TLC:** *And so you just ended up staying?*

**JS:** Yeah. I wanted to go back to **Challengers**, but I found out he had given the **Challengers** to Mike Nasser, and wanted me on the **Legion** book permanently. So it wasn't just a fill-in. But luckily I thought, "Wow! This has such potential!" I didn't want to go back anyway.

**TLC:** *And Mike used to spell you on the Legion, too.*

**JS:** Yeah, they expanded the book to 34 pages from 21, and they had him doing the back story and me doing the front story. Then, I think at some point I took on some other project that didn't allow me any time. I think he did the whole book. They put a fill-in of his in, and after that came the "Earthwar." I'd been working on an idea and I told Paul, "Let's do this thing where the Legion gets into a war [and] each time the Legion win a battle they find the bad guys are only a front for somebody else. We find out somebody's behind somebody else behind somebody else. The Dark Circle is operating, manipulating the Khunds, who in turn are manipulating the Resource Raiders..." and he said, "Yeah, that sounds like a good idea. I think we can do that." But it started going in a direction that I didn't want it to go in, into magic. DC 'magic.' Magic to DC is/was kind of an escape clause. When they didn't have the imagination to explain something they said, "It's magic. You don't have to explain it." Their editorial point of view

of magic kept them safely away from real stories and anything with substance and meaning. And [then] Paul wanted to have Mordru the Magician come in and do the finale. I [said], "Ahhh! No! No! You have the Legion and the readers go through this epic battle, waiting issue after issue to find out the reason all this is happening to them only to find out it's magic?" [*laughs*] "Let's keep it real!" And he didn't want to do it.

**TLC:** *Is that why you didn't finish that storyline?*

**JS:** Yeah. I felt he was using me at that point. It finally dawned on me that it wasn't gonna go where I wanted to go, so I tried going on strike, so to speak. Plus, there were things going on in the sidelines and behind the scenes. There were 1976 copyright law changes, and in 1978 comic book artists were starting to organize, to fight for our rights and for creator-owned books, so we could own the rights to the characters. Not to DC characters and Marvel characters, but to our own characters. To this point, they had just been using our ideas for new characters without compensation. So it was kinda at the same time doing comics all fell apart for me. It fell apart for me in comics, but as far as everything else, my career just took off.

**TLC:** *Did you intend on doing your own creator-owned work then?*

**JS:** I had planned to, but I'd been so involved in other, better projects that taking time out to do those things seemed kinda silly.

**TLC:** *Paul Levitz tells me that you designed the Major League Baseball logo.*

**JS:** Yes. I did. I didn't know he knew that. [I did] a couple of others, too, but they didn't get as famous as that one. A grocery store chain... a couple of car company logos... [the] ShopRite

*Play ball! James Sherman designed both the Major League Baseball logo and the ShopRite logo.* MLB logo TM and © Major League Baseball; ShopRite logo TM and © Wakefern Food Corporation.

"I FEEL AN INCREDIBLE *VITALITY* COURSING THROUGH ME! BUT... IT'S SOMEHOW *DIFFERENT* THAN BEFORE!"

logo, and one for AMC (American Motors Corporation), but the AMC logo didn't get accepted, so other people got credit for that. I did a final execution for the National Basketball Association...

**TLC:** *You did their logo, too?*

**JS:** Yeah, but not the one they're using [now]. And logos for several magazines and small companies, things like that. But you wouldn't know those. I couldn't even remember the ShopRite logo, but there you go. I remember what it looks like, I just couldn't remember the name.

**TLC:** *I don't really remember you doing much work for DC after you left the* **Legion**.

**JS:** I did a few things for Marvel, but it was always guest-shots. [They'd ask] "Can you come in and do a series for us?" and I'd say, "Well, I can do one issue. Which issue do you want me to do?" Usually it was a number one or a special issue of something, where the characters were going to

do something different, like not wear uniforms that issue. But I just didn't have time to do comics. Every time I did do one, it got me in financial trouble.

**TLC:** *You did do the first issue of the* **Fly** *relaunch.*

**JS:** Yeah, I was gonna do the whole series. There were six issues slotted to be done, but a week into it the editor called up and said, "We need this done next week." I was supposed to do the pencil, ink, and color. I was supposed to have three months to do it, not one more week after just starting. So I ended up having only two weeks to pencil and ink the whole issue. So that was another situation where I didn't get any sleep. And then I found out that he had farmed out the second half of the first story (because it was a two-parter in the first two issues) to somebody else. The first eighteen pages, I think, were mine, and then somebody else did the rest. I just said, "Well, you can't do that to me. I don't need this headache."

**The Fly** was a book I came across when I was thirteen years old. I spent the summer running around with a beach towel cape, swim goggles, and a ray gun water pistol playing the Fly. That was the only super-hero comic I had ever seen as a kid. I mean, I'd seen **Superman** on TV, but I'd never read super-hero comics. But **The Fly** was among the ones my parents caught—the collection they caught and took away from me. Jack Kirby had done the artwork. Great stuff.

**TLC:** *You must have been really disappointed, then, to not have an opportunity to finish the series.*

**JS:** I was pissed for about 2 minutes. That was all the time I had to think about it. I already had two other deadlines on my drawing board and I had chosen to sacrifice my social life and my sleep time to do **The Fly**. So it was a good thing I didn't get to do more of **The Fly**. Although I was enjoying the hell out of collaborating with the writer, Jack C. Harris, the editor and the company were quickly revealing themselves to be a nightmare to work for. But I was in and out before I experienced any real damage.

**TLC:** *You said when you were working on the* **Legion** *with Paul that he was taking the story in a direction you didn't want it to go...*

**JS:** Only in the end. He gave me a pretty good free hand up until then. He'd write the stories, and I'd make minor visual

changes as I wanted to. Some of the stuff, they'd take it and make little changes back, which was fine, but at least I was getting a free hand until that point. So, that was kinda a stupid thing on my part to say, "I'm not gonna do this unless you give me my way." And that was just at the very end.

**TLC:** *Did you leave on bad terms?*

**JS:** No, I don't think so. It was just a casual comment. I really didn't think it was gonna be anything, but they [were] a lot more serious over there than I'd thought.

**TLC:** *So things are resolved today?*

**JS:** There was nothing to resolve. It wasn't a big deal at all. The fact that I couldn't stay in comics was my own turmoil, not theirs. I just had other projects and other deadlines that were impinging on me getting any work done for the comics. [The situation was], "I really want to do this, but if I want to keep my life together, I gotta pay the bills." So they had no clue what was going on with me. I just said simply, "If I can't do it the way I want it, what am I doing comic books for at all?" So it wasn't like, "Hey, DC: this is my situation, this is my stand." We were getting that way on the outside with comic book rights, but I

*A life-long fan of the Fly, Sherman was able to illustrate the character in 1983.*
The Fly TM and © 2003 Joe Simon.

wasn't even at that point yet. I think I wrote Paul a letter about that, but no biggy. It just kinda coincided with it in hindsight.

**TLC:** *In a perfect world, how long would you have stayed on the title?*

**JS:** I don't know. It's one of those things that I saw going far into the future. [*laughs*]

**TLC:** *A lot of artists have burned out on the* **Legion**.

**JS:** I can see why.

**TLC:** *But that didn't happen with you?*

**JS:** No, I was just beginning to hit my stride. They were laughing that I had Legionnaire's disease, 'cause I was just fascinated about all the possibilities. I mean, you've got twenty-four main characters, about every super-power possible, all their villains, and a universe in the future where you get total freedom to create entire civilizations that they're gonna meet and go up against. But my ideas were too big for what was going on. I had to go there slowly. In the "Earthwar," we started to get there, but I had to cut it loose to save my family and home.

**TLC:** *You had a few different inkers during your run. Did you change your penciling at all, depending on who was going to ink you?*

**JS:** Only with Jack Abel. Jack's stuff was my favorite, although I wasn't excited about it in the beginning. He was one of the few inkers who really knew what he was doing. The other guys had a lot of flair, but Jack knew what he was doing. His draftsmanship was amazing. I decided to pencil a splash page just the way I thought Jack would ink it so he wouldn't change anything. In fact, editors were saying, "Someday we want to print in one of the issues a page with all your tone values intact." They were gonna shoot my pencil drawings. Of course, that splash was the page they chose to print as pencil only. So it's penciled for Jack; it's not penciled for me.

**TLC:** *Do you remember what was on that page?*

*Published directly from the artist's pencils, a splash page from* Superboy and the Legion of Super-Heroes *#236.*
© DC Comics.

**JS:** It was Lightning Lad and Saturn Girl on a bench together, and he was going to hand her a rose and propose his marriage to her. I don't remember the title of the story, but that was the situation [*"Words Never Spoken," SLSH #236. —Ed.*].

**TLC:** *Was it understood that you were the regular artist on the* **Legion**?

**JS:** I don't think so. I had a two-year run on it, but I think it was always [up in the air]. It sort of dawned on me later on that Paul had big plans, and that somehow I was being manipulated toward that goal, but I always felt that it was myself and Mike Nasser and other people all working on the **Legion** at the same time.

**TLC:** *Joe Staton mentioned to me that when he took over the* **Legion***, the idea was that you and Mike and he were going to rotate on the title.*

**JS:** Yeah, there was always a sense of rotation on us, because it was just a huge deadline to do so many characters in one

book, especially a thirty-four page book. I mean, that's more than a page a day, and usually it takes four or five hours to do one panel in those books.

**TLC:** *Then shortly after you left, they dropped it back down to normal size again.*

**JS:** [*laughs*] Yeah, he would do that. [*laughs*] I think Paul was great. Paul was right for the book. I'm not sure I was right for the book, but Paul was right for the book. Paul was more of a fan than I was, and I had no background, no history until he showed me the first script. In fact, he gave me a bunch of background issues, [something] like two years worth of the **Legion** leading up to the script that he gave me, and when I read through it, I just started connecting the dots, going, "This stuff is amazing!"

But not so much what was in the book. It was the characters, their mix of powers, and all the design possibilities. **Star Trek** never went there. They started at least visiting other civilizations, and communicating with the aliens, but it just didn't seem to be going in a direction where you could escape humanoid-isms. But because it's comics, you're not limited to make-up for humans. You could do anything, and I just saw all kinds of potential there, but the script kept calling for humanoid this, humanoid that, and then, even when I got a chance to do other sci-fi books, I found writers didn't want anything but human-type aliens anyway. I thought that was very strange.

So I never really got a chance to do it until I got called in for the movie **Men in Black** to design aliens. It was my first chance to go wild. [But] when the movie came out, they had rehumanized them. I was told, "We don't want anything humanoid. We don't want anything insect-toid. We don't want anything anyone's seen before." So I went crazy and designed forty different aliens for them that nobody's ever seen. Some touches of it were still there. Like the little alien inside the guy's head that had all the controls? That was still there. That was close to intact, but they made him cute and lovable. He was supposed to be a 'good guy' alien, but they

The "cute little E.T." referred to by the artist. Men In Black TM and © 2003 Marvel Characters, Inc. and Lowell Cunningham.

Dawnstar's **Who's Who** entry, courtesy of Steve (Greybird) Reed. Dawnstar TM and © DC Comics.

**TLC:** *Did you work on both* **Men in Black** *movies?*

**JS:** Just the first.

**TLC:** *After you left the* **Legion**, *you did come back on a few occasions. You drew Dream Girl twice: once in* **Who's Who**, *and again on the cover of #300. Did you single her out?*

**JS:** No, they asked me. Dream Girl was not my favorite character. It was fun to draw her, because she had this silver suit, this kind of reflective skin, and I just thought it was fun to draw reflective stuff. But the inkers, when they don't understand the dynamics of it, they tend to fudge over it and do some comic book gimmick that they've done all along. So that took the fun out of drawing her. I think I got to draw the **Who's Who** and #300 Dream Girl by default. Pencilers weren't actually drawing reflections. Before I got into comics, all the mirrors and the windows on street storefronts—anything that was reflective—they would just do slash lines on a white surface. I think James Sternanko did some reflections in **Nick Fury, Agent Of Shield**, so I can't say I'm first, but I'm just saying,

made him cute and more humanoid. I'd made him more like a little squid in structure. He looked like something that was deep in the sea and had never seen light inside this guy's head. I wanted to open the head up and see this grotesque little alien, not a cute little E.T.

in general, comic book reflections didn't exist.

**TLC:** *I remember a specific panel in the issue which introduced the Infinite Man [*SLSH* #233. —*Ed.*] which had a mirror in it, and my reaction was, "My God, how long did it take this guy to draw this thing?"*

**JS:** That's why I say it took hours to do one panel. It was stuff like that. Not every panel, but near every page. I would get comments from editors saying, "You can't do that stuff in small panels." Then I would get letters from people saying, "Wow! Those panels are amazing! I felt like I could step right through them!" Other inkers were coming [up to me, asking], "Can I ink your stuff?"[and I would say,] "Hey, let me just get the job done. Leave me alone!"

**TLC:** *What were the logistics of doing that cover (#300)?*

**JS:** They called us into the office, actually. We had to do it right there in the editor's office.

**TLC:** *You also drew a chapter in that issue. Was it comfortable slipping back into that role?*

**JS:** It's ironic, because I didn't want to do Mordru the Magician, and that's what it was about. Paul said, "Here, why don't you get a chance to finish what we were gonna do?" and because there was no hard feel-

A panel from Superboy and the Legion of Super-Heroes #233 showcasing the use of mirrors. © DC Comics.

ings with this—it wasn't a big deal—I said, "Yeah, sure."

**TLC:** *Who was your favorite Legionnaire?*

**JS:** I can't tell you that. [*laughs*] I'm very fickle on who was my favorite, but she was definitely female.

**TLC:** *You did also draw Dawnstar in Who's Who.*

**JS:** Yes. Shrinking Violet kept becoming my favorite. I really had a lot of fun with her. I had a whole story written featuring her, but Paul didn't want to use it.

**TLC:** *So the two of you would collaborate?*

**JS:** Yeah, he'd hand me a plot and I'd say, "Hey, can we do this? Can we do that?" He'd say yes or no. I'd come in with stuff I'd written down, entire different plots that I came up with, and it went back and forth. I saw, in the years after [I left], some of the plot ideas were used, but I didn't get to draw them.

**TLC:** *Anything in particular?*

**JS:** No, just the way that the relationships would go between various Legionnaires.

**TLC:** *Did you ever try to introduce any new Legionnaires of your own design?*

**JS:** Oh yeah, but there was this copyright process they had to go through—lawyers and stuff—before they could appear. Apparently, they had enough trouble getting Dawnstar in there, which was Mike Grell's creation, but he didn't even get a chance to draw her.

**TLC:** *And the Legion did have a cap on members, too. Plus, they tried to limit the number of characters who would appear in one issue.*

**JS:** The whole thrust of the stories was teamwork, so it was good to get as many

*The first appearance of the Infinite Man, as illustrated by Sherman.*
© DC Comics.

in as you could, because they would mix and use combinations of powers to defeat the bad guy. That was a problem because the Legion always looked like they overpowered the bad guy, and outnumbering the bad guy was not a good American ethic. In other countries, you could have several people gang up on the bad guy [and] it's not a problem, but in America, the fans want to see one individual go up against a horde and come out on top. In the **Legion** it was reversed, so that was always a problem, but the thrust of the story was you had to use teamwork.

**TLC:** *You drew a story which introduced a few new students at the Legion Academy. Did you design those characters?*

**JS:** I designed them all. [Power Boy] was introduced along with Shadow Lad, Shadow Lass's brother. Shadow Lass was one of my other favorites. I thought she was really cool and a hard ass, real kickass tough, but they didn't want her to do anything nefarious.

**TLC:** *Do I detect a little bit of a Kirby influence in Power Boy's costume?*

**JS:** No. Wasn't even thinking Jack Kirby. My tip of the hat to Jack Kirby was in the issue with the squid-like alien that the Legionnaires trapped in a fire cage in the end [*Sden*, in **SLSH** #233 —**Ed.**]. I did a whole bunch of Jack Kirby stuff which the inker paid absolutely no attention to, but his designs are all over it. [In the end,] it absolutely resembled Jack Kirby not at all.

**TLC:** *Were you aware of all the Legion fans out there?*

**JS:** No. In fact, I was blown away that there'd been a waiting list group—I forget what they're called [**Note:** *Sherman is referring to Interlac.* —**Ed.**]—that only allowed three hundred members. I thought that was amazing. So I wasn't the only one who saw potential. At that point, I felt I wasn't crazy. They kept saying, "You've got Legionnaire's disease. Ha ha, you're really sick." I thought, "Wow! If there's this kind of group out there, then other people can see the potential as well. So I'm not alone."

**TLC:** *You know, your whereabouts have been a recurring theme among Legion fans for years. Some people will say, "Where did Jim Sherman go? That guy was really good!"*

**JS:** No kidding. Really? I never heard anything like that.

**TLC:** *Do you still keep in contact with the industry?*

**JS:** Yeah, [it goes] back and forth. I've talked to people about stuff, but my schedule is not that I can pinpoint a specific date to start a project and end a project. I have so many things going on at the same time, it's difficult for me to take time out and do a comic. Anything that takes more than three days [to do], it becomes a deadline conflict.

**TLC:** *Did you ever talk with any of the other Legion artists about the difficulty of drawing the comic?*

**JS:** No. I've talked to Joe Staton, though we didn't talk about the **Legion**. We never talked about the **Legion**. For that matter, we haven't talked about any comic books. For some reason, talking about comics is sort of a taboo subject now. I don't know why. I think everybody's afraid of ideas being stolen.

**TLC:** *Did it take you a while to get used to drawing the Legion?*

**JS:** No, no.

**TLC:** *How about learning all those costumes?*

**JS:** Nah, that was easy. But I wanted to change them. In fact, I got a chance to do that in one of Mike Grell's big issues, one of those over-sized issues where somebody got married [**All-New Collector's Edition C-55**, a.k.a. "That Damned Tabloid" — **Ed.**]. I got to do three pages of what the Legion should look like.

**TLC:** *You changed Element Lad's costume in that.*

**JS:** I changed everybody's costume, but for some reason the lawyers complained, and most of the inking got changed so that the costumes were [changed] back. I don't know why some got changed and some didn't, but instead of having what they should look like, it was sorta like, "This is what the Legion does look like, and we'll have modifications, maybe." [*laughs*] So it was a big disappointment that it came out the way it did.

**TLC:** *Did you have any fun designing the villains that you introduced?*

**JS:** Yeah, every villain. [The Infinite Man] was a ball, but unfortunately there was no regress. We never came back to him again.

**TLC:** *Is there a bit of a Hindu influence in his design?*

**JS:** No. In fact, I actually had read the Tao by then, which doesn't have any reflection on Hindus, but no. There might have been a Taoist influence on a subconscious level, but that was it. I was just trying to see how far I could stretch the costume limits. You weren't allowed to show a lot of skin, especially on male characters, so I was just trying for something that was way out there. Because it was a villain, they let me do it.

**TLC:** *You're one of only a handful of Legion artists who got to kill off a Legionnaire.*

**JS:** Chemical King, right.

**TLC:** *How well do you remember that two-part story?*

**JS:** I definitely remember that.

**TLC:** *Did you change your approach to that story at all, maybe treat it as though it was more important?*

**JS:** They were all important to me. I was fresh in comics. I had done maybe a dozen issues by the time that I got to the **Legion**, and most of the stuff wasn't being seen by anybody, but just doing comics for me was special. I didn't see a differentiation as a more special story then, even the "Earthwar" stuff. What's special to me is where I was given a freer hand, or more open possibilities to designing something that wasn't pre-established in the **Legion**. So that was my only basis for upping my level of excitement.

**TLC:** *When was the last time you dug those old issues out and took a look?*

**JS:** Let's see... when was the last time I was single? [*laughs*] It's a problem digging comics out when you have a family. It's kind of a no-no, almost as bad as subscribing to **Playboy**. There's a stigma attached to comics. Only in America.

**TLC:** *There used to be, but it's coming out of that now.*

**JS:** Is it?

**TLC:** *Oh, yeah.*

**JS:** I've been hearing the industry's having hard times. I've been in Forbidden Planet [*A NYC comic book store.* —**Ed.**], in and out. Whenever I've got spare time and I'm in the neighborhood, I'll jump in there.

*Top: a convention sketch by Sherman. Left: Element Lad's new look, from **All-New Collectors' Edition C-55**. Element Lad TM and © DC Comics.*

Nothing on a regular basis. I've been looking for Alan Moore's stuff, 'cause that guy was in my brain. I started reading his stuff, and I said, "Geez, this guy is already doing what I'd been thinking of."

**TLC:** *They are making* **League of Extraordinary Gentlemen** *into a movie now.*

**JS:** Good! It's nice that comics are being made into movies. I think that's kinda why I thought the industry was flailing, because so much of the stuff is becoming movies instead of "Who wants to read?" The only thing missing from a comic book is the motion. Every attempt to draw a comic book is to create a sense of motion. I mean, if we could capture what Jack Kirby did in his comics, we'd all be having a great time, and there'd be no need to see movies. But the magic that Jack Kirby did, and Walt Simonson still does, is a dying art. I almost cried when I saw **Spider-Man**. I said, "Geez, they finally did it right." I thought Marvel or DC was always going to get their fingers in the pie and ruin everything, but **Spider-Man** was like watching Steve Ditko's and Stan Lee's job come alive. That was great.

**TLC:** *Are you aware of the* **Legion Archives**?

**JS:** No.

**TLC:** *They've been reprinting all the* **Legion** *stories going right back to its first appearance.*

**JS:** No kidding?

**TLC:** *They've been releasing them in these fifty dollar hardcovers.*

**JS:** [*laughs*] I guess they don't want anybody to read them. [*laughs*]

**TLC:** *They're on the verge of reprinting your work.*

**JS:** No kidding. [*laughs*] So it'll finally see light of day? I don't think there was a big audience for the **Legion** when I was doing it.

**TLC:** *Actually, it was one of their more popular titles.*

**JS:** Okay... They wouldn't tell me anything like that. I would ask, "How's the sales doing?" "Just doing a little bit better than it was doing last month," was the only answer I'd get. But when I discovered this fan club of three hundred, [I thought], "Wow! [We've] gotta be doing something [right]. Maybe there's only three hundred people buying it, but it's gotta be going somewhere if there's a fan club for this and nothing else like that."

**TLC:** **Legion** *fans are legendary. They're sort of like* **Star Trek** *fans.*

**JS:** Yeah, they would have to be, wouldn't they? I'd like to meet some. I think one of them came out of the crowd at a convention one time and introduced himself, but I can't remember if I've actually met one of them.

**TLC:** *Every so often, the topic of "Who was your favorite* **Legion** *artist?"comes up among* **Legion** *fans, and you'd be surprised how well you do in that.*

**JS:** Yeah, I would be surprised.

**TLC:** *In fact, there are still people who hold out hope that you will draw a* **Legion** *story again someday.*

**JS:** Huh. Well, [*laughs*] it'd have to be where I left off. I mean, if I'm gonna do comics, I gotta do it my way, because there's not much point in doing comics as far as paying the bills goes. Although Frank tells me he's doing great, and I'm sure Walt Simonson is doing great, but I don't know many people doing comics. [If I came back,] it would have to be under my terms. My terms are no big deal, I just want a chance to put some stuff down there that I want to put down there, instead of working on somebody else's [ideas]. I mean, whatever Paul Levitz wants to do is okay with me, because he was willing to collaborate with me. I hear that there's a lot of people out there who just argue back and forth "You didn't do this! You didn't do that!" That'd take all the fun out of it for me.

**TLC:** *Do you miss working in comics?*

**JS:** Oh, yeah. There's nothing that engages your imagination like doing a comic book. I've always said that doing a movie, you've got at least fifty people on the movie project, and it goes through so many changes, because you've got so many people in charge along the way that the original concept is barely there. But in comic books, [there's] one or two people in concert. [It's] like you're up on stage, and you get to do your thing. But I found that many of the comic book writers don't want to do it that way. They want you to be their hand, and they don't want anything different. You stray off of the script, or you come up with your own idea, [and] they get nervous. I've had many people over the years come to me with projects, and if I come back with ideas, they go, "Never mind." They take it as if I'm pointing out their shortcomings instead of my chance to design some-

*The first appearance of Shvaughn Erin, from* **Superboy and the Legion of Super-Heroes** *#241, courtesy of Mike Napolitano.*
© DC Comics.

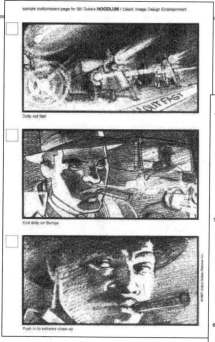
sample motionboard page for Bill Duke's **HOODLUM** / Client: Image Design Entertainment

Dolly out fast!

End dolly on Bumpy

Push in to extreme close-up

RDA: P5

*Samples from Sherman's commercial art portfolio: storyboard sequences from the movie* Hoodlum *and an untitled video game.*
Hoodlum © 1997 United Artists Pictures, Inc.

thing cool.

**TLC:** *Overall, how would you rate your time on the* **Legion***?*

**JS:** That's a tough question. I was so into it, the rest of the real world went away. I had so much fun, but I was turning down jobs unless I actually needed the job to pay a bill. I wasn't excited about advertising—never was excited about advertising—but advertising is a job where they call you at five o'clock in the afternoon and say, "We need the job done by nine o'clock in the morning." So you're up all night and they pay you thousands of dollars to do it. Those would come along in the nick of time to keep the groceries on the table and heating oil in the furnace, so I would have to take those. Everything else I was turning down so I could do comics. Complicated answer, huh?

**TLC:** *Do you know that they eventually instituted royalty programs at the companies?*

**JS:** That was after my tenure.

**TLC:** *Would that have made it easier for you to stay?*

**JS:** Hell, yeah. Although talking to various people about how much royalties they got, I'm not sure. You would have to be on a good-selling title to make any money off of that. I heard the average royalty was a thousand dollars, which [is] good for a week. Paying bills is far more expensive then an iffy thousand dollars a month royalty, especially living in New York City.

**TLC:** *Are you one of those artists who*

can't stand to look at his old work?

**JS:** I learn from looking at the old stuff, as well as the stuff I did last week. But more from sketching from life and magazine photos and TV dramas and movies. I carry a sketchbook almost everywhere. There's a constant learning process that goes on in my work, and I look at the old stuff and realize, "Here's what I could've [done better]." Back when I was doing comic books, you get caught up in all the details, and it's hard to see the big picture, 'cause you're always delivering the job as soon as you're done. But when the finished comic appears in the stores, the big picture slaps you in the face with what you could have done better, and you find yourself studying it for how to pencil it better for the inkers to understand the shadows and lighting and reflections and subtleties of anatomy forms you were going for. But I don't get a chance to look at the old stuff much anymore. One, there's no chance to do comics, and two, [laughs] up until what you just said, there's been a stigma attached to pulling out old comics, especially at my age.

**TLC:** *Is age a factor in advertising?*

**JS:** I'm only halfway through my life cycle, but when I go out there to meet potential clients, especially in the advertising industry, where everybody's hardly over twenty-four and life expectancy in advertising is about three years—an illus-

trator is already thirty-something before he's good enough to pull off the subtleties required in storyboards—they look at me like some dinosaur just got dragged in. "Who called this guy?" y'know? [But] when they see my portfolio, they go, "Oh, okay. Now we know." Most of the guys I know who are working in advertising are doing everything they can to look young. They'll dye their hair, put on the young clothes and dress like they're hip-hop, or whatever's twenty-something, and I'm like, "C'mon, guys!" [laughs] "It's just your portfolio that counts." But try to get your portfolio through the door, that alone is tough enough. Hiding their age gives them an edge. I'm left surviving on recommendations alone.

**TLC:** *Do you still do sketches at conventions?*

**JS:** Yeah, that's fun.

**TLC:** *Have you given any thought toward doing commissions?*

**JS:** Yeah, sure, I'd do that, but I'm not sure if I have time.

*A recent (2003) convention sketch by Sherman, courtesy of Vladimir Fiks. Art © 2003 James Sherman; Shadow Lass TM and © DC Comics.*

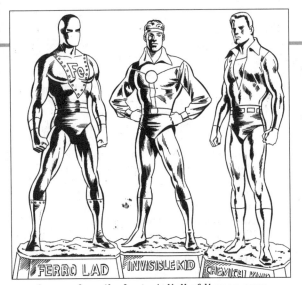

A scene from the Legion's Hall of Heroes, courtesy of Mike Napolitano. Ferro Lad, Invisible Kid and Chemical King TM and © DC Comics.

**TLC:** *Most artists take a while to get around to their commissions, anyway.*

**JS:** It's difficult. They often pay less than comics and they intrude on existing deadlines. I think I'm one of the guys who's stayed awake the most trying to get everything done on time. I probably do two or three all-nighters a week. I'm so busy that I don't even know what weekends are. For me, it's just another work day. Every year, from September to December, I am just so busy, I have to steal time to sleep.

**TLC:** *I guess that's one of the disadvantages of freelancing.*

**JS:** Yeah, during those months. But other months, you've got three months to go travel the world, which I usually do. I haven't been to the Far East or middle Asia, but I've been almost everywhere else. Most of Canada, all of the United States except Utah, and everywhere down South. I haven't been to South America, but I've been through all of Mexico and most of Central America. I've hiked through most all of it. I've taken months to trek through everywhere.

**TLC:** *It sounds like you're doing what you want to be doing.*

**JS:** Oh, yeah. That's a big advantage to freelancing. Meet your deadlines, pay your bills and you can do exactly what you want to do. Mess with that formula, life spins out of control.

**TLC:** *Do you have any plans of ever returning to comics again?*

**JS:** There's always hope. Hope lives eternal that I'll be able to do comics, but the logistics of doing them is just very complicated.

**TLC:** *So if you won the lottery tomorrow....*

**JS:** Yeah, I'd be doing comics for the rest of my life. I have a whole line of comics that I was gonna do, and right now they're sitting gathering dust. I have all these treatments and character designs and stuff, but there's just no time. I'm doing projects that are paying the bills. I'm doing projects that are paying way better than the bills. I'm doing projects that are paying for my travels. Like I said, when I was doing comics there was trouble keeping the oil in the furnace and food on the table, and forget about it if you've got a family.

**TLC:** *How closely did you follow comics after you kind of drifted away?*

**JS:** I followed them for about ten years. I would make the rounds to the comic book shops up until about 1990.

**TLC:** *That would take you up to a few years before the bottom fell out of the industry.*

**JS:** I thought the fall was because the sharks came into the pool. You know, the guys like Perelman and Icahn. Sharks strip a company down to only what sells and squeeze the blood out of those. Comics used to have a homegrown life of its own. My whole theory about why comics went, or were going, down the tubes is simply because they started renumbering the system, [and] nobody could follow the universe anymore. Sharks think: "A number one sells really well, so let's do a whole bunch of number ones. Let's renumber everything." The only way to keep track of the universe was to follow the numbers of the issues so that you would know where to tune in on the characters when you had time to catch up. There was always this sense that there was this alternate world of action and amazing deeds going on. Grabbing this or that num-bered issue, you knew where it fit into the universe and how it all worked together. You could even time-travel around in the grand opera when you collected comics. But when they started renumbering things, [it became] "O-kay, lost track, can't find my place."

**TLC:** *If you had to do it all over again, would you make the same decisions?*

**JS:** Yeah, in a heartbeat. In a New York heartbeat.

**TLC:** *No regrets?*

**JS:** If good times ran in a continuous flow who'd know they were having a good time? But I'm lucky. I have a great family and great friends and I've met a lot of very talented people. I'm too busy with interesting assignments to dwell on regrets. And when I'm not busy we're out exploring the world. I'm having the time of my life.

The death of Chemical King, from **Superboy and the Legion of Super-Heroes #228**. From the collection of Steven Weill. © DC Comics.

# Jim Starlin

Born in Detroit, Jim Starlin travelled to New York City to become a comic book artist after his release from the Navy in the early Seventies. After memorable stints on **Captain Marvel** and "Adam Warlock" for Marvel, he left the publisher for DC Comics, where he illustrated a variety of titles, not the least of which was **Superboy and the Legion of Super-Heroes**. Although his time on the title was brief, it is still fondly remembered by Legion fans today. The following interview was conducted by Glen Cadigan on November 15, 2002, and was copyedited by Starlin.

**TLC:** *You're probably best known for your work at Marvel in the Seventies. Why did you leave?*

**JS:** When you work in comics, editors change, different things happen, and I don't remember at that particular time what the exact story was, but you have fallings out with the editors at different places, and I had fallings out with the people at Marvel on several different occasions. [*laughs*]

**TLC:** *How did you end up at DC?*

**JS:** I believe it was mostly Al Milgrom, [who] was working up there as an editor at the time. I don't think he was the editor of the **Legion** books. I actually think I got the job through Joe Rubinstein, who was inking a lot of those.

**TLC:** *What drew you to the Legion?*

**JS:** I read them when I was a kid, back when there was a John Forte and an occasional Curt Swan job, but I was never really a big fan of them. I suspect it was more that they needed a fill-in, and Paul, who was the writer on it, needed fill-ins, [so] they asked me if I wanted to do one. He was a little bit busy, so I remember I sort of plotted the story, drew it, and then Paul scripted it and Joe Rubinstein inked it.

**TLC:** *Was there any particular reason why they didn't let you script it as well?*

**JS:** It was Paul's book. He was the writer on it, and he was also the president of the company or something like that [*laughs*], so there was never any question of me being the scripter on it.

**TLC:** *It's well known that you're a fan of science-fiction. Drawing the Legion must have been a pleasure for you.*

**JS:** It was fun. It was that futuristic stuff. One of the things I hate drawing is people in suits, cars, and modern day stuff, so this worked out quite well. It was something I was happy to do.

**TLC:** *How well do you remember the story?*

**JS:** Well, I remember [Ultra Boy] was accused of murder or something like that, and it turns out it's someone else who's the killer at the end. I can't actually remember if we did one story involving that or if it was a two issue thing, 'cause I did a giant thing for them later on, and that got split up into [two issues]. It was supposed to be one giant issue and it got split up. There were a lot of other problems with it, [so] I asked my name to be taken off of it, and used a pen name, "Wolfgang Apollo" or "Steve Apollo."

**TLC:** *Who came up with "Steve Apollo?"*

**JS:** It was mine. They said, "We've got to put some name down there," and I said, "Well, put Steve Apollo's name down there."

**TLC:** *There was about a year's difference between the publication of the first story [SLSH #239] and its sequel [SLSH #'s 250-251]. Did you do them back-to-back?*

**JS:** Fairly close, as I recall. Like I said, the second part was inked by Dave Hunt. Paul couldn't get around to scripting them, and so they sat for a long time. Joe Rubinstein was off on some other project at that point and couldn't ink them, and that's how they ended up with Dave Hunt.

**TLC:** *How satisfied were you with the final product?*

**JS:** The first one I enjoyed. The thing I did with Rubinstein was a nice little story, as I recall. We set up a mystery, and eventually resolved it. But there was that big lag between it, and I remember not being involved—I went off to do other things—

*Starlin's wraparound cover for **Superboy and the Legion of Super-Heroes** #238. From the collection of Simon Bollinger. © DC Comics.*

ALEGIONNAIRE ... ACCUSED OF MURDER MST FOUL!

Above: Starlin's rough for the cover of "Murder Most Foul." Below: the printed version, as penciled by Mike Grell and inked by Joe Rubinstein. Thanks to Al Milgrom for the rough and Jonathan Mankuta for the original cover art. Superboy and the Legion of Super-Heroes TM and © DC Comics.

and the sixty-four page story that I had laid out for Joe Rubinstein to finish off (because he had worked off my layouts before, and I knew what I could lay out and he could fix-up) [was different than] what I should [do] if I was working with somebody else. And out of that sixty-four pages, I think they used forty-eight or something like that. So not only was the artwork done by somebody who wasn't prepared to have to deal with what I had left him, the story was pretty truncated. So I wasn't too happy about the second part of it, and, as a result, never did come back to do anything on that particular series.

**TLC:** *That basically soured you on the* **Legion**.

**JS:** When something goes bad, you just don't want to go back and revisit it.

**TLC:** *Whatever happened to those pages?*

**JS:** I put them up for sale at conventions. There's probably still some of them floating around somewhere, but I haven't got any actual copies of them anymore.

**TLC:** *Do you think that someday that story will be printed the way that you intended for it to be printed?*

**JS:** Oh, no, because a lot of those pages were never inked.

**TLC:** *They could always get someone to ink them, though.*

**JS:** Yeah, but they're long gone, so whatever was going to be is never going to be. Besides, it's all DC stuff, and DC is not going to go out of the way to do something like that. [laughs]

**TLC:** *One of the things which strikes me about the first part of the story [* **SLSH** *#239] is how much it really resembles an annual. It was over-sized, self-contained, and centered on a single plot. Did you think while you were doing it that it was going to be something special?*

**JS:** Other than it was going to be a good-sized book, no. In fact, to tell you the truth, I wasn't aware that it was anything special. I'd sort of forgotten about the story a long time ago.

**TLC:** *You left an impression, though, because a lot of* **Legion** *fans still remember it.*

**JS:** Well, I'm glad they enjoyed it. It just doesn't hold that much in my memory pan here. [laughs]

**TLC:** *You also worked on Superman, in* **DC Comics Presents**.

**JS:** Yeah, I had fun with that.

**TLC:** *Why do you think people don't remember your DC work as well as your Marvel work?*

**JS:** It didn't seem to have the impact that the stuff I did at Marvel had. DC works a bit differently. I never got as much of a free hand over at DC as I did at Marvel. Mostly, I had that at Marvel during times of chaos, [and in] times of chaos, they'd tend to slacken up on their editorial control.

**TLC:** *Why didn't DC allow you to script your own material? Your* **DC Comics Presents** *issues were always scripted by someone else.*

**JS:** Yeah, I got a different writer on that it seemed every week. [laughs] I think I did two with Len [Wein], one with Marv [Wolfman], and one with Paul.

**TLC:** *Was it frustrating not being able to script your own work?*

**JS:** No, I don't think I was looking for it at that point. All those were supposed to be fill-in jobs.

**TLC:** *Do you see the work which you did at DC as a continuation of the themes which you explored at Marvel?*

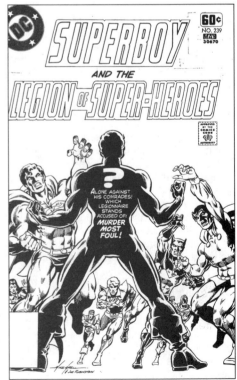

Superboy and the Legion of Super-Heroes TM and © DC Comics.

Starlin's creation Wyrd, the reluctant warrior. Wyrd TM and © 2003 Jim Starlin.

Remember these guys? Vanth Dreadstar and company, from an uninked page by Starlin. Dreadstar and related characters TM and © 2003 Jim Starlin.

**JS:** No, I usually came in with something different. Like with **Cosmic Odyssey**, they asked me to make a map of their outer space universe. Apparently somebody was doing something similar with their mystic characters at the time. I just took it, and I paid no attention to their request at making a map of the universe. I think I worked a map in there somewhere in the story. I had a pretty good time with that, and [**Batman:**] **The Cult**, and a few other things, but most of the time they never quite worked out as well as some things elsewhere did.

**TLC:** *Would you ever consider returning to do another* **Legion** *story?*

**JS:** Nooo, I have all sorts of other things to keep me busy. I'm ending the Marvel Universe right now. [*laughs*] I'm working on a double-page spread with Thanos sucking in the entire cast of the Marvel Universe right at the moment coming to conclusion.

**TLC:** *Is Thanos your favorite character?*

**JS:** Well, he's my baby. I created him while I was in college, taking a Psychology course, and then brought him over to Marvel when I came. Every time I come back to Marvel, I usually do something with him. I think of all the characters I've created along the lines, he has been my favorite.

 Thanos. Thanos TM and © 2003 Marvel Characters, Inc..

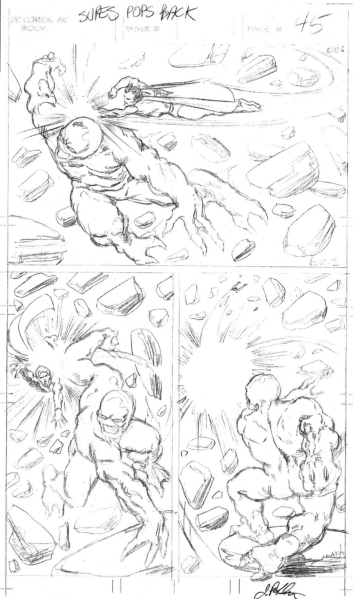

An unpublished page from the sequel to "Murder Most Foul," featuring layouts by Starlin. Courtesy of Bryan Hawkins. © DC Comics.

# Joe Staton

After beginning his career at Charlton Comics, Joe Staton came to DC via Marvel in the mid-Seventies. A collaborator with Paul Levitz on the Justice Society feature which ran in **All-Star** (and later **Adventure**) **Comics**, Staton made his way to the 30th Century to briefly work with Levitz again, this time on **Superboy and the Legion of Super-Heroes**. He was interviewed by Glen Cadigan on December 4, 2002, and copyedited the following transcript.

**TLC:** *You and Paul Levitz have something in common: you both began your **Legion** careers on the same issue: **Karate Kid** #1. How did you get that job?*

**JS:** I had been working at Marvel doing finishes on the **Hulk**, and Paul was looking for people to do finishes at DC. He kind of promised me if I did finishes for a while, I'd be able to do some penciling as well. That's why I wound up on **Karate Kid**.

**TLC:** *So that was your first DC assignment?*

**JS:** Yeah, I think it was.

**TLC:** *How much of the finished product was you and how much was Ric Estrada?*

**JS:** I remember at the time Joe Orlando told me that I stayed a lot more

in line with Ric's work than a lot of the finishers did. Wally Wood would pretty much completely obliterate Ric. But I think I kept a fair amount of his basic stuff.

**TLC:** *Have you ever gone back and looked at those old **Karate Kid** issues?*

**JS:** Not recently. [*laughs*] I haven't dug them out in a while.

**TLC:** *Did you get the Legion assignment based upon your work with Paul on the "Justice Society"?*

**JS:** Pretty much. I always worked well with Paul, and really liked working with him. But originally when I came onto the **Legion**, I wasn't supposed to be the only artist. There were supposed to be a bunch of us rotating on it—I think Mike Nasser and Jim Sherman and maybe Ed Davis—but one by one everybody disappeared, and I was left on my own. So it was just a question of working well with Paul, and people disappearing, and me just being left there.

**TLC:** *[laughs] So you were left holding the bag?*

**JS:** Yeah, that's kind of how that turned out.

**TLC:** *How much did you contribute to the plot?*

**JS:** None at all. I just drew what was given me.

**TLC:** *The **Legion** was one of DC's better-selling titles when you took over. Were you aware of that at the time?*

**JS:** I believe so. I don't really remember, but I remember it was doing well.

**TLC:** *Did you feel any added pressure because of that?*

**JS:** I don't remember any pressure in those terms.

**TLC:** *You came on board partway through a multi-part storyline. Did it take you a while to get your bearings?*

**JS:** Actually, since it was Paul, I just kind of picked up with what he was going with. I trusted him, and went on from there.

**TLC:** *How long did it take you to figure*

*Top: Staton in the Seventies, in a picture originally published in* **Alter Ego.** *Above: a convention sketch of Mordru by Staton. From the collection of Steven Weill. Art © Joe Staton; Mordru TM and © DC Comics.*

LEGION OF SUPER-HEROES

A THOUSAND YEARS IN THE FUTURE 25 SUPER-TEENS WILL BAND TOGETHER AS THE... LEGION OF SUPER-HEROES

BUT YOU CAN THRILL TO THEIR INTERPLANETARY ADVENTURES TODAY!

SEE:
✳ COSMIC BOY ✳ SATURN GIRL
✳ LIGHTNING LAD ✳ DUO DAMSEL
✳ PHANTOM GIRL ✳ CHAMELEON BOY
✳ COLOSSAL BOY ✳ BRAINIAC 5
✳ ULTRA BOY ✳ STAR BOY
✳ SHRINKING VIOLET ✳ SUN BOY
✳ BOUNCING BOY ✳ MON-EL
✳ MATTER-EATER LAD ✳ ELEMENT LAD
✳ LIGHT LASS ✳ DREAM GIRL
✳ PRINCESS ✳ KARATE KID
PROJECTRA ✳ TIMBER WOLF
✳ SHADOW LASS ✳ DAWNSTAR
✳ WILDFIRE
✳ TYROC

ALL IN THIS MIGHTY MONTHLY DC COMIC—AT THE BARGAIN PRICE OF 12 ISSUES FOR THE PRICE OF 10! MAILED FLAT IN PROTECTIVE WRAPPERS!

SEND TO: DC COMICS INC., SUBSCRIPTION DEPT., 155 ALLEN BLVD., FARMINGDALE, N.Y. 11737
PLEASE SEND ME 12 ISSUES OF:
LEGION OF SUPER-HEROES (Code #3)
I ENCLOSE $4.00 ($5.00 OUTSIDE U.S.)
NAME_____ AGE____
ADDRESS_____
CITY & STATE_____
ZIP CODE_____
OFFER EXPIRES OCTOBER 1, 1979
FULL REMITTANCE MUST ACCOMPANY ORDER. SEND CHECK OR MONEY ORDER, NOT CASH. PLEASE ALLOW 8 TO 10 WEEKS FOR DELIVERY OF THE FIRST ISSUES

Above: Artwork from a DC house ad selling a year's worth of **Legion** issues. Right: Staton designed the League of Super-Assassins, featuring Blok as a member. Both pictures and all characters © DC Comics.

out which Legionnaire was which?

**JS:** [*laughs*] To this day, I have no idea. Once you get past Lightning Lad, I'm kind of lost.

**TLC:** *Is that one of the reasons why you asked to leave?*

**JS:** I had just really burnt out on the title. It was a lot to keep up with, and in lots of ways, I never really got the hang of it. It wore me down pretty well.

**TLC:** *Why do you think that you didn't take to it as well as, say, the Justice Society?*

**JS:** I guess it wasn't really one that I had followed that much. I was always more at home on Earth-2, anyway. And the writers changed, so it was harder to keep my bearings there.

**TLC:** *How closely did you work with Gerry Conway?*

**JS:** Again, not at all. I just tried to work with what scripts I was given.

**TLC:** *How hard is it to draw a comic if you just can't get it straight in your head?*

**JS:** Even if you don't really understand the concept, if you're working with somebody like Paul, who you have a track record [with], and you know what they're doing, you can kind of get your traction that way. But I didn't really have any record with Gerry, and never really figured out how to approach his stuff. So that way I was kind of at sea on the concept, and [had] no real handle for the writer. It's a lot worse that way.

**TLC:** *Just about every artist who's drawn the **Legion** on a regular basis has added one new member to its roster, and you're no exception. You designed Blok.*

**JS:** [*laughs*] Well, good for me. I had forgotten that.

**TLC:** *Did you know in advance that he was going to become a Legionnaire?*

**JS:** I'm sure I didn't.

**TLC:** *Weren't you involved in science-fiction fandom before you got involved in comics?*

**JS:** Oh, yeah. I had a long run in science-fiction fandom.

**TLC:** *Was that an aspect of the **Legion** which appealed to you?*

**JS:** I never really made a connection between the Legion and science-fiction fandom. I guess I should have, but I never really made that connection.

**TLC:** *You worked with a few different inkers during your stint. How satisfied were you with the quality of inks which you received?*

**JS:** I always thought I was a real good team with Jack Abel. He had a real nice balance of abstraction and decoration [while] still looking convincing. So, Jack was my favorite, and others were more or less from that.

**TLC:** *You only inked yourself once on the **Legion**. Do you find yourself putting in more or less effort into your pencils if you're not going to ink it yourself?*

**JS:** I try to put more effort—more finished pencils—into things I'm not going to ink myself. The problem is, when I ink something, I always see things after I'm done that I want to go back and work on some more. So it's always good if I'm working with an inker who realizes, "Okay, if he'd worked on this a little longer he would have thought of something else." Maybe the inker takes up a little slack. There's always something you can think of, and when you're inking yourself, you can go back and work on that.

**TLC:** *I know that the **Legion** wasn't your favorite assignment. That being said, were there elements of it which you enjoyed?*

**JS:** I really enjoy working with Paul, and I really enjoyed Jack Abel's inking. Occasionally, when they'd get into aliens, I really liked making up aliens. So that was fun.

**TLC:** *What are you doing today?*

**JS:** I'm a regular on **Scooby-Doo**. I have been, I think, for five or six years now.

**TLC:** [*laughs*] *That's a bit of a stretch from the **Legion**.*

**JS:** [*laughs*] It's all comics.

Blok

Lazon

Mist Master

Neutrax

Silver Slasher

Titania

# Gerry Conway

A prolific writer during both the Seventies and the Eighties, Gerry Conway has, at one time or another, written virtually every title published by both Marvel and DC during those two decades. The co-creator of the Punisher and the man who wrote the death of Gwen Stacy in *Amazing Spider-Man*, Conway is also known for his long stints as the writer of record on *Justice League of America* and *Firestorm*. When Paul Levitz stepped down as *Legion* writer (for the first time), it was Conway who took his place. Now working in the entertainment industry and living in Southern California, Conway was interviewed by Glen Cadigan on December 17, 2002, and he copyedited the final transcript.

**TLC:** *Do you remember your first professional sale?*

**GC:** That was a three-page short-story sold back in 1968 to Murray Boltinoff for a suspense comic that he was doing.

**TLC:** *How old were you at the time?*

**GC:** I had just turned sixteen.

**TLC:** *What happened when Murray found out that he was your first sale?*

**GC:** [*laughs*] He was very upset. He thought that Dick Giordano had been working with me. Actually Dick had, but he hadn't bought anything from me yet. Murray discovered that he had taken my cherry and was very distraught [*laughs*], although he concealed it well.

**TLC:** *Did you also try to sell stories to Mort Weisinger?*

**GC:** I did. Not with any real success.

**TLC:** *Would you actually go up to the offices?*

**GC:** Yeah. They used to have a tour at DC Comics in the summers back in the

1960s, and once a week they would bring people back into the offices and show them how things were done. I would go on this tour every week and slip away from the touring party, and then go out and try to solicit editors into letting me do stories for them.

**TLC:** *How seriously did they take you?*

**GC:** Not very, I don't think. But persistence won some of them over.

**TLC:** *Who gave you your big break overall at DC?*

**GC:** That would have been Dick Giordano.

**TLC:** *What did you do for Dick?*

**GC:** Dick encouraged me to write, and after I learned the ropes, he gave me my first steady assignment, writing intros and wrap-arounds for *House of Secrets*.

**TLC:** *What was the atmosphere like in the office back then?*

**GC:** It was strange, in that there was the old guard, who were mostly men in their forties and fifties— and some in their early sixties—who had been doing this since the 1940s, and were very professional, white shirt, tie, jacket-type people. Then there were the young snots, as we referred to ourselves, who were, for the most part, counter-culture types with long hair and jeans, and not a very respectful [*laughs*] attitude. The two groups didn't really

mingle that much. But, over time, the counter-culture group pretty much took over, so it didn't matter if we mingled. [*laughs*]

**TLC:** *Growing up, were you much of a fan of the Mort Weisinger Superman family of titles?*

**GC:** Y'know, I really wasn't. I liked some of the stories that Jim Shooter did. I liked his "Legion" in particular. I think he did some

*Top: Conway relaxing at home circa 1984. Above: a page from one of Conway's early Legion issues, #234. From the collection of Peter Hansen. The Legion of Super-Heroes TM and © DC Comics.*

Above: Jimmy Janes' finished pencils for the cover to the **Legion of Super-Heroes** #272. Below: the accompanying cover rough. Both pictures are from the collection of Miki Annamanthadoo. © DC Comics.

good work—the stories that Curt Swan drew—and that was about it. I was not a huge fan of Mort's stuff, and while I had read the "Legion," I hadn't really latched onto it as my favorite book.

**TLC:** *Didn't Shooter indirectly inspire you to become a writer?*

**GC:** Yeah. I discovered that there was this thirteen-year-old kid out there writing comics, and I was thirteen, and I thought, "I could do this, if he could do this." So, in that sense, he opened the door for a lot of us.

**TLC:** *So you weren't totally unfamiliar with the series when you took it over.*

**GC:** No, but I was pretty unfamiliar. [*laughs*] I had read it sporadically. I wasn't a fan the way that Paul Levitz was a fan, for example. I enjoyed it, but I was probably more a fan of Paul's stuff than the series itself.

**TLC:** *You followed him on the title. Did that influence your decision to take it over, the fact that you had been following his work?*

**GC:** No. I think what mostly influenced [me was that] I had written a number of group books, and was considered somebody who could handle group book dynamics. At

least in the beginning, it was mostly just an assignment. I had, at that time, a contract to do quite a bit of writing in a given month for DC, and that was one of the titles that they gave me to feed that voracious maw [*laughs*] that was my typewriter.

**TLC:** *How many comics were you writing a month?*

**GC:** Well, I was under contract to do 150 pages a month. So that would break down to, say, six or seven titles a month.

**TLC:** *Did you write your scripts Marvel style?*

**GC:** I did a bit of each. With **Legion**, I believe I wrote mostly scripts in advance.

**TLC:** *You actually did a few fill-in issues before you came on as the regular writer, including a couple with Ric Estrada in which you started to introduce a sub-element that maybe some of the United Planets didn't get along with each other as well as we had been led to believe. Do you remember that?*

**GC:** Well, if I did do that, I was probably responding to my desire to have conflict in the otherwise very **Star Trek**-ian universe that was being represented by that material. And it could also just be that I wasn't as [*laughs*] on the material as I probably should've been. I don't think that there was a master plan operating.

**TLC:** *One of the things that I noticed about your **Legion** run, especially some of the stories after Superboy was written out of the*

title, was that they had a real **Adventure Comics** feel to them. They were usually self-contained, with the occasional two-parter thrown in. Was that intentional, or was that just the way that it happened?

**GC:** I think that was mostly [**Legion** Editor] Jack [C. Harris]'s desire. Jack was somebody who had been trained by Murray Boltinoff, [and] Murray was never a fan of the continued stories as a way of doing comics. I think Jack sort of inherited that point of view, and preferred the self-contained stories. They were also easier to organize, because I'm not sure that we had the same artist on all the issues. We had a number of artists coming in and going out, so doing a self-contained one or two-parter enabled you to hand them around.

**TLC:** *How did that affect your approach to storytelling?*

**GC:** My tendency has always been to do

*Part Two of the Reflecto saga in this previously unpublished version of the cover to the **Legion of Super-Heroes #278** by Jimmy Janes. From the collection of Miki Annamanthadoo.*
Legion of Super-Heroes TM and © DC Comics.

stories that are referential to the material preceding it and following it. The idea that you should be able to pick up an individual issue of a comic book and never have read one before and never read one again doesn't really appeal to me. I think that you need to have enough material in there for a new reader to feel welcome, but you should also have enough continuing material so that they have an incentive to keep reading. It also makes for a richer and stronger and longer storyline.

**TLC:** *You did get to add some subplots while you were writer. The first one involved the Dark Man, whom you had mentioned back when Blok and the League of Super-Assassins first appeared. [**SLSH** #253 —**Ed.**] It was said that he had given them their powers, and then you didn't actually bring him in until about a year later. How far in advance were you planning?*

**GC:** To be honest with you, I never plan anything [*laughs*] in advance. I may have

some notions that I want to play out, and they're just notions. For the most part, what I do is I sprinkle seeds. I set myself little challenges that I'll have to resolve later without any thoroughly worked out storyline in a Joe Straczynski sort of way. The Dark Man that you're talking about was probably designed as a device initially just to explain these characters, and then knowing that I needed to have some explanation for that character, I would then play [that] out at a later stage when I had some further development of what that notion was.

**TLC:** *So it was a lot like improv?*

**GC:** Oh, absolutely. When you're doing six or seven titles a month [*laughs*], improv is all you've got! It was far too much work for any one person to be doing, and I shouldn't have been doing it, but I did.

**TLC:** *Did you always plan to make Blok a hero later on?*

**GC:** Actually, my experience with villains that later become heroes is that the more interesting that you make the villain, the more likely you will want to turn him into a hero later, because you fall sort of in love with the character. Blok, as I recall, was kinda like a Thing type of character, and that chip-on-your-shoulder, not one-of-the-gang mentality that can turn somebody into a bad guy can also be very useful among super-heroes.

**TLC:** *It's interesting that you should mention the Thing, because as originally conceived, Blok was a human who had been turned into Blok, but later on you said, no, he had always been a rock creature.*

**GC:** Yeah, probably. [*laughs*] This is why the mythology is so effervescent. What you have to realize is, with the exception

of people who are so dedicated to the logic of the material—people like Paul Levitz, for example, who had, when I took over **Legion**, something like a hundred and twenty pages on the different characters. Incredible details, backgrounds, story points that had never gotten anywhere because he had not had an opportunity to use them, and storylines if I had wanted to—and in some cases, I did—would have provided me with material for the future. Then there are people who didn't know whether they were going to be writing the next issue [*laughs*], and were just simply trying to do the best story they could at the time. The mythology sort of developed by the seat of our pants as we were going along. It wasn't thought out. It was far more common, certainly at DC and at Marvel, because I don't think Stan even remembered from one month to the next what stories he was writing. [*laughs*] Roy [Thomas] was the one who was very fixed on that. The rest of us really weren't.

**TLC:** *Were there any Legionnaires that you enjoyed writing more than others?*

**GC:** To be honest, none sort of stand out in my mind. Probably Blok was made a hero, at least in part, because I wanted to have something that I could put my own

*The published version of the cover, as rendered by George Pérez. From the collection of Steven Weill. © DC Comics.*

imprint on. But most of those characters before Paul came on the book were so one-dimensional. There was no character there to speak of. [laughs] Ultimately, what was the difference between Lightning Lad and Saturn Girl? One had long blonde hair, and one didn't. [laughs] In terms of personality, it was really Paul who gave them personality, and I just sort of tried to follow that. I didn't really have an overriding agenda.

That was a book that was, for me, a second-tier book as a writer. As opposed to **JLA**, which was my primary book that I

was paying attention to. That was my passion. That was the book that I had read as a kid, that I wanted to write as an adult.

**TLC:** *How obligated did you feel to follow the Adult Legion stories which Jim Shooter wrote?*

**GC:** That's always a question, because whenever you have what amounts to future future history, where things are locked in—like a character you know is going to do x or y when time passes because you've seen this future future story—it's kind of a trap. It really eviscerates any suspense, and doesn't allow anybody who follows you

to invent something creative on their own. So I have a tendency to kind of ignore those stories, or to assume that they might happen, but they might not, because they might be in an alternate universe in which this all might take place. I think I was influenced to the degree that I liked what was done, and if I liked it I might use it, but if I didn't like it, I didn't necessarily feel an obligation to it. Unless my editor insisted that I follow it.

**TLC:** *One element that you did introduce was Reflecto. Roy Thomas has said in the past that what he did with the character was not your original intention.*

**GC:** I'm not really sure what my original intention on that might have been.

**TLC:** *Was that was another open-ended plot for you?*

**GC:** Yeah. As I say, I sort of throw these things out there, and whatever sticks, sticks. When I was working at Marvel, there were a lot of story points that I never tied up, but if I had stayed, I might have picked them up at some point and used them as a springboard for something else. I never liked things to be that neat. [laughs] I really don't.

**TLC:** *Why did you leave the **Legion** when you did?*

**GC:** I think I left because I was in the process of leaving DC entirely. It was part of a continuing disaffection with the company. I think we were all sort of figuring that I had been doing too much work and needed to cut back.

**TLC:** *What are you up to today?*

**GC:** I'm working on a television show called **Law and Order: Criminal Intent**.

**TLC:** *I guess you reach a lot more people with that than you did when you wrote comics.*

**GC:** Yeah, but fewer know my name. [laughs] That is the weirdest thing about being around a long time. The things that you're remembered for are not necessarily the things that did the best for you.

**TLC:** *Do you miss working in comics on a regular basis?*

**GC:** I miss being twenty-five years old. [laughs] I don't necessarily miss the constraints, because there are constraints. It's peaches and pears. It's different entities. It's really hard to say.

*An early rendition of the ladies of the Legion of Super-Heroes by a young George Pérez.*
All characters TM and © DC Comics.; art © 2003 George Pérez.

# Jimmy Janes

As the Eighties dawned, the Legion found itself without two key elements: Superboy and a regular penciler. Enter Jimmy Janes. For close to two years, Janes provided the **Legion** with some much needed stability as the penciler on both the regular title and the **Secrets of the Legion** mini-series. For many **Legion** fans in their third decade, Janes was the artist who introduced them to the **Legion**. The following interview was conducted by Glen Cadigan on December 18, 2002, and was copyedited by Janes.

**TLC:** *Let's start with some biographical information first. Where and when were you born?*

**JJ:** I was born on Staten Island, New York, July 17, 1947.

**TLC:** *Were comics something which you were always interested in?*

**JJ:** Yeah. Always.

**TLC:** *What artists influenced you?*

**JJ:** Jack Kirby was one of my main influences, and Steve Ditko. At that time, they didn't really sign their names to the books, so a lot of the artists didn't get credit. A lot of the stuff went by, and [you didn't know who drew it]. But basically, Jack Kirby.

**TLC:** *So you were basically a Marvel fan?*

**JJ:** Yeah, Marvel was a beehive of energy. I also bought DC titles. I grew up reading DC. Two great companies.

**TLC:** *What titles did you follow?*

**JJ:** I followed mostly the early **Tales of Suspense**, **Astonishing Tales**.

**TLC:** *At what point did you*

decide that you wanted to become a professional comic book artist?

**JJ:** I think about ten years old.

**TLC:** *And how long after that did you try to break in?*

**JJ:** Actually, I really didn't think that there was hope for me, because I didn't get really serious until later on. I basically got into advertising for about ten to fifteen years, and then I segued into comic

*Another version of the cover to* Legion of Super-Heroes *#270 by Janes. From the collection of Miki Annamanthadoo.* Art © 2003 Jimmy Janes; Legion of Super-Heroes TM and © DC Comics.

books. I went to work for DC in the production department, with Sol Harrison and Jack Adler.

**TLC:** *How old were you then?*

**JJ:** I think I was about thirty-two, thirty-one.

**TLC:** *Was the* Legion *your first big break?*

**JJ:** Actually, I got my first break from Bill DuBay at Warren Publications doing the horror stuff for their magazines. **Creepy**, **Eerie** magazines.

**TLC:** *So how did you end up on the* Legion?

**JJ:** Early on I had met Joe Orlando, and he laughed when when saw my artwork because I had filled up every part of the page with some kind of stipple effect, [or] crosshatching. It was just way over the top, and he laughed and he told me to go home and basically simplify my stuff. He gave me the regular speech. I had done some samples, and I came back and he loved it. But Joe Orlando was a big inspiration to me. I visited him at his house when he was doing "Adam Link," and Joe kinda guided me along. So when I finally did learn how to draw, Joe was pleasantly surprised, and they were trying to break me in to do **Superman**, so they put me on the **Legion** as a starter. It was also a pleasure working with guys like Paul Levitz and Jack C. Harris.

The first thing, actually, they gave me was romance. Dorthy Woolfolk and Vince Colletta. Vince was inking my stuff at the time. Then Joe Orlando gave me the **Legion of Super-Heroes**. I went on from there to do some of the horror stuff, some of the sci-fi stuff.

**TLC:** *Were you a fan of the* **Legion** *before you became its artist?*

**JJ:** I didn't run out to pick up the latest **Legion**. But if a friend had one, I'd borrow it.

**TLC:** *How much input did you have into what went into the title?*

**JJ:** When I was working with Roy Thomas, I would work from a synopsis, and I would plot it out myself. I liked doing it that way.

**TLC:** *Did you ever try to introduce your own characters?*

**JJ:** Actually, I tried to do that. Early on they gave me stories, and there was a character in one of the books called Dagon the Avenger. I got to design his costume, and

it was sort of a Jack Kirby-style thing with horns on his helmet. It was pretty bad, but I had fun doing it. That's the only freedom I had.

**TLC:** *You worked with a variety of different inkers during your* **Legion** *run. Did you have any favorites?*

**JJ:** I thought Bruce Patterson was pretty damn good. I also liked Dave Hunt. I kinda liked his style.

**TLC:** *Did you get to meet any of the people that you worked with?*

**JJ:** I met Bruce, and I met Dave Hunt. They're the only guys that I really met.

**TLC:** *Take me through the process of designing a* **Legion** *cover.*

**JJ:** I was a little crazy at the time. What I would do was I would actually do three or four finished pencils, and bring them in, and they'd choose one. The others I'd take home and I'd ink it, or one of my friends would see it and they'd say, "Can I ink it?" So they would ink it. I sold a couple of those on eBay not too long ago.

**TLC:** *There was a period there before you took over the book where they had a lot of fill-in artists. When you came on board, you stayed for almost two years. Did they tell you that they were looking for someone to stay on the title for a while?*

**JJ:** Yeah, they would have liked me to stay on the title for awhile, but what happened was I did three books on the **Secrets of the Legion**, and besides doing the regular books, alternating with Steve Ditko, I kind of fell behind and I got burned out.

I didn't really consider myself a very good penciler. I had to work real hard to make the pages what they were, and a lot of times the pages were... I call it taking it

*The debut of Dagon the Avenger, from* **Legion of Super-Heroes** *#263.* © DC Comics.

*The pencils to the cover of* **Legion of Super-Heroes** *#270. Dick Giordano would ink the finished version. From the collection of Miki Annamanthadoo.* © DC Comics.

down to the lowest common denominator. You put a line over it. It was just a line. It wasn't a good line by some of the inkers. I won't name names, but a lot of the stuff just had that flat look to it, and a lot of the detail was left out. A lot of the mouths were just like they took a brush and they put a slash across it instead of contouring lips and putting in shadows that I had put in. Some of that was left out. It was simplified to the lowest common denominator. When I had been working for Warren Publications, a lot of that stuff Rudy Nebres and Alfreda Alcala inked of mine, and [they] had put all the detail in it. The lighting and the shadows, and lips that made sense, and effects in the background, and textures. I didn't get that with a lot of the stuff that was inked at DC. So I felt a little let down.

**TLC:** *Is that why you left the title?*

**JJ:** Actually, I left it because I had fallen behind on schedule, and I got kinda burned out. I had been up 18-24 hours a

*Another unused Janes cover, this time for* Legion of Super-Heroes *#267. From the collection of Miki Annamanthadoo. Art © 2003 Jimmy Janes; Legion of Super-Heroes TM and © DC Comics.*

day sometimes, days on end, trying to get the books done.

**TLC:** *The* **Legion** *has that effect on a lot of different artists.*

**JJ:** Yeah, there's a lot of characters to draw, and on the **Secrets of the Legion**, I did how the Legion got their powers, their first costumes, their second costumes, sort of the evolution, and it was a lot of detail, a lot of back story there. There were a lot of characters to do and it just became too much for me.

**TLC:** *Did you have any favorite Legionnaires to draw?*

**JJ:** Oh, yeah. I loved Dawnstar. I really liked Timber Wolf. I thought that Timber Wolf was like Wolverine. They could have done so much more with that character. Also, I really liked Lightning Lad. His costume was really cool.

**TLC:** *When did you leave comics?*

**JJ:** I think it was the end of 1980.

**TLC:** *So when you left the* **Legion**, *you pretty much left the industry?*

**JJ:** Yeah. I basically left the industry. I got into animation. First I went back into advertising. I did the Bruce Lee posters for the Kato movies that came out, and that was very exciting for me. I worked for Larry Berl at the Monsty Times, and I did a lot of their poster work. I did the movie posters on the B movies. I got to do a lot of Kung Fu movie posters—**14 Bronze Men, 5 Fingers of Death,** and then I got to do **Bruce Lee Son of the Dragon** and **Fury of the Dragon.**

**TLC:** *What animated series have you worked on?*

**JJ:** Oh, God. I was the main model artist on the **Fantastic Four** for the second season at New World. I drove people crazy by trying to make the characters consistent with the way that Jack would do it. I did **Spider-Man, X-Men, Batman: The Animated Series, Gargoyles, Hulk, the Avengers, Mummies, Ghostbusters X, Cyber X, Sherlock Holmes 2000, The Roswell Conspiracies, Ace Ventura, Biker Mice From Mars, G.I. Joe**—I think I did five tours of duty on that show...

**TLC:** *I notice a lot of super-hero names on that list. Did you seek out those jobs, or did they seek you out, due to your comic book background?*

**JJ:** A lot of people knew me for that, and I have a certain style of inking that's a comic book style. I like using the Pentel to finish things off, and a lot of the guys like my line on these things. I have a sort of Jack Kirby-ish feel.

**TLC:** *When did you move out to California?*

**JJ:** I think about '85.

**TLC:** *Do you ever feel an urge to get back into comics?*

**JJ:** Yeah, I would love [to]. In fact, I just finished a book called **Prime Squad**, which is gonna be a **Final Fantasy** type 3-D show. We're doing that for Mult Studios in India. Of course, headed up over here by Bill DuBay.

**TLC:** *Overall, when you look back at the time you spent in comics and on the* **Legion**, *how would you describe that experience?*

**JJ:** I thought it was incredible. I really thought it was incredible working with guys like Neal Adams, Murphy Anderson, Curt Swan, Vince Colletta—I loved Vince as a person—Sol Harrison, of course. There was Carmine Infantino, and Don Heck, and of course Steve Ditko, all those guys who I looked up to for years. Just being in the same place with them was a real kick.

*The Legion flys into action by Janes, with inks by Bruce Patterson. From the collection of Miki Annamanthadoo. © DC Comics.*

# Roy Thomas

Perhaps best known as Stan Lee's heir apparent at Marvel, Roy Thomas also wrote the **Legion of Super-Heroes** for a brief period in the early Eighties. Originally a fanzine editor with **Alter Ego**, Thomas revived the magazine in 1998 and continues as its editor today. A longtime Justice Society fan, he also edited the **All-Star Companion** for the team's Sixtieth Anniversary. The following interview was conducted by Glen Cadigan on April 16, 2003, and was copyedited by Thomas.

**TLC:** *You have a **Legion** connection which a lot of people don't know about. You used to work for Mort Weisinger. What was that experience like?*

**RT:** As I've written and said at various places, it was two weeks of sheer hell, only one of which I was ever paid, which made it worse.

**TLC:** *How did you end up there?*

**RT:** He's the one who offered me a job in New York while I was teaching in St. Louis. I had exchanged only one or two letters with him, [and] a lot more with Julie, but I guess I'd been sending him and other editors copies of **Alter Ego**. He was a good friend of Julie's, and he knew that I had been corresponding with Julie a number of times. I guess he was looking around for an editorial assistant, so he suddenly sent me an offer in the mail out of the blue one day in '65.

**TLC:** *Did Otto Binder have anything to do with you getting that job?*

**RT:** I doubt it directly. I think he would of if he could have, because he was writing for Mort at that time. In fact, I went out to lunch during that couple of weeks I was there once with Mort and with Otto, because I'd been corresponding with him, but I think it was mostly just Mort's decision. Maybe my correspondence with Julie

had something indirectly to do with it, [and] my correspondence with Otto and with Gardner Fox probably less so. Of course, he had seen the letters and things from Otto in **Alter Ego**, so indirectly [maybe that influenced him] a little bit because there was a little connection there.

**TLC:** *Where was E. Nelson Bridwell during all of this?*

**RT:** Nelson, although I didn't know this until I got to New York, was the person I was supposed to replace. He was going to be taken off staff, and he was, for that one week. [He] was just trying to line up free-lance assignments. When I quit, Mort hired him back. I suggested that when I quit, but I don't think that's why Mort did it. I think he was just desperate, so Nelson had that job for another few years.

**TLC:** *How many years were you at Marvel?*

**RT:** Fifteen.

**TLC:** *Around when did you go back to DC?*

**RT:** My contract ran out in fairly late fall in '80, so I began to work for DC then.

**TLC:** *Was the **Legion** one of the first things you were offered?*

**RT:** No, because that came about six months or so later. I don't know the dates offhand, [but] I started doing two books of my own creation: **Arak, Son of Thunder** and **All-Star Squadron**, and they gave me **Batman**

to do, which I quickly got out of. But **Legion** came along pretty soon there. I just don't remember the exact start.

**TLC:** *What was the appeal of the **Legion** job?*

**RT:** Mostly just it was a job. I'm just not a **Legion** fan. I respected the fact that it was very popular, and I liked groups, [but] it just wasn't my thing. It wasn't a book I was eager to do because I never really followed it, but an assignment was an assign-

*Top: Roy Thomas, circa 1997. Above: Superboy returns to the Legion in this cover by George Pérez and Dick Giordano. From the collection of Steven Weill. © DC Comics.*

NAME: _____ ISSUE: 277 VOLUME: ____ DATE: ____

*An unused rough for the cover of Legion of Super-Heroes #277, Thomas' first issue. From the collection of Miki Annamanthadoo. Art © 2003 Jimmy Janes; Legion of Super-Heroes TM and © DC Comics.*

ment, and I enjoyed the half a dozen issues I did.

**TLC:** *Did you have to do a lot of research before you started writing it?*

**RT:** Yeah, I bought a complete set of everything that'd been done to date on the **Legion**. I had that for the few months I wrote the book, and then I sold it off when I left the book.

**TLC:** *What's the difference between writing a book with a large cast like the **Legion** and a book with a large cast like **All-Star Squadron**?*

**RT:** Well, I had a lot more freedom [with **All-Star Squadron**]. The **Legion** was pretty well established when I got in there. Also, I never felt I was going to stay with it that terribly long, [and] although I obviously did all that research for it, I was not that wild about doing it. I wasn't going around thinking, "Boy, I'm gonna think about what I'm going to do over the next few years with this." It was sort of a month-to-month assignment, but I had fun enough when I did it. I don't remember that much about it. I remember we brought them to the

Twentieth Century in one story. That was all right [*laughs*], and a few other things.

**TLC:** *Were you around long enough to get any fan feedback?*

**RT:** Not really, because by the time the last stuff was coming out, I was probably already leaving.

**TLC:** *You inherited Gerry Conway's "Reflecto" storyline. Did you know going in who Reflecto was supposed to be?*

**RT:** I think so. Whatever it was, I'm sure that was something that they told me at the time, and I don't think that I changed that.

**TLC:** *You were also the writer who brought Superboy back into the Legion.*

**RT:** Again, it was something I was in favor of, but it wasn't just my idea. It was whatever they were wanting to do at the time. Maybe it was already a plan that was in place when I came back. I don't know. I was in favor of that, but I don't think it was my idea. I suspect it was something that somebody else wanted, too.

**TLC:** *Do you think it was more of an editorial decree?*

**RT:** Yeah, probably so.

**TLC:** *Did you follow the comic after you stopped writing it?*

**RT:** A little bit. I followed all the comics to some extent, especially the first few issues [after] Paul [Levitz] took it over. He

*A convention sketch by George Pérez featuring the major players in the Reflecto saga. From the collection of Steven Weill. Art © 2003 George Pérez; characters TM and © DC Comics.*

DON'T DARE PEEK AT OUR ULTRA-SPECIAL **LAST PAGE** GUEST-STAR IN THIS ISSUE OF THE **LEGION OF SUPER-HEROES™**

50¢ ALL NEW! NO. 279 SEPT.

WE'VE FINALLY UNMASKED **REFLECTO**—

—AND WE HAVE TO SAVE HIS LIFE... BEFORE IT'S **TOO LATE!**

BUT... BUT **HOW?**

*The Reflecto saga draws to a close in this cover by George Pérez. From the collection of Steven Weill. © DC Comics.*

**RT:** Well, it was one of the first books that really had a legion of very young people that were somehow like **Superman** meets **Archie**. [*laughs*] It was a squeaky clean kind of book in the squeaky clean future, and I think that it just had a nice, optimistic, fun feel. In a different level from the Marvel books, it had the same kind of soap opera elements. It was not played in as heart-rendering a way, but [it] showed there were romances, there were occasional deaths or tragedies, and heartache and intrigue and all those things. I think in some ways it was a precursor of the feeling that **X-Men** tapped into some years later, especially from the middle Seventies on, which **X-Men** hadn't really tapped into in the Sixties.

Give Weisinger and the other main people there the credit for it. They knew what they were doing when they got it going, and they knew how to milk it for quite a few years. It basically had its own book for quite a few years, and it was one of the best-selling books in the company. I don't know if they plan any more, but they [had] eleven volumes of the archives, [and] that's more than any other book has had, and at least as many as any other character has had. I think that says something for the appeal. The fact that it wasn't my cup of tea doesn't make me think any less of the fact that it was a good idea.

Of course, they didn't think it was going to grow into anything, but just like Stan did later at Marvel and other good editors [do], when you see something's going, you kind of follow it and see how you can take advantage of it. I think they found people who liked it as readers, they found people who liked it as writers and artists, and

they just went with it and had a very good success for a number of years.

**TLC:** *So how would you evaluate your* **Legion** *run, looking back at it years later?*

**RT:** It's hard to say, because it was such a short period of time. I think they were a handful of reasonably good stories. I think it was probably better than some [other] work on the **Legion**, but I never got into it the way that [Jim] Shooter and Paul Levitz and maybe one or two other people did. I just tried to do a good job on it as long as I could, but it was something that I knew I wasn't eager to do in the long haul.

*A recent Ultra Boy commission by George Pérez, courtesy of Michael Lieb and Spencer Beck at* **www.theartistschoice.com.**
Art © 2003 George Pérez; Ultra Boy TM and © DC Comics.

had more of a passion for it than I did, and I think it worked out pretty well. Different people are interested in doing different books. Paul had a special thing for the **Legion** just like I did for **All-Star Squadron** or the **Avengers**.

**TLC:** *What was your feel for how important the* **Legion** *was to DC back then?*

**RT:** I thought it was a reasonably important book. I think it had been quite a seller. I don't know if it still was then. It seemed like it was selling pretty well at that time. I didn't feel like it was some minor, unimportant book. It just wasn't a book that I had a great desire to do myself.

**TLC:** *What do you think the appeal of the* **Legion** *is to its fans?*

# Pat Broderick

After drawing for both Marvel and Seaboard/Atlas during the 1970s, Pat Broderick started working for DC Comics professionally in 1980. He became the artist on the Legion of Super-Heroes in 1982, and although his stint was short, he did get to illustrate the prelude to "The Great Darkness Saga" during his stay. After returning to Marvel in the Nineties to illustrate titles such as **Alpha Flight** and **Doom 2099**, Broderick left the industry altogether during the mid-Nineties, returning only recently to illustrate **Peacekeeper** for Future Comics. The following interview was conducted by Glen Cadigan on Jan. 8, 2003.

**TLC:** *While doing research for this interview, I was surprised to see that your career goes all the way back to the early Seventies. What was your first break in the industry?*

**PB:** My first break was back in '73 at DC Comics. I won a contest called "Junior Bullpen," and they sponsored an internship in the Fall of '73 and '74.

**TLC:** *Your career really took off when you went to Marvel. Had you followed Jim Starlin's work on **Captain Marvel** before you got the job?*

**PB:** Yes, I had. I was a big **Captain Marvel** fan/Jim Starlin fan. I just loved his work.

**TLC:** *Were you intimidated at all to follow in his footsteps?*

**PB:** No, it was inspirational to work on the character, because we both loved Gil Kane's work so much. It was nice working on a character in the field that I felt at home in.

**TLC:** *Then you moved onto **Micronauts**. Given the title's popularity, did you feel any pressure there?*

**PB:** No, not at all. I also loved the **Micronauts**. It was a great series. It started out with [the Michael] Golden issues really well. I came on at issue nineteen, and had a very enjoyable run with it. I think I went up to about [issue] thirty-five. [**Note:** Broderick's last **Micronauts** issue was 34. **—Ed.**]

**TLC:** *Why did you leave Marvel for DC in 1980?*

**PB:** At the time, DC had made me an offer. I felt I'd been on **Micronauts** three years [and] it was time to move on.

**TLC:** *Did DC offer you the **Legion** then?*

**PB:** No, they just told me that work was available, so I wanted to come over. I surprised them by coming over. They gave me "The Creature Commandos." I think that was the first thing I did for them, and then it was right after that I got the **Legion**.

**TLC:** *How long did you intend on staying?*

**PB:** I intended on staying at least for a good year, to get used to it, but then they had expanded their line and they offered me **Firestorm**. It was, I felt, a good move to make. But I did enjoy doing the **Legion**. I went back and did a few fill-ins and always liked the characters. It was a good book.

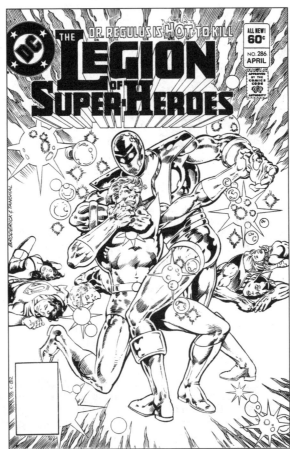

*The cover to Legion of Super-Heroes #286 by Broderick. From the collection of Steven Weill.*
© DC Comics.

**TLC:** *Were you a fan of it before you drew it?*

**PB:** Yeah. I read all the [Dave] Cockrum issues. I was also there at DC when Mike Grell came on board, and he had started with the **Legion**, so I watched him produce his episodes of it.

**TLC:** *So it was an assignment you were looking forward to?*

**PB:** Yeah, absolutely.

**TLC:** *Do you regret now leaving when you did?*

**PB:** No. I had a lot of fun with what I went on to do. I did regret seeing that it had taken a story change in a direction I would have liked to have had a more involved hand in, instead of just being able to do the introduction of it.

**TLC:** *And that would be "The Great Darkness Saga."*

**PB:** Yeah, but I truly did enjoy reading it. I thought it was Paul Levitz's best work.

**TLC:** *Did you and Paul collaborate on any ideas?*

**PB:** No.

**TLC:** *You drew some pretty striking covers during your run. Did you design them yourself?*

**PB:** Actually, the covers were designed by either Dick Giordano or Ed Hannigan. Ed was the cover editor, if memory serves me correctly.

**TLC:** *You mentioned your fill-in work a few years later.*

**PB:** Yeah, I had come in to help out. I believe at the time Karen Berger was editing the book, and she had asked me if I was interested in helping out on a story arc. I jumped at the chance. I enjoyed it.

**TLC:** *When you're penciling a comic, do you change your style at all depending on who's going to be inking it?*

**PB:** Sometimes you do. During those

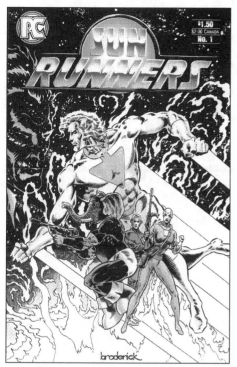

Broderick's attempt at creator-owned comics, the **Sun Runners**. Sun Runners TM and © 2003 Roger McKenzie and Pat Broderick.

days, I didn't.

**TLC:** *One thing I noticed about your career is that when you take over a title, you usually stick with it for a while, the* **Legion** *being the obvious exception. Do you think it's important that when a fan buys a comic they know month in and month out that the same artist is going to be there?*

**PB:** Yeah. I always told them if they liked the book, buy it, if they don't like it, then don't buy the book. I always felt if the reader had a continuity in the storyline—also with the creative team, and not just the story—then they enjoyed it more. I know I enjoyed it more. I enjoyed exploring each title that I drew. That's why I would generally stay on a book for about three years.

**TLC:** *Of all the titles you've worked on, which one did you enjoy the most?*

**PB:** **Doom 2099**. [*laughs*] I had a long and enjoyable run on it. It was also three years. I believe I did probably some of the best work of my career on the first twelve issues in that series. I thought I was definitely cooking at the time.

**TLC:** *Do you think the fans remember you for that?*

**PB:** No. **Doom** was a very popular book, but I believe I'm probably more well remembered for my work at DC. The **Green Lantern** series, **Firestorm**, and then at Marvel, **Micronauts**.

**TLC:** *You've drawn a variety of different titles in a variety of different genres. How hard is it to switch gears from one title to the next?*

**PB:** Sometimes it's difficult. Doing the war comics was difficult in the sense of getting all the reference correct. Switching into the fantasy titles was something I was more comfortable in. So even though the subject matter may have switched around a bit, I still felt comfortable wearing those shoes.

**TLC:** *You've done a lot of science-fiction in your career. Is that something which you look for?*

**PB:** I just feel comfortable in it, whether it's comics or animation. I always felt comfortable in it.

**TLC:** *Which is more rewarding for you: working on material which you own yourself, or working for the companies on already established characters?*

**PB:** It's very rewarding to be working on a series at a company that you've always wanted to work on. I always felt that it brings the most out of any creative team, be it a writer or artist or an inker. Working on your own work is also extremely satisfying. It's something that you can control. You don't just have [it] for one moment when it's published. You have it forever.

**TLC:** *Is creator-owned work something which you see yourself doing again someday?*

**PB:** Oh, definitely. I currently have two projects underway: two sixty-page graphic novels, both science-fiction. I have both of them written and both of them halfway penciled and inked. I'm just taking my time with those two stories. Also, I'm doing production designs and storyboard work for movies and some animation work. I like doing my own stuff.

**TLC:** *Why did you leave comics in the Nineties?*

**PB:** Comics, at that time, definitely took a sales turn which affected the industry worldwide, and within my field personally, with my co-workers and friends. A lot of people were basically left without work, and without means of finding more work, 'cause the companies [had] shrunk in size tremendously. You had, generally, about three hundred or four hundred people that were out of work. It made it, at that point, very difficult to get back in. The industry had to grow again, [and] you can't wait around. I got into advertising, got into animation, [and] now I'm also teaching.

**TLC:** *What projects did you work on in animation which people would recognize?*

**PB:** I worked on **Jimmy Neutron, Boy Genius** in the production design department. I designed his two-seater spaceship, his gadgets, the cars, [and] set designs that were later animated into Lightwave.

**TLC:** *When you work in comics, your name is always on the work, but animation has more of an assembly line approach. So which do you prefer: comics or animation?*

**PB:** Well, in the production end of it, it's not assembly, it's more creative-concepting. That part I enjoyed. It's more like comic books. It's just thinking and drawing, creating and designing, capturing the feel of an atmosphere [and] being able to instill drama into it. So it's a good crossover. And it's the same with storyboarding. During my years in comics, I also did storyboarding and advertising at the same time. Some of the first storyboard work I worked on was with Neal Adams at Continuity, back in '75, '76. So they both worked hand in hand. Storyboarding is fun. You're able to tell a story. There's a difference between storyboarding for commercials and for movies, and they're both enjoyable, both challenging.

**TLC:** *Are there any characters out there which you've never drawn that you'd like to get the opportunity to draw someday?*

**PB:** Yeah, I would love to do Kirby's Demon. I've always loved Kirby's characters. That would be enjoyable.

**TLC:** *Do you ever see yourself drawing a* **Legion** *story again?*

**PB:** Only if called.

**TLC:** *But you'd be willing?*

**PB:** Oh, of course.

**TLC:** *When you look back, do you wish that you had a chance to draw the* **Legion** *more than you did?*

**PB:** There were a lot of things I wish I could have drawn more than I did. [*laughs*] You know, the books I didn't even have an opportunity to draw. I did then, and as an artist, still regret missing the Darkseid saga. It would've been incredibly fun to have done. I would've enjoyed handling the characters in that storyline. I do regret, in a sense, having missed out. But I couldn't draw everything.

# Keith Giffen

## Part One

Of the many artists who have worked on the **Legion of Super-Heroes** during its forty-five year history, probably none have produced a greater fan reaction than Keith Giffen. From his early days on the **Legion** drawing "The Great Darkness Saga" to his "Five Years Later" take on the title, Giffen's name has become almost synonymous with the comic which he once drew. Also responsible for the creation of characters such as Lobo, Ambush Bug, and Trencher, Giffen was interviewed on April 7, 2003 by Glen Cadigan, and he copyedited the following transcript.

**TLC:** *I'd like to start with the early part of your career. You broke in at Marvel, correct?*

**KG:** Yeah. I think the first thing I ever sold for Marvel was an inside front cover for **Deadly Hands of Kung Fu**. The first actual comic book story [was the] "Sword in the Star" back-up in an issue of **Marvel Preview** [#7 —Ed.]. I know that "Satana" was the cover feature.

**TLC:** *How did you end up at Marvel?*

**KG:** Boy, talk about doing everything wrong. I was working at Hoffman & LaRoche as a hazardous material handler. I always wanted to break into comics, so I slapped together a portfolio and figured I'd make the rounds. In my naïveté I figured I'd call first, not realizing that if you call it's easier to say "No." Again, I looked at the list of comics and I thought, "I don't want to start right at the bottom calling someone like Charlton." I didn't want to start at the top, either, because I really didn't figure that I stood a chance at getting into Marvel. This is when Atlas was still publishing, so I called Atlas and I said, "I was wondering if you'd be looking at art samples," and the receptionist there was just wonderful. She was so personable and nice and kind. "Oh sure, come on

down, but you better come down soon. We're going out of business." And I thought, "O-kay," then I hung up. I thought, "Screw it."

So I called Marvel and I talked to the receptionist, and she said, "Tell you what: just bring it in and drop it off. Johnny'll look at it and then you can pick it up tomorrow." Real encouraging. So I go into the city and I drop it off with the receptionist, and she just shoves it into a desk drawer. I go, "That's the last they'll see of that for a while," and I go home. The next day I'm about ready to go back in and get my portfolio, but then I thought, "Nah. Let me give it another day." Like another day's really gonna matter if some guy just walks in off of the street. I go in the day after. I don't call first, I just go in to get it, and I walk into the lobby. The secretary leaps up from her desk and starts yelling at me, haranguing me about being a professional and being stupid. I thought, "Whoa! Where did this come from?"

As it turns out, Ed Hannigan had just left the "Sword in the Star" series, and the deadline was tight and they needed a warm body. Bill Mantlo saw my portfolio when it was in John Romita's office because John Romita, God bless him, really did look at the stuff. He wasn't a con guy just sitting at a desk somewhere. He really looked at it, and they were trying to

get ahold of me, but in my consummate professionalism I had not put my name [or] address [on it]. No contact [information]! I just dropped it off! There was no way they could get in touch with me. And I landed the first "Sword in the Star" script, and it's pretty much been downhill since then.

**TLC:** *When did you cross over to DC?*

**KG:** I did a handful of things for Marvel. My chronology's all screwed up. I don't know if the **Defenders** thing I did was

*Top: would you buy a vacuum cleaner from this man? Keith Giffen at the DC offices circa 1984. Above: the Legion remembers its roots in an homage to the cover of **Adventure Comics** #300. © DC Comics.*

© DC Comics.

before I wandered over to DC the first time or after. I suspect it's after. [*He's right. — Ed.*] I know I did "Woodgod," and I might have done one or two other things. Bill Mantlo realized I wasn't going to be getting a lot of work at Marvel, so he reached out to Gerry Conway, who was an editor at DC that he knew, and he said, "Take a look at this guy's work," and I wandered over there. Gerry put me on *All-Star Comics*. So here I am, new in the business, I've maybe done three comics in my entire life, and I'm working with Wally Wood. On top of that, I'm doing breakdowns and doing the storytelling for Wally Wood. I landed there, and then it was a long, drawn-out, agonizing period of doing everything wrong and blowing myself completely out of the business in about a year. I could've written a book, *What Not To Do*. I wound up down in south Jersey selling Kirby vacuum cleaners door to door.

**TLC:** *How long did that last?*

**KG:** About six months. Then I got into repossessions because I was small and thin and I could fit through half-open car windows. There's nothing like sneaking into some guy's parking lot by his apartment building down in Atlantic City in the dead of night [and] hotwiring a car in front of an applauding audience of hookers and junkies. I used to work with a neanderthal man who would actually carry a gun. I was the small, skinny guy who could do this kind of stuff, [and] he was there in case it got hairy-knuckled.

[Then] I came back up North and I got into phone collections and a series of dead-end jobs. My wife-to-be had been dating me for three months and didn't know I could draw. That was how firmly I had shut the door on it. When she found out, she started campaigning with me to get back into it. Finally, what won me over was she said, "Don't you at least owe them the opportunity of hanging up on you?" 'cause I had slinked out of town, tail between the legs. I just disappeared.

So I called Joe Orlando, figuring Joe was the one I did the most damage to, and Joe just said, "Come in and we'll talk." He sat me down, and he liked what I had to offer, but I screwed up so badly I had to be [put] on a probationary period. He said, "If you're willing to do that, we're willing to give you another shot." And I've been at DC pretty much since. I owe a lot to Joe Orlando for taking a chance on a guy who was a complete and utter screwball. What a foul-up! Goldbrick, you name it! And [also] to Dick Giordano, [because] at that point he was editing some ghost books, as well as one or two other things, and he was the one who hooked [me] up with [Robert] Kahniger to do some stories to see if I could match a deadline.

Then Mike Barr offered me the "Dr. Fate" back-up [in *Flash*], and then Paul Levitz was kind enough to let bygones be bygones and give me a shot on the *Legion*.

**TLC:** *How familiar were you with the Legion then?*

**KG:** I was very familiar with the Legion. I'd been a fan since the John Forte days, but I was more familiar with the Legion as vast untapped potential. I kept looking at that book, thinking, "You could really push this. No one's really thinking it through." Paul was trying to in a lot of the stuff he was doing, but a lot of the artists didn't seem to understand it. In the Thirtieth Century, if it's got wheels, it's wrong! And he had some great artists there, but I just kept thinking, "If I get my hands on that book, I know I can make something of it." And they gave me the opportunity. It was like, "Put your money where your mouth is."

**TLC:** *How long was it before you started playing an active role in the plotting?*

**KG:** Almost from day one, if the artist wants to be involved in the plotting, Paul brings [them] in. Paul used to give me the co-plotting credit, but you have to understand, that was nothing more than chatting

*The Servants of Darkness, from **Who's Who in the Legion of Super-Heroes** #6. Courtesy of Mike Napolitano.*
© DC Comics.

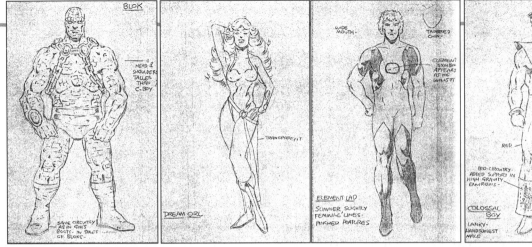

Samples from Giffen's model sheet, circa 1983. Courtesy of Mike Napolitano.
Art © 2003 Keith Giffen; characters TM and © DC Comics.

with him in the hallway or talking on the phone. He's always been really, really generous in terms of giving credit. Paul would write a plot. I would take Paul's plot, and I might poke around with it a bit, [maybe] take a scene that he thought was a throwaway and try to add a bit more juice to it. Eventually it did evolve into "Can you top this?" where we would be bouncing things off of one another. I was never actually a co-plotter in terms of sitting down and working out the stories with him, but he gave me a lot of latitude to play my little games. In terms of the one-upmanship thing, he beat me soundly when he wrote the one caption that froze me in place. It was a caption in one panel of "The Great Darkness Saga," and this was the art direction: "The population of the planet Daxam rises off of the planet." At that point I realized that he could do me much more damage than I could do him.

**TLC:** *When did you start to realize that "The Great Darkness Saga" was shaping up to be something special?*

**KG:** When Paul said, "I want to use Darkseid." The minute he said, "I want to use Darkseid," I didn't even have to hear the story. It was like, "I'm on board. Ab-solutely." The idea of introducing that character into the Legion's mythos, I just thought it would be a great story, period, over and out. I never knew that it would generate the response that it did. At best when I was doing the stuff, I just thought we were doing a fun comic.

**TLC:** *Did you pay attention to how popular the book was becoming?*

**KG:** Yeah, because I always had one eye on knocking [*The New Teen*] *Titans* off its perch. Stay ambitious! I just thought, "Boy, [let's] just take one month to do that, to knock it off." We never did, of course, because Marv [Wolfman] and George

[Pérez] were the juggernaut back then. They were unstoppable.

**TLC:** *When you were first drawing the* ***Legion***, *you were also drawing* ***Omega Men*** *at the same time.*

**KG:** Yeah, that was a mistake.

**TLC:** *Why do two science-fiction books at once?*

**KG:** Stupidity. There's really no other answer for that. I thought it was an interesting concept, and I was actually dumb enough to give it a shot. [*laughs*] It didn't last very long. I realized probably by the end of the second issue I'd bitten off more than I could chew.

**TLC:** *When did you start to feel like the title was yours to play around with?*

**KG:** Not until it became mine to play around with. Karen Berger called me into her office and said, "Paul's going to be leaving the ***Legion***. Would you like to

take over?" When you're collaborating with somebody on a book, especially somebody who's had a long run on the book, who am I to come in and go, "Now, Paul, we'll do it this way." You defer to the guy who has the most experience with the book, and as long as the guy's doing good work—which Paul was—I had no problems with it at all.

**TLC:** *Did you have much contact with* ***Legion*** *fans initially?*

*For many Legion fans, the Levitz/Giffen era really began with* **Legion** *of Super-Heroes Annual #1. From the collection of Steven Weill.*
© DC Comics.

*Giffen's art style began to evolve while on the Legion, as shown in this page from LSH #311. From the collection of Mike Napolitano. © DC Comics.*

**KG:** At first, not really, but it grew gradually. I don't even remember how I got connected with **Legion** fandom, but Harry Broertjes' name keeps floating to the surface. Harry, Tom and Mary [Bierbaum], Ken Gale... I don't recall exactly how it reached the point wherein I started interacting with Legion fandom, mostly through an APA called **Interlac.** I guess it was a gradual process. And Legion fans get a bad rap. They can be opinionated and arrogant and half-crazed, but that's the charm! [*laughs*] I wouldn't have it any other way! If they thought you were coasting, they'd crucify you.

**TLC:** *Do you remember when you found out that they were adding another monthly **Legion** book to the schedule?*

**KG:** Yeah. I remember saying, "No way!" I had learned my lesson on the **Omega Men.** I believe that was when we started

plundering **New Talent Showcase.** People like Terry Shoemaker, Karl Kesel, and various others. I think Steve Lightle came out of that period. I love new talent. I used to go down and look through the **New Talent Showcase** all the time. I have no memories as to why they did that. That was during the period when the book was agony for me to do. That poster came along and blew me out of the water. Every line was just like sweating blood. That period, I mostly remember it as I was winding down off of the book and really not having a good time.

I really enjoyed doing the **Legion,** and I probably would ably would have continued doing the **Legion.** Everyone wonders, "What happened? Why did you leave the **Legion** the first time? Was there friction? Was it [because] you and Paul started fighting?" Nothing could be further from the truth. I left the **Legion** the first time because I did that **Legion** poster and fried myself. After I was done with that poster I thought, "I don't want to do this anymore," and sort of wandered off. The **Legion** was a good time. I often wonder what would have happened had we not peaked early with "Great Darkness." After "Great Darkness," everything was, "Can you top that?"

**TLC:** *Did you follow it after you left?*

**KG:** No. I never followed **Justice**

**League** after I left, I never followed **Lobo** [after I left]. I don't follow stuff after I leave, because all I'd then be doing is going, "That's not the way I'd do it!" Well, of course it's not the way *you'd* do it. You're not doing it! Why make yourself crazy?

**TLC:** *Your last **Legion** story arc featured the Legion of Super-Villains. Did you change your approach to that storyline, given that it was the launch of a brand new title?*

**KG:** Not really. Like I mentioned before, by that time I was pretty much fried, and I was running on autopilot. I gave those books as much attention as I really, honestly could, considering the circumstances. I had one foot out the door at that point. I guess if there's any different approach to be seen, it was just trying to keep myself interested. And it had nothing to do with story, it had nothing to do with the writing, it had nothing to do with the book. It was just after doing that poster, I was fried.

**TLC:** *You also redesigned some of the members of the Legion of Super-Villains for that storyline.*

**KG:** Yeah. Some of them looked really hokey. I mean, c'mon!

**TLC:** *When you would do something like*

*A favorite target of Giffen's while on the **Legion** was the Legion of Substitute Heroes. Note the redesign of Chlorophyll Kid by the artist.*
Chlorophyll Kid TM and © DC Comics.

More samples from Giffen's **Legion** model sheet, from the collection of Mike Napolitano.
Art © 2003 Keith Giffen; characters TM and © DC Comics.

that, would you have a backstory in mind?

**KG:** Nope. It would be, "Okay, let's see now: this was first drawn in 1950-something. Maybe we should update it a little." As quaint and nostalgic as the Legion could be with their upside-down rocket-ship and their two-fingered salute to the Legion flag, and their very early old-school costumes, it was time to move on. It took Dave Cockrum to take the first major step in redefining the Legion, and at that point I figured, "These are young kids! Don't kids always tinker with their looks?" Even the Legion of Super-Villains, which was an older group, were still basically the opposite Legion. People play around with their visuals, and play around with the way they look, and play around with their fashion sense. I didn't see any reason for these people to still be wearing the same costumes that were in vogue in the Fifties, or whatever the 30th Century equivalent would be.

**TLC:** *Karate Kid was killed during that storyline. Why did you dislike him so much?*

**KG:** Well, you have to choose one, don't you? Super-karate. It stuck in my head like a burr. Even when I was a kid, I just didn't like him. Oddly enough, my favorite color is orange, but still, I never could wrap my head around that character.

**TLC:** *So was it a disappointment that you didn't get to draw that issue yourself?*

**KG:** Ultimately, it was. But it happened, so I'm okay. But he's back, anyway. Comic book death starts to be an oxymoron. It's something that I don't think anyone really takes too seriously. I just wanted to see him get it. If I was on the **Legion** today, I'd want to kill that snake.

**TLC:** *Are there any **Legion** stories from your first run that you wish you had a chance to do over?*

**KG:** I guess the latter issues of the run, when I was running out of steam. I'd like a chance to go back and do those right. And when it comes to beyond that, definitely "The Magic Wars." I'd like another chance at it, because I think I really dropped the ball on that one.

GIFFEN/MAHLSTEDT

Previously published in **Interlac**, this group scene of the Legion of Super-Heroes was contributed by Harry Broertjes and Kevin Gould. Art © 2003 Keith Giffen; Legion of Super-Heroes TM and © DC Comics.

# Paul Levitz

## Part Two

In Part Two of our interview with Paul Levitz, we cover his second run on the **Legion**, his relationship with Keith Giffen, and what he thinks of the Legion today. Like Part One, the following interview was conducted by Glen Cadigan on March 13, 2003, and was copyedited by Levitz.

**TLC:** *Gerry Conway told me that when he took over the **Legion**, you gave him something like a hundred pages of story ideas and character developments.*

**PL:** I used to keep a big blank book, and I had pasted into it pasted versions of Neil Pozner's old **Amazing World Legion** issue, and whatever my scribbled

*Polar Boy by George Pérez, courtesy of Spencer Beck.* Art © 2003 George Pérez; Polar Boy TM and © DC Comics.

notes were. Words that a particular character would use to build the vocabulary, backstory thoughts, plot scenes, whatever came to mind when I was working on the book organized by character or by theme. I don't really remember how it was set up. I guess I gave a set of that to Gerry.

**TLC:** *How far in advance were you planning as a writer?*

**PL:** As I say, I rarely was planning in advance more than a half-dozen issues, but with a book that I loved that much, every time I would sit down and read the run of pre-existing **Legion** stuff—and I must have read the whole run six or seven times in my life, including at least a couple of times during that period when I was doing that first run—you just scribble stuff down. A lot of it you never end up using—you change your mind, it would never particularly fit, or it was, on reflection, a dumb idea—but periodically, that's where you would get something rich to throw in.

**TLC:** *You know, in the three years that you were gone, they didn't hold a single leadership election.*

**PL:** Yeah, I think I remember that vaguely.

**TLC:** *You used to try and drum up support for the elections in the letters page.*

**PL:** I thought the Legion leadership elections was a very cute tradition, so I was always very fond of that. I had loved doing letters pages. I think I've ended up writing more comics letters pages then maybe anyone in my career—a dubious distinction—and the **Legion** letter pages had more potential to be fun than most, because of things like the election, or the old "Bits of Legionnaire Business." Not things that I had instituted, but things that I wanted to keep around.

**TLC:** *Did you feel that it was important that fans had that sort of a direct connection to the title?*

Above: a rare Legion cover by Brian Bolland. From the collection of Steven Weill. Legion of Super-Heroes TM and © DC Comics.

**PL:** I think it helps.

**TLC:** *Let me put it to you another way: were you often influenced by what people would say in the letters page?*

**PL:** I think there were several occasions where ideas that someone sent in made their way into the story, and when somebody told me I was doing something stupid, I had a reaction to it. Part of the problem is you've got an enormous time lag, and fan mail tends to focus on the story itself, rather than what the underpinning of the story is. But there were certainly occasions where it had some influence.

**TLC:** *So what were the circumstances around you returning to the **Legion**?*

**PL:** I think what happened was Mike Barr had taken over editing the **Legion** somewhere in between, and Roy [Thomas] was

*A Legion romance which came to an end during Levitz's tenure on the title. From the collection of Dylan Clearbrook.*
Art © 2003 Steve Lightle; Timber Wolf and Light Lass TM and and © DC Comics.

writing **Legion** to keep busy. [He] didn't particularly care for the book at all. Mike asked me if I was interested in taking it on. I wasn't expecting to ever go back to the book, so it was kind of an odd [experience]. I was writing the [**Superman**] newspaper strip, [and] I hated writing the **Superman** newspaper strip. I just found it an incredibly painful assignment, so we were able to work out a triple-swap where Roy got whatever Gerry was doing— maybe that was **Wonder Woman**—I got **Legion**, and Gerry got the newspaper strip to write. And the one thing I was bound and determined to do coming back to it was not f*ck it up. This time I wasn't gonna blow a deadline. This was gonna be basically the only assignment I was gonna take on, and I was just gonna stay 'til it was done. I'm very proud of how long I lasted without interruption on it.

**TLC:** *When you returned, you had to work on the Reflecto storyline. Did you have any input into how that was wrapped up?*

**PL:** I think I just got to dialogue the story,

so you can do some patchwork in the course of that, but there's limits to what you can do.

**TLC:** *When you first wrote the **Legion**, your first issue was also Jim Sherman's first issue. When you came back to the title, your first full issue was also Pat Broderick's first issue. Is it just a coincidence that whenever you take over the **Legion**, a new artist also joins you?*

**PL:** Definitely the first time, 'cause as we said a minute or two ago, the theory was Mike Grell was still gonna be on the book. Maybe after taking one look at me, the incumbent artist turns and runs, but I don't think that's the case. I think Mike [Barr] was just in the process of figuring out how to make **Legion** a better book, and he thought Broderick would be an interesting artist to do it.

**TLC:** *Did you keep up on the **Legion** as a reader once you stopped writing it?*

**PL:** No. As a matter of almost religious principle, I didn't read the book after I stopped writing it. In the case of the Seventies, I didn't read it for the two years until I was given the assignment again, and then I went back and read all the intervening material and made my notes. When I gave it up in '89, I think it was about four, five years before I looked at it again, and then it was at the editor's request. Because I've got the day job, too, I didn't want to be bringing any unnecessary emotional baggage about my view of how the book was doing.

**TLC:** *When you came back to the **Legion** in the Eighties, how did you adjust to the changes that had occurred during your absence?*

**PL:** The characters I liked out of what had happened I tried to take full advantage of. The characters I liked less I tried to change in a way that would make them more entertaining to me, and hopefully, to the reader in the deal.

**TLC:** *It wasn't too long after you returned that Keith Giffen came on board.*

**PL:** Keith was the back-up artist almost from the beginning. He may have done the back-up in the second issue that I did. Keith and I had some old history from **All-Star** where we had gotten along not particularly well, so I was a little nervous about working with him again, but he had changed enormously, as had I, in the years since. It was really some wonderful magic fun that we were able to play together.

**TLC:** *Why do you think the two of you worked out so well?*

**PL:** I got in a conversation with Stan [Lee] once, asking him about the Golden Age of Marvel when he and Jack [Kirby] and Steve [Ditko] were just doing such awesome work, and at some point in the conversation, he basically shrugged his shoulders and said, "You know, for a few years there, it just seemed like we couldn't do anything wrong." Not comparing my work to theirs, because it doesn't deserve to be, but one of the peculiarities of comics as a collaborative medium [is] sometimes you're just in tune. The fertility of Keith's imagination, which is one of the truly great imaginations in our business, the passion he was able to bring to the work made me do better work than I probably would have done otherwise, or that I have done otherwise with many other artists. Whatever I was doing in terms of the way the stories were structured [and] the springboards were set up funnelled his imagination in some productive directions. Although we didn't agree on everything during the course of the time, we just had a lot of fun playing, "Can you top this?" "Here's an idea: what if we do that?" "I don't know, but what if we did it that way with whipped cream on it?" "Okay!"

**TLC:** *When did you decide to bring Darkseid to the 30th Century?*

*Part 1 of "The Great Darkness Saga" by Keith Giffen and Frank Giacoia. From the collection of Steven Weill. © DC Comics.*

*A page from Levitz's long-running Shrinking Violet story-line. Art by Keith Giffen and Kurt Schaffenberger. From the collection of Mike Napolitano. © DC Comics.*

**PL:** Probably when I plotted the story. The little back-up that I did with Pat that led into "The [Great] Darkness Saga" was probably the first time I thought about it.

**TLC:** *So when you wrote that story, it was your intention then and there that it would be Darkseid?*

**PL:** Oh, yeah.

**TLC:** *Why use Darkseid? Why not come up with another villain?*

**PL:** I'm not great at creating villains. If you take my lifelong track record for that, I don't think you'd come up with one first-stringer. I did a decent job, I think, in **Legion** at modernizing some of the old villains. Taking an old name and giving them some more contemporary approach, or then-contemporary approach. I was a great fan of Jack's work on **New Gods**, and at that point I guess we had cancelled the then-last attempt to revive it maybe a year before. It's hard for me to work the dates out in my head. So that whole mythology was lying fallow.

**TLC:** *Do you think that story-line is responsible for making Darkseid one of DC's heavy hitters?*

**PL:** Nah. Everything that's great about Darkseid is Jack's.

**TLC:** *Were you trying to top yourself on "Earthwar" with that?*

**PL:** I don't know whether [it was] top myself or get it right this time. You know, "Okay, this time let's do a multi-part story and really pull it off!" And I certainly didn't know as I was writing it that it would end up being the most respected work of my career as a writer, but somewhere along the line as it started pulling together, it began to feel like certainly by far the best thing I had done on **Legion**.

**TLC:** *Why did it take so long to put that back in print?*

**PL:** **Legion** hasn't been a hot book for a long stretch, so the first question in our planning meetings usually hasn't been, "How do we get some more **Legion** material out there?"

**TLC:** *Just before "The Great Darkness Saga" the first **Legion Annual** came out.*

**PL:** Yeah, I loved that one. I think that was just one of those writer's jigsaw puzzle stories. "How do you get every Legionnaire into the story, [and] pull the team back together?" That constraint of doing basically the one page about each was just such a fun way to plot.

**TLC:** *Was there a conscious effort to make it appealing to new readers?*

**PL:** I had a conscious effort, I think, when I came back on **Legion** from the beginning that we should make it not just a new beginning for me, but a friendly entry point, 'cause if I was trying to bring some new vitality to the project, hopefully that would be an invitation for people to come in.

**TLC:** *That annual introduced the second black Legionnaire. Was that your way of righting the wrongs of Tyroc?*

**PL:** I don't know about righting the wrongs of Tyroc, but at least getting a black character in the book who I was comfortable writing. I think the lack of a rational racial mix in comics has been a big problem for a long time, and I've tried both as a writer and an editor to take some steps about addressing it. In retrospect, looking back at my writing career, I didn't try nearly hard enough, but it's consistent with a lot of other things that I've done to want to get a more diverse cast of faces out there.

**TLC:** *Are there any **Legion** stories which you've done which you feel like you've really missed the boat on?*

**PL:** Oh, yeah. Start with the one with the playing with [the] dynamics of aging—[**SLSH** #] 235, or something [like that]—where we tried to explain that, "No, these guys really can be thirty years old, but they're still being called kids because the definition of what a kid is has changed." Well intentioned, not necessarily badly reasoned from a historian's point of view—our definition of childhood has changed a lot over the years, and may continue to—but not a very good comic book story.

*A convention "sketch" of Mongul by Brian Bolland. From the collection of Steven Weill.*
Art © 2003 Brian Bolland; Mongul TM and © DC Comics.

In 1984, if you weren't reading the **Legion of Super-Heroes**, you weren't reading comics. From a DC house ad promoting the relaunch of the title. Legion of Super-Heroes TM and © DC Comics.

**TLC:** *When did the **Legion** become a candidate for DC's hardcover/softcover program?*

**PL:** I think when we came up with the idea of doing it. It was probably our second most profitable title at the time, so it was a logical thing to do.

**TLC:** *So DC did see the **Legion** as one of its more valuable properties?*

**PL:** There's a dichotomy between being a valuable property and being a successful publishing venture. **Wonder Woman**'s never been an extraordinarily successful publishing venture, but it's an extraordinarily valuable property. **Legion**'s never been an extraordinarily important property outside of comics, but in its good years, it's been a very, very successful publishing venture.

**TLC:** *When you started off the new title, that was the first time that you actually used the Legion of Super-Villains.*

**PL:** Was it? Yeah, I guess it might've been.

**TLC:** *Why did you wait so long to use them?*

**PL:** Beats me.

**TLC:** *They are the logical counterpoint to the Legion.*

**PL:** They're an appropriate story. One of the challenges of the **Legion** is you start off with twenty-five characters and a few supporting characters running around in a book, so adding a dozen villains doesn't necessarily make it any easier for people to understand what's going on. I didn't do a lot of villain groups for that reason. My bias in the **Legion** was most often to have a single villain behind whatever was going on, [with] some exceptions.

**TLC:** *There was one new villain who appeared in that storyline, and people have been wondering about him ever since. Who was Terrus?*

**PL:** [He] might've been a modernization of a later generation of Scarecrow. If I was naming him Terrus, maybe it had something to do with terror.

**TLC:** *Karate Kid died in that storyline. You said you liked him as a character.*

**PL:** Yup. A lot.

**TLC:** *So why'd you kill him?*

**PL:** I think he was valuable enough emotionally that it had surprise power. He didn't have a lot of unduplicated strengths relative to the Legion. In many ways, I think he worked better as a character who was sort of a counterpoint to the Legion then he was as a member. And you've gotta give up the good ones sometimes, or people think you're only gonna kill the Chemical Kings.

**TLC:** *Did you intend to bring Projectra back when you had finished that storyline?*

**PL:** Oh, yeah. Eventually.

**TLC:** *So when did you get the idea to start adding some new Legionnaires?*

**PL:** When is always a difficult question on any of these things, because when you're writing a regular book... we talked before about the notebook I used to work off. You'd wake up at three in the morning, or you'd finish reading something and say, "Wouldn't it be cool if I did this some day?" and you scribble it down. The idea may come up then and not be used for years, or it may come up just as you're sitting there. "Okay, need a plot for next month's issue. What the hell are we gonna do, and this is due tomorrow morning?" Unless you do incredible documentation or have an extraordinary memory, you have no idea of what happened when.

**TLC:** *Did you have definite ideas of who you wanted to join the group?*

**PL:** Probably not anything more complicated then a desire to have greater diversity.

**TLC:** *So how serious were your attempts to bring Supergirl to the 30th Century?*

**PL:** I'd forgotten most of it until I read about it in some fanzine article fairly recently. I don't know if it was an interview with John [Byrne], or somebody writing about the **Crisis** period.

**TLC:** *But she was originally supposed to be Sensor Girl?*

**PL:** I think so. I haven't gone back and dug out the plots to look, but I think that was the plan at one point.

**TLC:** *One of your trademarks when you were writing the **Legion** were your long sub-plots. Take me behind the scenes of one of them. For instance, the Shrinking Violet storyline.*

**PL:** The basic approach I would take [was that I would] usually keep about six or seven issues rough sketched out in advance. What that would amount to is an 8½" x 11" paper with, let's say, eight columns. The headings of the columns two through eight would be the next seven issue numbers. The first column would be a list of open story items. I don't have the run in front of me, and I can't recreate it in my head, but whatever the major storyline would be for that issue might be up there as the first line on the left—whoever the villain would be—and then you'd have four or five open sub-plots or character developments. Somewhere there'd be a line that might say, "Lightning Lass" or "Lightning Lass/Shrinking Violet," and it would scribble out the beats. The theory I tried for is that each time you would visit with that subplot, something would progress. You would learn some new information, there would be a new development, but it wasn't just a character moment, it was a plot in motion. Would it end up being the lead story someday? Probably most of them matured into that. Not all of them did.

**TLC:** *There's one thing which people have speculated on for a long time, and that's the relationship between Lightning Lass and Shrinking Violet. Would you care to clarify that?*

**PL:** I speculated on it, too. Sometimes the characters write themselves.

**TLC:** *Did you have any destination in mind, or were you basically just going with the flow?*

**PL:** Most of it, as it went along, started as an outgrowth of whatever happened between Timber Wolf and Saturn Girl in that "Cold and Lonely Corner of Hell" story [*LSH* #289 —Ed.]. So you had a logical alienation between Timber Wolf and Light Lass, [or] Lightning Lass, whichever she was at the time, and from then on it began to write itself.

*Are they or aren't they? Even Levitz isn't saying for certain. Courtesy of Dylan Clearbrook.*
Art © 2003 Steve Lightle; Lightning Lass and Shrinking Violet TM and © DC Comics.

**TLC:** *How much input did you have into what happened to the Legion during* **Crisis**?

**PL:** To the extent that it was the Legion as itself, an awful lot. To the extent it was juggling Superman, juggling Supergirl, the things that weren't the books I was working on, fairly limited. Then we got into some debates back and forth on that as I tried to find solutions, and John tried to structure his **Superman** material in a way that made sense, rolling forward. I had very good relationships with all the people who were working on **Crisis**. They were all good friends, but I kinda had my corner of the universe, and they had the rest of it.

**TLC:** *So when did you learn that Superboy was going to be written out of continuity?*

**PL:** Probably whenever John decided to do it.

**TLC:** *What was your reaction to that?*

**PL:** I wouldn't have been happy.

**TLC:** *Did the wheels start spinning right away about how to fix that problem?*

**PL:** As I remember, we had a couple of weeks, or months, of debates back and forth about the different ways it could be dealt with to accomplish his goals for **Superman**, and maybe still leave me with what I needed to work with for **Legion**. Ultimately, we came up with whatever we came up with, and it didn't quite work.

**TLC:** *How important did you feel that Superboy and Supergirl were to the Legion?*

**PL:** I don't know that Supergirl was ever particularly important to the Legion. It was fun to write the relationship between her and Brainiac, 'cause it was such a perfect counterpoint moment for Brainiac. He was this enormously controlled, all intellect person, succumbing to a set of emotions that were completely beyond his control, but I don't think it had any resonance beyond that. She didn't have any interesting powers, [or] differentiation to work with that way. Superboy I

*With John Byrne's reboot of* **Superman**, *changes were in store for the* **Legion of Super-Heroes**. *From the collection of Steven Weill.* Superboy and the Legion of Super-Heroes TM and © DC Comics.

always found to be an important character for the Legion because he was the emotional centerpoint, the inspiration. I had a lot of fun writing him. One of the relatively few pages I have of my **Legion** run hanging up is one of the ones from [#] 231 where it's basically a narrator's monologue about Superboy's sense of guilt from Krypton having died, and he's just not gonna let that happen again as he goes off and bounces against some spaceship. It's a lovely, I think Jim Sherman/Jack Abel page hanging in the basement somewhere.

**TLC:** *What was your original plan for Rond Vidar?*

**PL:** Somewhere along the line I came up with that stunt for making him the contemporary Green Lantern, which I thought was a lot of fun. I'm not sure how early on I came up with that, or whether Keith or someone else [had something to do with it].

**TLC:** *When you killed him, did you intend to leave him dead?*

**PL:** No, I don't think so, because we didn't do a real enough death. I have a personal writer's rule that if I kill someone on-panel, they stay dead. So the fact that I had that as an off-panel [death] was clearly a set-up in my head for whatever mystery was gonna be built around it.

**TLC:** *How do you shoot a Manhunter robot with a Kryptonite bullet?*

The effect of inter-company crossovers on the Legion: Laurel Kent becomes a Manhunter in this **Millennium** crossover. From the collection of Miki Annamanthadoo. Legion of Super-Heroes TM and © DC Comics.

**PL:** I don't know.

**TLC:** *Remember the **Millennium** crossover? It sort of contradicted the "Who Shot Laurel Kent?" storyline.*

**PL:** Well, you can still get shot by a Kryptonite bullet.

**TLC:** *But it did put her in the hospital...*

**PL:** Shoot most things with a Kryptonite bullet and it'll end up in the hospital. I'm entirely sure that any thorough rereading of my run will find a variety of contradictions and goofs.

**TLC:** *Did you welcome those intrusions into your own little corner of the DC Universe?*

**PL:** I spent most of my writing career looking for places where I didn't have to pay attention to what the other writers were doing, so it was never fun to do that. On the other hand, those issues tended to sell fairly well, so you made a few extra bucks in royalties, and particularly in my job description, I couldn't exactly throw a snit against company cooperation with my other hat. I understood the economic

importance of it to the business.

**TLC:** *Did you end up keeping any of those new readers?*

**PL:** You never really know for sure, particularly with a book that's already relatively successful. If you've got a book that's failing and you do some kind of stunt like that, you get a trackline that says, "Oh, well, the last batch of issues we had almost no readers, now we have a decent number of them. We gotta assume that's not a coincidence." If you have a successful book, the jumps are likely to be much smaller. Historically, when stunts like that were successful, they had a much more disproportionate effect on the sales of the lower end titles than the high end titles.

**TLC:** *You've mentioned before that you were going to leave the **Legion** with #50, but you were persuaded to stick around another year.*

**PL:** I had a couple of issue numbers in my head at different points that were gonna be where I was gonna wrap up.

**TLC:** *When you did leave, was it a case of you had run out of gas?*

**PL:** No, it was a point that my kids needed me. I didn't leave the **Legion** to do anything else. My kids were five and three at the time, [maybe] a little younger, even, when I made the decision finally to give the book up. We'd moved to the suburbs to give them a better place to live than growing up in the city easily permitted, so I had to commute. Most of my writing was being done on the weekend. I was losing most of three Sundays a month to writing the **Legion**, and my kids were at an age where there was a lot to be done with them. Selfishly, because they were at a magic point that they wouldn't be at again in terms of actually wanting to play with their father, and unselfishly from wanting to be the dad. So I said, "This isn't the time to be doing a

regular body of writing." At the same time, my day job here had gotten successful enough that I couldn't justify to myself that I needed the money. You can always find something to do with a few extra bucks, but it wasn't the difference between any particular lifestyle that we wanted or another, so I just said enough's enough, and I think timed it out so that it would be with the one hundredth issue in a row.

**TLC:** *Did you have a lot of stories left over that you wanted to tell but never got the chance to tell?*

**PL:** I've never been an enormous writer out of inspiration. I'm more a writer out of perspiration, so I'm sure that there were a long list of half-baked ideas, or seeds of ideas, scribbles in my notebook that I would have loved to having gotten around to doing. Explore this character a little more, or that character, see where this relationship was going... but there was nothing sitting there that was, "If only I could get this done." I'd had the chance to work with Curt [Swan] on a couple of big projects, which was a phenomenal treat. He was enormously gentlemanly and tolerant, 'cause he did not like drawing the **Legion** particularly at that time in his

Who shot Laurel Kent? A story which would later have to be reworked in light of the **Millennium** mini-series. From the collection of Miki Annamanthadoo. Laurel Kent and the Legion of Super-Heroes TM and © DC Comics.

career, and still willingly stepped in on those things. I'd had a chance to write the characters that I'd loved. I had a chance to do a long run. It was an honorable time to put the typewriter down.

**TLC:** *Was "The Magic Wars" set up to be your big send-off?*

**PL:** Well, I definitely knew that was set up to be my end, to give me a clean endpoint. Somewhere along the line, Keith came up with the conceit of, "Let's come in after a multi-year gap," so also, at some point, it began to take shape to set that up, as well.

**TLC:** *You mentioned that you didn't read the comic again after you left it until many years later. What was your reaction when you saw the **Legion** again?*

**PL:** We used to do an approach, sort of an editorial review of titles, where you'd read the previous year or whatever of the book, and the four or five of us who had some seniority would sit around with the editor then and toss out our concerns, our criticisms, our suggestions. KC Carlson was editing **Legion** at the time, and I had offered to recuse myself from our doing the **Legion** because I knew that I would have a prejudiced approach. He said, "No, no, no. Please..." So I pulled out my copies and read whatever it was—the four or five years that had been done since my run—in a weekend, and I've used the remark before I don't think I've had a more painful weekend that I didn't spend in a hospital.

But that's a writer's prejudice. These were my kids and somebody else had brought them up. It wasn't necessarily that the stories were by any objective standard bad [or] wrong, they just weren't where I would've gone with those things, and it feels very weird to see somebody else bring your kids up in an utterly different way.

**TLC:** *How much of a role, if any, did you have in the **Legion**'s reboot?*

*Atmos by George Pérez, Courtesy of Spencer Beck.*
Art © 2003 George Pérez; Atmos TM and © DC Comics.

**PL:** None that I can remember.

**TLC:** *Was that another situation where you recused yourself?*

**PL:** With the exception of one lunch with [Dan] Abnett and [Andy] Lanning at one point, and maybe one or two conversations where someone working on the book has been curious about my philosophy of the Legion, I've stayed pretty far away from the title. It's not fair to the guys who are on it. If I wasn't a senior executive of the company with some weight, and I was just a writer and they wanted me to come in and kibitz and argue, fine, but it's not fair to have your boss, or one of your bosses, sitting down and telling you how to do your job in something where it's based on as personal a set of prejudices as writers feel for characters that they've lived with for so many years.

**TLC:** *But do you think that necessarily disqualifies you?*

**PL:** Yeah. I mean, I might be right in everything I believe about it—I certainly think I am—but there's nobody who can objectively say whether I am, and that's not good for process.

**TLC:** *A few years ago the **Legion** was cancelled, then brought back as a mini-series, then brought back as another mini-series, then brought back as a regular series again.*

**PL:** I don't think it was cancelled *per se* as much as sort of replatformed that way.

**TLC:** *If the mini-series had not done well, could there have been a point where the **Legion** could have gone away and stayed away for a while?*

**PL:** It's always possible. I think when you've got a

A page from **Legion of Super-Heroes #300**, showcasing the storytelling team of Levitz and Swan. From the collection of Mike Napolitano. © DC Comics,

book that's had that kind of longevity, it's hard to imagine it going away for any length of time, but you can lose your audience.

**TLC:** *Has there ever been a point past the reboot where DC has considered telling stories which took place before it?*

**PL:** Probably.

**TLC:** *So it's not something which is necessarily written in stone "This will never happen again!"*

**PL:** Nah. I don't think anything like that's ever written in stone in this business.

**TLC:** *Do you think you'll ever write a **Legion** story again featuring your Legion characters?*

**PL:** The guys want me to every couple of years. Keith would love to do one in collaboration. At least once or twice a year, when he pokes his head in, he takes a baseball bat to me about it, and it'd be fun. It's hard to find the time. I didn't write any stories last year. I wrote, I think, two short stories the year before [that]. I don't think there's been a year that I've hit more than eight pages of comics writing in the last seven [years]. I hope to be a full-time writer again at some point in my life, and if the door's still open for it, it would be fun to do some **Legion** work then, but who knows when that day'll be.

**TLC:** *You did write a short **Legion** story a few years ago which took place in the current continuity. [LSH #100 —Ed.]*

**PL:** Yeah. That was a lot of fun.

**TLC:** *Did you have to do a lot of research for that?*

**PL:** Some. Not too much, because I think that KC was still on that book at that point, so it must have been fairly shortly— a year or two years—after I had gone through the exercise of reading all the material, and he asked me to do a very specific thing. It was to set up a particular type of situation that he thought I was a good writer of, that they could then use over a period of issues. So, I think I probably deliberately set it up using characters who had changed relatively little [to] make life a little easier for myself.

**TLC:** *What do you say to the **Legion** fans who have become disenfranchised with the series due to its various retcons and reboots?*

**PL:** You have my total personal sympathy. Me, too.

**TLC:** *Would you care to elaborate?*

**PL:** In the same logic, I'm not reading it as a fan.

**TLC:** *But is that because you used to be a **Legion** writer?*

**PL:** It's hard to tell. You know, is there some version of the **Legion** that might have been a more linear extrapolation from Gerry's, and Ed Hamilton's, and Jim's, and mine that I'd be able to read and have fun with? Maybe. Or it might be that there would be nothing that would make it comfortable for me.

**TLC:** *How high or low is the **Legion** a priority at DC today?*

**PL:** That's kind of a *non sequitur*. Fans, I think, have this image of DC or Marvel as though the company was a living organism with a hive mind. The reality is that most books in the history of the company have been shaped by the people who are actu-

ally working on them. When **Superman** was the rent payer that was the heart and soul of DC economically in the 1960s, on one level you could say that was the company's highest priority, but on another level you could say whatever was done creatively was whatever Mort Weisinger had going on in his room. It wasn't like the staff of DC gathered around to say, "What can we do to help **Superman**?" So it doesn't really relate to how the real world works.

**TLC:** *What did you take away from all your years as a writer?*

**PL:** The enormous fun of people remembering what I did. There's just nothing better then the moment when someone comes up to you who you've never met and starts talking to you about a story you did years ago that mattered to them for one reason or another. Brad Meltzer, who just did that **Green Arrow** series for us, came into visit DC for the first time about a year ago, and Bob Schrek brought him around and introduced him. He started going at me about the twists in the Sensor Girl mystery versus the twists in "The Universo Project," and which were better and why I did this or that. Here was a guy who is a better writer than I am, an accomplished prose writer reaching a large audience, [and] he remembered this stuff from when he was a kid and liked it. The way I told mysteries was interesting enough that it made him think about it in a mind that later turned into a mystery writer. To have been along that trail of somebody's life... Wow! That's just so much fun. Having written is enormously more fun than writing, and having written things that people remember and care about, that's just the greatest stuff.

**TLC:** *Do you look forward to doing that again someday?*

**PL:** I certainly hope so. I have a very good life lesson [in] my high school English teacher, who was Frank McCourt. Here's a guy who didn't start his writing career 'til he was in his sixties, retired from teaching, and goes out there and knocks it out of the park for a Pulitzer Prize on the first book. Frank McCourt led a vastly more interesting life than I've led, and he's an awesome writer who's a great anecdotalist and storyteller as a teacher, so I don't aspire to anything like that, but if he can pull that off as a home run, maybe there's a single out there for me when the day comes.

*This picture is entitled "Long Live the Legion!" and it's easy to see why. From the collection of Mike Napolitano. © DC Comics.*

# Mindy Newell

Back during the "double your pleasure, double your fun" days of the mid-Eighties, producing two monthly **Legion of Super-Heroes** books proved to be more than **Legion** writer Paul Levitz could handle, and so newcomer Mindy Newell was selected to script (and sometimes plot) **Tales of the Legion of Super-Heroes**. Also known for her work on **American Flagg!**, **Catwoman**, and **Wonder Woman**, Newell became the first woman to ever write the **Legion of Super-Heroes**, and her three-part Dawnstar story is still remembered by Legion fans today. On March 8, 2003, Newell was interviewed by Glen Cadigan, and she copyedited the following transcript.

*Two Legion ladies, aptly illustrated by Steve Lightle, courtesy of Steve (Greybird) Reed. Art © 2003 Steve Lightle; Dawnstar and Dream Girl TM and © DC Comics.*

**TLC:** *How did you become interested in writing comics?*

**MN:** I read comics my whole life. I'm forty-nine, so I go back to I guess what's considered the Silver Age. I have a very, very, extremely faint memory of some comics that I had that were ten cents. Most of the comics I really remember first reading were of the twelve cents variety, so I guess that would be the very late Fifties, early Sixties. Like most kids, I discovered DC first, and I'm not really sure why. I remember reading "Superman" in **Action** [**Comics**]. I loved "Supergirl," and I loved "Superboy," and that's where we all discovered the Legion. I was just always a voracious reader, and I had very cool parents who encouraged my reading. They let me read anything I put my hands on, frankly. They never said, "You can't read comics because they're trash." In fact, my uncle [was] a principal in the New York school system, and he told my parents that he thought it was just great that I was reading because comics were a wonderful way for kids to really discover what they called "the joy of reading." Y'know, "Reading is *fun*damental!"? But I was just a natural reader anyway, so it wasn't anything that I was forced to do.

**TLC:** *Which comics where your favorites?*

**MN:** I never read that much Marvel, but I liked **Thor** a lot, because I liked the Asgardian aspects of it. I remember reading **Thor**, and I didn't read all that much **Spider-Man**. I think **Spider-Man** was really geared towards young teenage boys, and maybe that's why I didn't read it. I never really stopped to think about it. You know what's really funny? I hated **Wonder Woman**. That was one of my big things, writing **Wonder Woman** with George Pérez, [because] everybody was going on about how I

was the first woman to write **Wonder Woman**, and at the time when I was a kid, I hated **Wonder Woman** because Diana Prince was such a nerd. I had no interest in reading about Diana Prince whatsoever, so I wouldn't read **Wonder Woman**. I would skip all the Diana Prince parts, and read the pages where Wonder Woman herself appeared. But Diana Prince, there was nothing about her that would appeal to a young girl. She was everything negative about being a little girl right there in print. I mean, she was nerdy, she was whiny, she pined after a man who didn't want her...

I've said this before at comic conventions when I've been on panels with women in comics: when you're reading it, you never think about, and when you get older, you start thinking about things. Someone asked me what I really liked about Supergirl, and I think on some level, the fact that when Supergirl first appeared, she was very young—she was supposed to be twelve or thirteen years old—and she was Superman's secret weapon. She was the one who pulled his ass out of the fire on numerous occasions. When I think about it now, that was a very appealing and positive message to send to little girls. You could be strong and powerful and be the hero. I'm sure that when the writers were writing these stories, nobody was thinking along those psychological lines. They were just telling good tales. I think that was the appeal of Supergirl to me.

**TLC:** *Was there a point when you made a decision to become a comic book writer as opposed to a writer in other forms?*

**MN:** No, I just fell into it, frankly, which is going to be very discouraging to all those people out there who are busting their chops to become comic creators, whether as a writer or an artist. I just completely fell into it. It was just one of those things that, "Well, I guess this was part of the plan." The big plan of Mindy's life was that, "She's a nurse, and she's a single mom, and she's also going to be a comic book writer."

**TLC:** *So how did you break in?*

**MN:** Basically, I had stopped reading comics for a number of years, although I

Speech bubbles in comic panel: "YOU STOLE IT? WHEN? WHERE?" / "LAST NIGHT. IN THE MALL, FROM THE RANGERS." / "BUT WHAT IF THEY COME LOOKING FOR IT?" / "DON'T WORRY, WEEZIE. THEY'VE GOT OTHER PROBLEMS." / "WE'RE GONNA DIE!" / "SHUT UP, RAUL!" / WHUP WHUP KRUP WHUP WHUP WHUP KRUP

*Above: Newell also worked with Howard Chaykin on* American Flagg!. *Below: Another famous Legion couple, also courtesy of Dylan Clearbrook.*
American Flagg! TM and © Howard Chaykin, Inc; Cosmic Boy and Night Girl TM and © DC Comics.

still would like 'em, and I would sort of browse them, but I never actually picked them up. I still loved science-fiction. This is a time period around the time when *Alien* came out, and *Star Wars* came out, and then *Superman* came out, and *Close Encounters*… y'know, that whole period of the late Seventies, very early Eighties. So I was still reading all that stuff, and watching those movies, and reading science-fiction stories. I had just stopped reading comics because, basically, I didn't know where they were. There weren't any real comic book stores that I knew of, and they really weren't around. But anyway, I was working as a nurse, and one lunchtime I went down [to] the hospital's hospitality shop, and lo and behold at this particular hospital, the hospitality shop had this huge array of comics. I mean, everything. They had all the Marvels, all the DCs, [and] I think they even had some First Comics. I think I remember seeing an *American Flagg!* there, if it was out yet. They just had a really good display, and it was just one of those things. I was like, "Wow! Cool, comics!"

So I just picked up a whole bunch of them, and I went back upstairs. I was just sitting in the staff lounge reading them at lunchtime, and I do remember that everybody was grabbing them, going, "Oh my God! I haven't read this in long time!" So there you had all these supposedly very serious, professional people sitting there reading comics. I always thought it would be very funny if the patient who was waiting for her heart surgeon to come out saw him at lunchtime with his nose in *Flash*. She would probably get very nervous.

But anyway, in the DC comics of that month, Dick Giordano used to have an edi-

torial column, and in that particular column he was talking about the new talent program, and how they were looking for writers and artists and yadda yadda. He mentioned in passing what they were looking for. You couldn't use any of the established characters, you had to come up with your own [for] a six- to eight-page story, the whole thing. So I didn't really think too much about it, but it must've been there cookin' under my brain, because a few days later, [or] maybe a week later, it was just a rainy Sunday and I didn't really have too much to do. I just sat down and wrote out this story, and I sent it off. Basically, three weeks later I was sitting in front of Karen Berger at DC—she was the editor of *New Talent Showcase*—and it was the proverbial stone rolling down the hill. It just gathered steam from there.

But I do remember Karen saying to me, "What do you do?" "I'm a nurse." "Did you ever take any writing classes?" I said, "Yeah, y'know, one or two." "Well, do you know what a script looks like?" I liked writing, but I never really did anything professionally—never attempted anything profession-

ally—[and] she's asking me all these questions. "Do you know what a script looks like?" "No." Basically, every answer that you could think of in relating to putting a comic book together, my answer was, "No, no, no, and no." "Do you understand what an artist does? Do you understand what an inker does?" "No." Well, I mean, I could put it together, 'cause I wasn't an idiot, but in terms of [previous knowledge], no, I had no idea. "Do you know what a Marvel style plot is?" "No." "Do you know what a full script is?" "Well, I know what a script is, but I don't know what a full script is." Everything was, "No, no, no, no, no."

Len Wein came into the office while I was there, and I knew his name, but for the life of me, I couldn't remember what he did or who he was. I just kinda knew his name [*laughs*], and so I fudged [it]. I was like, "Oh, Len, it's so nice to meet you, Mr. Wein, and blah blah blah," which Len knows, because I got to be friends with him, and I told him how I lied my ass off when he walked into the office, that I

Art © 2003 Steve Lightle; Cosmic Boy and Night Girl TM and © DC Comics.

really didn't have any idea of who he was. And that's really basically how it started.

So I started doing stories for **New Talent Showcase**, and then Paul Levitz, God bless his soul, came in and asked me to dialogue [his back-ups in **Tales of the Legion**] over his plots. That's how it started. Really, when I stopped to think about it, I was like, "Oh, man, I cannot believe I am writing the adventures of Lightning Lass and Chameleon Boy and Timber Wolf...." It was a real kick! I loved it! I basically just kinda walked around with my [head in the air]. I was just really happy. I was like, "Wow." I was walking around pinching myself all the time, that type of thing. And it just kept steamrolling from there.

TLC: *Did you get a sense then that DC was breaking you in?*

MN: Oh, absolutely! They were absolutely breaking me in. I'm very, very loyal to DC for that reason. I'm not saying that I [have] tunnel vision about DC, or any other corporation. I just will always feel a very, very strong loyalty to DC, and to particular people. To Karen... Karen is Karen, and I love her dearly. I think she's a brilliant editor, and she's a really good friend. Karen and I had this really great relationship where we started out as editor and writer, and then we became friends, but we were always able to put aside the friendship part, and when we were in the office, she was the editor and I was the writer. We could talk business without it interfering with our friendship at all. I think that's one of Karen's special skills, her ability to separate business and friendship and not let the two hurt each other at all. I'll just sit here and sing my praises of Karen for the next half hour. [*laughs*] And also the other person I have to thank is Paul, because if Paul hadn't given me the **Legion**, which was really [what] put me on the map—if I'm on the map at all, it's because of the **Legion**. That was all Paul. That was Paul and Karen.

TLC: *Do you know that you were the first woman to write the **Legion of Super-Heroes**?*

MN: I was? I didn't know that.

TLC: *Do you think being a woman gave you a different perspective on the title?*

MN: My first impulse is to say yes, because I'll be honest; I do naturally drift to women characters when I'm writing. But when I stop and I think about when I actually write the characters, the actual

process of putting words in the mouth of Lightning Lad or Cosmic Boy or Braniac 5 or whoever, there was never a process where I said, "Okay, this is a man talking, so how would a man say this?" To me, first and foremost they were people before I divided them into genders. What I'm saying is that if I have any talent at all, I seem to have this ability to really be able to put down on paper the way everybody naturally talks.

One of the stories I did—this is really embarrassing, because I don't remember the name of it [*"Triangle?"* in **TLSH** #320 —**Ed.**], but it was a little back-up where Sun Boy was, for lack of a better word, the chauvinist of the Legion at the time, and we did this little back-up in **Tales of the Legion** where Gigi Cusimano and Yera set him up. I had a lot of fun writing that story, 'cause whether you're a man or a woman, if you've ever gone into a bar on a Saturday night, you've heard the conversations that went on, you knew the conversations that went on, you participated in those conversations, so I just basically sat down and wrote it. It was real easy for me to write Sun Boy's dialogue because we all know men like that, and frankly, I know women that are bitches, too. So it was just very easy to write that story, and then it was so cool because I found out that it made "Best of DC" for that year. I was like, "Wow!" y'know? It was just a cute little throwaway story, but it was really easy for me to write, because it was just someone who needed a kick in the ass getting his kick in the ass. It could have just as easily been Dream Girl, who a lot of people considered very horny, getting a kick up her ass.

TLC: *The Legion* story you're probably best remembered for

is your three-parter with Dawnstar.

MN: Yeah. [*laughs*] I don't know whether that's a good thing or a bad thing. [*laughs*] I think that was a case of I had great ideas, but I wasn't able to carry through on it all as much as I wanted to. I think that was a case where it wasn't a horrible story, and it certainly wasn't the worst story I ever wrote—believe me, there's one or two others that I kinda wish I had used a pen name [on]—and there was some really, really nice parts of it, that I'm very proud of, [but] I don't think I was ready to do a big three-part story on my own like that, to be honest. I think there was some great ideas in there, but I wasn't completely ready. Paul and Karen helped me enormously, and Paul helped me a lot in the plotting out, but I didn't have the discipline at the time to take all these ideas and hone them down to one thing. It takes

A DC house ad promoting the Legionnaires 3 mini-series. Newell would script all four issues, and would play a part in the plotting, as well. © DC Comics.

*WITHIN THE VOID OF DEEP SPACE:*

*BRAINY, I'VE FOUND THEM!! YOUR MACHINE WORKED!!*

*ELEMENT LAD AND THE OTHERS ARE DOWN ON THAT PLANET! I'M SURE OF IT!!*

A panel from Newell's three-part Dawnstar story, specifically *TLSH #321*. © DC Comics.

discipline. So that's how I feel about it. It was part of my learning experience.

**TLC:** *How did you go from scripting over Paul to plotting and writing yourself?*

**MN:** The Dawnstar trilogy was like the first shot that I got of doing a whole big, three-part story. I'm not really sure, but I guess people in the office thought I was a good writer. I guess I had a pretty good reputation at meeting my deadlines and everything. What might have scared some people off from working with me is that I've never been one to keep my opinions to myself. [*laughs*] That's why I say it was sorta like a stone rolling down a hill and just gathering more and more speed. I guess basically I was pretty good on meeting my deadlines, and even though I was pretty upfront with my opinions—and

I'm still like that. I still pretty much say what I say, and it gets me in trouble sometimes—I guess people just felt, "Let's give her a chance. Let's see what she can do." I guess that's really what it was all about.

I didn't really go out searching. There's the other thing. I think in some ways it was too easy for me, 'cause everything just sort of happened. I mean, I never really took a class in writing. I kinda learned under fire, and I never really sat down and said, "Okay, [this is how you write a story]." Remember I said that my plotting was weak? That's because I think at that time I never really sat down and started from scratch. People would just come up to me and ask, "Would you like to do a story?" I remember Len Wein had "Tales of the Green Lantern Corps," and he said to me, "Would you like to do a story?" and I think by that time I was in the business for about two years, [and] I had gotten a pretty good solid handle on writing eight-page stories, or even one whole comic, but I still needed practice and development in writing an ongoing series. I hadn't reached that point yet. But people were very willing for me to do a fill-in story here and there, and I wasn't gonna say no.

Sometimes I would get an idea for a story, like one line or one scene just kinda pops into your head, or sometimes you see the ending before you see the beginning, and you'd mention it to somebody, and they'd say, "Oh, okay. Work it up into a plot, and we'll see." It was like that kind of a thing. Either someone would approach me, or I would just mention in passing to someone that I had an idea. But pretty much everyone was incredibly encouraging. We all have horror stories to tell, but all in all, I was treated really well while I was freelancing there.

**TLC:** *Wasn't there supposed to be a sequel to that Dawnstar story?*

**MN:** Yeah, there was, and it just kinda fell to the wayside. I think *Tales of the Legion* stopped publishing after a while, and Karen got busier and busier with what I call "proto-Vertigo," so I think it just fell by the wayside. I don't really know whatever happened to it. It might be interesting to do it now. I'd be interested, actually, in

seeing what I could do with it now, 'cause as I said, I feel a lot stronger as a writer these days.

You know what I am really proud of? *Legionnaires 3*. That was really cool. I loved working on that. That was a really fun story to write.

**TLC:** *Was that another series that sort of fell into your lap?*

**MN:** Keith came up with the idea, and you'd have to ask Karen this, but I don't know who suggested me for dialoguing it. I remember Karen saying to me, "Keith has this idea for a *Legion* mini-series, and he wants to work with you on it." I don't know if Keith brought it up, or if Karen suggested it. I'm not really sure what happened, but I ended up [working on it]. Keith is another one who's a very cool guy, and he also is on my list of life-long friends and business associates. It started out originally where Keith was gonna plot the whole thing, and then I was just gonna dialogue over him—which is fine—but I would come up with specifics, so I honestly can't answer that. Keith did the majority of the plotting, but I know that there's stuff in there that I threw in, and he was like, "That's a really good idea. Okay, let's do that," so I'd have to check on the credits of that. I might even have co-plotter status on that. I don't remember.

That was so cool. I loved that story. To me, that was a real space opera, because it had everything. It had family crisis, and mega-villainy, and mega-threat, and for some reason, I just loved running Lighting Lad through the ringer. The poor boy, he just [*laughs*]... you know, it all started when he lost his arm. Ever since then, he's never really got back his balls. [*laughs*]

**TLC:** *What's the difference between working with Keith and working with Paul?*

**MN:** Let's see: I found them both really cool to work with. Keith is all over the place. Talking with Keith when he's on a roll plotting, and he's getting all excited and his eyes light up and everything, it's like talking with someone who's dropped a hit of acid. [*laughs*] I don't mean that in a bad way, I just mean that he's just really...

**TLC:** *Animated.*

**MN:** Animated, yeah. Whereas Paul is as thorough, and gets as excited, but he's quieter about it. I'm not saying that Paul doesn't get excited. Obviously, he wouldn't have written the *Legion* for like twenty years if he didn't love the book, but he was just quieter about it. Keith was just very animated. I can't think of another word off the top of my head [that's] the opposite of animated. You take the total opposite of animated and it makes it sound like Paul's a stick in the mud, and he's not.

**TLC:** *He's more laid back.*

**MN:** Laid back, yeah. [*laughs*] To keep the drug analogy—which I'm sure you're gonna love to use, and I'll probably hear about it—talking to Keith is like talking to someone who dropped a hit of acid, and Paul's more like he's smoked a big doobie. He's just real laid back, man. [*laughs*]

**TLC:** *And, of course, you're saying all this in your capacity as a nurse.*

**MN:** [*laughs*] And by the way, I don't do drugs anymore. [*laughs*] I haven't done any drugs in like twenty years. [*laughs*] Kids! Don't do drugs! This is not an advertisement for drugs! [*laughs*] Drugs don't help you write! [*laughs*]

But to me, that's like a great way to describe it, y'know? It's not that Paul's not excited about it, but he's just more laid back. That's exactly it. So that was the difference. And poor Karen was like the cops at Woodstock [*laughs*], trying to keep control of 500,000 stoned out people. [*laughs*] And she did a very good job, too. [*laughs*] But that was really the only difference, the way they reacted when they knew they were on to a good thing. That was it. I never found either of them [were], "No, I'm the boss here, and this is how you're gonna write it." Neither one of them ever gave me anything like that at all. In fact, all I heard from them was praise, to be honest.

**TLC:** *When you're scripting over someone else's plot, how hard is it to put your own stamp on it?*

**MN:** Not hard at all, because—boy, this sounds so egotistical—but before you put words in the characters' mouths to make them come alive, they're cyphers. They're pretty pictures on bristol board. When I sat down to write something, I never thought about, "Oh, I have to live up to Keith's aspirations, I have to live up to Paul's aspirations." Well, maybe a little bit that was in the back of my mind. If I actually had to be totally honest, maybe that was in the back of my mind a little bit. But that was not there in the forefront at all. Really, when I would sit down to write it, I would read the plot, and it was like watching a movie

without sound. Then when I would sit down to write it, when you're really lucky—and I'm one of those lucky people, because it happens more often than not for me—it's like you're watching the movie on the screen and you're transcribing it as you go along. You just hear them talking to each other, and you're like the secretary, and you're just writing down really fast what they're saying. So no matter who I wrote over, whether it was plot over Keith or over Paul, with the ***Legion*** I guess I just, having read the book for years and years and years and knowing these characters so well and everything else, I could just sit down and it was like I would see a scene and I could hear them in my head talking, and it was the characters speaking, not Paul or Keith. It was them, and I would basically just transcribe it.

It makes it sound so easy. Of course I would sit there and reread it and say, "That's not quite exactly what Garth Ranzz said. I have to change it." So it's not like I wrote it down and I never rewrote it. I'm just saying that the process was the characters speaking and not Paul or Keith speaking.

**TLC:** *Are there any scenes which stand out in your mind where you put something in it which wasn't there? You know, it wasn't in the plot when you got it, but it was in the script after you left?*

**MN:** Yeah, I felt like with ***Legionnaires 3***, even though I was ostensibly hired to dialogue over Keith's plot, I was so involved in the book—and I can't remember exactly places where this happened—but there were things where [I said], "This is what [happens here]." There was one or two scenes where, when Keith wrote the plot, and then I handed the script in, Keith'd say, "Well, that's not what I meant, but this is great. She put a different spin on what they were saying," [and] it stayed, because it worked so well.

But I think that relates to what I was saying before, about how when I sat down to write a plot, whether it was by Paul or Keith, it wasn't Paul or Keith telling me what to write, it was the characters themselves who would take over. I think you speak to any writer, and I don't care if it's a comic book writer or a novelist, or a screenwriter, to some extent the characters themselves take over, and you start hearing their voices in your head. It's like the character gets to a fork in the road, and in your head when you thought about the scene and everything and wrote the plot out, the character is gonna take the

left fork. Well, the character gets to the fork, and he says, "F*ck you, I'm taking the right fork." You can't do anything but go along.

I said to John [Higgins] the other day, "Writers are like controlled schizophrenics," 'cause you hear all these voices in your head. It just flows right through you.

So there are definitely scenes in ***Legionnaires 3***, like the scene where they discover that the Time Trapper's taken the baby. That was one page where it just came right out of me. Maybe that came from being a mom myself—but Keith is a dad, and Paul's a dad, so I'm sure they could have written it just as well—but because I was a mother, and being a nurse, and having worked with abused kids, maybe that's where it all came from, 'cause originally—I may be wrong on this, but originally I think that Saturn Girl was supposed to be really, really strong, 'cause she was like the Iron Butterfly. "Oh, we're going after him, and f*ck the Time Trapper," y'know? And if I remember correctly, she breaks down and just cries in Garth's arms, and I remember saying, "I don't care how strong a person you are. I don't care if you're the first woman President of the United States. [If] your kid is kidnapped, you're gonna be a mess. You'll regroup, but your first impulse is gonna be, your whole world is destroyed, and you are gonna be an emotional

© DC Comics.

mess." So I remember that I did rewrite that scene that way. And everybody loved it, and they said "Okey-dokey. No problem." And I think it worked.

**TLC:** *You wrote the text pages for that mini-series. Didn't you also write the letters page for* **Tales***?*

**MN:** Yeah, I did the letters page for **Tales**, and I did the text pages for **Legionnaires 3**. That was a lot of fun. I loved doing that. I love talking to people. I think one of the biggest mistakes DC has done is dropping the letters column. I cannot understand how they did that. I just don't get it. With comics facing so much competition these days in getting kids attention, one of the best ways to capture and to keep the kids' attentions— [and] I don't mean kids only, but adults also. [I'll] use fans. That's a better word—is to have a dialogue. Give a feeling to the fan that there's a dialogue going between the creators and the reader. It involves the reader so much more, and it helps continue the process of them being readers, and being involved in comics. I totally, totally disagree with that move, and like I said, this goes back to my understanding the corporate bullsh*t. I'm not even in the business anymore, except in a very, very, very ancillary way, but I could probably give you, right now, five reasons why they did it, and it all comes down to finances. I can understand that completely, but it doesn't mean that I have to agree with it.

But yeah, I loved writing those pages, and I loved getting the letters. I would say that ninety percent of the letters were very positive about what I was doing, and who doesn't need an ego boost like that? It's great! Plus, as I said, I always had a big mouth, and then Karen says, "Here, I want you to write the text pages for four issues," and here I had two pages to mouth off. [*laughs*] So yeah, I loved writing the text pages. They were just really [great]. I guess I am a writer. I guess I just like putting words down on paper.

**TLC:** *Did you have much contact with the artists with whom you were working?*

**MN:** Well, I did with Keith, because he lived in the New York City area, which I do, too. So he would go into the office all the time, so I would see the pages, and I would see Keith and stuff. When I was writing the Dawnstar trilogy, I don't

*Every parent's worst nightmare, as depicted by Keith Giffen, Ernie Colón, and Karl Kesel. From a suggestion by Newell.*
© DC Comics.

remember talking to the artist very much. I think Karen was basically the go-between, if I remember correctly. I met Dan [Jurgens] later on, but Dan doesn't live in the New York area. I did meet him when he came in. We got along, no problems at all, but while I was writing Dawnstar, I honestly don't remember if I spoke to him or whether Karen, as the editor, was the go-between. Keith was a different story

because we both live in the New York area, and more often than not we'd hook up at the office. So that was an entirely different situation.

**TLC:** *When did you stop following the* **Legion** *as a reader?*

**MN:** Probably three or four years ago. I know the last time I was reading it regularly, Tom Peyer was still writing it.

**TLC:** *So you kept reading it for a good long while.*

**MN:** Yeah, I did. And then I think I kinda lost interest in it when they started drifting away. This is gonna sound like I'm an old fart [who's] not into new things, which isn't true at all, but I kinda drifted away from all comics at the exact same time. So that might've been maybe '96, '97. I'd say from about '97 to 2001 I didn't read any comics at all, and then starting late 2001, 2002 I started reading one or two again. I started reading **Promethea** and I think I came in on the tail end of **Preacher**, but I wasn't reading a lot, and it's really only in the past six months now that I've started reading again. Even though I go once a month and get the whole big stack and then come home and read it, I'm still not reading them in any kind of regularity again. I haven't picked up the **Legion**. This is why I'm saying that maybe I sound like an old fart, but from what I've seen of it, it's changed so much from what I remember, it doesn't feel like the **Legion** to me anymore. "Well, in my day..." y'know? "They don't make 'em like they used to." But for some reason, I just feel like the characters now... I can't even say it fairly, because I haven't picked it up in so long, but I think when I heard about the new reboot, I was sort of like, "Again? I can't believe they're rebooting it again. How many times are they gonna reboot it?" I don't know. There was just something in me that just was like tired of reboots, and I don't really know [why].

I can't give you a real yes or no, and now I'm feeling terribly guilty, and I'm going to go down and buy like the last five issues of the **Legion**, and call you up and say, "Hey Glen, add a little P.S.: Mindy started reading the **Legion** again and she really loves it!" [*laughs*] I don't know. Maybe I just outgrew it? Who knows? I just don't know why I'm not reading the **Legion** anymore. It does have something to do with the reboot, but it may have something to do with I just lost interest in it. I still love the idea of the Legion and all that, but it's done for me. I don't know, but I promise I will go check it out and see if I enjoy it. I do promise that.

**TLC:** *When you were writing the **Legion**, who were your favorite characters to write?*

**MN:** Like I said before, I definitely found myself inclining towards the women generally, and I also did love beating up on poor Garth Ranzz. I don't know why. Like I said, it's just something about the poor boy.

He's like a schnook. You know when you want to hit a wimp and say, "Stop being such a wimp!" [*laughs*] That kinda thing?

I loved writing the originals. I loved writing all the characters that I grew up on, the ones that were in the yellow rocketship headquarters. So, of course, right away that's Saturn Girl, Cosmic Boy, and Lighting Lad. I loved Cosmic Boy. This is gonna sound incredibly geeky, but I remember as a kid I thought he was so handsome. [*laughs*] I always did go for those dark-haired types. Maybe that's why I didn't like Garth, because redheads have never done anything for me. [*laughs*] Cosmic Boy always seemed to me to be the mature one, the really smart one, still-waters-run-deep type of guy? So I always liked writing him.

I loved writing Sun Boy because he was such an arrogant, cocky son-of-a-bitch. He was a lot of fun. I liked writing Lightning Lass, and Brainiac 5 was actually kinda tough for me to write, because he was this genius guy, and it was very hard for me to imagine how he sounded. Was he like Spock on **Star Trek**, or afraid to show his emotions? I tried to write him in a very stilted, scientific method type of characterization, and that's kind of boring to me.

I liked writing the odd ones, like Bouncing Boy. The ones in the Legion of Substitute Heroes [*laughs*], because they were like the Avis "We try harder!" type of things. When you're growing up and you're playing basketball or softball, they were always the last ones chosen. [*laughs*] So I always kind of liked writing them because I always liked to show that, "Yeah, he's a real nerd, but y'know what? He's gonna grow up to be Bill Gates," you know what I mean?

**TLC:** *Do you think that your time on the **Legion** opened many doors for you?*

**MN:** Oh, absolutely. Without a

doubt. They talk about the tripods of DC being Superman, Batman and Wonder Woman. I actually think it's not a tripod, it's a cube, or a square, if you're thinking two-dimensionally. I think the Legion of Super-Heroes is part of that premier echelon that helped build up DC. At least that's my personal opinion. That might just be speaking purely as a fan, but I really believe that.

**TLC:** *Did you have many **Legion** stories in you that you never got a chance to tell?*

**MN:** Sure. Have them call me right now. [*laughs*] The trouble is, the **Legion** stories that I would tell, that Legion doesn't exist anymore. So the first thing I would have to do is immerse myself in the Legion of today and see if any of the stories that I had in mind for Duo Damsel or whoever would be right for the characters as they are now, and then approach the editor. That's the only thing that I can think of. All the stories that I think about, I guess they take place on Earth-2 these days. [*laughs*] And I know Earth-2 doesn't exist, so no wisecracks. [*laughs*]

**TLC:** *You've collaborated with some pretty big names throughout your career. You've worked with Paul and Keith, and you've also worked with George Pérez. Did you learn something new from each person?*

**MN:** Absolutely. Actually, this doesn't really have that much to do with writing, *per se*, but on a personal viewpoint: I was talking with George one day, and I think I mentioned that I was a single mother, and George said to me—I don't even know in what context this came up, but he said to me, "You're a super-hero." I said, "Whatd'ya mean, I'm a super-hero?" and he said, "Because you're a single mother, and in my opinion, all the single mothers are the super-heroes of the world." And I was like, "Wow! Thank you, George!" My first impulse was to laugh it off, but in truth, it really kind of nestled in me, and when things were tough, I honestly used to remember him saying that to me. So that's not like a writing thing, but it certainly was a great help to me.

As far as writing, George's pencils were so incredible. I would look at the boards, and I know I said before about how I sit down and the characters are just talking and I transcribe it, but when you have magnificent artwork like George gives you, where the characters [are] like photographs, it just made it so much easier to write, because I knew exactly what George was thinking as he drew that grimace on Diana's face. I knew exactly what he was

*From the collection of Dylan Clearbrook.*

Art © 2003 Steve Lightle. Sun Boy and Gigi Cusimano TM and © DC Comics.

thinking. It just made it so incredible, so I guess one thing I learned from him is that great art can save a bad writer, but a good writer cannot save lousy art. In other words, it truly is a visual medium, so that you are dependent, to some extent as a writer, on the artist's skills of portraying what's happening. So that's what I learned from George, both on a personal level and on a professional level.

**TLC:** *Did you make a decision to stop writing comics, or did you just sort of phase it out?*

**MN:** What happened was that I was hired at Marvel as an assistant editor, and one thing about Marvel at the time, to some extent it was a really incestuous boy's club. It was very, very hard for me to get [writing assignments]. I mean, Ralph Macchio was great. Ralph was very open to me doing some writing and stuff, but I found it very difficult to get any writing done at Marvel. And then, of course, once I was on staff at Marvel I couldn't do freelancing for anybody else, so as I became more involved with the editing side of it, I wasn't doing as much writing. The old Marvel, frankly, was a very incestuous boy's club. There were a few women writing there, but the way they handled their writers was very different from DC.

*Dawnstar by George Pérez, courtesy of Spencer Beck.*
Art © 2003 George Pérez; Dawnstar TM and © DC Comics.

Maybe it's also because I work full-time and I make a very, very nice salary working as a nurse. I love being a nurse. I really enjoy it. I came back to it after like a ten year break, so I'm really enjoying it. When you don't have the wolf at the door, it can be very freeing in one way as a writer, because you can really work hard and feel like, "I'm gonna write until I feel it's right," and I don't have to worry about "Hurry up and get it in so I can get paid, so I can buy some food." On the other hand, it's destructive because you do have a regular paycheck coming in, so you don't have that impetus of, "I don't feel like writing today, but I have to write because that's my job. If I don't write, I don't get paid." So it's definitely a double-edged sword of working full-time and trying to be a writer on the side, 'cause it's real easy to procrastinate.

But in the past year or so, something has come alive again in me—whether it's this egotistical need to see my name in print, or whether it's all of a sudden I have all these stories in my head again that I want to tell—and I have started writing again. So far the only thing that John and I have sold is the one [story] to **2000 AD**. We do have something in at Marvel, but I'm not even gonna talk about that because it's on somebody's desk. I do know that it passed one desk and got passed on to someone else's desk with a recommendation, but it could be another six months before

I hear something about it. So that's about as far as I'm gonna go with that.

**TLC:** *What did you take away from all your years in comics?*

**MN:** Great times, great friends, great memories. I sound like a Kodak commercial [*laughs*], but it's true. I'd have to say that the time where I was really into comics and doing a lot of writing, and was in the office at least twice a month, maybe more, up at DC, [was great]. I flew all over the place. I flew all over the United States. I met people that are still my friends, and, in fact, I met John in 1989 when I went to London for UKCAC—'cause I had just written **Catwoman**, so that's when I met John—and twelve years later, John and I are [*sing-song voice*] in love. [*laughs*] So who knows? Comics turned out to be a major, major part of my life in ways that, frankly, as they say in comics, "I could never have foreseen!" [*laughs*] And I loved it. It's a lotta fun. It's an exciting industry to be in. It changed my life, literally. It literally changed my life.

*Newell also scripted the origin of the White Witch, who appears here from the collection of Dylan Clearbrook.*
Art © 2003 Steve Lightle; White Witch TM and © DC Comics.

# Terry Shoemaker

A relative unknown when he was chosen to replace Keith Giffen on **Tales of the Legion of Super-Heroes** in 1984, Terry Shoemaker was one of the first graduates of DC's new talent program. He would go on to illustrate a variety of titles in the industry, including **X-Factor**, **Strange Tales**, and the **New Mutants**. Still living in California, Shoemaker was interviewed by Glen Cadigan on April 14, 2003, and he copyedited the following transcript.

**TLC:** *How did you become involved with DC's new talent program?*

**TS:** [By] reading DC comics and seeing that they were having a talent search. I sent some of my work in, [and] they sent me out a script of "Class of 2064" [**New Talent Showcase #'s 7-8 —Ed.**]. I still have all of that stuff. It still holds up.

**TLC:** *Had you done anything in comics before that?*

**TS:** Actually, I had been drawing for a company in Newfoundland [which published] a TV guide. They wanted to create their own Newfoundland super-hero characters. That's where I got my start. Myself and my brother were [telling our parents] that we were going to college, signing up for classes and not actually going. Instead, we were going to the library to draw. Well, our parents found out that we weren't taking classes, and they told us we had to get jobs. We opened up the newspaper, and I think it was that week or the next week [that] there was an ad looking for somebody to create super-hero characters. I thought, "That's odd!" That was a stroke of luck.

So we both sent our stuff in, and submitted it for work. We got invited to [the publisher's son, G. Scott Stirling's] house. I walked into his home, and he's got every comic book that was ever printed that month laying all over the floor. It seemed to me like he had a whim to say, "I'm gonna create super-hero comics!" He was interested in creating comic books that could be printed in their TV guide. He was starting this business, and he's trying to learn about how to do this. Myself and my brother were lucky enough to get chosen. I was drawing something called "The Golden Gladiator."

**TLC:** *Did it ever see print?*

**TS:** Yeah, I think it was about a year's worth of TV guides, which is about fifty-four pages. And it was fun. I was drawing my own character, and that character happened to be me. [*laughs*] That's how I got started. That's where I learned how to tell a story, really. I used to do it just for fun, creating these stories about myself and my friends having these wild adventures. I actually worked for the **Newfoundland Herald** for a year before I got a job offer with a regular company. We were only doing a page a week, and I forget how much he was paying us for drawing, writing, and inking. Basically, we were doing it for exposure. I appreciated the money, but it wasn't that much. [*laughs*]

I accepted a regular job at a place that I had been copying my work at. I'd taken it in to get statted, and I had the president of the company come up to me once and ask me if I wanted a job. I thought he was joking. "Oh, they're just making fun of the comic boy," [*laughs*] and when I came back again, he made the same offer. So, myself and my brother both got hired to work for this company, and we worked for [it] for a year and a half, and it was pure hell. [*laughs*] It was a good reminder of just how bad it can be if you've got a regular job. That's gonna sound like I'm spoiled—which I probably am [*laughs*]—but it was a year and a half of hell, and when the company moved to Florida, we stayed behind. We got on unemployment for a year and a

*Shoemaker's first published work, The Golden Gladiator, from May, 1980.* Golden Gladiator TM and © 1980 Apache Communications International.

*A recent sketch of Legionnaires by Shoemaker, courtesy of the artist.*
All characters TM and © DC Comics.

DC Comics, Inc.

*Above: the second page of Shoemaker's three page **Legion** try-out. Below: the published page, as illustrated by Keith Giffen.*
The Legion of Super-Heroes TM and © DC Comics.

half, back when everyone was unemployed in the Eighties, and I figured I had until my unemployment checks ran out to get into the business. That's pretty much how it went. They kept extending the unemployment benefits because everybody was unemployed, and I finally got work accepted through Marvel and DC at the same time. I think I sent in two or three packages [before I got accepted].

I thought it was a sign when I was in trouble and needed a job that that week there just happened to be an ad for this particular thing and we happened to get it. In both respects, I got recognized for my ability to draw by [Stirling], and also by DC, when I moved on. Actually, that stuff, [because] it's my own character, and "Class of 2064," I'm probably the most proud of, other than the **Legion**. All those pages that I have from then I kept, 'cause I knew that was the start of my career. And it's fun to look back, 'cause then you think, "Oh, man," [laughs], "I've improved somewhat."

**TLC:** *Weren't you the first graduate of DC's new talent program?*

**TS:** I don't know. I think I was, or one of them. The thing was, they stopped doing **New Talent Showcase** [because] they were running out of talent. Otherwise, it would have been a great idea, especially nowadays. It's probably something that they should relaunch, considering [that] there's more of an interest in the field, and there's a lot more people drawing.

**TLC:** *When did you become aware that they were looking for someone to draw the **Legion**?*

**TS:** I didn't know until the last second. When myself and my brother started drawing when I was twelve, we collected **Legion**. They were the coolest kids in the universe, and they were the first ones that we drew. My brother challenged me to draw one of the **Legion** characters, [and] that's when I started drawing. I personally didn't have an interest in drawing, but I was interested in the challenge. I've been drawing **Legion** characters since I was twelve. You probably hear from a lot of people who've worked on the book, "I'm the biggest **Legion** fan." I never knew there were so many people interested in these characters, or the book, until just recently when I started doing cons again, and people were asking for the pages.

**TLC:** *Didn't you have to audition for that job?*

**TS:** Yeah, I did. I did three sample pages, which I thought were awful when I sent them in, but they liked them. And when I started doing the book, they had me work through Keith Giffen's thumbnails for the first three issues. So there was a transition. I was slated to do twelve issues, and it was my first book. I looked on the newsstand [when it came out], and I was like, "Man, it's great! I started drawing **Legion**, and now I've got a book on the stand." I

picked it up and I opened it, and this happens a lot with artists, especially ones who are just starting out, [but] they take the art very personally. What I found out when I went to the newsstand [was] they had changed some faces on some of my characters. [They had] adjusted them. They had told me that they wanted a little more expression, [and] I think that's 'cause Giffen was working on the book, and he's really comical, in a way, in his approach to working with the characters. Mine tends to be more subtle. So I was told that I should draw a bit more extreme faces, and I started to, but they had changed some of the faces in the first issue, and not told me about it. [laughs]

Art is a very personal thing. It's the only thing I was doing, and I took it too personally. I called up Karen Berger on a Sunday night—I wasn't even aware of the time difference, [so] it was like two o'clock in the morning—and I quit. [laughs] That's the only regret that I have in my career, that I didn't finish out the twelve issues, because the **Legion** is so much fun to draw. I never knew as a young person how important these characters were to me until I got a little older and got a little more perspective on it. I'd draw **Legion** today right now, and it's probably the only book I collect right now. I would love to draw the book again. **Legion** has always been my one big regret. If I had just waited twenty-four hours and thought about it, I

© DC Comic

would have never called her, and I would have stuck it out and done the rest of the issues. Working on the book had been incredible.

**TLC:** *Didn't DC fly you in when you first got the job?*

**TS:** Yeah, they did. They showed me around the studios, and it was great. I was kind of in shock that I was actually there, and that people were actually going to pay me to draw.

**TLC:** *Were you aware of how popular the* **Legion** *was when you took over?*

**TS:** No, I didn't. I knew that there was what was described as a small, loyal "legion" that followed the book, but I never knew how important it was. I only knew how important it was to me. It always struck me on a personal level that this was a book that was enjoyable, but I never really considered that there was how many other people following this book.

**TLC:** *When you first got the assignment, what was your approach to it?*

**TS:** That I didn't know what the hell I was doing, and that I was gonna do whatever Giffen and Karen wanted me to do. I wish I had a little more confidence where I would've changed some things, not stuck so precisely to his thumbnails, because when I look at the last three issues, which are totally mine, I can see my style of storytelling, and it's just a lot of fun. Giffen's stuff was great, too, but his approach is more extreme, and my approach [is more subtle]. My biggest pleasure in working in comic books is expressing relationships between people. Every opportunity I had to show some kind of affection between the Legionnaires, I'd take advantage of that. That's been true throughout my career. I can think of every pivotal point where there's been an emotional scene between two characters where I thought it had an impact on the book, and that would be true with "Class of 2064," where at the very end, the daughter hugs her father. I think that's what impressed Karen as far as me working on the book.

**TLC:** *Did you deal exclusively through Karen, or did you speak with the book's plotters personally?*

**TS:** I'm not very good over the phone. I've always had difficulty calling people up or being caught off-guard, so I've never learned to network. In fact, I used to work with Bobbie Chase for a number of years at Marvel, and she was the only person I got work through [at] Marvel. Since she's [left] I really haven't called Marvel for any work, even though I know it's probably there, and I know if I ask for it enough, I'd probably get it. But I [also] know there's a lot of artists out there that are struggling right now because of a cutback in book titles. I'm sure that's changing now.

**TLC:** *Were you influenced by any former* **Legion** *artists?*

**TS:** When Curt Swan was drawing it, [he] was my favorite artist at DC. I tried

© DC Comics.

to emulate him, because there was a certain softness, or realism, to his work between characters. So that was an influence. All the retro stuff, all the costumes that [Dave] Cockrum designed and when Mike Grell was doing the book? That's when myself and my brother were collecting it as teenagers, and that only added to the legend of the Legion. It was kind of comforting and fun to have Curt Swan doing it, and it's just great stuff, but then suddenly Dave Cockrum came along and he designed all these costumes, and the characters came to life. And then there was Mike Grell, who didn't know anything about anatomy, but his stuff was supercool. Even I could tell that. You had these incredible artists, and it's just a fun book to follow. I think that's part of the reason anybody would kill to get on the book. I had no idea that was the case when I was [doing it]. I just knew that I had a childhood dream that was coming true.

**TLC:** *So you didn't see yourself as a link in the chain?*

**TS:** I thought part of the reason why they chose me [was] my style was kind of cartoony, and was kind of close to Giffen in a way. So I didn't think of myself as a link in a chain, no. I thought of myself as a pinch-hitter. You know, you can't compare yourself to Curt Swan or Dave Cockrum or Mike Grell, or even James Sherman. I actually met James Sherman in a studio with Walt Simonson and Howard Chaykin when I had switched over from DC and quit the **Legion**, [when I] moved over to Marvel, and

*Above: the third page of Shoemaker's three page* **Legion** *try-out. Top: the published page, as illustrated by Keith Giffen.*
The Legion of Super-Heroes TM and © DC Comics.

that was a big thrill. Here's a guy who draws the way I like to draw, which is more close emotional moments between characters, and not so much the *Rambo* stuff. There was a connection [there], and I think a lot of people feel that connection. Assuming you're a teenager and you're reading the book, you want to feel like you belong, and here are a group of characters that accept anybody. The majority of them are all white [*laughs*], [but] you've got to remember when they were created. I kind of miss the old Legion in a lot of ways.

**TLC:** *Did you get a chance to draw all the Legionnaires which you wanted to draw?*

**TS:** It's kind of hard to complain about not being able to draw a certain *Legion* character when you know you got a chance to draw all these other characters, like Mon-El and the original Invisible Kid. It's easier for me to focus on all the characters that I got a chance to draw. Now that I think about that, yeah, there's a couple that I do want to draw. They're my favorites, and a lot of [other] people's: Ultra Boy and Phantom Girl. I've got a lot of drawings of them around the house because they seemed like a stable couple. I always thought of Ultra Boy and Phantom Girl as having a natural chemistry. They'd sit together, and they would fight on a superficial level. So they're my favorite characters. I don't know if I actually got the chance to draw Ultra Boy, but how can you complain when I drew twenty-seven of the other ones? I still draw them today, and I get fun out of it.

**TLC:** *Do you draw them at conventions or do you draw them as commissions?*

**TS:** I haven't started drawing them as commissions. I would love to do commission pieces for people who want their

favorite character drawn, but unfortunately every time I draw a *Legion* character, I keep it for myself [*laughs*], 'cause I'm a big fan. I love the Legion, and when I sit there and I draw a character, it doesn't matter that I've drawn it, it's the fact that it's the Legion. I'm always impressed that I can do it. When you think about it, when I'm ninety or whatever, if I can still sit down and draw a Legion character, that's the meaning of life. I've worked on a number of stuff throughout the years, and [it's] always been one of my favorite books. It's the start of everything.

**TLC:** *Which aspects of the job did you enjoy more than others?*

**TS:** I guess just drawing the Legion, drawing the characters interacting between each other. I'm looking at the stuff where Mon-El's battling in a city in the sand, fighting these invaders [*TLSH #318* —**Ed.**], and that was fun. Him throwing things around, getting to use his super-powers, going mad and flying through space, all that stuff was fun. When I really think about it, the greatest pleasure I got out of drawing the Legion was showing them interrelating with each other. Close moments.

When you think about it, with Curt Swan you got the PG version of the Legion, and I don't really think that's a truthful way of presenting the characters. I think even today when you look at the characters, they're too clean-cut. It's too unrealistic. It's almost like watching *Star Trek*, and you're sitting there [thinking], "This is great, and I love it," but at the same time, it's devoid of any sort of sexuality. I think that's an injustice to the characters. It doesn't have to be lude or explicit or anything like that, but on a more realistic, more emotional level. I can see them not wanting to do that while they're out there fighting and saving the world, but behind closed doors, I would think that all this battling and all this combat would make them closer instead of at each other's throats.

**TLC:** *You were one of the last artists to draw Supergirl before she died in* **Crisis.** *Is that something that you're glad you got a chance to do?*

**TS:** Absolutely. My only problem with drawing Supergirl is the fact that she had that headband. That costume always freaked me out. Even when I was working on the book, I was looking at stuff and I was saying, "This is awful. This needs to be changed." Like in that issue where they had the Dark Circle [*TLSH #315* —**Ed.**], I always thought that could've been a little less campy, perhaps developed along the way a little more. But being an artist who was just starting out, I really didn't have the confidence to take any chances in changing any designs. I certainly had a lot of fun telling the story when they let loose the reins. I always considered myself [to be] a good storyteller in the first place because of my previous work, but since I was supposed to do twelve issues, they wanted a smooth transition from Keith Giffen's work to mine. It was done for the fans, mostly.

**TLC:** *You even managed to squeeze in an issue with the Substitute Heroes.*

**TS:** Oh, yeah, isn't that great? You know, all your life you read about these charac-

*Left: a convention sketch of Mon-El, courtesy of Steve Mohundro. Top: more recent Legion sketches, courtesy of the artist. All Legionnaires TM and © DC Comics.; art © 2003 Terry Shoemaker.*

*Above: A gathering of Legionnaires, featuring Superboy. Below: Shoemaker's favorite Legion couple, Ultra Boy and Phantom Girl.*
All art © 2003 Terry Shoemaker; all characters TM and © DC Comics.

ters who are losers [*laughs*], but they're heroes in their hearts. And here's Cosmic Boy, who is one of the founding fathers of the Legion, and he's dating somebody who isn't on his level. I'm not trying to bag on her or anything like that; you just feel a little sympathy for her and those characters. I always thought that was kind of cool, especially when you don't focus on the powers, you focus on the relationship.

**TLC:** *What was the coordination between the two monthly* **Legion** *comics?*

**TS:** That is something that Karen Berger would know about. I don't think there was any. There wasn't any connection between the two books as far as I know, storyline wise.

**TLC:** *So you weren't told specifically, "Don't draw this character because they're in the other issue?"*

**TS:** No.

**TLC:** *Did you get the impression back then that DC was breaking you in on the title?*

**TS:** When I broke into the business, I got offers from both Marvel and DC to work for

them, and I went specifically with DC because they had offered me the book that I grew up on, the book that I wanted to draw. It wasn't an issue of money. I was offered more money at Marvel. It was an issue of, "I'll probably never get this opportunity again," and I wish I'd written that down on my desk. But I look back at those pages now and I'm very proud of the work I did. Hopefully one day in the future I'll get to do a fill-in issue or something. I was trained for this job. [*laughs*]

**TLC:** *After you left the* **Legion**, *you pretty much worked for Marvel exclusively.*

**TS:** Well, I think I had burned a bridge with DC. I was embarrassed. I had reacted out of inexperience, and made it too personal. Instead of thinking on a business level, I took it personally that they had changed my faces. And it wasn't the fact that they changed them, it was the fact they didn't tell me they were gonna do it. So when I picked up that first issue on the stands, I overreacted, and you know the rest.

**TLC:** *Did you ever get a chance to mend fences with the people at DC?*

**TS:** Yeah, I did. I did actually apologize. I think I've apologized twice to Karen about that, and she kind of laughs about it, but at the time I'm sure it wasn't funny. [*laughs*] She gave me the sense that this was normal, and after talking to other artists, it is kind of normal to react badly, because art is such a personal thing that a lot of young people make that kind of a mistake. That doesn't make the regret any worse on my part, but there's always hope for the future. I certainly can still draw the characters for fun.

**TLC:** *What's your take*

on the business today compared to when you first broke in?

**TS:** When I started in the business, I always got the feeling that the comic book industry was more of a family kind of thing. Now that it's got more exposure, and the people who originally read the books have grown up and have the monetary means to buy their childhood back, the interest in comics and characters has become almost nostalgic, in a way.

I think there's a better understanding of how the industry works today. When I started, it was a mystery. I drew comic books as a kid, and I never thought of it as a job, because that's for the people who work in New York. Now it's a lot easier. There's more exposure of the material, and there's also a lot of pressure to draw well. So in a way, you're always an art student. You're always improving and trying to take your work to another level. At the same time, that makes it more time consuming to do a page, and that's what slowed down the industry. It took forever to do these incredible pages. That's what Image was all about, and that's how they failed. They created this incredible work that very few people could match, and if they did, they took a lot of time doing it. That sunk their boat. They couldn't get stuff out on time or a regular basis, and the fan base lost interest.

But that's the thing about comic books. It's kind of a double-edged sword. The comic books I used to read, I could buy ten or fifteen of them at a time. Now you've got [a situation] where you can only buy one or two with the same amount of

*Above and below: more panels from* **The Golden Gladiator**, *featuring Shoemaker himself in the title role.* Golden Gladiator TM and © 1980 Apache Communications International.

money. But the work is incredible. I've never seen work like this before. Part of the fun of being in this business and drawing, besides the fact that you're creating work that, in your mind, will last forever, [is] the other work that you see of your peers. I think there's a better understanding of how this business works, and it is a business now, as opposed to being a family. I got more of a family sense when I went to DC and Marvel, where everybody was working closely together to create product that was fun and affordable. That changed in the Nineties. Then you had speculators in the market buying comic books and all these little business tricks.

As far as the reason why I went over to Marvel, it was because they paid so much better. They had royalties, which DC really never had. So I was drawn by the money, [and] drawn by the characters. I didn't know it at the time, but when I worked on **X-Factor**, that was a splinter book of **X-Men**. I had no idea of the historical significance of that in itself, but it was explained to me by Chris Claremont at a past convention. He said that **X-Men** at the time was like eighty percent of the marketplace, or eighty percent of the sales, or something crazy like that, and Marvel wanted to take advantage of that sales figure. So that's why they splintered off into the original **X-Men**, which was **X-Factor**. I had been working with Louise Simonson on a book called **Spellbinder**, and Walt [Simonson] was drawing **X-Factor**, and I was lucky enough to know his wife. That's what I mean by a family kind of thing. There wasn't a sense of, "This is business." And that's, I think, the direction that this is going in. That's good in a way, because what they're producing is of higher quality, but at the same time, it doesn't have the same sort of friendly feeling in the business.

**TLC:** *How important is it to you to keep in contact with your fans?*

**TS:** I think I never knew how important it was, because I personalized comic books. I never really went around and talked to

other people about super-heroes and stuff like that. So these past few years doing [the San Diego] Comic-Con, yeah, I got a better sense of just how important it is to them and me, and to our childhoods. So now I know, and I'm appreciative of the people who are interested in the field. In my day, when I was drawing, I knew nothing about comic books, and it was just trial and error. I knew nobody to call, so when I do meet somebody who is struggling, if I can help them, I try to give them that help. Every so often I teach a class at the community college in the area where I grew up, just so I can meet some of the kids who are interested in art and have questions, because I had those same questions and there was no one there to talk to.

**TLC:** *Are there any comic book characters out there that you haven't drawn yet which you would like to get a chance to draw?*

**TS:** Yeah. This past couple of years I've wanted to draw my own characters again. When I originally started, when I drew for the **Herald**, I was drawing one character,

and that's how I started. That's how I would like to finish my career, drawing a book that's my own. Unfortunately, I picked a project that's kind of epic in a way. At least that's how we all consider it when we start out a project. It's a matter of cutting it down to size [and] focusing on what's really important. That's taking some development on my part. That's what I'd like to do next. It's a new book that's gonna be a lot of fun, and get back to basics for me, which is drawing science-fiction. I think part of the reason why they choose me for **Legion** was that I was good at drawing science-fiction stuff, which was what "Golden Gladiator" was all about, and also "2064."

**TLC:** *So to sum it all up, if your phone rang tomorrow and they offered you a* **Legion** *job, your answer would be "Yes"?*

**TS:** Absolutely. The **Legion** is something that I can draw very well. The **Legion** is still [about] the coolest kids in the universe. I always said that, and it's just fun. After all these years working for Marvel and a number of different companies, that's what [the fans] ask for, and I never knew that. So that was a big shock, and it put a smile on my face. The funny part is that I still have all my **Legion** pages. I'd never part with them. People keep asking, "Where are those pages, and how can we get our hands on them?" I don't personally own any art of any other artist. I've never done that, but now that I've connected with the fans, I can see how it's important to them.

Golden Gladiator TM and © 1980 Apache Communications International.

# Dan Jurgens

A longtime **Legion** fan, Dan Jurgens is probably best known for his work on **Superman**, an association which lasted over ten years. Having since moved on from the Man of Steel, Jurgens was happy to discuss his **Legion** days with Glen Cadigan on Jan. 28, 2003. The following interview was conducted via phone, and was copyedited by Jurgens.

**TLC:** *The first place I can remember seeing your name associated with the Legion of Super-Heroes was in the letters page of an old issue of* **Superboy and the Legion of Super-Heroes** *[#205 —Ed.]. Do you remember getting a letter published when you were a kid?*

**DJ:** Oh, yeah. [*laughs*] I think I probably had all of five letters published, and I believe two of them were in **Superboy and the Legion**.

**TLC:** *Do you remember what that letter was about?*

**DJ:** I think I wrote in a couple of times, one when Cary Bates and Dave Cockrum were doing the book, and then right around the time that [Mike] Grell took over for Cockrum. It may have been in relation to that, as a matter of fact.

**TLC:** *It was. You wrote in to say that they should sign Mike Grell to a long-term contract.*

**DJ:** And Mike still owes me money for saying nice things about him. [*laughs*]

**TLC:** *Didn't he give you your first break?*

**DJ:** He was certainly instrumental in it. The first work I ever did professionally was with Mike, when he was writing **Warlord** and I became the artist on it. As a matter of fact, back when Mike had first taken over **Superboy and the Legion**, I wrote him a fan letter, and at that time he sent me back just a great Superboy sketch, which I still have. Years later, I certainly am in debt to him just because of that. But yeah, my first professional work was with Mike on **Warlord**.

**TLC:** *So it's safe to say that you're a* **Legion** *fan from way back.*

**DJ:** That's more than safe to say. Absolutely correct.

**TLC:** *When did you first start following the* **Legion**?

**DJ:** It certainly would have been during the Shooter/Swan era. The first **Legion** stuff I remember actually buying was right around the first Fatal Five story—you know, with the Sun Eater and everything [**Adventure Comics** *#'s 352-353* —Ed.]—and I don't remember exactly what issues I got first and all of that, but that's right around the time when I came on as a reader.

**TLC:** *What was the appeal of the Legion to you?*

**DJ:** Well, I think it is probably the same as it is for everyone. First of all, as a kid, I think I was attracted to the fact that they were younger characters, but more than that, I think I was attracted to the fact that there were a number of them. Part of liking the Legion has always been the fact that these guys aren't just three or four of them—there's an army. It gives you more as a reader to investigate and find interesting in them. And then the other part of it is, it was a thousand years in the future, and it was a future that was very, very bright, and very, very optimistic. I think that's what attracted me to the book.

**TLC:** *Tell me about your relationship with Curt Swan.*

**DJ:** First of all, I would never claim to know Curt well by any means, but I live in Minnesota, and Curt was a Minnesota native. Back when he was still alive, he would travel here from time to time because he still had relatives in the area. So when he came through town, we would try and get together, which we did on several occasions. Certainly we were able to collaborate on a couple of **Superman** projects, and above and beyond all of that, he is an artist whose work I have always... to say greatly admired would be an understatement.

**TLC:** *Is he still the* **Legion** *artist?*

**DJ:** To me he probably is, but I kind of think of it differently, because the Legion has been so different in different eras. I'm very comfortable saying, on the one hand,

*Top: Jurgens at a convention, circa the mid-Eighties. Above: the cover to the* **Legion of Super-Heroes Archives** *Volume 8, courtesy of Fred L. deBoom.* The Legion of Super-Heroes is TM and © DC Comics.

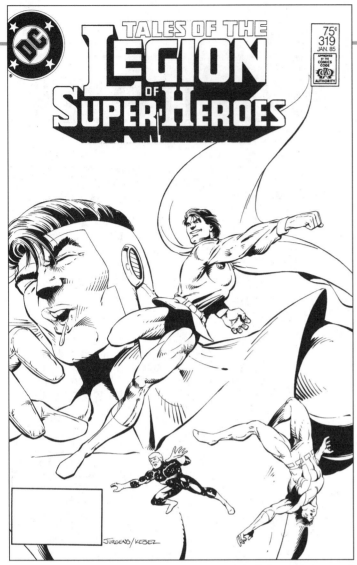

Above: the original, unaltered cover to *TLSH* #319 by Jurgens and Kesel, courtesy of Fred L. deBoom. Below: the published, corrected version. All art and characters © DC Comics.

that Curt Swan was *the* Legion artist. I could also say Cockrum was *the* Legion artist, or perhaps even Grell, and certainly Keith Giffen. I can say that because the versions of the Legion that each of them worked on were so different from one another that I look at them as different properties in much the same way that you can pick it up and say with *Spider-Man*, Steve Ditko was *the* Spider-Man artist. Well, I can find other guys I would say that of as well, which takes nothing away from Ditko. It's just that their versions can be different enough that they can still be rather iconoclastic.

**TLC:** *Did you ever bring up the Legion when you talked with Curt?*

**DJ:** I think we discussed Superman for the most part. We might have touched on the Legion every now and then. I think Curt saw himself as so much the Superman guy, I was under the impression that, to

him, the Legion was more of an assignment that he even looked at more in terms of Superboy than the Legion in and of itself. I don't want to put words in his mouth by any means, but that was the impression that I always had.

**TLC:** *Was the* **Legion** *something that you were looking to draw once you became a professional?*

**DJ:** Yes. I think that out of all the properties that DC has, the *Legion* is one of the most visually interesting. Not only do you get to draw what for me is fun stuff, [but] when you're an artist, to deal with alien worlds and different cultures, that is fun because you get to let your imagination run wild. I think in many ways comics don't have as many forums like that for artists anymore. I always wanted to draw the *Legion*, always wanted to run with it, and it's something I'd still like to do, because my time on it was actually somewhat minimal.

**TLC:** *How did you get the job on the* **Legion***?*

**DJ:** As I recall, when I first started drawing *Warlord*, Karen Berger was the editorial co-ordinator at DC, which meant that rather than being a specific editor with specific books, she was working to coordinate all the books and the talent that worked on all of them. In a couple of conversations, we probably chatted about things I would like to do and things I might like to draw above and beyond just *Warlord*. Then later, when she moved over to the *Legion* as editor, [she] gave me a call and asked me if I wanted to step in. I was more than happy to.

**TLC:** *Do you think that the work which you guys did on the newsstand version was overshadowed by the direct sales version?*

**DJ:** Oh, I'm sure it probably was, and it should have been. At that time, the direct version was being done by Paul [Levitz] and Keith, and they were just coming off a tremendously successful run on the other book in which they really pushed the *Legion* to a whole new group of fans and had great success with it. So yes, we were overshadowed, and yes, we should have been overshadowed by it.

**TLC:** *Did you have any input into the plot of the stories which you worked on?*

**DJ:** No. I've always given [Paul Levitz] a great deal of credit for writing plots that are very well fleshed out for artists, but that also left enough room for the artist to contribute. Paul manages to find that perfect balance of information. Some writers give the artist too much information, other writers don't give nearly enough. Paul found a real good balance. Obviously, he had a long association with those characters and I wasn't about to call him up and say, "Are you out of your mind? Star Boy would never do that!" Not my style.

**TLC:** *Did you deal with the writer, or did you just work through the editor?*

**DJ:** Primarily it went through the editor. I do remember us having a couple of chats. I don't even remember what about in terms of the specific characters or anything else, but I do remember us talking about things in fairly general terms.

**TLC:** *You know, you're part of the first generation of* **Legion** *artists who were fans of*

© DC Comics.

the title as children. What do you think that helped bring to the title?

**DJ:** Commitment. I think anytime you put a group of talent on the book that has been a fan of a particular book or a character, it's entirely possible that you may not like the spin they bring to that group of characters or that particular title, but the one thing you always seem to get is a real, true sense of commitment from the creative team, and I think that's something I had.

**TLC:** *You drew the Dawnstar series-within-a-series in* **Tales** [*#'s 321-323* —**Ed.**]. *Was there ever any serious talk of doing a sequel to that?*

**DJ:** Not that I recall.

**TLC:** *That one* was *sort of open-ended.*

**DJ:** There may have been different ideas of maybe we'd do a follow-up story at some point, but I don't recall anything beyond that. I remember talking with Mindy [Newell] about a couple of things at that time. I believe that would have been one of her first works for DC, as she was just coming into the system.

**TLC:** *You also used to contribute to the Legion's* **Who's Who**. *Did artists ask for specific characters in that, or did you just take what you were assigned?*

**DJ:** I think it was a little bit of both. When it first came up as a project, I have a dim memory of a couple of phone calls where they had a list of fifty characters—or more, probably—and [it was like] "Do you want to do this one?" "No." "How about this one?" "No." "This one?" "Yeah! Okay." But I couldn't remember the particulars of who it was and who it wasn't.

**TLC:** *You've also managed to work the Legion into other projects that you've done over the years. I'm thinking about* **Booster Gold** *here.*

**DJ:** The Booster Gold origin actually involves the Legion because originally he brings a Legion flight ring back from the future to the past, and that gives him the power of flight. Some of that had to be reworked because when Booster was originally conceived, it was before **Crisis on Infinite Earths**. Then as things progressed, certainly some of that was adjusted. John Byrne came in to redo Superman, which kind of ended up wiping out the idea of Booster working in a Superman museum later in the future. So it's been adjusted from time to time.

**TLC:** *You also had the Legion appear in "Time and Time Again." Was it fun playing around with the different versions of the Legion?*

**DJ:** Yeah. It was one of my all-time favorite projects, just because what appealed to me about it (for anybody who remembers it) was it was a series of issues that ran through the **Superman** books at that time, and we actually dealt with different versions of the Legion. So we had the Curt Swan-type version, [and] later we had the crew dressed in some of the classic Cockrum-type outfits. It was Superman encountering the Legion at different points in time. We also played around with the whole notion of the Sun-Eater then, so that was a real favorite of mine. That was a lot of fun to do.

**TLC:** *I want to ask you a specific question about that story: at that time, Superboy had been written out of Legion continuity, and yet Superman still made references to him. What was the situation there as far as Superboy and the Pocket Universe were concerned?*

**DJ:** Oh, boy. First of all, I'm not even certain that I can remember that with a hundred percent clarity. I think the way we approached it at the time is that if you look at it from the Legion's point of view, we played it up so that they had had some association with Superman. The question was, had they really dealt with a Superman or a Superboy? What was their awareness? Because, of course, if you go back to the original Legion stories and their origin, their inspiration for putting on the costumes and doing what they did came from the idea that Superboy was a great super-hero when he was a teenager, [so] you can do it too! So I think when they referred to him, we played it from the angle that, at first, they were just aware of

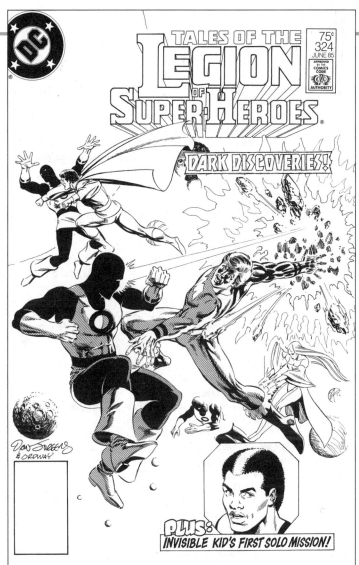

Another Jurgens cover, this time inked by Jerry Ordway. From the collection of Fred L. deBoom. Legion of Super-Heroes TM and © DC Comics.

a super-character, then the Pocket Universe story all came up. I didn't have anything to do with the writing or creation of that story, and it was, as I recall, something they put together to deal with the inherent contradiction of the changes in Superman when Byrne did come and overhaul the character, because the property that really was drastically affected by that, ultimately, was the Legion of Super-Heroes. Once Byrne said there had never been a Superboy [laughs], it kinda made things difficult for thirty years worth of Legion history to reconcile all that.

**TLC:** *There was a point beyond the Pocket Universe story where Superboy was removed from continuity altogether and Valor took his place, and "Time and Time Again" did take place after that.*

**DJ:** You know, that was one of those situations that, because of the overhaul done to Superman, it seemed to change all the time. You did go through the Pocket Universe thing to the Valor thing, to "Was it Superman who was there?" and there were a lot of different ideas bounced around. I'm not sure we were ever consistent, and quite frankly, to me there was probably just never a good solution to be had there. Whatever we did, it seemed very obvious that we were just desperately looking for an answer to throw out there because we realized that there's not a good explanation that we can give you.

**TLC:** *How involved were you with what happened to the Legion during* **Zero Hour***?*

**DJ:** Actually, not nearly as involved as you might think. The way we worked on **Zero Hour** is, when we went ahead and decided to do the project, I remember sitting down with all the DC editors and pretty much said, "Here's the basic idea of the story: in terms of what happens to your individual characters, you tell us," meaning myself and KC Carlson, the **Zero Hour** editor, "what you want to have happen to them, in terms of a resolution, and we will try and build that in." And so, in the case of the Justice Society, for example, where a couple of characters died, or went through changes, that was actually given us by someone else at DC. In the case of Hawkman, I believe that was put together by certainly Archie Goodwin and whoever was writing **Hawkman** at the time. And by the same token, with the Legion and their final disposition, again, it was the same thing. It was whatever the particular creative team and editors wanted at that time. We tried to accommodate them within the context of the story.

**TLC:** *Which is more important to you: the concept of the Legion of Super-Heroes, or the execution of that concept?*

**DJ:** Not to cop out, but that's a very hard question to answer. I think the concept of the Legion of Super-Heroes is great. When you boil it down to a base essence— here's a world one thousand years in the future, a group of kids from a variety of planets who come together to do good—I think [it] is very, very strong, but the problem is, you can take the best concept in the world

and not execute it properly, and you end up with a lousy book. By the same token, you can take a poor concept, execute well and end up with an okay book. I think it's hard to define. What's interesting to me, in terms of the Legion, is that at various times throughout its history, the execution and the view, the slant of the creative teams, has taken it so far away from the base concept that it doesn't work. I will say that.

**TLC:** *Given how long you've been in the business, why haven't you ever been the regular writer/artist on the* **Legion***?*

**DJ:** No one's ever asked me. [*laughs*] It's a very simple answer. No one has ever asked. You know, I most recently played with them in the **Teen Titans/Legion of Super-Heroes** crossover project that was a four-part, bookshelf-type mini-series. But beyond that, no one has asked. Sometimes it's as startlingly simple as that, where it's quite possible that whoever's editing the book at any given time looks at it and either doesn't think I'm right for the book, or that I couldn't do it the way they see it, or something like that. So those things happen.

**TLC:** *So if you were asked tomorrow, "Dan, we need a new writer/artist on the* **Legion***. Are you interested?"*

The Legion of Super-Heroes TM and © DC Comics.

**DJ:** Oh, I'd always be interested, and I say that because it's one of my favorite properties in comics. I suppose to a certain degree that over the course of years, the kind of books and themes I enjoy exploring most are in the bigger than life-type stuff. I think when it functions well, that's how the **Legion** functions best. You can go all the way back to the Sun-Eater story I mentioned earlier, and that's a great example of it, or what Paul and Keith did years later in the Darkseid saga. When that book functions the best, the stakes are really, incredibly high. You weave that all in with the idea that you have a number of interesting, compelling individual characters, and to me there's no excuse for not doing a good, interesting book. I really think the concept is that strong. I always liked that about it.

The other part of it is—and I do think this is a good thing—that if you come from the angle that the future is a positive place, that in terms of the human condition, we're gonna be better off in a thousand years than we are now, I think that's every bit a part of it, too. To me, part of the fun should be that you should see tricks that make life more fun. I don't know, maybe if it's even an individual jet pack-type thing. [*laughs*] I would never go that far, but you know what I mean? That there should be some fun aspects to the future. We ought to be offering something.

And the other part is, it's got to be separated. I know within the past several months I picked up a book in which one of the Legion characters was wearing a baseball cap backwards like you used to see thirteen-year-old kids wearing five years ago, which they don't do so much anymore. I thought, why? That's the world according to 1995, not a thousand years from now.

**TLC:** *What's keeping you busy today?*

**DJ:** I am currently writing **Thor** for Marvel, and I am drawing a mini-series for Top Cow at present, based on one of the **Rising Stars** characters of Joe Straczynski. So that's what's keeping me busy these days.

# Steve Lightle

## Part One

When the decision was made to produce two monthly **Legion of Super-Heroes** comics in 1984, DC Comics began the search for a second **Legion** artist. What they didn't know at the time was that the man whom they passed over for the **Tales** job would soon become the artist on the main **Legion** book itself. Hailing from the Midwest, Steve Lightle inherited the **Legion of Super-Heroes** mantle from Keith Giffen and went on to establish a career for himself as both an interior and cover artist. On February 19, 2003, Lightle was interviewed by Glen Cadigan, and he copyedited the final transcript.

*Originally published as a portfolio plate with the hardcover edition of **The History of the DC Universe**, the above piece is reprinted here for the first time.* © DC Comics.

**TLC:** *When would you say that your comics career began?*

**SL:** [*laughs*] I've been drawing comics all my life, it seems like. It's actually been twenty years now. Probably what you're expecting me to say is the **Legion**, because it was one of the very first assignments I ever did. It was certainly in my first year. I went from **New Talent Showcase**, which was DC's tryout book, and did an issue or so of **World's Finest**, **Batman and the Outsiders**, and then I was offered the **Legion**.

**TLC:** *Didn't you do some self-publishing when you were younger?*

**SL:** [*laughs*] Yeah, I did! **The Power Masters**, and a few other oddball things. The strange thing was, I wanted to be the youngest comic professional, and then when I found out Jim Shooter had started writing at the age of fourteen, that kinda dashed my hopes, 'cause nobody was wanting to hire me that early. So about the age of fifteen I started getting ready to publish my own comic, and scraped my pennies together. [*laughs*] So, in a way, it's another **Legion** connection.

**TLC:** *Didn't you also do some work for Americomics?*

**SL:** Yeah. I got chastised once in print for deserting the independents to go work for the major companies. The funny thing was, I didn't do that. I got my start at DC on the new talent program, and was already working pretty regularly for them when I found out that Jerry Ordway and some other guys I had worked with in my fan days were doing stuff for Americomics. So just on a lark I called up Bill Black, who I'd never spoken to up to that point, and said, "Y'know, what'd be kinda cool is if I could pencil something and Jerry could ink it." [*laughs*] So yeah, I did a few covers for them early on.

**TLC:** *How did you hear about DC's new talent program?*

**SL:** That's a real good question. I had always been a big fan of the DC books. When I was a kid you couldn't find Marvel comics reliably, so their continued stories made it difficult for me to get into them. I wanted to know what happened to Spider-Man, but if I couldn't find the next three issues, then.... And their distribution was really bad in those days, [which] I think everybody admits now. So DC just seemed to be the natural because you could get an entire story in one issue, and I could follow those characters. I could also follow the books more consistently, so I kinda became a DC fan, and that really stayed with me for years. So I was probably reading a DC comic [*laughs*] when I saw it announced.

**TLC:** *Were you a **Legion** fan from way back?*

**SL:** Oh, yeah. One of the oldest drawings that I've got was done in second grade, and it was a massive Legion fight scene that I probably did sitting at my desk when I should've been doing my work. [*laughs*] I think I was first introduced to the Legion by a friend on the playground who wanted to play like we were these characters. So it's going back to first grade, and this guy on the playground said, "I'll be Brainiac and you can be Chameleon Boy," and I'm like, "Who are these guys? What's all this about?" [*laughs*] At that time, I think Sun Boy sounded really cool to me because he could shoot fire, and I basically knew about that from the **Fantastic Four** cartoon which was probably running at the same time. "You shoot fire." "Okay, that's cool."

**TLC:** *When you decided to become a professional comic book artist, was drawing the **Legion** one of your goals?*

**SL:** It was one of my favorite strips, [but] at that early stage, I didn't have such high

One of Lightle's covers for Americomics, inked by Jerry Ordway. *Bolt and Starforce Six TM and © 2003 AC Comics.*

goals. I thought it would be tremendous, but I thought it was unattainable. I really would have been happy to do the back-up "Green Arrow" strip in **Detective Comics**, or some humble little job in comics. Just rubbing elbows with these great comic geniuses would have been fine with me. I didn't need to have a glory job, but the weird thing was, out of the **New Talent Showcase** program I met Karen Berger, who was also editing the **Legion**, and so when they needed somebody to replace their regular artist, they started casting for it. [*laughs*] At that time they were doing the hardcover/softcover program. They were going to go into this stage where they'd have two **Legion** books a month, [and Keith] Giffen was supposed to be doing one, and the new guy, whoever he might be, would be working on **Tales of the Legion** [*of Super-Heroes*]. So the deal was, I was given a three-page script from an upcoming issue, one that hadn't seen the stands yet, and told, "Show us what you can do on these three pages." I turned them in and I was told very kindly, very politely by Karen that the samples blew them away, but they weren't gonna give me the job because they didn't think I drew enough like Keith Giffen, and they kinda wanted the **Tales** book to resemble what Giffen was doing on what they considered the main book, what was gonna be the Baxter book. So I didn't get the gig, but

they said, "Don't feel bad. It's not a reflection on your art. Your art's good, but it's just that it's not 'Giffen' enough."

So okay, I went on and did a couple of issues of **World's Finest**, and I think I did a **Batman and the Outsiders**, and was offered **Infinity, Inc.**, I believe, at that point. [It's] a little confusing because I got offered **Infinity, Inc.** and I got offered **Legion of Super-Heroes**, and was already doing **World's Finest**—I was supposed to be the regular artist on that—[so] all these things came at me at once. The **Legion** job, though, was really odd, because when they finally offered me the regular **Legion** book, Karen called again and she said, "We'd like you to do the **Legion**," and I thought, "Well, I didn't get the gig, so it must be a fill-in." I'd already done a couple of fill-ins on other books by that time, so I was familiar with the idea. I thought, "Great! I get to draw the **Legion**, even though it's just for one issue," and about fifteen minutes into it, she says, "You do realize I'm talking about the main book," [*laughs*] and so somehow I managed to lose out on the second-string book, and ended up getting the main book a month or two later.

**TLC:** *When you took over, Keith Giffen was given credit for layouts. How closely did you have to follow what he had done?*

**SL:** Well, [*laughs*] I'll set the record straight, I guess. In those days, what happened was several issues had been solicited in advance, and they had been solicited with Keith Giffen's name as the artist. The problem was that according to [DC's] own policies, if the artist changed in a book that had been solicited for retailers, then that made the book returnable. So if they solicited books and said Keith Giffen was doing the book, and then suddenly some new guy that nobody had heard of started doing the book, then theoretically retailers could have sent the book back and gotten a refund, and DC could have ended up losing money. So what they wanted was, since they were definitely not going to have Keith Giffen drawing it—by his own choice—but they had already com-

mitted to several issues drawn by him, they had to find some way to keep Giffen's name on it. What they did was they had him do thumbnail sketches. Some were a little more elaborate than others, but they were all very tiny, suggesting where the panels should be, and what the basic layout of the panel was. These were all really small, [a] little bigger than index cards. They handed those to me and said, "Okay, take these and don't slavishly follow them. If you feel like he's doing something really good, go with it. If not, go your own way."

Specifically, I think on the first issue they picked seven pages out and said, "Don't do them like Giffen did. Do something different." So the first issue, with the exception of those seven pages, was pretty much Giffen's thumbnail sketches guiding me through. With the next issue, I'm remembering that it was something like a third of the issue, or a half of the issue was in thumbnails, and then the rest of the thumbnails never came in the mail [*laughs*], so I was kind of on my own. The third one that he was credited on, he was credited as "Consulting Artist," which I

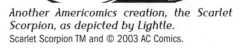

Another Americomics creation, the Scarlet Scorpion, as depicted by Lightle.
Scarlet Scorpion TM and © 2003 AC Comics.

guess meant that should I have needed anyone to give me advice, I could have called him. [*laughs*] I'm always hearing different dates for when Steve Lightle started as the regular artist on the **Legion**. In my mind, I started at issue three, and I read somewhere online that issue seven was the issue where Steve Lightle became the regular artist on the **Legion of Super-Heroes**, which is [*laughs*] annoying at best.

**TLC:** *You must have been bewildered back then, considering it was your first regular assignment.*

**SL:** Well, it was interesting. I remember specifically on **World's Finest**—which was actually, technically my first regular assignment, even though I only ended up doing two issues before jumping to the **Legion**— the thing that kinda weirded me out was I felt very insecure as a new artist. I was constantly asking people, "What do you think of this? Is this good enough?" and I kept waiting for the editor to call and say, "Change this panel, this is all wrong. We don't do things like this at DC. You don't know what you're doing, kid. Change this, change that," and nobody did. I went through a little bit of insecurity, thinking, "Surely I must be doing everything wrong and nobody's telling me." But I never had that moment where they took me to task and set me on the DC path. It was really pretty easy for me. I can't complain.

**TLC:** *Wasn't the **Legion** behind schedule when you got the assignment?*

**SL:** Yeah. What happened was the book was several months behind schedule, and while I was working on number three,

number two was actually on the stands. I don't think that should ever happen. That's really an oddity, that the previous issue should be on the stands while you're working on the next one, because usually you're five months ahead. So that meant we had three months of catch-up to do, which is why there's a lot of fill-ins in my first few issues. Joe Orlando was working on his fill-in while I was probably working on my first issue. It was just the understanding that, "Hey, we're way behind, and whatever we can do to get caught up..." I think a few issues after that there were a couple of issues where they were split [into] two stories per issue by different artists.

**TLC:** *And to make matters worse, you had to draw a storyline which featured the entire Legion of Super-Heroes and the entire Legion of Super-Villains. Did you ever get the feeling that you might have been in over your head?*

**SL:** [*laughs*] I just ate it up. I still enjoy things that take a lot of research, [although] I should take that back quickly, because if it has to do with historical research—if it's a period piece—then it drives me nuts, because then it's like, "How can I be accurate? How can I trust my source?" Sometimes you think you're getting good reference on a historical period, and it turns out not to be. Usually you don't get any reference material from your editor or writer, so you're kinda trying to run around to different libraries and such [*laughs*] while you're supposed to be drawing. But when it comes to just imaginative craziness, or if it's something that's got comic reference, where I know, "Oh,

John Forte drew the costume this way in such-and-such an issue, and I can go find it," I love that stuff. And, of course, I had a friend who had every appearance of the Legion, so I even went and borrowed his collection at one point to make sure that I got every little thing right.

**TLC:** *One of the things which you had to do immediately after you took over was to kill off Karate Kid.*

**SL:** One of my favorites, yes.

**TLC:** *How bittersweet was that?*

**SL:** That was horrible! I kept thinking, "There's got to be some really good reason for this." Ferro Lad, previously, had been one of the few heroes in comics who had died, and [it] had a tremendous impact on the book. Here Karate Kid was going to go the same way, and I thought, "Man, this is monumental. This is something that you do with trepidation." When I found out that, basically, [*laughs*] Giffen just didn't like Karate Kid, and one of the last things he wanted to do before leaving the book, he told me, was to kill him off because he thought he was just such a lame character that he didn't belong in the book, I thought, "That's great for you, but I'm the one who actually has to draw it 'cause you're jumping ship, and he's my favorite character, thank you very much." [*laughs*] So it was horrible, not only because I was killing off a character that I really liked, but because I didn't agree with the reason for it.

**TLC:** *In retrospect, are you glad that you*

*The death of Ferro Lad, penciled and inked by Lightle. A published version of the same picture appeared in **Who's Who in the Legion of Super-Heroes** #2, featuring inks by Dick Giordano. Courtesy of the artist.* © DC Comics.

The execution of Nemesis Kid, proving that Legionnaires can kill, under certain circumstances. Courtesy of the artist.
© DC Comics.

*were the one who got to draw that story?*

**SL:** Oh, yeah. I tried to make it as worthwhile as possible. The strange thing about that story in retrospect is that, at that time, certain things weren't done in comics, and for years afterward there were rules in comics, like Marvel's rule about if you show blood, it can't be red. It has to be black, or it has to be [something else], but no gore. Red was considered too frightening, too gory. There was this anti-violent thing. When I had done a ***World's Finest*** issue where I had Batman fighting a bunch of armed guards, when one of them hit him with the butt of a gun, I had a trickle of blood running from Batman's mouth. Nowadays, an editor would tell you, "Oh yeah, throw in more gore! Let's break his back!" Do whatever, you know? But in those days they actually asked me to take the blood out. "No, it makes Batman look too weak if he bleeds."

So in the same year, when it came time to kill Karate Kid, there was a lot of concern that maybe I was taking it too far, and Paul Levitz, actually, was the one who said, "No, no. Let's be gutsy about this and go ahead and run it as is. I like it the way it is. I like it the way Steve's drawing it. Let's make sure the blood stays blood." At one point I remember him saying that he thought that when blood was flying out of Karate Kid's mouth somebody might get scared and end up coloring it as saliva, so he made notes himself to say that, "Make sure this stays gory. This should be a dramatic scene." I guess it was a big deal, because I got a call from Jerry Ordway saying, "Oh man, this was an amazing issue. I showed it to everybody at the studio, and told them this is what a fight scene should be," and stuff like that. [*laughs*] So I guess for the time it was really earth-shattering, but I think anybody who's reading comics now and looks back at that issue won't get it at all. It's changed so much now that dramatic violence and gore is much more commonplace. [It's] less shocking nowadays.

**TLC:** *How did you approach drawing the execution of Nemesis Kid?*

**SL:** Of course, you remember that Jeckie broke his neck, and I thought, "That's gonna be hard to bring off. That's gonna be hard to convince everybody that this scrawny little girl who casts illusions is breaking this guy's neck when Karate Kid couldn't knock him down." So I remember trying to bring it across visually so that what really won the day wasn't her strength, it was the fact that Nemesis Kid saw something in her eye that made him

fear [her]. I tried to bring that across in a sequence of panels where, instead of just showing them going into battle with each other, I got this scene where she looks him right in the eye, and then the camera pulls completely into the pupil of her eye until the panel is full black, because I just wanted to get this feeling that, from Nemesis Kid's point of view, he saw something there that frightened him, and we don't know exactly what that was. The strength of her anger, her conviction...

**TLC:** *Do you think the fact that it was drawn off-panel made it more effective?*

**SL:** Right, because after he looks into her eyes we see her grabbing him by the throat, and then what I did was I tried to pretend that I was a cameraman instead of a comic artist, and I did something a little unusual. I decided, "It's just gonna look so goofy, so comic booky, if she just reaches up, grabs him by the neck, and we see her twist and 'Uhhh,' he falls. It could be very hard to believe." So I thought, "You know what is really effective? When something happens off-panel." I've believed this ever since I've seen the old Universal monster movies where they used to pull away as Dracula would take his prey. You know what's going on, so I just took the camera and panned down until you saw the body of Karate Kid lying there on the ground. The somewhat corny, cartoony sound effect—which I probably penciled myself, so I can't blame anyone else—of Nemesis Kid's neck cracking in the same panel... Yeah, I was going for a poignancy that wasn't typical of comics at the time, but it was partially motivated by feeling that maybe it would come off as way too corny if we just simply saw the act of her breaking his neck.

**TLC:** *When you took over the **Legion**, it was DC's second best-selling title. Was that something you were aware of at the time?*

**SL:** Yeah. It spooked me a little bit, because at that time, I think John Byrne was doing ***Fantastic Four*** and George Pérez was doing [***The New***] ***Teen Titans***, and I felt like, "Man, the league I'm in all of a sudden is frightening!" At that point, ***Batman*** and the ***Justice League*** [***of America***] weren't selling very well, and so here was a book that was outselling ***Batman*** and ***Justice League*** and ***Superman***, and here I was, just some guy trying to do his best and not embarrass himself too badly.

**TLC:** *You were part of the first generation of **Legion** fans who became **Legion** artists.*

*What do you think that helped you bring to the title?*

**SL:** Well, just having an incredible love for the characters. You just can't beat that. You've gotta respect the characters, and if you already love them going in, you're going to bring that much more to it. There's no guarantee, of course. I worked on other books where I was fond of the characters, and [I] don't think I did my best work, and then there are books where I've worked on characters which I wasn't very crazy about, and the test then was finding something about that character that I could relate to. With the **Legion**, it was easy, though. With the Legion, I already loved their history, I already loved their personalities, I loved their potential... I really loved the idea of all these varied and different people coming together with a common purpose. It seemed a very promising future, to think that a lot of the things that divide us now would be done away with by that time, and aliens and odd-looking fellows, green people and antennaed people [*laughs*], that all these different people could come together and never seem to have any problem with their differences. That was really attractive to me.

**TLC:** *When did you start collaborating on ideas with Paul Levitz?*

**SL:** I was fortunate—and I've only realized in the years since how fortunate I was—because in my first meeting with Paul, he said that he was used to collaborating that way with Keith Giffen, and he welcomed it. So if I had any ideas, to feel free to contact him with them. So it was almost immediate. Now, the first script or two were already in the can, and they were expected to be drawn by Keith Giffen, so I had no real input other than things like Karate Kid's death that we've already discussed, but as far as plot points, those didn't come until a few issues later. But I was encouraged to suggest dialogue bits, [and] in some cases I would add entire scenes. I would just give Paul the courtesy [of a phone call]. I would call and say, "Do you mind if I do this?" and he'd either say yes or no. I can't remember an instance where he said no, but I always thought he had the option of saying "No." He'd say, "Oh yeah, go ahead, do a scene where the Proties are trying to get their independence and their sentient status. Go ahead and do a scene like that in this issue. Take half a page here if you can fit it in," or whatever. And so I was really very fortunate. Paul was very generous as a creator, I thought.

**TLC:** *When did he tell you that he was going to start bringing in some new Legionnaires?*

**SL:** As far as what issue we were working on, or when it came up, I don't know. We discussed a lot of things. At one point I thought that we should have a Khundish Legionnaire, and we were kinda keen on that idea, or at least I was. I'm not sure [if Paul was]. It was a phone conversation, so he may have just been nodding, going, "Steve's out of his mind." [*laughs*] But I thought that it was a cool idea, and we'd just throw around these ideas constantly, and it would be for future things. Paul had this system where, because of the nature of the book, because it was kinda a soap opera and things developed over time, he would make charts on a large board in his office, and if we'd discuss a point, he'd write it down on the chart. So the story-points that we would bring up, it wasn't, "Well, we're gonna wedge this into this current issue," it was, "This is something we can work in down the line, wherever it fits." And so we probably talked about it long before it happened.

I know that I was really pushing that we should have non-humanoid Legionnaires. By that time, something had happened. I remember way back with [Pat] Broderick, when he drew a few issues, it seemed like suddenly the aliens around the Legion that they interacted with became tentacled creatures and things with eyes on stalks, and things like that. They became very inhuman, and Giffen continued that when he came onto the book, so it seemed like to me the Legion was operating in a world that was not only friendly to aliens like the orange-skinned, green-skinned fellows that had joined previously, but they were

also around these non-humanoid peoples, and they were interacting with them. So if they're interacting with them and this is commonplace in the 30th Century, it almost seemed like an injustice that none of them were in the Legion. So I really pushed the idea that we should get some of these non-humanoid characters into the Legion, that it shouldn't just be pink-humanoids running around. [*laughs*]

One of the things that attracted me, I guess, to the Legion was the way it included all these different races. But then as the background races became even more diverse, it started to look like the Legion wasn't keeping up with the diversity around them. It seems ironic, really, to think that a book that was all about different people from different cultures coming together started to look, in a

*Cover artwork to the **Legion of Super-Heroes** #14, featuring Lightle creations Tellus, Quislet, and Sensor Girl, among others.*
© DC Comics.

strange way, that it was exclusive. So that's one of the things I pushed, was "Let's change that," and Paul was open to that idea. And so we brought in Tellus and Quislet.

**TLC:** *Take me through the process of each new character you created, starting with Quislet.*

**SL:** I wanted to do it in such a way that made sense. I wanted a character that really made sense from a practical standpoint. So many Legionnaires had powers that were shared amongst their entire race, and it was because their world was dark, or one aspect or another of their world demanded that they have a certain ability. So I thought, okay, that's fine, but some of it's hard to understand. Like why does everybody on Cosmic Boy's planet have magnetic powers? What exactly was the reasoning behind that? And sometimes they would apply a reason, and it didn't seem particularly persuasive. So my idea was, create the world first and then create the entity that would come out of such a world. And that's how both Tellus and Quislet came about in my mind.

It might've just been silliness on my part, really. Think about it: it's a lot of wasted effort and time, and nobody ever knows about it [*laughs*], but my thinking

with Quislet was what if you broke the opposable thumbs rule, the idea that an intelligent species could only rise to ascendency [if it had opposable thumbs]? The idea was if a sentient species was required to have opposable thumbs, then whatever it was, it had to have hands, it had to be very humanoid. I wanted to throw that out, so I thought, "Okay, here's a world where they can manipulate things without hands." Well, that suggests the power has something to do with manipulating matter right there. So then I thought, "Okay, if you can manipulate matter, then obviously it changes your entire approach to life. If you physically manipulate matter without touching it, then you wouldn't build things the same way."

Anyway, I laid out this whole weird thought process, and came up with a world where these creatures could create things out of the sand of the earth beneath them that would carry them from place to place. They would create things, since they had this ability to alter matter and form matter by sheer thought. Then, ultimately, many of the things that we build, they would've built in a different way. Protection, for instance. They could've built armor about themselves at all times, and I thought, "Wouldn't it be really strange if because they have armor, they're so fully protected they don't even require a skeletal structure because they don't need muscles to move, because they can cause the very world around them to become their toy?" [*laughs*] So what I came up with was this hideous little creature that had no muscles for movement. All the muscles that he did have were to maintain his internal organs. So basically, he became a sack of organs. There's also this theory that all creatures are basically tube-shaped, that there's a place for taking in food, and [*laughs*] you know how that goes. So anyway, all this went into it. All this weird thought went into the idea that, well, he had no bones, he was basically a sack of organs, and if the

entire species revolved around the idea of manipulating matter, then probably they would be either incredibly speculative about the supernatural, or they would just be very sensual.

Quislet TM and © DC Comics.

My idea with Quislet was that he should be incredibly sense-oriented, a sack of sensory organs [*laughs*] going from one place to another enjoying himself. [*laughs*] What I got was this hideous thing that nobody could possibly associate with, this horrible, ugly little creature. So I thought, "Hmmm. This is something I could just say, "Look, I put this thing together, and isn't it unique," and everybody's gonna hate it because they can't associate with it, or I can put it in a cute little ship [*laughs hard*] and make the mystery that nobody knows what he looks like inside the ship." So the thing was, inside my mind, inside this ship was this hideous little entity that would probably make it difficult for you to make it through a meal if you were at the same table [*laughs*], and because he was from an entirely alien atmosphere, the ship had a purpose. It was a life-support unit. He literally couldn't survive in our atmosphere without being entirely encased in this technology that supported his life. So that's Quislet the way I created him. Ultimately, after I left the book, they did a story where it turned out that inside this ship was a little spark of energy, and to me, that's not the real Quislet, but to the world who followed the book after I left, that's what he became.

**TLC:** *How about his attitude?*

**SL:** I gotta pin that mostly on Paul. Maybe something in my saying that he was entirely sense-oriented and in it for his own experience and fun and that sort of thing, that might have influenced it. Paul took it into this cutesy, happy-go-lucky guy, so I guess we were, in that sense, kind of on the same wavelength. I just never imagined that he would go around saying, "Boop-a-doop," and things. [*laughs*] So yeah, that one I'll put at Paul's doorstep.

**TLC:** *How about Tellus?*

**SL:** They had done something already. They had shown the Legion Academy and said that there was an Academy student that was so alien that he was in his own room and he couldn't breath our atmosphere. Nobody saw him, or knew anything about him. I was really curious when I read that

Tellus TM and © DC Comics.

issue, so I asked Paul, "Let's bring him out of there! What is he?" and he said, "We don't know." [laughs] "We have no idea what he is or who he is or why he is. We just said that because it seemed like there probably should be somebody really alien around, and it would be kind of interesting, but we didn't have anything in mind." So the next time we showed the Academy, I slipped in this strange looking creature that had a helmet, and I assumed a tran-suit, which is this invisible suit that the Legionnaires wear when they're in space. It helps them to survive that environment. I thought, "Well, if that's the technology, then obviously Tellus, this strange Academy student, could wear such a suit

Even Sun Boy likes the Beatles. From the collection of Dylan Clearbrook. Art © 2003 Steve Lightle; Sun Boy TM and © DC Comics.

to survive in our atmosphere." So I assumed he's covered entirely in this suit, and he has some helmet which has dual purposes. I assume that he's really alien in his language, so why not have the suit not only take care of his needs as far as the atmosphere goes—heating and cooling, and keeping his body moist, or whatever the needs of his species [are]—but also translates his language into ours so that he speaks with a mechanical voice? So that's what was all tied into the helmet.

Anyway, I put all this into that one panel. It was just one panel. I showed this guy amongst the other Academy students, and I said to Paul, "If you don't mind, this was the guy that was behind the wall," and he says, "Oh, that's cool," and we went on [from there]. So when it came time to bring somebody into the Legion, I, of course, said, "Remember that guy that I just created for one panel that was based on your idea that there was an alien student? Well, that's him. Let's bring him in."

**TLC:** *Did you come up with their names, too?*

**SL:** No, that was Paul. Paul came up with both Quislet and Tellus. He also came up with some other names, too. [laughs] See, I would describe these characters to him, and then I'd say—feeling guilty that I'd already gone too far without him—"So, what's your input? What do you want to call him? What do you want to do with him?" I would have vague notions [of what to call them]. With Quislet, I really wanted to call him 'Dybbuk,' and the thing is, foolish gentile that I am, I didn't realize the ramifications of choosing a character from Hebrew mythology. Both Karen and Paul were kind of like, "Hmm, I don't know if we should do this, because, yeah, it means 'mischievous spirit,' but more than that. It also means 'demonic presence' and stuff like that, so we don't know if we want to go there." But I thought 'mischievous spirit' would suit the character perfectly, which was the interpretation I had been given of the word 'Dybbuk.' And Karen also said, "Well, I'm Jewish, Paul's Jewish. It's gonna look like we're just calling him this Jewish name." Then he wanted to call him 'Starworm,' and I thought, "No." [laughs] "How can I gently say this? 'No.'" Because I thought it's not a good idea to take somebody and bring them in because they're different, and we want to show how accepting of the different we are, and then name them after an Earth-thing they resemble. He also suggested that we should call Tellus, or that unnamed char-

In addition to being a huge **Legion** fan, Lightle is also a huge Beatles fan. Art © 2003 Steve Lightle.

acter that became Tellus, 'Mind-Monster' [laughs] because he had mental abilities and telekinesis, and I thought, "Oh, man, how do we not do 'Mind-Monster'?" And so I gave meager and pathetic excuses why it just didn't sound right to me, and he came back with 'Tellus,' which I thought, "Hey, this is so much better than 'Mind-Monster,'" [laughs], "go with it!"

And the same thing with Quislet. When he came in and said 'Quislet,' my first worry was that people would assume he was a quisling, that it was a play on the name 'Quisling,' and I didn't want them subconsciously thinking of some war criminal, some Nazi traitor. I didn't want that going through people's minds. I said, "They're gonna think that he's an obvious traitor in the Legion. It's going to be a negative association," and I think he said something like, "No, no, no. It's not that at all, but it wouldn't be bad if they thought that. If [we] went down that road, [and] let 'em be misled a little bit. They like that. Let them think they know what's going on, and then we can surprise them later." "Well, okay, we'll do that." I liked the idea, and I'm pretty sure that he was thinking of 'Quislet' as not the base word being 'quis-ling,' but being 'quiz,' or 'question,' because by that time I'd expressed to him that I really wanted the core of this character's interest to be how unique he was, and that nobody really knew what he was inside that ship. So I've always thought 'Quislet,' okay, the base word that we're drawing it from is 'quiz,' a question, a mystery.

**TLC:** *Was it your idea to give Polar Boy a new costume?*

*One of Steve's own creations, Catrina Fellina.*
Catrina Fellina TM and © 2003 Steve Lightle.

**SL:** [*laughs*] Yeah, and I tried it twice, if you noticed in the book. The first time I drew him in just a couple of panels. I think I tried to streamline some of the designs, but I still kept the silly fur around the cap and things like that. I just subtly tried to change it, and put a little more design into the costume. At that same time, Keith Giffen was given free reign with the Substitute Legion, and they were appearing in **DC Comics Presents** with Superman and Ambush Bug [*laughs*], and I think they did that Substitute Legion special after I had redesigned Polar Boy in that one scene. Giffen came in, and suddenly the character had spikey ice hair and things like that. What he was into, at that point, was farce. He was taking these characters and playing them farcically as pathetic losers who meant well [*laughs*], and I so completely disagreed with that approach, because to me the nobility of these guys who tried and weren't quite up to the standards of the Legion but didn't let that deter them from doing what they thought was right, I thought that was something incredibly heroic. They capture your heart in a way that the Legion doesn't because they really are bucking the system by even attempting to continue and fight the forces of evil in the universe. This is after their heroes have said, "Nah, it's okay. Go home," [*laughs*], and they're like, "No! We really can do something!" There's something very admirable about that, so I disliked that they were being played for comedy. When it came time to bring in more Legionnaires, I thought, "Can we finally say he's good enough? Can we finally take one of them [and put him in the Legion]?" I always thought he had powers that were easily as good as many characters who were in the Legion, whom I won't mention, so "Let's bring him in and let me change him so that you can respect him. Let's take the spikey hair, let's take the fur-lined boots," or whatever he had, "and all these silly things that make him

seem pathetic, and let's strip him of those and streamline him."

I always tried to draw inspiration from what went before with a character, so that my designs for characters that previously had existed usually have an element of what had gone before in them, not because I'm unoriginal in my thinking, but because I always had such respect for what had gone before and the people that tried to do these things before, and also just for the simple consistency of character. This is an element of him, and let's keep some element in the new design. I don't want the readers thinking when they see a redesigned costume that it's a totally new character. I want them to think the old character put on a new costume. And so there's a little bit of the old Polar Boy here and there in the color scheme. I probably should have pushed more towards something a little bluer, a little colder, but other than that, I thought it was a fairly decent design.

**TLC:** *You must have been proud when the fans voted him Legion leader.*

**SL:** Oh yeah, I got a great kick out of that, 'cause to me, that was like, "Yes! They don't think these are just comedy characters for throwaway laughs. This is a vote for treating the Legion of Substitute-Heroes with respect." I thought that was cool.

**TLC:** *Tell me about Sensor Girl.*

**SL:** Sensor Girl was mostly Paul's baby. Paul really wanted to keep as much of the older elements of the Legion as possible, and yet, with the changes in the Superman universe, we were kept from using Superboy as much as we would have liked. We couldn't use Supergirl because she was going to die in **Crisis**. It still hadn't happened yet, but we knew it was coming up. It was going to eventually be published, and we knew she was gonna die, so Paul thought, "Steve, I want you to think of Sensor Girl as Supergirl having survived **Crisis**, but

she doesn't remember who she is, and her powers have been almost entirely wiped away, with the exception of her sensory abilities." So, at that time, I think he was suggesting that she had heat vision, x-ray vision, and super-breath, maybe. I don't know. [She would have] these powers that were thought of as Supergirl's sensory powers, and that it would somehow be Kara, Supergirl surviving, and only known in the **Legion**. She would appear in the future and never return to the 20th Century, so that they would still mourn her as dead. Of course, you know she has blonde hair [*laughs*], which was supposed to be the clue that it's actually Supergirl. It was the only thing I showed of her. There was no skin showing in the costume, just her hair, and it was just that little tip of the hat to Supergirl.

But a few issues later—or a few weeks, whatever it was—Paul says, "We can't do it. It can't be Supergirl. Jennette Kahn laid down the law. She says, "If they die in **Crisis**, they're dead. That's it. Nobody brings

*A recent commission by Lightle of Sensor Girl, courtesy of the artist.* Art © 2003 Steve Lightle; Sensor Girl TM and © DC Comics.

Art © 2003 Steve Lightle; Sensor Girl TM and © 2003 DC Comics.

the **Legion**. I was actually asked to return several times after I had removed myself from the book, and in retrospect, looking back at my motivation for this, I think, "How foolish I was!" in some respects, because I loved the book, I loved the characters, I loved working with Paul—the collaboration we had gotten was just more than I could have hoped for—yet I had this sneaking suspicion that I was somehow holding the book back. I had convinced myself that my inability to do everything I wanted in every issue was somehow meaning that I was delivering less than a hundred percent, and therefore I shouldn't be on the book.

Let me explain what I mean by that: I wanted to take four weeks to pencil each issue, which they were cool with, but it meant that occasionally we'd have to have a fill-in, because normally they'd like me to keep to a three week schedule on doing the pencils. Well, they knew going in it was gonna take me longer because I was new, and they even addressed that before they offered me the job. They said, "We know you're not gonna be able to do every month, but it's an easy book to do fill-ins on, it lends itself to guest artists very well, and we don't think it'll be a problem."

So I took the book, but the thing is, somewhere along the line—and I don't want to place the blame anywhere—but I started hearing from people that, "They want you to do every issue. The readers want you to do every issue," and I always felt like, "Okay, I can rush through the issue I'm doing and do it in three weeks," and I would do that—and I won't tell you what issues, but there are issues that I felt rushed on—and then I'd look back at them and think, "Man! If I'd done this, if I'd taken a little more time, if I'd fixed that…" I'd look at the issue and think it fell short, and I would feel like I needed more time. I wasn't doing my best work, and I started feeling like I was caught between a rock and a hard place. Either I compromise my abilities and give ninety percent, or eighty percent, or seventy percent of what I knew I was capable of to meet a deadline, or I miss the deadline, and then they have to bring in a fill-in, and then they're unhappy because they've gotta have a fill-in. So I convinced myself, in a strange way, that although I

loved the book, and it was probably the best thing I'd ever work on—at least, that's how I felt at the time—I better just step away from it and let somebody else jump in that can meet their expectations and get the book done every issue and not have to have any fill-ins.

So, the funny thing is, looking back, I can't even understand my own thinking on this. I understand I tortured myself over it, and I tortured myself into making the wrong decision. I probably should have stuck to my guns and said, "You told me when I started that it would be all right to have fill-ins every six months or so. Let's do that," but instead I kept trying to meet expectations they thought I was capable of achieving [and] I thought I wasn't, [namely] doing every issue. I thought, "Well, I'm letting them down. I don't want to work at this and feel like I'm letting them down all the time." So I quit. Now, the strange thing is, I really should of stuck to my guns and done eight issues a year, or ten issues a

them back." So that changed that. What I didn't tell Paul was I kind of appreciated her stance. I liked the idea that if something happens, you treat it seriously, even if you don't like it. Y'know, don't bring Karate Kid back in the next issue just because you'd rather have him around, even though you killed him off. None of that stuff. So I kind of sympathized with that, but then we had this character that nobody knew who she was underneath the thing. We knew it was a mystery, but we had thought it was Supergirl. Now we're gonna have to come up with "What could be the mystery behind Sensor Girl?" and we really didn't know at the time I designed the costume who it was going to be. Paul came up with the Princess Projectra thing entirely on his own. I didn't have any input into that at all. So Sensor Girl, designed by me, [was] Paul's baby all the way, as far as motivation and personality and that sort of thing. All that I brought to the personality of the character was that I wanted her to carry herself with a sense of power. And maybe, in a way, this regal quality suggested Princess Projectra, but to guess somebody else's thought process is just ludicrous, so I have no idea if I had any input at all in that.

**TLC:** *You hardly got a chance to draw your new characters before you left. Is that a regret of yours?*

**SL:** You know, I've been asked, "Why did they take you off the **Legion**?" and this and that, and the fact is, I took myself off

*An updated version of Dawnstar, courtesy of the artist.* Art © 2003 Steve Lightle; Dawnstar TM and © DC Comics.

year, and stayed with the book for a good long run. Instead, I bowed out, and they asked me back to do covers, and they asked me to do the interiors as well. I've gotta say, they were not as hard on me as I was on myself, because apparently they didn't mind having me back despite my doubts. Karen and Paul both asked me to come back as the regular artist on a few occasions, and each time, whether [it was] stubbornness or self-doubt, I said, "Nahh, you know..." It may have also been other commitments, because I was doing **Doom Patrol**, and I was doing covers, and this and that on other books. So I never came back whenever they'd ask me. [*laughs*] I would instead just look at this book that I loved being done by other people, and I would do the covers for it. [*laughs*]

**TLC:** *Did doing the covers kind of soften the blow?*

**SL:** Yeah. I still felt like I was being involved in some way. I remember I was a little stubborn in some ways, because I would see them going off my designs. Like on Tellus, I'd see them giving him fingers and hands and making him act more human, and I would think, "Oh! Well, on the next cover I'll have to make sure I make it very clear how his hands look!" [*laughs*] "I've gotta make sure that the anatomy on this character is just so, so that some way, somehow, somebody gets the message that this is how the guy who designed him thinks he should look." Little things like that. I remember Polar Boy's headgear got changed by the interior artist—and he had every right to change it. He's the interior artist—but I would look at it and I'd think, "No, I don't think that's an improvement. I'll just draw it the way I did before." It's a subtle difference. [*laughs*] So he had a slightly different look to his costume than he did inside, but it was the same costume, just a different interpretation of the costume.

When it really got funny was later on when Giffen came back to drawing the book's interiors. He would work so close to deadline that when they wanted me to do the covers, nobody had any clue what the costumes were gonna look like, 'cause he would be changing them without telling anybody. I think they knew that he was making changes, and I suppose they gave him that permission to do that, but they didn't know what the costumes would be when he turned them in. As I was drawing covers before the issue was finished, there were always these strange circumstances

*From the collection of Dylan Clearbrook, Mon-El by Steve Lightle.*
Art © 2003 Steve Lightle; Mon-El TM and © DC Comics.

where I'd call the editor, or I'd call the assistant editor at that time and I'd say, "Art, I've got to draw this character. What does he look like inside the issue?" And he'd say, "Well, I don't know. Let me call Keith." And he'd call Keith [*laughs*], and he'd call me back and say, "Well, Keith says he's gonna put some kind of a vest on him," and I'd go, "Oh, man! Some kind of a vest?" [*laughs*] I'd go, "Okay, based on what we've been seeing from Keith, I'm gonna try and guess what he's doing, and I'm gonna take the vest and I'm gonna try and draw it in this Keith Giffen style of the moment," the way he was doing things at that time. So there are some real inconsistencies, as far as the interiors on those later Giffen issues and the covers, because I was guessing. I mean, on characters like Magnetic Kid and Timber Wolf... several of these characters had complete changes in their look on the interior, and there was no reference for me to do, so I was drawing them on the cover, not knowing what they were going to look like inside, hoping that I was second-guessing Keith Giffen's artistic intentions.

**TLC:** *You also did the reprint covers on* **Tales.**

**SL:** Some of them.

**TLC:** *How did that come about?*

**SL:** At the time, I was looking to do a lot more covers, and I was trying to develop a series of my own on the side. DC was showing some promising signs of wanting to have me write and draw another series, so I was working on that, but it wasn't pressing. So I wanted to do a lot of covers, and I was doing various covers on **Flash** and **Suicide Squad** and things like that. It seemed a natural, since I was already doing the covers on the regular **Legion** book to want to do the **Tales** covers also.

**TLC:** *Did you see any of those covers as an attempt to do a better job the second time around?*

**SL:** Every time. I'm not sure I was always successful, but that's what you try to do. Tomorrow I'll try and do a better job than I do today. I'm drawing the **Legion** right now, [and] the funny thing is, they've gone through so many changes. Like it or hate it, there's

been some major changes in continuity, and the characters have been recreated, and they're not the same designs, and I've got to try and look at the designs that are current. In a sense, I'm trying to do better than the guy before me [*laughs*], and I'm trying to do better than I did twenty years ago when I did the book. I'm trying to do better than I did on my last assignment, and I think that's what motivates you to improve, is just this feeling that there's always room for improvement. No matter how good you think you are, or how good you think you did something, you can always do it better the next time.

**TLC:** *Are there any* **Legion** *stories which you've drawn which you're especially proud of?*

**SL:** There's one that comes to mind first, and that's because I also got credit for co-plotting it. Quite often when I would contribute to an issue it would be a bit here and there, but when we did "Back Home In Hell," [**LSH #23** —**Ed.**] the story about Mon-El developing an immunity to the anti-lead serum that allowed him to stay alive in the 30th Century, it just seemed as I looked at current medicine, the human

Peking Tom & Bobbi Sox TM and © 2003
Steve Lightle.

body develops immunities to things that you keep putting in your body. Eventually you develop a certain amount of immunity to them, and I thought, "Well, he's been taking this drug for some time. What if his body, being this super-human Daxamite body, has developed an immunity to this serum, which means that now it can no longer help him? Now he's at risk of dying of lead poisoning again? What if, as a stop-gap measure, they decide, 'To save your life, we've got to put you back in the Phantom Zone?'"

Just the idea that this well-adjusted, most Superboy-like character of Mon-El... what if there was more to him? What if the idea of going back into the Phantom Zone terrorized him? What if it was so deeply scarring that this rational, sensible man couldn't be rational and sensible about the idea of going back into the Phantom Zone? I thought, "Man, that just makes him such a more interesting character!" I also told Paul, "There's something that's been over-looked about this character. He spent a thousand years waiting for his friend to save his life, waiting for Superman to develop a serum, and this is Superman's biggest failure. He never developed a serum. He put this kid in there, and every issue of Superman is an issue he fails Mon-El." That's how I put it. I said, "Every issue that Superman saves the world is an issue he fails Mon-El, because he told this guy, 'Trust me. I'll save you,' and he puts him in the Phantom Zone surrounded by criminals from Krypton's past."

Mon-El is in this place where he's

cursed to see a multitude of worlds, but not be able to touch anything. He's surrounded by evil forces that he's opposed his entire life. It's like putting Gandhi in prison—because he's a moral person—only imagine Gandhi wasn't so well-adjusted. Imagine Gandhi as a teenage boy, and throw him into prison with all these crazed psychopaths, and he's waiting for his friend to help him, except—unless Superman lives eternally—he sees his friend grow old and die and never save him. He sees worlds decay. In one panel I drew Darkseid standing over these humans who were naked and grovelling on the ground, and there's a tear in Mon-El's eye because he's a hero! He's got a heroic personality, he has a heart for these people, and he can't touch them. He can't help them. He can't do anything. A thousand years pass. I'm thinking, this should shatter most minds. If his mind was not shattered, then he had to have been affected in such a deep way that perhaps he's even repressed it, and it's the idea of going back into the Phantom Zone that brings this trauma to the surface. So that's one you can tell I'm rather proud of. It probably should have been played as more than just a single-issue story, and I've noticed that a lot of people have tried to pick up on elements of it since, but that was something I was proud of.

**TLC:** *Have you ever given any thought toward writing yourself?*

**SL:** I've always toyed with the idea of writing my own stuff. The strange thing is, the last time I turned in a script—and I won't mention the editor because I'm still too annoyed by it—I was actually told, "Well, go ahead! You write this and draw it," and I turned it in, and after a while they said, "Are you incorporated? Because if you're not incorporated, then we can't have you both write and draw it, because technically, that gives you more of a claim over the end product, and we don't want you contesting the copyright. But if you're incorporated, then we can make a deal with the company." That's how the writers and artists do it in comics, typi-

cally, is that they form a corporation, and so DC Comics actually works with them, and the writer and the artist are entities that work for the corporation. It's some loophole, and he's trying to explain this loophole to me.

He says, "Well, I suppose you could write an issue, and we could get somebody else to draw it, and you could draw somebody else's issue, and we could get somebody else to write that, and so we'll be doing two separate issues. One you'll write, and one you'll draw," and I thought, "Aw, man, this is not good," but I still believed in the story enough that I wanted to go ahead with it. So I did rewrites, and I changed the story, and I altered this, and I fixed that to make it fit within the continuity of this book, and I turned it in. Ultimately he says to me, "Well, you know what the problem is now? Since you're not drawing it, you're an unknown commodity as a writer, and therefore we don't think it'll help sales of the book to have your

©Copyright, 2003, Steve Lightle

*Top and above: Two more of Lightle's creator-owned properties: Peking Tom & Bobbi Sox and Justin Zane, both published by LunaTick Press. For more information on LunaTick Press, visit www.geocities.com/lunaticks2001.*

name as writer. If you're not drawing the book, it doesn't do us any good." [*laughs*] "So when it comes out in Diamond, and your name is as the writer, they'll be insecure, because they're looking for you to be an artist, and they don't know if you can write, and it'll hurt sales." So, there's this incredible catch-22 that I found incredibly frustrating. Yeah, I just keep feeding ideas to people that write [*laughs*], and hope that somehow, by osmosis, I get credit for standing around with them.

**TLC:** *One thing I noticed about your* **Legion** *run was that outside of the first story arc, you didn't really get a chance to draw a lot of villains.*

**SL:** That's an interesting thought. We certainly didn't create very many villains, did we? I can't remember one offhand. I know that there were a lot of villains recycled shortly after I left. They brought back Starfinger, and stuff like that, but as far as creating all-new villains, no, they were more like villains of the piece. There were villains there, but they weren't classic comic book villains. I think McCauley appeared for the first time while I was drawing it, 'cause I vaguely recall designing him, but he was just a businessman at that point. There was no super-hero costume or anything, there was just this evil businessman with a slightly angelic look about him. I always found it a lot more interesting, the idea that people can be evil and not appear evil.

**TLC:** *Is that an area that you would've liked to have made more of an impact in?*

**SL:** Not really. To me, the story's always more important then the idea of superficial things. It would've been nice to have a greater legacy walking away and say, "Oh, I created all these new characters, and all these new designs," but at the time—and I still feel this way today—the most important thing you're called to do is tell a story, so let the chips fall where they may. If you get pages that sell as original art, or if you get a design that somebody will laud you for later, that's all nice, but you can't let that get in the way of telling a good story.

**TLC:** *Which* **Legion** *artists influenced your interpretation of the group?*

**SL:** Everybody's. Everybody I've seen, that is. Now, since I quit the book back in the Eighties and started doing covers, at the point where they retooled everything and had the Five Year Gap and all of that, I kinda lost track of it after that for years. I've seen Jeff Moy's work, and stuff like that since, [and] there's a lot of guys I'm sure I've never seen, but everyone I've seen I'm sure has had some influence. To me, it was just really weird. "I'm the keeper of the **Legion** for while I'm drawing it," is how I felt, "and all these other guys created it. All these other guys brought it to this point." So the idea of completely ignoring what they had done would never have occurred to me. When I did flashbacks, it was always important to me that, "If we're flashing back to a story that happened in 1964 in a particular issue, [and] there was a guest artist on that issue, and instead of long gloves, he drew short gloves on a character, in this flashback, I'm going to make sure she's got short gloves, because *that happened*. In that moment, in that artist's mind, that's how she looked, and that's how she was presented. As far as I'm concerned, that day she went out and she put on short gloves." [*laughs*] If Night Girl's beehive hairdo was different in one issue, well, when you flashback to that, it's different for that issue. You don't find, "There's the classic Curt Swan look. Let's stick with that for every flashback." They didn't always look consistent, and it's the inconsistencies that make things interesting, anyway.

**TLC:** *So you basically saw yourself as a link in the chain.*

**SL:** Yeah. I just wanted to polish that one link up as best I could, and present my work as best I could, and keep it interesting. But I always felt like I was adding on to some existing work.

**TLC:** *I noticed that various alien races used to keep popping up in the background.*

**SL:** Well, that was because I would notice things. As a fan, I would notice things. Going all the way back to the Sixties, there'd be an alien, and he'd have a nose on his forehead, and you'd see him, and he'd appear for one issue, and then you'd never see that alien race again. I'd think, "How funny," because it seemed so fake. You just create an alien race for a moment when he's necessary. It rings so false, because in reality, you wouldn't say, "Let's have a Hispanic person in this story, but we've never done anything with Hispanics before, and we're not going to have anything to do with Hispanics again. But for this one story, we're going to have a Hispanic out of nowhere." The sensible thing is to realize that the world consists of a multitude of races, and to draw these people in the background so that they don't look like they were just cobbled together for one moment. My thinking was, "To create a more consistent world, to create a more natural environment for the heroes to exist in, everything should be sensible." If there's a particular style of architecture that's typical of one planet, then any time you visit that planet, that kind of architecture should be there. If there's a particular type of technology, then everything has to reflect that technology. That's why when I designed Quislet's ship, I didn't go nuts and go, "What kind of a ship could it be? It could be streamlined, it could be this, it could be that, it could be..." and design something

*Another Legion couple, from the collection of Dylan Clearbrook.*
Art © 2003 Steve Lightle; Star Boy and Dream Girl TM and © 2003 DC Comics.

Another character from the mind of Steve Lightle. Courtesy of the artist.
Tim Can TM and © 2003 Steve Lightle.

entirely different. I looked at all the stuff that was in the backgrounds, and thought, "Okay, here's the technology of the 30th Century. It's gotta reflect this." So my choice became limited, but I thought it was worthwhile, because it made it seem like a more consistent universe. You think, "Here's what exists."

Maybe Giffen's great contribution to the **Legion**—at least artistically—was that he created a consistent look for the technology of the 30th Century. I do remember trying to be consistent with that look, because to me he had accomplished something. He had fallen on to something that made sense. Y'know, "Here's a particular look that's the technology of the 30th Century," and with alien races it was the same thing. I kept going back, and there's one issue where they're rounding up all these space pirates, and I took one and I dug him out of an old Dave Cockrum issue. "Here's one of the pirates. He looks exactly like these characters that Dave Cockrum drew in one issue that never appeared again." And then, "Here's this other race. He's this stupid looking three-legged thing that only appeared in one story," and I'd bring back these characters that were just peripheral throwaway things and have them appear again.

**TLC:** *While you were doing the covers on the **Legion**, there was a period there when you stopped and Ken Steacey started doing them. What happened there?*

**SL:** For the life of me, I don't recall what happened at that point. It may have just been that he was available, and that [I was busy]. I think he did a cover for an annual, and I think that he had probably expressed an interest in wanting to do more. I don't know. I'm just guessing. I don't remember there being any specific problem, and I don't remember why I moved on and did other things. It may have had something to do with conflicting schedules on my part. Probably what happened is that I probably said, "Gee, you need this cover next week? I'm gonna have a real hard time getting it done by next week, but I'll do what I can, because I've got this other commitment, and if you need it next week, then it'll be late next week," and probably the reaction to that on Karen's part was, "Oh, well if you need more time, then I can get somebody else to do that issue." It was probably something real simple like that, and it just turned into several issues out of convenience.

**TLC:** *You occupy a unique perspective. You're a preboot **Legion** artist who has returned to the book postboot. How difficult, or easy, was it to make that transition?*

**SL:** There was a time when I thought I'd probably never draw a **Legion** book again. What made me think that I could draw the **Legion** again is that I look at what's being done with the **Legion** today, and I think, "Okay, granted it's a whole different continuity, but I had considered changing continuity, or being part of it, when they first considered changing the continuities," so I was somewhat sympathetic to what they were going for. Face it: they destroyed the Moon. They destroyed the Earth. They made the Legion depressed and dysfunctional, and that was all good if you liked reading about a depressed, dysfunctional Legion, but if you wanted to read about the Legion that we all grew up with, and the Legion that, I think, other people would like to grow up with, the Legion of young, positive-minded characters with a tremendous amount of potential, and a tremendous energy to meet it, if you want that kind of Legion, you either have to say none of the Five Year Gap stuff happened—which I'd of been perfectly happy with. You could have just simply said, "Well, that's an alternate future. That's what could have happened," and then go back to "The Magic Wars" and continue telling stories from there—or you restart everything.

So I was sympathetic to what they were going for, [which was] bringing the **Legion** back to it's original concept: the positive group of young people from diverse backgrounds who pulled together with a cause and were willing to fight for it. It was a predominately positive view of the future, and I keep saying positive, because that's the word that describes the **Legion** best to me. If the current **Legion** is different from the **Legion** I worked on, well, that's fine. At least it's a positive vision of the Legion. It predominantly is a positive view of these characters who have come together with a purpose, and there may be details—we may be betrayed by having some of our continuity written out—but it's closer to the Legion I know than what came after I originally quit, so it didn't seem like a big betrayal of the original continuity. It gave me pause, but ultimately I had to think, "We've gotta salvage the **Legion**. We've got to bring it back to some kind of hopeful future again." I think that when they did reboot the Legion, they kept that in mind. Most of the time, it was with that goal [in mind]. That was a long time coming, and I was glad to see it. So, I admire those that ended up recreating the Legion for keeping that in mind, for

*The* FATAL FIVE

The Fatal Five TM and © DC Comics.

keeping the positive view of the future in mind.

**TLC:** *How important do you feel that **Legion** fans are to the success of the **Legion**?*

**SL:** Well, I could just read it to my family, but that wouldn't sell a lot of books. [*laughs*] You're talking about the fact that **Legion** fans, above and beyond any other fans in comics, are enthusiastic and vocal and involved, and they take their characters to heart. I think that's incredibly sustaining, because there have been moments in **Legion** publishing history where it's faltered. There have been moments when it hasn't been as good as it should be, there have been moments when maybe they've lost sight of their direction, or the creative team was not a hundred percent into what they were doing. There were times when I could swear that it looked like they were on automatic pilot. The fact that the book never collapsed completely, that the fans never allowed it to disappear, is as important to the **Legion**'s longevity as what was done by the creators, as important as Dave Cockrum recreating the Legion, because they brought the **Legion** through times that maybe it didn't deserve to continue, and yet they saw potential. So yeah, you've gotta give the fans credit. I don't know of any other comic fans that would be as loyal. When I sell original artwork, I'm

always inundated by people who want to see **Legion** stuff. Even after fifteen or sixteen years of not working on the book, I'd say seventy-five percent of the people that I talk to about my original art are interested in **Legion** work first.

**TLC:** *How rewarding is that to you?*

**SL:** I don't know. It's one of those things where you just feel good to have been involved in something that meant something to someone. I'll tell you what: it's nice to meet somebody and have them say, "Your depiction of Timberwolf is the one that I remember. That's the character I like," or "The way you portrayed Lighting Lass with so much power, and yet, such a small, physical presence...." Things like that. When people tell me, "Blok really appeared sensitive despite his obvious size and strength. You brought across an aspect of the character better than this person or that person," that really feels good, especially when you consider that it was done so long ago.

The flipside is, I once encountered a would-be comic publisher, a man who was putting a great deal of money into starting a publishing company, and he said, "I want you to do a book for me, and you can do any book you want, I don't care, but I want you to draw it the way that you drew the **Legion**, because that was real art!" So I thought, "There's a flipside right there. I guess what I'm doing now isn't." [*laughs*] So if people are obsessed with the **Legion**, and they think the **Legion** is all that's important, well, that's cool, but it can also lead them to say things like, "I've never seen anything you've done outside the **Legion**." [*laughs*] So that's the frustrating other side to the coin. There are people who love my work, and only remember the **Legion**, even though I haven't drawn the **Legion** in years. If I say, "Well, I drew **Spider-Man**. Did you see that issue?" "No. I don't read **Spider-Man**." "Well, I did 'Wolverine' [in **Marvel Comics Presents**]." "No." "The **Doom Patrol**?"

*From Lightle's return to the Legion: a page from **The Legion** #24.* © DC Comics.

"No." [*laughs*] "Well, did you at least see the covers I did on [**Flash**]?" "Well, maybe." "I did **Red Sonja**. Did you see that?" "No." [*laughs*] "But when you did the **Legion**..." So it cuts both ways.

**TLC:** *How would you sum up your time on the **Legion**? Are you satisfied with the work you've done?*

**SL:** It's part of the problem we were talking about earlier. You're never satisfied. As an artist, you're trying to recreate a universe that's already been created, and you're trying to add things to perfection already, so no, you're never satisfied because you never get there. I always feel like I could do better, and one of the reasons why I'd come back and do more **Legion** work now, and am doing more **Legion** work now, is because I feel like I can do it better now than I did when I was twenty-three. I think I've learned things since then. But overall, my view of the **Legion** and my involvement with it.... I just have to say that it's an extension of my being a fan of the **Legion**. I've just felt very excited about it. I'm very pleased to be involved with something that I hold in high regard.

© Robert E. Howard Properties, LLC, 2000

*The Robert E. Howard character de Montour, published by Cross Plains Comics.*

# Ernie Colón

When the newly launched **Legion of Super-Heroes** direct sales title fell behind schedule, one of the artists called in to help out was Ernie Colón. A longtime Harvey artist, Colón is probably best known for his work on **Amethyst, Princess of Gemworld**. He would go on to be the artist on both Legion mini-series which appeared during the middle part of the decade (**Legionnaires 3** and **Cosmic Boy**),as well as write and illustrate his own original graphic novel, **The Medusa Chain**. Still active in the industry today, Colón was interviewed by Glen Cadigan on March 2, 2003.

**TLC:** How long have you been working in the industry?

**EC:** About forty-five years.

**TLC:** Do you remember what your first paying job was?

**EC:** It had to be the Harvey work. It was on Richie, **Richie Rich**.

**TLC:** How many years did you stay at Harvey?

**EC:** Twenty-five.

**TLC:** And how did you end up there?

**EC:** They actually advertised for a letterer. When I went up there, they realized that I couldn't letter to save my life, and I still can't. Luckily for me, there was a woman up there called Vicky Lauren who eventually married Alfred Harvey, and I had known her briefly a couple of years before. She told Leon Harvey that I could draw, and not to let me go, and to hell with the lettering. [*laughs*] So they did, and I stayed.

**TLC:** Did you always want to be an artist?

**EC:** Oh yeah. As far back as I can possibly remember.

**TLC:** Are you self-taught?

**EC:** Yes, unfortunately.

**TLC:** [*laughs*]

**EC:** Well, when you're self-taught, you have a tendency to reinvent the wheel. It's the long way around. It always sounds good when you say that to people, but it's the long way around. I had a good mentor at Harvey Publications, Warren Kremer, who was a wonderful craftsman.

**TLC:** I understand that your days at Harvey were far from boring, in the sense that there was some tension going on behind the scenes in the front office...

**EC:** Oh, yeah, the two brothers didn't like each other at all. In fact, they detested each other, and they were twins [*laughs*], but it affected us only in the sense that the company should have remained viable for much longer. At that time, there were movie studios doing what they are doing now, which was they were courting the Harveys to make movies out of **Richie Rich** and **Casper** and so on, but they were so crazed with their emnity towards each other that they weren't taking advantage of it. In fact, at that time, Ricky Schroeder was being picked for **Richie Rich**. That's how far back it goes.

**TLC:** How did you go from working for Harvey to working for DC?

**EC:** Actually, I started with Marvel, then moved to DC. I sent Jim Shooter a letter. I think I drew Casper on his knees with his hands clasped together, begging, "Please, get me out of here! I've been here for twenty-five years!" [*laughs*] and he responded immediately. He put me on **John Carter,** [**Warlord**] **of Mars**, for starters.

**TLC:** Didn't you work for Seaboard, too?

**EC:** Atlas/Seaboard, yeah.

*Top: Colón in a contemplative mood. Above: a rare **Legion** cover by Colón, from the collection of Fred L. deBoom. © DC Comics.*

**TLC:** *I know that you like drawing science-fiction and fantasy. In that regard, working on the* **Legion** *must have been right up your alley.*

**EC:** It was. I think that Keith Giffen did a far better job on it than I did. Mine was a kind of generic cartoon, whereas his had a lot of personality. The kind of science-fiction that I really love to do was like the graphic novel that I did, **The Medusa Chain**. That was for DC, and that's the really hard science-fiction that I like. They used to call it "science-fiction opera," or something like that.

**TLC:** *Keith Giffen was credited with the layouts on* **Legionnaires 3**. *How did that work? Did he do thumbnails, or...*

**EC:** If I remember right, they were thumbnails.

**TLC:** *So did you have to follow them religiously, or...*

**EC:** No. The reason I did it is because he's the kind of storyteller where he doesn't like figures jumping out of panels and stuff like that. He really likes straight ahead, panel-by-panel storytelling, and at that point, I wanted to follow his stuff because I liked that. If you remember, **Watchmen** was like that—very straight ahead storytelling—which I still think is the best way to tell these stories. I'm not that fond of the very imaginative panel layouts.

**TLC:** *One thing that I noticed about your* **Legion** *work was that you used to put Interlac everywhere.*

**EC:** Did I? [*laughs*] I think I was writing letters in Interlac at that point.

**TLC:** *You must have had fun on it, to spend that much time doing it.*

**EC:** Oh, I did. I did have a lot of fun with it, and, as I say, it was just great working with Keith. Working with him was a big pleasure. We keep threatening to work together again, but we never seem to get around to it.

**TLC:** *Didn't you and Keith also briefly work together on* **Amethyst**'s *regular series?*

**EC:** [I think] I only did the twelve issue series [**Note:** *Colón actually returned to* **Amethyst** *with #9. Giffen became the plotter of the series with #13.* —**Ed.**] After that, DC brought her back, and I understand they killed her. I'm not sure, but they never called either the writers or me to redo it, or to ask us about it. They were a pretty cold-blooded lot up there at that time.

**TLC:** *You know, they eventually ended up tying* **Amethyst** *into the* **Legion of Super-Heroes**.

**EC:** Did they really?

**TLC:** *They said that the Sorcerer's World in the Legion's time was actually Gemworld a thousand years from now.*

**EC:** Well, good luck to them. [*laughs*]

**TLC:** *I've heard that you used to destroy some of your original art.*

**EC:** That goes around a lot, but the fact is, I really destroyed stuff that I didn't like. I didn't destroy stuff that I thought was good. The stuff that I thought was good I gave away. I've given it all away, of course.

**TLC:** *That stuff goes for a pretty penny now. Do you wish that you had hung on to it?*

**EC:** I don't like to go to eBay [*laughs*] because I see my stuff all over the place selling for fairly nice money. Of course, my wife tells me that I'm a complete idiot, and I probably am. A lot of the stuff I gave away as gifts, and unfortunately it's winding up on eBay. But I guess if they needed money, that's the way it goes.

**TLC:** *Weren't you also briefly an editor at DC?*

**EC:** Yeah, I was there for one year, two weeks, and three days. [*laughs*]

**TLC:** *Which titles did you edit there?*

**EC:** I was editing **Green Lantern**, **Wonder Woman** briefly, **Blackhawk**, and **Flash**. You know, I brought Dave Gibbons in from England? I called him from DC, and nobody was doing that at that point. I saw his work and I called him up, and he couldn't believe it! "Oh, my God! You're calling me from New York?" He came in, and made a big success of himself, but he never spoke to me again. [*laughs*]

**TLC:** *Was editing something you aspired to?*

**EC:** No, it was handed to me by Jenette [Kahn], and I thought I'd try it. It was the corporate structure. I'd never been in it before, and I've never been in it since. I didn't get along with it at all. I didn't get along with the politics, with the silliness, favoritisms... y'know, the usual garbage that happens in corporate structures. I didn't go for it.

**TLC:** *You mentioned the* **Medusa Chain** *graphic novel, which you also wrote. Do you prefer working with other writers, or writing your own stuff?*

**EC:** Oh, if the writing's good, I'll take anybody. I actually wrote my own stuff generally when I couldn't get anybody else to

*Amethyst in evening wear, as illustrated by her designer.* Amethyst TM and © DC Comics.

Above and below: from the **Medusa Chain** graphic novel, Colón's foray into writing and illustrating.
Medusa Chain TM and © 1984 DC Comics.

write it. I liked the idea of the **Medusa Chain**, [but] I couldn't get a writer, so I wrote it myself.

**TLC:** *Even when you're not writing your own stories, do you find that the writers with whom you work are open to your ideas?*

**EC:** Yeah, they are. That doesn't mean that you can get things started, because projects are so difficult to start. A huge percentage of the industry is not original work, it's maintenance work. You know, you draw your Mickey Mouse, or you draw your Superman, or Batman, or whatever. Original ideas are very difficult to sell.

**TLC:** *Tell me about your Doodlemovies.*

**EC:** [*laughs*] I was working at a crappy job for a while, and there were a couple of hours where I sat at the desk doing not much, so I started doodling—which I never do. I only draw—but the doodles kind of took their own form. In other words, I'd do a drawing, a doodle of something, and then I'd say, "Well, what if I had to make a story out of it?" and I would just go on with it with a ballpoint pen—no pre-planning—and a couple of stories came out. I got in touch with Komikwerkz [*www.komikwerkz.com* **—Ed.**]—Keith told me about them—and they put 'em up. They're still up there, somewhere. I have a whole bunch of them here that I promised I'd send them, so I better get busy with them, now that you've reminded me.

**TLC:** *Is the Internet a way to get around the traditional politics of comics?*

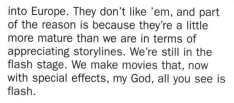

**EC:** The thing with the Internet, as with print, is you have to be a businessman, and I'm not. You really have to pay attention to the business end of things. I'm kind of dopey that way. I'm not good at business. I never was. I just sit there and draw like an idiot, like a drudge. I call myself a "monk illuminator of manuscripts." But the fella whose name I can't remember now... he has a science-fiction [strip] up there daily...

**TLC:** *Steve Conley?*

**EC:** Yes, that's it. He's a great businessman. You read that interview [which he did in **Draw!** #2 **—Ed.**], and he's unbelievable. So from that standpoint, to answer your question the long way around, if you're a businessman, you can make it in the Internet, you can make it in print. It doesn't really matter.

**TLC:** *You mentioned Keith Giffen's style of layouts before, where storytelling comes first and illustration comes second. Would you say that a lot of the time, artists lose sight of what their true goal should be?*

**EC:** Absolutely. They're under the impression, as I was for a long time, that the art is more important, and it isn't. Even though it's a visual medium, the fact is that a pretty picture only lasts for so long, whereas a good storyline will always grab attention. You look at something like **Tintin**, [and] there's a straight ahead storyteller. No flash, nothing extraordinary in terms of panel layout. The panels are really like a movie screen. It doesn't change. [Hergé] may give you a full page, [or] something like that, and it's all story. The art is cute, but it's very repetitive. Once you've seen Captain Haddock, you've seen him. Front view, side view, that's it. He's not gonna get any weird shadows, or any weird perspectives, so that's a perfect example of something that is hugely internationally popular. I mean, that book has sold millions of copies in sixty different countries, and Marvel and DC can't get their superheroes into Japan or

into Europe. They don't like 'em, and part of the reason is because they're a little more mature than we are in terms of appreciating storylines. We're still in the flash stage. We make movies that, now with special effects, my God, all you see is flash.

**TLC:** *So if someone waved a magic wand and put you in charge of the industry, what would you do?*

**EC:** [*laughs*] What a question! I guess I would do what I tried to do when I was at DC, which was talk to writers, talk to people who needed a break in writing. I had guys like Robin Synder [and] Todd Klein, who was a letterer but who wanted to do some writing. I had him write some stuff. Then I hired guys like Dave Gibbons, who told a straightforward story. The stuff that appeared at that point, I think, because of their talents, was superior to anything else that was going on at that time at DC. So I guess I would do the same thing if I was in charge of Marvel or DC, God forbid. [*laughs*] That's what I would do. Concentrate on storyline and storytelling so [that] the story is clear, lucid, and don't give me all the flashdance.

**TLC:** *Of all the things that you've worked on throughout the course of your career, what would you say you are the most proud of?*

**EC:** In terms of the return from the reader—in other words, meeting people later in life at parties or whatever— the greatest response I've gotten has been for the Harvey work. I think I'm most proud of it because those characters really entertained kids. They were hugely, hugely popular, and they still would be today excepting that the company that bought the characters isn't printing them. They're simply looking for a way to make that very big dollar in the movies and in marketing and licensing. They're being very shortsighted. But that's tangential. The answer to the question is I guess I would have to pick that, simply because it really entertained so many kids for so long.

**TLC:** *Do you consider yourself to be retired today?*

**EC:** No, no. I'm never retired. I'm working now with CrossGen. I'm inking a book called **Cross-overs**. A fella named Morris Set is penciling. I'm inking it, and I'm penciling a book called **Mendy and the Golem** [*www.thegolem.com* **—Ed.**], which is a Jewish-oriented comic book which is looking to go a little bit mainstream.

# Greg LaRocque

Less than two years after the debut of the Legion's direct sales only series, the title received it's third regular artist in the form of Greg LaRocque. A former Marvel illustrator best known for his work on **Web of Spider-Man**, LaRocque adjusted to life in the 30th Century and became the sixth regular penciler to work with Paul Levitz on the title. He would stay for almost three years before moving on to the **Flash**, where he helped redefine the character with Mark Waid. On March 16, 2003, LaRocque was interviewed by Glen Cadigan, and he copyedited the following transcript.

**TLC:** *Where are you from?*

**GL:** I'm born and raised right here in Baltimore.

**TLC:** *So were you always interested in comics?*

**GL:** Yeah. I go back to the early days of Marvel—1963, **FF** #1—and I've been hooked ever since.

**TLC:** *Which comics did you follow growing up?*

**GL:** I was a Marvel fan, so pretty much everything that Marvel put out, I collected. I was one of those guys that collected everything, basically, that they put out. I kept 'em in my bedroom, numbered, in bags and everything, so I was a pretty big Marvelite. My favorite book back then was **Thor**.

**TLC:** *Which artists would you say influenced you the most?*

**GL:** Probably Neal Adams. When he came on the scene, he changed the look of comics, and I think overall, he's been my favorite artist of all time.

**TLC:** *When did you make the decision to give comics a try as a pro?*

**GL:** I was an art student coming out of high school, and once I graduated the school that I was

going to, I knew that I had to make a decision of what to do. I got married, spent a few years here in Baltimore, did a little bit of advertising work, wasn't really happy doing advertising, and as things worked out, my wife at that time was from Newburg, New York, which is close to the city. Once I moved up there, I said, "You know, it's time to give comic books a chance." I knocked on the door, showed some samples, [and it] took me a little while to get some work, but after talking to some people there at Marvel, I got my first assignment in 1980, and was lucky enough to keep working for a long while there.

The two things were a perfect match for me, having always been a comic fan [and] always been interested in art. I never really took the idea of working in comics

very seriously until I did get married and realized, "You know, you've got to make a living here. What do you want to do with the rest of your life?" So that's when I decided to go ahead and give it a shot and knock on the door.

**TLC:** *When did you head over to DC?*

**GL:** Actually, the very first job I got was from DC. I showed my work to Marvel. Al Milgrom was the editor there at that point. He was working with me, he saw my samples, called me in and said, "We really like your stuff, but you do need to work on a few things." He introduced me to storytelling, and while I was doing that, he says, "We don't have work for you here at Marvel right now, but why don't you let me send you over to DC?" He gave Joe

*The then-current Legion of Super-Heroes, featuring members both past and present.*
The Legion of Super-Heroes is TM and © DC Comics.

*A sample of LaRocque's post-DC career, courtesy of the artist.* © 2003 its copyright holder

Orlando a call, and actually walked me over, [and] took me into the offices there. Of course, this goes back to 1980, when things were done a little bit differently, and Al is one of those guys that's just a prince. Other editors and other people in the business don't really encourage that kind of friendship between the two companies, but Al had started with DC, went over to Marvel, was doing **Spider-Man** at that time, and he just didn't have any problems with saying, "Hey, we've got this young guy. Maybe you can find him some work?"

He took me in, sat me down with Joe, [and] Joe was nice enough to walk me around the office that day. Len Wein was actually the first guy who offered me some work. I got work from him, and I got some work from Jack C. Harris that day, so my first paying assignment came from DC. I was with them for a little while, but it wasn't soon afterwards that Marvel started offering me some work. [So] I was with them for a little bit first.

*TLC: Were you a fast artist?*

**GL:** Editors have always called me fast. Going back to those first few years in the business, I had certainly a different way of getting the work done. I used to work over a light table, on trace paper, redraw the stuff two, three, four times until I felt comfortable with it, and then transferred it to the Bristol paper. But in the twenty years I've been working in comics, I've never missed a deadline, so I think "reliable"

would probably be a better description. If I told the editor it's gonna come in on such-and-such a date, it came in on that date, so I think that they considered me fast because I was always able to meet my deadlines.

*TLC: How did you get the **Legion** job?*

**GL:** I was with Marvel doing **Spider-Man**, and it was at a time when there was a lot of craziness going on at Marvel. This is the days of Jim Shooter basically looking over the editors' shoulders and really running the company the way he wanted. If he didn't like an artist, he didn't work. I had been doing **Spider-Man** at that point for like two years. He wanted some changes on the book, changes were made, and when I was taken off of **Web of Spider-Man**, I just made some calls. I called Karen Berger over at DC, [and] went over to see her. There happened to be a spot available at **Legion**, and she offered it to me. So I made the jump to DC.

*TLC: How familiar were you with the **Legion** when you took it over?*

**GL:** Actually, **Legion** was my favorite DC book. As I said, I grew up collecting Marvel. The titles that I did collect at DC happened to be **Superboy** and **Legion**. So when I was offered that job, I was thrilled.

*TLC: Did it take you a while to get comfortable on the title?*

**GL:** Because there's so much history there, and it was one of my favorite books—Curt Swan was always my favorite DC artist—and **Legion** has just always had good quality artists, good quality stories, it was a little bit intimidating, and I just wanted to do my best work. I was coming from Marvel, coming from **Spider-Man**, so I felt confident. At that particular point [they were] doing the Baxter book, which was an experiment for them. It was kinda the prelude to Image quality books. We were doing things different with the color, doing things different with paper.

We really wanted this to be a fresh, huge book, and they let me know that going in. I was very complimented, you know, [by] the fact that they would choose me to handle that particular assignment. So I really gave it my best shot, and really enjoyed the book.

If you think back at that particular time, there were twenty-seven Legionnaires, so it can be a little bit difficult doing a book with twenty-seven characters and that much history, but also the greatest thing about it was you were dealing with a universe where there were certain things established, and Keith Giffen [had] established a certain look and feel of the things. It's just really nice to be able to not have to draw the New York City skyline and street lights, and be able to just invent the universe. So there was some tough things about the book, and there was also some things that artists love to do, so I looked at it as a challenge, but enjoyed the challenge.

*TLC: What was your relationship with Paul Levitz like?*

**GL:** I've always told people that **Legion** was my favorite book to draw, and one of the reasons was Karen Berger and Paul

*A convention sketch of Sensor Girl, courtesy of Miki Annamanthadoo.* Art © 2003 Greg LaRocque; Sensor Girl TM and © DC Comics.

Levitt. If you wanna talk about a guy being professional, Paul was as professional as it comes. I mean, I'm not sure what his title was at DC, but he was the boss. He basically ran the show. [He was an] extremely, extremely nice, professional guy. We had a working relationship where we knew a book had to get done every four weeks. The way we did it was he would hand me a script, I would work for two weeks, and then when I was two weeks into the assignment, [I would hand half of it in] and then the rest two weeks later. So basically they were getting a package from me every two weeks. We were knocking out a book every four weeks, on schedule. His script was always available as soon as I turned in the final pages of the assignment I was working on. I never, ever had to wait for a script for him. I think in the years that we worked on the book together, there might have been three pages where he asked for changes. He was just a prince to work with. Very professional, very nice. Every few months we would get together and he would tell me what was coming up as far as what he had in mind, [and] ask me if I had ideas. Most of the time those ideas ended up in the story. It's good to work with a writer who respects your opinion, and not only that, looks for ideas from you. It was just a joy all the way through.

Karen did it all with [class] when I was with Karen. She was the editor on the book. She was the one who hired me on the book, so I had a great relationship with her as well. What we all worried about was putting out a great book, and I think we did.

Wildfire gets a new look courtesy of LaRocque.
Wildfire TM and © DC Comics.

**TLC:** *How much latitude were you given to add things visually to the script that weren't there to begin with?*

**GL:** When I first started, Paul did full script. After a few months on the book— I'm not really sure how long—he actually changed over to more of a plot, like the old Marvel style, recognizing the fact that I do like taking scripts and adding things to it. When you've got a writer who respects that and can work with you, it makes it nice for an artist like me. I think it's best, and I think comic storytelling works best when you have an artist who has enough confidence to be able to contribute. Some writers are threatened by that. Paul was not. Karen was not, and I think, for me, the job was better. The job was easier. So yeah, I was not only eventually given that role as far as our relationship, but I was encouraged. Paul's scripts loosened up a bit and really gave me a lot of room to contribute. For me, I couldn't thank him enough. It was just great.

**TLC:** *There were a few new villains introduced during your run. Were those characters your designs?*

**GL:** Starfinger, yeah. I designed Starfinger. Paul would just dig these guys up and rewrite 'em and reintroduce them, and it's one of the things that I really did enjoy doing, taking the old characters and giving them a modern spin. The Time Trapper, actually. There was a new look given to him. I just said, "This guy's been around for a long while. Let's give him a little bit more ancient, ragged look." I talked to Karen about it, threw it in there, and I was really surprised to see that that was kinda his new look. [There were] a couple of aliens as well. They were always looking for new ideas, things that work. Whatever was gonna make the book better.

**TLC:** *How about Wildfire's new costume?*

**GL:** I walked in one day, and had an idea for it, showed it to them, and they said, "Cool! This is outstanding!" The whole idea about that human form was actually mine. What we wanted to do was expand on Dawnstar and his relationship. We started a few things. Unfortunately, as other things got developing we didn't push it too much. But yeah, the whole look there [was mine]. When Paul would pull

me in and we'd talk about things that we'd want to do, there was a scene where Dawnstar saw the new form and still rejected him. That was basically my idea, and it ended up in the story as well. It was really great when Paul would do that.

**TLC:** *A lot of times when an artist takes over the* **Legion**, *they have their own ideas for a new Legionnaire. Did you ever try to add anyone to the cast?*

**GL:** No. [*laughs*]

**TLC:** *I guess you figured they had enough already.*

**GL:** They had enough, and I figured Paul had a good handle on what he wanted to do with the book. It was enough for me to take what he handed me and work on it. So as far as that goes, I left that to Paul.

**TLC:** *Did you have much contact with* **Legion** *fans while you were the artist?*

**GL:** No. I didn't do very many conventions. They used to forward me the fan mail, so I would read some stuff like that, but I do know that **Legion** fans are very loyal. They've been very nice to me. It's been great.

**TLC:** *What was the appeal of the* **Legion** *to you?*

**GL:** The history of it, the costumes, the fact that Superboy was there, the whole unexplored universe of looks, aliens, having a book that's outside the established Marvel or DC universe where it's its very own universe, that is what I think is probably the most exciting thing about it. As I said, you don't have to draw the New York City skyline. There was a definite look to Legion headquarters—their portals, their machinery, their transportation and

Blok

Element Lad

Bouncing Boy

Ferro Lad

Brainiac 5

Invisible Kid I

Chameleon Boy

Invisible Kid II

Chemical King

Karate Kid

Colossal Boy

Lightning Lad

Cosmic Boy

Lightning Lass

Dawnstar

Magnetic Kid

Dream Girl

Duo Damsel

Matter-Eater Lad

© DC Comics.

such—things like that. But still, because there's so many fresh things that Paul would throw into the book, you're just constantly being asked to invent things. New aliens, new everything. So it was an artist's dream to be able to constantly be challenged to come up with this stuff.

**TLC:** *You had to draw the death of Superboy.*

**GL:** Yes.

**TLC:** *How did you approach that assignment?*

**GL:** Well, knowing what was coming up, I talked to Karen and we worked a schedule out so that I could actually have a little bit more time with those two particular books. As I've said before, Superboy was my favorite DC character. Knowing what was happening with that.... it was a weird assignment. Knowing that that history was changing, and that the Superboy that we knew was not the man that's destined to become the Superman that's currently in the books.... I can't say I was very happy with the storyline and the way that worked out, and actually can't say that I'm very happy with some of the history of **Legion** since I've left the book. I think that there are some **Legion** fans that agree with that, that would really like to see that story revisited and maybe some of this stuff changed. Maybe that shows my age, the fact that I'm loyal to the Curt Swan Superboy that I grew up with, but I think Paul provided a great story. I gave it my best on the pencils, and I hope people were pleased with the outcome.

**TLC:** *Which characters did you enjoy drawing the most?*

**GL:** Dawnstar was easily my favorite. Whenever I would do the conventions—and I would do a few more conventions later on after I left **Legion**, during my **Flash** days— easily my two most requested sketches were Dawnstar and Dream Girl. I liked drawing both of them. I liked doing Timber Wolf. Mon-El was always a favorite, 'cause he was so close to the Superboy thing, and also Superboy.

**TLC:** *Were there any characters who were just a pain to draw?*

**GL:** I hate to even mention it, but probably Quislet was my least favorite. [He was a] weird little character. We did have some fun with him going into his dimension, and that's where we changed Wildfire, but he probably was the least interesting character to draw.

**TLC:** *Is there any one story arc or issue that you're especially proud of?*

**GL:** Well, "The Death of Superboy" [**LSH #'s 37-38** —**Ed.**], of course. I remember one particular issue which featured Ferro Lad and Princess Projectra and Karate Kid from the old days [**LSH #31** —**Ed.**], and probably that has something to do with me, again, going back to drawing a story of the Legion when I was reading it, as a fan there. The Sensor Girl trilogy where it was revealed that she was Princess Projectra, probably that one. Of course, also the Emerald Empress. She was fun to draw. Just so you'll know, I liked to sometimes assign actresses and actors to the characters so that I'd get a feel to what I wanted to do with them, and Sybil Danning was my Emerald Empress.

**TLC:** *When you were working on the **Legion**, could you separate yourself from it as a fan and look at it through the eyes of a professional?*

**GL:** For me, that was pretty much impossible. I'm just a comic book geek fan from way back, and it was always fun whenever the book would come out. I'd be waiting anxiously for days, and then when it came out I'd pick it up even though it's my own work, and it's just weird to do that. I was still a fan of the book. I'd just look at it and pore over it. You have to try to separate it so that you do your job, but still, being a fan is a big part of enjoying the job, and it was always fun.

**TLC:** *Why did you eventually leave the title?*

**GL:** I was on the book for, I don't know, sixty issues, maybe? [*Actually, it was 32.* —**Ed.**] I had talked to Karen about if there was something else available, **Flash** became available, and I did think it was the right move at the time. Even for that time, sixty issues on the book was a long run. I mean, it's unheard of today that an artist is going to stay on a book for sixty issues. People jump now after just a few issues—six issues—and you just need sometimes to get the battery recharged by doing something different. So it was just the right move.

**TLC:** *You bring up an interesting point: today if an artist stays on a comic for twelve issues in a row, it's considered to be a big deal. When did that start to happen in the industry, and why do you think it occurred?*

**GL:** I just think that nowadays the continuity that we used to cultivate in comic

books has been thrown out the window. You used to be able to take a book, find a writer, find an artist for it, and the readers of that particular book knew what they were getting every month. Storylines ran for years. **Flash**, of course, was a different book, but the growth that you saw in Wally West over the five years that I did that book were very easy to chart from the beginning. We saw him go from a mixed-up teenager to a man, and it took literally five years to tell that story. Nowadays, because of the change in just everything—and where that change came from, you can point to a lot of things: the change in storytelling in movies,

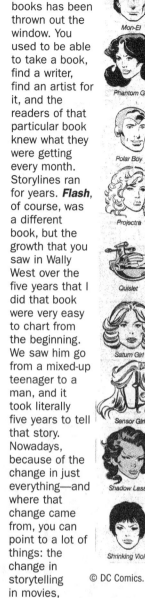

Star Boy
Mon-El
Sun Boy
Phantom Girl
Superboy
Polar Boy
Supergirl
Projectra
Tellus
Quislet
Timber Wolf
Saturn Girl
Tyroc
Sensor Girl
Ultra Boy
Shadow Lass
White Witch
Shrinking Violet
Wildfire

© DC Comics.

the change in storytelling in television, where people want this immediate gratification—it's [become] "What can you put on the table this month that's gonna make the reader pick this book up and buy this book?" So, it's more like a singular issue thing, as opposed to, "Let's cultivate a reader that's gonna come back every month." Where that came from and why it's infected the comic book industry as much as it has, it's gotta go to the editors. The editors were competing against each other, and they just wanted to give the special of the month, [or] the hit of the month. They still do seek out storytelling and continuity, but it's just not as important as it used to be.

**TLC:** *But why do you think a lot of artists just can't draw a title month in and month out?*

**GL:** I really don't know. That's a good question. I've talked to some young guys, and they have such a problem meeting their deadlines. They just get tired of the book real fast, [they get] tired of the work real fast. I don't know if it's just something inherent in the generation of people as they've changed. The work can be a grind. Very often you're sitting alone in your studio or your room, and you gotta churn out the work. It can be difficult work, and it's challenging work. You have to look at it as a profession, and be a professional. Some people have the makeup and the personality to do this kind of work, some people don't. It seems like this generation of artists just aren't going to invest the time and the work, and are always looking for that fresh project so that they always have fresh energy and fresh enthusiasm. Maybe it's good, maybe it's bad. There's good parts to it and there's bad parts to it. I do kinda miss a long run of a particular artist on a book where you see that continuity and that growth. But there's Jim Lee doing **Batman**, [and] now that's the coolest thing in the world. So, there's good and bad to it.

**TLC:** *How would you rate your **Legion** expe-rience now, looking back at it?*

**GL:** I think it's some of my best work. It's some of my best super-hero work, and it was, as I said before, some of the most enjoyable times I've had in comic books, working with Paul, working with Karen. DC is, without a doubt, the greatest company in the world to work for, and I have nothing but pleasant memories of it.

**TLC:** *Is it something that you'd like to draw again someday?*

**GL:** Without a doubt. I actually was up in the DC offices a few months ago. I haven't worked for DC or Marvel, as you probably know, for a few years here. I've been keeping my feet wet in the independent market, but that can be torture [*laughs*], let me tell you. I've actually turned down some assignments because I'm just tired of being taken advantage of here on the lower end. That's why I decided to knock on the door up there and see what might be had. I'm actually talking to Mike Carlin, and I want to get some samples to show around and see what could be available up there.

**TLC:** *So you're still working in comics?*

**GL:** Yeah. I've always been lucky enough to get an assignment here and there. I did some self-publishing. I did some work for London Knight Studios, for Avatar, for a smaller company by the name of Peregrine, but these books are really hard to find, because some independents are that hard to find.

**TLC:** *Where do you see yourself five years from now?*

**GL:** Well, I work a full-time job. I work for a company that does license work. We do work for Nickelodeon characters. It's an art studio. We design toys, we do stickers, that type of work, but this is a little bit different genre. With this company, I've actually been able to learn a lot because my skills with DC and Marvel were penciling chores, and you sit down with a blank sheet of paper and you draw with a pencil. Now that I'm in here with this company, I've been learning computer skills, learning PhotoShop, Illustrator, and Quark, so that's actually unleashed a whole different side of my talent. I'm doing a lot more color work now. When I did my independent work as well, I was doing some color work. So I'm kicking out commissions as far as portraits and individual work like that.

I've actually just finished a graphic novel for a publisher. The work that I did a few years back, the character was Crybaby for XL Studios—that's my studio—and I've put together an eighty-page graphic novel for that now. The publisher ran out of money, so we weren't able to get the book published, so I'm gonna be shopping that around. I hope to get that published, or I may just go ahead and go out on the limb and just arrange something on my own, but comic book sales right now are not the best, so I would hate to see the book sit there and not get published. I've gotta get together with some people and just see if it's financially feasible for me to go ahead and do this. I just want to keep myself working, [and] see what comes along as far as assignments go. If DC or Marvel could throw something my way, I'd try to fit it in, but I am working full-time for another company to pay the mortgage on the house, and to keep running the studio.

*Continuity housecleaning does what no super-villain could: Superboy is laid to rest in this double-page spread by LaRocque. From the collection of Fred L. deBoom.* © DC Comics.

# Keith Giffen
## Part Two

In Part Two of our interview with Keith Giffen, he discusses his return to the title in the late Eighties, his revamp of the book through the early Nineties, and what went on behind the scenes during his "Five Years Later" version of the title. As with Part One, Part Two was conducted by Glen Cadigan and copy-edited by Giffen.

**TLC:** *So what made you return to the* ***Legion*** *in 1988?*

**KG:** I'm tempted to say another paycheck. The *Legion* is a book that's always exerted this weird kind of siren song on me. I just keep returning to it eventually. I wouldn't be all that surprised if I wind up doing *Legion* work down the line again someday.

**TLC:** *That was the period when you gave all of the Legionnaires new costumes. What was the reaction to that?*

**KG:** If I remember correctly, it was the usual reaction to any change in a long-running series: shrieks of outrage, followed by this grudging acceptance, followed by a handful of people stepping up and going, "Well, I kinda almost sorta like it." Legion fans, God love 'em, they're definitely a vocal bunch. I remember coming on the *Legion* and being told, "You're no Pat Broderick!" And then when I left the *Legion*, Greg LaRocque was going, "My God! They're all over me because I'm not doing it like you!" Then when I came back on the *Legion*, I was told, "You're no Greg LaRocque!" [*laughs*], so that's part and parcel [of the job], and it was just part of why I enjoy *Legion* fandom so much.

**TLC:** *You mentioned earlier that you'd like a chance to do "The Magic Wars" over again. What went wrong there?*

**KG:** For the life of me, I can't remember. If you go by limited recollection, I think it might have been just a scheduling thing

that I had to really, really rush my way through it, and I shouldn't have. There may have been more to it than that, but for the life of me I can't put my finger on it right now.

Keep in mind, most of these things that happened that had to do with the artwork or the approach or my side of the book, ninety percent of them were my fault. You know, your head's in the wrong place, or you take on too much work, or you don't walk when you should have. There are so many things that can impact the art and impact the book. I never wanted it to get thought, "Well, Paul was writing those stories, and therefore [it's his fault]." No, no, no, no. Most of the problems I had on the *Legion* were *mine*.

**TLC:** *When you returned to the* ***Legion***, *did you know going in that Paul was only going to stick around for another year?*

**KG:** Yes.

**TLC:** *Were you one of the people who tried to convince him to stay?*

**KG:** No. When Paul makes up his mind, you can joke around with him about it, but you are not going to change his mind. Paul digs his heels in, and that's it. He pretty much figured it'd run its course. He knew he had other stuff that was going to start demanding the

lion's share of his attention as he worked his way up the corporate ladder, and he had the professionalism to say, "Rather than do it at fifty percent, I'll leave."

**TLC:** *So did the two of you put your heads together and come up with a year-long plan?*

**KG:** Not really. When I worked with Paul, I followed Paul's lead. I'd kibitz and add little things and make suggestions, but Paul

*Top: Giffen in the early '90s. Above: the Legion assembles for a group photo in this* ***Who's Who*** *piece. The Legion of Super-Heroes TM and © DC Comics.*

A scene from **Invasion!**, complete with missing word balloons. From the editor's collection. © DC Comics.

was always very, very generous with the co-plotter credit across the board.

**TLC:** *How did **L.E.G.I.O.N. '89** come about?*

**KG:** At the end of **Invasion!**, we were waiting for people to come and want to do spin-off books, because at the end of any crossover, a lot of spin-off books come out. Nobody stepped up. The reason I did **L.E.G.I.O.N. '89** and **JLE** was because there were all these openings for spin-off books, and I felt, "Well, if no one else is going to do them, I'll grab them." I think Bob Fleming came up with **Blasters**, as well. You have to understand, **Invasion!** as a mini-series was not very popular among the professional rank and file up at DC. I guess nobody wanted to play in our playground. **L.E.G.I.O.N. '89** was an idea waiting to happen. "The Legion's in the 30th Century. What would a Legion in the 20th Century be like?" Once I found out I could use Vril Dox and steal Phantom Girl, and also [use] Lyrissa Mallor, then it all just fell together.

**TLC:** *Did you ever feel like your hands were tied on that title because it all had to line up with the **Legion** a thousand years later?*

**KG:** Nope, I never felt I had to line it up with the **Legion** a thousand years later because I was dealing with the reality now. I kept a weather eye on it, of course, but no. The first year of **L.E.G.I.O.N. '89** was just sheer enjoyment. It was really just flying by the seat of your pants and having a ball.

**TLC:** *Why, exactly, did you return to the **Legion** then?*

**KG:** I guess I went back then to really try to do something, really, really, really different with the book, and it sounded like DC was really ready for something radically different to be done with the **Legion**. I went in figuring, "Let's give it a shot!" but I didn't want to be too radically different, which is why I brought in Tom and Mary, who were very much of Legion fandom, and had great affection for Legion history. They were pretty much there to temper my more extreme ideas.

**TLC:** *Why take the Legion five years further into the future?*

**KG:** Just the chance to try something different. And I told Karen what I wanted to do with the book, and she was for it. I guess it was my chance to try something different in terms of how you structure the story [and] what happened to the characters. Just take the book in a new direction. And it was also the home of the infamous nine-panel grid, which I was castigated for doing and Dave Gibbons, when he did it in **Watchmen**, was a genius! I guess people were trying to say, "Well, he did it better than you did." But I have never done anything as unpopular as that nine-panel grid in my career. And I'll tell you why I was doing it: because you're getting more story! Apparently not.

**TLC:** *How shortly after you relaunched the **Legion** did you start to feel that DC wasn't supporting it, or that the support which you had for it was slipping away?*

**KG:** I forget what provoked the confrontation, but there was a confrontation with the **Superman** group. I've often wondered, "Did I have anything to do with that?" 'cause I seem to remember walking in and finding out that we could no longer use any **Superman** mythos retroactively. And I thought, "What does that mean, 'retroactively'? [Does] that mean that I've got a group here that's been influenced by a character whom I'm [not] allowed to acknowledge?" And that was why that hourglass issue came about. [**LSH** V4 #5 —Ed.] But it was that early that everything started falling apart. It was just this real, dogged determination on mine and Tom and Mary's part to fix things so that we weren't doing the white event that everyone thought I was going to do. I think everyone really thought, "Oh, he's just going to erase it all and do it his way. He's such a maniac! He's got such a big ego!" and yet we struggled to try to salvage as much as was humanly possible in that book. There were times when I thought, "Why am I bothering? I'm over here, I'm trying really hard to respect the book, and I'm just getting nailed for it." But that's part and parcel [of the business].

**TLC:** *Didn't DC want you to start over from scratch at one point?*

**KG:** Yes. At one point, I was taken out to lunch, and they said, "Why don't you do a 'white event'? Just get rid of everything? It's too complicated." But that would have meant not only saying to the Legion fans, "Oh, by the way, the last thirty years? [*laughs*] F*ck you." It would also have meant doing what I brought the book five years ahead to avoid doing, and I couldn't do it. I remember saying, "Absolutely not," and that was the beginning of the end there.

**TLC:** *How far into the run was this?*

**KG:** It was probably not too far removed from the "Khund War" saga [**LSH** V4 #'s 15-17 —**Ed.**] when I quit the book for a couple of months.

**TLC:** *So those weren't just fill-in issues?*

**KG:** No, no, no. That was, "Oh my God, he's gone." I came back in time to do the covers. I walked off of that book many times. Most of the time it was just a one- or two-day walk off, but that one lasted a bit. It didn't even come down to supporting the book. It was just... it was like being pecked to death by ducks. It got to the point where it just got ridiculous. Everything I did was being second-guessed. Even Legion fandom was going, "Since when is Dream Girl this sorceress?" I'm thinking, "No, that's Glorith." "Oh, but she's got Dream Girl's hair." "Excuse me?" That was pretty much what I was putting up with on a day-to-day basis.

**TLC:** *What did you think people's reaction to the "Five Years Later" Legion would be heading into it?*

**KG:** I had no idea. I learned early on that my take on things is pretty far removed from the way things are gonna turn out. I have never had a success in the comic book industry that I didn't walk into thinking it was going to be an abject failure. I thought I was going to be fired for doing the **Justice League** the way that we did it. I thought **Lobo** was gonna be a disaster. **Legion**, I guess... I don't want the book to go away. I want there to be a **Legion**. And it was kind of shaky, in danger of maybe going away. Plus, like I say, I've always had a soft spot for the **Legion**. I guess I didn't know what to expect. I certainly didn't expect the open assault from every angle. You know, DC, fandom... [it was] like, "Jesus! It's just a comic book! Relax!"

The "Five Years Later" thing, everyone thinks was an act of ego on my part because I wanted my **Legion** to be mine, mine, mine, and not to build up to it. What it really was was I knew that I had to dismantle a lot of stuff that Paul had worked for on his run, [and] I didn't want to be the guy that did that. I wanted to boost my run on the **Legion** far enough away from Paul's that his run on the book would just remain his run on the book, and nobody would

screw with it.

**TLC:** *Were there any events put into "The Magic Wars" to set up your own run on the* **Legion***?*

**KG:** One, but I don't recall what it was. I recall specifically asking for one thing.

**TLC:** *Was it the death of Magnetic Kid?*

**KG:** No.

**TLC:** *So he wasn't killed to set up the events of Cosmic Boy's downward slide?*

**KG:** No, no, no, no.

**TLC:** *On a scale of one to ten, how close did you get to telling the story which you wanted to tell?*

**KG:** Five. I got about halfway there.

**TLC:** *So what would we have seen had you stayed?*

**KG:** Had I stayed and not been interfered with, the SW6 batch would be discovered to be the real Legion. The conspiracy theory was true. They were taken and stuffed aside somewhere—put in statis. My guys—the guys I'd been playing with—were clones. The war to free Earth would have been much bigger and more spectacular and had real moments of tragedy. Then when Earth was freed, the kids would inherit Earth and the United Planets, and whatever team was gonna continue with the **Legion of Super-Heroes** book would move it slowly back to that good future. My guys, what was left of them, would wander off to another solar system where they would become the last bastion of law and order before the unknown, and they would call themselves the

Omega Men, and we'd revive that team.

**TLC:** *Can you see why people might have been upset to learn that the characters which they had been following for years were clones?*

**KG:** Yeah, sure, but I don't care. That sounds cold, but I really don't care. It was the story that was being told. I sat down and thought about it long and hard, and I really wanted to give people back this young Legion. Cloning them and giving them young kids, well, that wasn't giving them back the Legion of Super-Heroes, now was it? Doing this, it gave them back the Legion of Super-Heroes. It was their Legion of Super-Heroes. It was the characters that they knew and loved, and if you wanted to play the continuity game, the fact that they were clones could cover

*The cover to Part Two of "The Khund War." From the collection of Miki Annamanthadoo.* © DC Comics.

*DC may have published it, but* **The Heckler** *is TM and © 2003 Keith Giffen and Tom & Mary Bierbaum. Courtesy of Spencer Beck.*

every continuity glitch ever since [way] back when. I could understand that [it would piss people off] just like I could understand the hourglass issue was gonna piss people off, and Laurel Gand was gonna piss people off, but then, what do they say? "If you don't piss people off, you're not doing your job."

Don't get me wrong: I did not want to make an enemy out of Legion fandom. I did not go out to deliberately ruffle people's feathers, but I didn't second-guess the story based on, "Oh, this might piss off a certain amount of people who really like this character," or "this might offend a certain amount of people," simply because you're going for the overall audience. You're going for the impact. And it's comics! It's a comic book! If I give Superman a third leg and people go, "Wow! I really hate the third leg!" I can take it away. So it's trying different things.

**TLC:** *What about Legionnaires who joined after the Silver Age? What was your take on them?*

**KG:** Those could be reintroduced as necessary. If they were wanted, then they would be left behind on Earth. It was going to be

a real, fair divvying up. I was actually going to take most of the duplicate characters.

**TLC:** *Have you heard the Keith Giffen hat trick rumor?*

**KG:** That was the whole deal. When we did the Earth war [aka "The Terra Mosaic," **LSH** V4 #'s 26-36], every Legionnaire's name was gonna be put into a hat, and I think five were gonna be pulled, and they would die. It was the only way to do it fairly. I had my favorites, and everyone had their favorites. I figured this was the best [way to do it]. Now, those characters that were critical to ongoing storylines would not make it into the hat, but there were certain characters [who would]. Yeah, that was true.

**TLC:** *Do you think that if you had told the same story, only using different characters like Alan Moore did with* **Watchmen**, *that it would have had the same reaction?* [**Note:** **Watchmen** *was originally based upon the then-newly acquired Charlton characters.* —**Ed.**]

**KG:** I never even thought of that. No, because I'm no Alan Moore, and Alan was at the top of his game then. I think that **Watchmen**'s success was due to the fact that at that point, Alan Moore and Dave Gibbons were at their peak. They were at the top of their game. It was just really mindbending stuff, some of the themes that Alan was exploring. If you break down my "Five Years Later" Legion, it pretty much dates back to the old pulp fiction stuff. Moore and Gibbons, they were on a whole 'nother level. I think they would have succeeded wildly with the Charlton characters or done as it was, and I think Legion "Five Years Later" wouldn't have that **Legion of Super-Heroes** backlash, but I maintain that it was **Legion of Super-Heroes** that kept it alive sometimes, just the fact that it was a marquee name. I don't know how it would have done if we had come out with all [new characters]. I have no idea what other name we could have used, but I think for the story I was telling, it had to be **Legion of Super-Heroes**.

**TLC:** *We've gone all this time and we haven't even mentioned the Legion of Substitute-Heroes.*

**KG:** Yeah, poor group. That's my bipolar group. When everyone wants to take them seriously, I turn them into buffons, and

when everyone thinks they're buffons, I introduce them in "Five Years Later" as an effective commando squad. It's just the whole idea of unfulfilled potential that the **Legion** was full of. All these wonderful characters just waiting for somebody to come along and give 'em a new twist. I used to love doing the Substitute Heroes stuff because it proved that Paul Levitz does have a sense of humor.

**TLC:** *Do you think you were unfairly criticized for turning them into comic relief?*

**KG:** Not at all. If the criticism is heartfelt, there's no unfair criticism, because criticism is an opinion. I can disagree.

**TLC:** *When you did leave your "Five Years Later" Legion, was it a case of you'd been worn down to a certain point?*

**KG:** I don't know if "worn down" [is the right term]. I did spend a lot of time during that run angry more than worn down. I know I left the book angry. I know that blowing up Earth was a temper tantrum, but I wouldn't say worn down. I guess "fed up" [is more accurate].

**TLC:** *Was that the one time in your career when you put your heart and soul into your work moreso than any other?*

**KG:** I always try to throw one hundred per cent of myself into the work, but I guess the Legion thing, there was a little bit more in there, a little bit more in terms of what I really wanted to do in terms of storytelling and tone in a book. I'm revisiting that territory now with the **Reign of Zodiac**, the large cast and the convoluted Byzantine storylines. Yeah, I guess that was. I guess out of all the work I'd done for DC up until that point, the **Legion** was the book that I put that little bit of extra into, that "Five Years Later" [run].

**TLC:** *Do you think that the work which you did during that* **Legion** *era has affected your chances of returning to the title one day?*

**KG:** Well, they say that in comics you're only as good as your last failure. I don't think so. If I were to go back to the **Legion**, I'd carry a lot of baggage with me. There are certain expectations, or prejudices people have by hearing that I'm going on the book, as opposed to hearing Jeff Loeb, or somebody else is going on the book. I guess it depends on who's editing it. Some guy who really loathed what I did is not going to give me the work, but some guy who liked what I did is going to be more amenable. It depends on

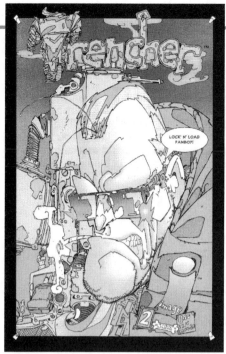

*Another of Giffen's creator-owned properties: Trencher is TM and © 2003 Keith Giffen.*

who's in the driver's seat.

**TLC:** *Are you reading the current **Legion** comic?*

**KG:** No.

**TLC:** *What was your reaction when you heard about the reboot?*

**KG:** I didn't do it. I'm clean. I'm innocent. That was pretty much it. I didn't want to do it; Abnett and Lanning found a way to make it work.

**TLC:** *How much consideration do you give to whoever has to write a comic after you've left it?*

**KG:** None. I tell the stories that I want to tell. When I don't want to tell the stories anymore, I usually walk away from it. Like on **Justice League**, I always maintain I stayed ten issues too long. I really should have left at number fifty, like I was planning on doing. When I left the **Justice League** book, that didn't mean that there were no more **Justice League** stories to tell, it just meant that there were no more **Justice League** stories that I wanted to tell. Whoever's gonna come on the book either picks up where I left off or discards it [and] sends it in a whole other direction. Unless the guy comes up and specifically makes a request, that's different. That's a direct request. But in terms of, "Okay, I know I'm doing my last issue, and I know that [so and so] is taking over," I'm not going to go, "Hmm, I wonder if I could set something up for [him]." No. That's ridicu-

lous. He doesn't need my help.

**TLC:** *Do you admit that you push the envelope?*

**KG:** Sure. You have to, don't you?

**TLC:** *Are you your own best judge of whether you've pushed it too far?*

**KG:** No. Not at all. Stuff I think is completely innocent, people go, "Oh, God, no." Stuff that I just figure is a nice little chuckle, people back away [from]. They're appalled. I'm not a good judge at all as to whether I've gone too far, which is why on a book like **Lobo**, I really need an editor, otherwise I'm afraid it's gonna go spiralling off into a weird place where we probably don't want to be. I've got billboards in the **Lobo** comic that [read], "I can't believe it's not yogurt; the only fertility clinic you'll ever need." That got taken out. *"Batman V: The Apology."* They didn't think that Warner Brothers would find that very funny. The funny thing was, *"Bulimia II: The Return"* stayed there. I guess I tend to project my tolerance, or trawling the gutter, onto other people. [But] I'll tell you, working the **Battle Royale** book? Twice helping translate that thing I've been poleaxed by what I've seen there, so I'm not the worst. There are people out there who are sicker than me.

**TLC:** *You left the industry there for a period in the mid-Nineties to work in animation.*

**KG:** There was no work. I wasn't getting any work. I had to. I had to survive. I couldn't get arrested.

**TLC:** *So what brought you back to comics?*

**KG:** I could get arrested. It was weird, because in my entire career in comics, I've only been offered a job three times. The rest of the time I've either had to find it for myself or I'm offered something to rework. I'm talking about offered a job that's already there. That was when Karen Berger said, "You want to take over the **Legion** after Paul is gone?" and Mike Barr said, "You want to take over the **Legion**?" There's two **Legion** references. And Peter Tomasi called and asked me if I wanted **Suicide Squad**. Other than that, it's always been, "You want to take over **Justice League**? You have to rework them from number one," or "You want to do this? It has to be from number one." I get these little damaged, f*cked up birds, and I gotta see if I can make them fly again. I kinda like that, but it would be nice if somebody goes, "Well, you know, you've been doing okay, so you want to do **Batman** for a

while?" But I never get that. I've never been offered any of that stuff. I think it might have a lot to do with the fact that I don't have the circuit breaker in my head that says, "This isn't appropriate for the book."

**TLC:** *You have been accused of reworking concepts a lot.*

**KG:** Yeah, and you know what? That's part and parcel of this field. I mean, [if] you stop growing, you stagnate. When I was doing **Justice League**, okay, [everything] was grim and gritty, **Dark Knight** and **Punisher** were *oooh, scary*, and we came out with a sitcom. But the deal was, I said, "If we're using your character and they walk into a **Justice League** book, we're gonna have a little bit of fun with them, but we'll return them to you in the same shape they were when they walked into the book. We won't f*ck 'em up." And even then, people were just, "Oh, but they're acting silly. They're acting funny." I thought, "No, they're acting human." And a lot of times, I'm called on specifically to rework a book. It's not like I go, "Oh, you offered me the **Flash**. I'll turn him into a Hispanic woman." I'm usually called on and said, "We'd like the Flash to be a Hispanic woman. Think you can work that?"

**TLC:** *So it cuts both ways?*

*During the mid-'90s, Giffen even spent some time at Valiant. Punx TM and © 2003 Acclaim Entertainment, Inc.*

**KG:** Yes. It amuses me how many people would actually rather see a book die then see the changes made to keep the book alive. I mean, if I hear, "Bring back Hal," one more time... Get over it.

**TLC:** *What's your take on the current state of the industry?*

**KG:** Super-heroes are dead. The cycle's played itself out, just like it did in the Fifties. Move on. There's horror, western, romance, humor. Let's start diversifying what we have out there. This might mean giving severe beatings to a lot of comic book shop owners, but I can live with that. With Tokyopop and Viz and the Shogun Weekly books embarrassing us in terms of sales, and the huge, phone book-like packages for $4.95 when two of our pamphlets are already up around six bucks... we're being slaughtered. We've gotta rethink it. Completely rethink it, and I think the first thing we have to do is say, "Continuity is a dirty word. Never invoke it again."

To me, it still should be Batman *and* Robin. They're perennials. You know what? You're thirty-two years old? You find it childish? You're supposed to find it childish! Archie still can't decide between the blonde and the brunette, and that book is still selling well! Charles Schulz died and Charlie Brown never kicked the football. There are books out there [where], yes, characters can develop. *Gasoline Alley* was a comic strip where people grew with the readers, but there are certain perennials. Batman and Robin. It's Batman and Robin, and Robin is Dick Grayson. *Superman* is basically about goofy Lois trying to find out that Superman and Clark Kent are one and the same. Use eight-page stories. All these books don't have to be stuff we like. They've got to be stuff that we recognize as commercially viable.

I think one of the most damaging things [about] the comic fan becoming the comic book professional is that they come in going, "I don't know. That seems old hat, because they always fight Dr. Doom that way," and yet every comic book is supposed to potentially be somebody's first. So the fiftieth Dr. Doom story could be some kid's first exposure to Dr. Doom. We gotta rethink the way we do business across the board, and I think part of it is just acknowledging we're comic books. We're kinda goofy, we're gonna stay that way, and there's room for Stan Lee-type *X-Men*, *FF* stuff, where the growth is gradual and they'll get mar-ried and have a kid and stuff like that, but there's also room for the perennial characters, the characters that become such an engraved part of the American junk culture landscape. I can go to Mogadeshu and stop the first person I see and go, "Superman," and he'll go, "Oh yeah, Clark Kent." Everyone wants that kind of recognition for their character, and yet now the character's unrecognizable. I'm sorry, [but] you marry Superman off to Lois Lane and it becomes the adventures of your parents. What kid wants to read that?

**TLC:** *So do you see yourself sticking with the industry for the foreseeable future?*

**KG:** I don't think I'll ever be able to put this industry completely behind me no matter how much I rail [against it]. Keep in mind here, I love the comic book format for telling stories. I love the medium. My problem is the business has grown to allegedly serve the medium, but has now become more important than the creative endeavor. When you have a support system that is more important than what it's been put there to support, you're in trouble. I used to think comics were dead. I don't think comics are dead anymore. I think the super-heroes are. I think we can survive. Just figure out a direction to go in and somebody brave enough to take it. Again, I could say, "Look toward Tokyopop. Look toward the books that are selling. Look toward the successes."

**TLC:** *One last question: How proud are you of your body of* **Legion** *work?*

**KG:** I'd do it again the same way without a second thought.

**TLC:** *Both runs?*

**KG:** Yes. Even if I knew that poster was coming to blow me out, I'd still do it. I like what I did on the **Legion**. I enjoyed doing the **Legion**. I even enjoyed the more obnoxious fans. It was fun. It was fun to do. It's something I'm glad I got a chance to do. It's something that, hey, don't be surprised if I wind up back there again somehow.

**TLC:** *Is it one of those comics that you just can't get out of your head?*

**KG:** I think so, yeah. Pretty much so. I don't pick it up anymore, but again, it'll just be me going, "That's not the way I'd do it." But you know what? If they called me tomorrow and said, "You want to come back?" I'd probably go. I have no idea what I'd do at this point, but I'd probably go.

*From a DC house ad advertising "The Quiet Darkness Saga," the thematic sequel to "The Great Darkness Saga." © DC Comics.*

# Tom & Mary Bierbaum

In 1989, longtime Legion fans Tom & Mary Bierbaum became the new scripters of the **Legion of Super-Heroes**, and along with plotter/artist Keith Giffen embarked on perhaps the most controversial era in Legion history. Loved by some, hated by others, the "TMK" era continues to be a hot topic of debate amongst Legion fans today. While some may disagree with their approach, the Bierbaums dedication to the Legion was never in question, and their extensive knowledge of Legion history proved to be an asset to them during their time as scripters.

The following interview was conducted by Glen Cadigan on Feb. 10, 2003, and although Mary's name is absent from the text below, she was present for part of the interview. That being said, Tom did all of the talking, and it is his comments which appear below. The interview was also copyedited by Tom, and in some places, reconstructed due to technical difficulties.

**TLC:** *When did you start following the Legion of Super-Heroes?*

**TB:** I was reading it from childhood. The earliest issue that I remember was **Adventure** [**Comics**] #310. I don't remember the name of it, but the one where the Mxyztplk character killed off all the Legionnaires, and at the end of the story, they used magic to bring them all back. I had read the Legion in childhood, and became a really dedicated fan about ten years later. One of my younger brothers really picked up the **Legion** at that time, and we started reading it together and getting interested together. As far as Mary goes, I think she read it casually as a kid, but really didn't read it regularly until probably the late Seventies, when she got involved in Legion fandom. We actually met through Legion fandom. She had friends who were in **Interlac** and other Legion-oriented groups.

**TLC:** *What was it about the Legion which made it catch your attention?*

**TB:** I think initially, at a young age, the number of characters. For me, I think it really gave you the opportunity to pick a favorite. I come from a large family, and there was always an attraction to a situation where we could all have our own favorite heroes. In the early days the characters were not that well defined, but that allowed us all to believe that whoever we picked was a great hero and a great guy, and as good as any of the other heroes.

I think the one that first caught my eye was Ultra Boy. At that point, his bright uniform [and] the emblem he had was really intriguing to me, and he became a favorite. I think the future had a lot to do with it, [too]. I think the setting in the future was exciting and the future was inviting. I think

that probably was what really got me hooked as a kid, and then later on when I really got deeply into it, it was almost, as much as anything, nostalgia for the Legion that I remembered from those earlier years. So really, the size of the group and the optimism of the future has always been part of the appeal.

**TLC:** *When did you start to become aware that there was an organized Legion fan base out there?*

**TB:** I guess I was aware of it very early, because they launched a Legion fan club and created **The Legion Outpost** in 1972, and I think within a year somebody sent me a sample copy of **The Legion Outpost**. I never knew quite the mechanism, but myself and my brother, who were Legion fans, were writing letters to the editor at that time, and they must have gotten our address out of the letter column. I think it was the third issue of **The Legion Outpost** that we received. We didn't really get active in fandom at that point. I actually submitted some stories and artwork to **The Legion Outpost**, but got turned down. It was several years later that I met somebody who was involved in **Interlac**. I'd sort of fallen out of touch with Legion fandom, and then I came across somebody who was a member of **Interlac**, so I got reintroduced into Legion fandom and became directly involved at that time.

In terms of my wife, I think she was involved in other APAs [*Amateur Press Associations —* **Ed.**], and met Legion fans in the other APAs, and then ended up becoming a member of **Interlac**, so I think that was when she became aware of Legion fandom.

**TLC:** *How did the two of you meet face to face?*

**TB:** I actually lived on the East Coast, and I moved out west to try and get work in the entertainment industry. I think I was still on the waitlist of **Interlac** at that time, and I was in touch with all the

*The Legion gets younger, courtesy of Chris Sprouse and Karl Story. From the collection of Royd Burgoyne.*
© DC Comics.

The Bierbaums first collaborated with Keith Giffen on *Wally Wood's T.H.U.N.D.E.R. Agents.* T.H.U.N.D.E.R. Agents TM and © 2003 John Carbonaro.

members that lived out there, and met them all, and relied on them for assistance. I was living in Delaware, and had gone to college there, and was looking for as much assistance as I could get when I went out to California.

**TLC:** *When did the two of you become a writing team?*

**TB:** Early on, we were living together and were both interested in writing. The first thing we wrote together was a Halloween story contest in the local paper, and we came up with an idea—it was really a Legion story—and submitted it and won that contest. Then pretty soon we started writing stories together for the APAs and submitting stories to the comics industry.

**TLC:** *So how did the two of you get involved with Keith Giffen?*

**TB:** Pretty early on in our writing, Keith had become the artist on the *Legion* book during the Paul Levitz era. Keith was excited about the assignment and very dedicated to it, and I'm sure Paul told him about *Interlac* and the Legion APAs. I'm not sure quite how—I think one of the

members spoke with Keith—but in some way we became aware he'd be interested in our ideas, and especially pieces of research any of us had about the background of the Legion universe. I sent Keith a letter, and the thrust of the letter was uniform suggestions for some of the Legionnaires. He used one of the uniforms that I had suggested [*Element Lad* —**Ed.**], and was looking for somebody who had a good background in the Legion and [who] was a member of Legion fandom as kind of a sounding board. So he enjoyed the chance to occasionally call and find out what I was thinking of the book.

Eventually he noticed in *Interlac* that we were submitting ideas to the comic book companies in hopes of working. He noticed that, and at one point he called up and said that he might be interested in working with us. He had an assignment for a comic called *Wally Wood's Thunder Agents* which Deluxe Comics put out in '84, [or] '85. They approached Keith and wanted to work with him, and asked him who he'd like to work with as a writer. He thought it would be cool to give us a break. He would plot the story and let us dialogue it, and that was really how it got started with us and Keith. We did five stories for that comic, and it was fun and didn't really necessarily lead anywhere, but then a few years later, Keith was given the chance to pencil the *Legion* and plot it and he needed a dialoguer. We were out there getting a little bit more work as time went on, and [adding] some more professional credits to our name, [so] when they asked Keith to discuss people he'd like to have as dialoguers, he mentioned several possibilities, and we were among them.

**TLC:** *Were the two of you a hard sell to DC?*

**TB:** I have no direct knowledge of that. I have heard people tell second-hand stories to imply that there was some considerable resistance, yes. I don't know that directly, but I've heard that there were some authoritative people who were not particularly convinced that we were the right people for the job. I know Dick Giordano, who was always

very supportive of us, did want to see a sample assignment from us before we would be given the assignment. In fact, they sent us the pencils to an upcoming *Legion* issue, and Keith ran through the plot with us and said, "Okay, dialogue the issue." We did, and they looked at it and it satisfied Dick. He was certainly not hard to satisfy, he just, very logically, wanted a little more indication that we were able to handle the job. As I say, we've heard stories—[and] we don't know how accurate they are—that there were other people who were somewhat more skeptical, and probably remained so throughout our time at DC, and were perhaps instrumental in ending our time at DC, ultimately. During our time there, there were people whom we were not very popular with, and were not that impressed with our work.

**TLC:** *Weren't you also involved with DC's new talent program?*

**TB:** That would be back in the mid-Eighties. Sal Amendola was running the new talent program at the time, and we did a number of scripts. We did some stories for *Elvira's House of Mystery*, and prior to that we had sold an original concept that would have run in *New Talent Showcase*. It [had] begun to be penciled by Kurt Schaffenberger. It was quite a thrill to work

The Legion Outpost 6

*Tom's first exposure to Legion fandom came in the form of a copy of **The Legion Outpost**. The* Legion of Super-Heroes TM and © DC Comics.

*More **Legionnaries** artwork, from the collection of Miki Annamanthadoo.* Andromeda and Chameleon TM and © DC Comics.

with him, but the book changed over into **Elvira** before that story ever saw print. Then we did a couple of **Elvira**'s, and I guess the program phased out. But yeah, actually our first DC work was with Sal in the new talent program.

**TLC:** *In the beginning of the **Legion** relaunch, did you feel like it had the support of DC?*

**TB:** There were always people for whom this was controversial, but I do think that when the thing was relaunched, by and large everyone at DC felt like it was an important project, and I think they put a lot of weight behind it. Whatever misgivings some people may have had, I think they put a very good push behind it. I think they felt it was important, and would have been very good for DC had it been a success. And it was quite a good success. Certainly that launch, and for the first several years [afterward], it did well. Only really over the course of time did it gradually go back down to the sales level that the **Legion** has basically maintained historically over the last decade or two.

**TLC:** *When did you start to feel the support of DC slip away?*

**TB:** It was a very ongoing situation. I think from day one, [there were] people who were not very pleased with the approach. Within just a couple of issues, there were specific objections or continuity conflicts that were arising that were creating difficulties with other books. So there really was negativity and controversy pretty much from the get-go. I don't think it necessarily got better or worse. Really, after five issues, I think it was basically the way it was gonna be, and what happened after that was that it played out it's course. Keith told the story for as long as he continued to want to be on the book, and when it got to the point where there were other things that Keith decided he was more interested in doing, he moved on. From that point on, I think the book was going to go in the direction other people at DC wanted it to go in. DC remained behind the book and supported it for as long as Keith was on it, and the company was willing to give him the chance to do what he wanted to do.

**TLC:** *What, exactly, was said about Superboy?*

**TB:** I don't know that I want to get a whole lot into any details, other than to say that there was a decision made at some point that we should not be using identifiable elements of the Superman universe. Because of various continuity issues, the decision was made that we shouldn't be using elements of the Superman mythos in our book, and that put us into a position to say, "Should we just move on and tell stories with no mention of Superboy at all?" We had a lot of different storylines in mind that involved Superboy as an important element of the Legion's history. So probably one of the more interesting decisions that we made, and certainly one [which people] can second-guess, [was] that we would take Superboy out of the history of the Legion so that we could tell historic stories without the existence of Superboy there.

**TLC:** *You were given credit with co-plotting, along with Keith Giffen and sometimes Al Gordon. If you had to break that down into percentages, who would you say did what percentage?*

**TB:** It was absolutely Keith's book. People need to keep in mind that he gets the credit, and if you're upset with what he did, he probably gets the blame. He was certainly the person who had the vision that was being realized. Keith was generous, he was interested in the creative energy that you can get when you work together, so he allowed us all to have a lot of input, but he deserves the credit for the overall vision of the book. With that all as a preamble, Keith was probably 70% of it. Of the remaining part, we had a little more than Al. Tom McCraw had some input, as well. We had a little more than Al, Al had somewhat more than Tom. We had maybe around 15%, Al would get about 10% and we'll give Tom 5.

**TLC:** *Do you think the fact that you'd recently been Legion fans gave you a unique perspective on the title?*

**TB:** I think for Keith that was important. I think he felt that our background in Legion fandom, and our appreciation for the history of the Legion was really important. He had a tendency to sort of want to tear up the universe and do things that would really stir things up, and he relied on us to talk him down from it and say, "Okay, these are interesting ideas, Keith, but it doesn't really fit. This is not really the Legion. Legion fans are really going to howl over this." We tried to get a balance. We tried to get a book that was both revolutionary and consistent with the Legion's background. I think we did that enough. We had different ideas of what the ideal Legion was, but he was excited at the notion that he could take some of our perspective and some of his perspective, mix it all together and get a product that really had a unique voice to it, and a unique perspective.

**TLC:** *Were you aware of sales?*

**TB:** We were not given real specific sales figures, and we didn't have enough contacts to really know how to get them, so we were a little bit in the dark, but we were very interested. In our writing, we always try to deliver for the people who are paying us and give them what they need so our project makes business sense. We were trying to support ourselves as writers and took the business end of things very seriously, and knew that it was our job to give DC a book that made money for the company. We knew that our future as writers relied on that, so we took it very seriously. We knew that if sales were good, we had a big future, and if they weren't so good, a not so good future. And I have worked, beyond my comics work, covering television Nielson ratings for twenty years, so

Ultra Boy by Chris Sprouse, from the collection of Chris D. Snorek. Ultra Boy TM and © 2003 DC Comics.

I've really been trained for decades now in the importance of an entertainment medium reaching an audience, and that's how it supports itself. So that was always something that we were pretty keenly aware of, and tried our best to perform [well at].

**TLC:** *Overall, how much of a free hand were you given to just tell your stories?*

**TB:** I think we had a good deal of freedom, surprisingly so. But really, for the first whatever it was, it was really Keith's book, so we would try and create something within the scope of what Keith was looking for. There were one or two times where we did something that he kinda reined in because it just didn't match the tone of what he was doing, but we didn't disagree or resent that. We felt as if our job was to do things to help realize what he was trying to do. After he left, we were given quite a free hand, and I think what we would have rather had was more of a sense of, "This is the direction we want the book to go in. Let's work together and have you guys realize that with us." And what they did instead was see that we had a certain number of issues left on our contracts and say, "Okay, go write your issues, and if things work out, then we'll continue, and if they don't work out, we won't continue." It was nice to have a free hand, and to feel like we could do different things in those issues, but we would rather have them say, "Okay, here's where the book's going. Get on board and let's do it together."

**TLC:** *One area where you did get to fly solo was in the annuals. Did you see*

*those as an opportunity to show what you could do?*

**TB:** I don't think moreso than the fill-ins we did. We actually had a little more success with some of our fill-in issues, like #5, the hourglass issue, or the Matter-Eater Lad issues [*#'s 11, 14, & 49* —**Ed.**]. The very first [annual], the big Ultra Boy issue, was a story that we had come up with that we were really excited about, and that was really a wonderful story that was going to be hard to execute. The ultimate execution of the story didn't live up to what we still feel was an exciting concept, and it probably was a bit much for us at the time to take on this very long, very ambitious story. Then the annual we did after that, "The Legend of Valor," that one was a difficult one. The editor had pretty strong ideas about how it should be, and we just had to outline the story over and over. I think we did three outlines before we were able to get started plotting it. That one didn't feel as if it was our expression. That was probably one of the most over-deliberated plots we ever did.

Probably the one annual that we are very proud of, and I think really is something that is our voice and what we would have done more of given more time, was the annual that we actually shared with Al Gordon where we told the story of a reunion that they had on the planet Winath [*LSH V4 Annual #3* —**Ed.**]. It ended up being the story that Garth was revealed to actually be a Protean, and had been a Protean since way back in early Legion history. In that particular story, I suppose that was an annual that really was reflective of our sensibility.

**TLC:** *That was a very controversial story. Did you expect the reaction which you got?*

**TB:** [*laughs*] It was funny, because that idea has been in Legion fandom since the Seventies. The idea had been kicking around Legion fandom for that length of time. When we were starting on the book with Keith, and he was coming up with a lot of ideas and urging us to throw out interesting ideas that we could play with, we said, "Here's this idea from Legion history," and he said, "I love it, and the reason I love it the most is I get to blame it on you guys." And sure enough, we sort of

officially got credit for the idea because it was revealed in a story that was our plot, and I don't think Keith was directly involved with that story. From the get-go, we expected that to be pretty darn controversial, and not everyone's favorite idea. I think, left to my own devices, I'm not sure I would have done that particular plotline. We suggested it to Keith, and he loved it. I'm not sure I would have done it myself, but it was an idea we raised and he embraced. Ironically, when I remember that particular issue, that's the last thing I remember about it. What I remember about it is really the characters and everything else that went on in the story. The Protean twist, to me, is almost superfluous. Of course, it was the bombshell of the story, so that's what people remember.

**TLC:** *Which one of you two was the big Matter-Eater Lad fan?*

**TB:** [*laughs*] I'm guilty as charged. That's me, and, again, going back to the Seventies, when I really picked up the *Legion* again with my brother, I hadn't even remembered Matter-Eater Lad from my earlier Legion days. He just grabbed me right away. I just thought that it was such a wonderfully absurd power, but in a way that I felt could exist in the real Legion universe. His stories could be humorous without completely wandering off into absurdity to be funny. It was a power that was just credible enough that the audience could

© DC Comics.

accept it, but also was silly. I loved his name, and so when I started reading the **Legion** again in the early Seventies, and my brother and I were doing our own stories, I began coming up with ideas about different kinds of silly things that he could do. When we got on the book, I remember Keith had a very serious storyline about Matter-Eater Lad. It was going to be about some kind of a scandal that he was involved in as a senator from Bismoll, and I said, "Well, I guess that could be kind of interesting," and I very timidly, after one or two discussions of that plotline, said, "Would you mind if we could do a funny take on Tenzil?" and he said, "Sure!" So we started working on that, and I guess that was one of our earlier fill-in issues [**LSH** V4 #11 —**Ed.**]. That featured a kind of silly Matter-Eater Lad, and then shortly thereafter, we had to throw together another issue [**LSH** V4 #14 —**Ed.**]—I can't remember exactly why—and this one we got so lucky because we were able to roughly outline it and then Keith ended up drawing it. Just to take whatever humor we could put in it, and then put Keith's sense of humor on top of that. It was, I think, a very successful issue, and Keith's contributions had a great deal to do with it.

**TLC:** *Did you feel like the* **Legion** *needed a little bit of comic relief at that point?*

**TB:** That wasn't the specific motivation. I

think it helped, and I think it gave the whole universe a little more depth and diversity for those few years. But it wasn't specifically saying, "This dark universe needs comic relief." I think it's what we would have done in any instance, and you'll notice when we eventually did do stories that were ours, there was Matter-Eater Lad. He continued to be an important presence. When I was a kid, we would draw our own little Legion comics, and other character comics, and I always felt like humor should be part of the mix. For me, that was part of what comic book super-hero stories should involve.

**TLC:** *Didn't you guys also do the letters pages for a while?*

**TB:** Right. We pretty much did them exclusively through our whole time on the book. And there was some tension about the letters page. We would fairly often be told by the editors to do them a little differently, and I remember one time we did, in frustration, ask the editor to pick the letters. I think we did even end up doing that letters page, too. So I guess we did them all. And then we did not do them in **Legionnaires**, I guess.

**TLC:** *So was it a little weird being on the other side of that fence?*

**TB:** I would say mostly it was fun. We always loved comics, and Mary and I did write a fair number of letters to the editor, and it was a lot of fun to get the letters. There were generally quite a few more positives than negatives, so it was never too depressing to read the letters. For the most part, ninety percent of the negative letters were civil and respectful and weren't that mean to us. Doing the page itself was hard, because we made the thing very complicated. We tried to mention everyone if we could, and we tried to come up with interesting little bits that summarized what a lot of people were asking about. So it was a lot of effort, but we did enjoy it. It was fun.

**TLC:** *I want to run through a list of artists that you worked with on the* **Legion***, and I want*

*you to give me your impressions of them. First up is Keith Giffen.*

**TB:** Keith, to me, is probably the closest that I have worked with in life that I would call a genius. I think he just has an incredible creative ability that I don't know that I've ever seen anywhere else. He was an immensely unselfish creator. He was excited about the energy you could get out of collaboration. He was really open to diversity of viewpoints, and was great to work with. Like a lot of the best artists we worked with, it was always difficult for him to crank out a book a month, and that was sort of the curse of our time in comics. [It] was the really top-notch artists that just made the stories come out great. By and large, it was hard to do a monthly book in those circumstances, and that was always true with Keith. Working with him was a great experience.

**TLC:** *Brandon Peterson.*

**TB:** Brandon Peterson was a lot of fun. It was fun to see him develop and really become a very professional artist. I think the first story we did with him was one of his very early professional assignments. I don't know that it was his first ever, but it was one of his very early assignments. We enjoyed working with him. He was a nice friendly guy. It was fun to get on the phone with him and feel his enthusiasm. He put a lot of effort into the stories, and really added a lot to them. So that was a lot of fun, and it was neat to see him then move on and have quite a successful career beyond what we did with him on the **Legion**.

**TLC:** *Jason Pearson.*

**TB:** Jason brought a new and really valuable sensibility to those later issues of Keith's run, and I really thought the book was getting its rhythm during that time. Keith could lay out the book and Jason could pencil it on a pretty regular schedule, and it was great to just sit back and watch the stories unfold. I think Jason had a very distinctive approach, and also one that was really attuned to the contemporary market. He was also a really nice guy who was very easy to work with, and it was exciting to be one of the first writers to be able to work with a great new talent like him there at the start of his career.

**TLC:** *Stuart Immonen.*

**TB:** Stuart Immonen was very talented. He

*Kent Shakespeare gets the convention treatment in this sketch by Stuart Immonen. From the collection of Steve Mohundro.* Art © 2003 Stuart Immonen; Kent Shakespeare TM and © DC Comics.

really did a great job on some of our stories in the homestretch. He was one of those people whose depictions of the characters had the most life, the most personality. You could feel the emotion of the story through the faces he drew, which was very satisfying when you're the writer and you're trying to get the readers involved. When the editor sent us samples of different artists when we were looking for somebody new, Stuart's really stood out, and we immediately got back to the editor and said, "He's the guy in this stack that would be great to get." He really did a great job during the time that we were on the book. And again, it was exciting to be there in the very early stages of somebody who did go on to a good deal more success.

**TLC:** *Chris Sprouse.*

**TB:** Chris Sprouse was another person I can't speak too highly of. He just did a tremendous job. He put as much or more effort into every panel than any artist we've ever worked with. What I just said about Stuart—the characters, the emotions came right off the page. You could feel what they were feeling. He went through every panel with a real impressive amount of creativity and commitment. Personally, I just liked him tremendously and thought he was just a superb artist. We loved to go over the work that he did. It's just beautiful, and it was really an idyllic situation to be able to work for about a year on *Legionnaires* with him. I feel like we put out some beautiful looking books, and that when we gave him a story, every scene of every story we did with him got better when Chris got on it and drew it. When he was done with it, he did a great job.

**TLC:** *You even got to work with Adam Hughes for a while.*

**TB:** Yes, yes. [*laughs*] I'm running out of superlatives! Adam has to be right at the top of the list, too. Again, everything I've said about Chris in terms of how hard he worked on every panel, how much emotion and life the characters had, just his dedication to making every panel beautiful... it was beautiful to have our stories come to life with that kind of artwork. It was a pleasure to work with Adam. The one issue we did—I think it was #7 of *Legionnaires*—was a great experience,

because Adam was available and we got on the phone—the editor just got us together—and we said, "Anything you're interested in doing?" and he mentioned a few characters that he liked, and the kind of situations he would like to have them in, and we put our heads together and thought about a story. [We] took the character dynamics that Adam was thinking of, and it wrote itself. We sent it along to Adam, and he just drew it beautifully. It was really, [one of] the smoothest, easiest, funniest issues we did, and I think Adam got a great kick out of it. I think he enjoyed it a lot, and that was really a very positive experience. Then he was able to do groups of pages here and there in later issues, and the more we could get of his artwork, the better.

**TLC:** *There were quite a few new characters introduced during your run. Who came up with whom?*

**TB:** Starting with the *Legion* book, Mary came up with the character Kono, I came up with the character Devlin O'Ryan, Al Gordon came up with Kent Shakespeare, [and] the Bounty character as a separate entity from Dawnstar was Al's idea. Ivy was Al's too, I think. Celeste was Al's. Keith came up with the character named Vrykos, who was ultimately going to be a Legion member, but we never came close to making that happen. He was kind of a vampire assistant to Mordru, and we never

*Even Brainiac 5 was confused by the changes in Legion continuity in the early '90s. From the collection of Dylan Clearbrook. Art © 2003 Steve Lightle; Supergirl, Andromeda, and Brainiac 5 TM and © DC Comics.*

even came close to a storyline that would bring him in as a member. Tom McCraw came up with B.I.O.N. In *Legionnaires*, Jason Pearson actually created Catspaw, though Jason was never directly involved in *Legionnaires*. I guess Mary and I came up with the Kid Quantum character together, but Chris Sprouse created the visuals, which are really what made that character. Dragonmage was based on a character Mary and I wrote in APA fiction. I think that's most of them...

**TLC:** *You left out Laurel Gand.*

**TB:** I guess Mary and I, in concert with some friends of ours, [created her]. One of them, unfortunately, died a few years ago. Laurel is, in our minds, a monument to him, a good, good friend of ours called Arnie Starkey, who was a big fan of Supergirl. When we were visiting him and another friend named James Ricklef, we discussed the fact that we had this new history of the Legion that had emerged from the event that replaced Superboy in the timeline, and Arnie sort of innocently said, "If you have to put together Legion history, there's a hole in Legion history for Supergirl the same way there is for Superboy." Lightbulbs went off in the room, and we started brainstorming about what kind of character could fill the gap in Legion history that Supergirl once filled. I don't really remember exactly how we got the name Laurel Gand. I think we quickly figured it had to be a relative of Mon-El's, and I guess the Laurel name came out of Laurel Kent. We suggested it to Keith, and he was as happy with the idea as the rest of us were. Keith designed the visuals on the character, and the actual general idea came through our friends from us. That was a lot of fun. I think she was, rightly so, a very popular character, and one of the most fun characters to write of our run.

**TLC:** *You mentioned that Bounty was not originally supposed to be Dawnstar...*

**TB:** I probably confused you a little bit. I was trying to make the point that Al Gordon came up with the idea of Bounty,

204

and it was Dawnstar, but he came up with the idea that Bounty was actually a separate entity, and ultimately that entity was to leave Dawnstar. I don't even remember if we ever picked up on that plotline. So I don't think that the Bounty entity ever went anywhere else and became somebody else, but that actual entity independent of Dawnstar was something that Al did come up with.

**TLC:** *I've got to ask: why didn't anyone recognize her face?*

**TB:** [*laughs*] Let's see, I'll have to try to remember if we ever addressed that in the book. I think the attitude that we had at the time was that, for one thing, there were people thinking, "She sure looks like so-and-so." I don't know if that was ever in print, but I think that was part of it. The other was the thinking that if somebody acts totally out of character, you know, combs their hair differently, and just happens to be missing these gigantic wings that used to be sticking out of her back, that there is a sense of, "Yes, she kind of looks like so-and-so." I think that was as much our explanation as anything, that they kinda did recognize her, but there were enough odd things about her that were different that basically, everyone just sort of thought, "Well, she's somebody who looks a lot like so-and-so." But I'd really have to go back and read the run and try to figure out if we had a better explanation than that.

**TLC:** *I mentioned earlier that the Lightning Lad and Proty storyline was controversial, but I think probably the most controversial idea of your run was what was done with Shvaughn Erin. Could you explain some of the thinking behind that, and how it came about?*

**TB:** My understanding of what brought that about was that originally when Keith was doing issue #3, where Roxxas kills Blok, originally the person he was going to kill was going to be Shvaughn. When Al Gordon heard that, he said he really didn't like the idea of killing Shvaughn, that he thought Shvaughn was a good character and we shouldn't kill Shvaughn. Keith said, "Okay, but then you've gotta tell me something else to do with Shvaughn." You'd have to talk with Al if you get the chance, because I'm relating something second-hand, but I think Al basically, with barely even thinking, just worded out, "Well, he's a man!" And [*laughs*] from what I've described before, you can imagine how, the way Keith's mindset was, these kind of radical ideas that come out of the blue that are really bizarre but interesting are

the kind of ideas that grab him.

Well, of course that was that kind of idea, and it grabbed Keith and he thought, "Okay, great! That's a cool idea." And so very early on, we came up with this notion, "Okay, somehow Shvaughn is not really a woman." I don't think anyone knew exactly how we were gonna do that, but as the issues progressed and the storyline developed, I guess Keith got more and more of an idea of what he was going to do about it, and how he was going to do it. Ultimately, we came to the issue where we were gonna tell this, and it was plotted by Keith, Colleen Doran drew it, [and] it was based on Al's idea that Keith had laid out and plotted. Then we ended up dialoguing it. So it was basically an idea from Al, plotted by Keith that we had to write the words to and really hook it all together and make it work. So it really was a collaboration of three disparate approaches, and we tried to pull it all together and turn it into an interesting story. That's basically how it happened, and, as you say, the results were somewhat controversial. I think it was a great issue, and turned out to be a real intriguing addition to the overall storyline. And really, I think some of the most poignant writing in the series came when we explored what that particular character went through. It was really a challenge for us to get inside that character's head and figure out what he or she was experiencing.

**TLC:** *That issue even had some pages drawn by Curt Swan. I always kind of wondered what his reaction to that idea was.*

**TB:** I don't know that Curt had a whole lot of empathy for the approach we were taking. In fact, I saw him speak at a convention one time, and he had no idea we were in the audience. Curt was way too professional to have done this if he did, but someone made a disparaging comment about our approach on the **Legion**, and Curt agreed with it. That was a bit of a heartbreak for me, because Curt is one of my real heroes, and we worked very hard to try to get as much work thrown Curt's way as possible. There were times where we would come up with a story and just beg the editor, "Oh, please, give this to Curt Swan," and for whatever reason, it didn't end up going to him. He was definitely a hero, and we were very, very

pleased that he was able to do pages in that issue. I don't recall that he was involved in any way in any other stories that we did. I really, really wish that since he was around and productive at that point that we had been able to do a lot more with him.

**TLC:** *If Roxxas had killed Shvaughn, given his connection to Element Lad, wouldn't that have given more emotional weight to the story?*

**TB:** That may have been what Keith was thinking. And yeah, I think it would have been a little more direct to the point in terms of the relationship between he and Jan. So it might have worked better. I tend to think that there was already plenty of baggage between Jan and Roxxas, so I don't think it was necessarily a missed opportunity. I think there really is enough intensity between those two characters already. In fact, I have a lot of fondness for the fact that by the end of our run, Roxxas really had been partially rehabilitated, and he was somewhat sympatic, and Jan was sympathetic toward him. To me, that was a much more satisfying way to develop the story than to have increasing levels of hatred and killing and violence. That, for me, is not what I read comic books for. I

© DC Comics.

was really happy to steer that storyline in another direction.

**TLC:** *The Substitute Heroes reached new levels of credibility during "The Terra Mosaic." Was that a conscious decision?*

**TB:** I believe so. That was Keith, and I think Keith always enjoyed taking the readers in a certain direction, taking them a certain distance, and then just when the reader thought that they could predict what he was going to do, turn it around on them. And this would be a classic example of that. I think he really felt as if he had taken the Substitutes about as low as they could go—and certainly in some minds that was very controversial—and then he just felt it was an interesting twist [to] really treat them as a highly competent, very heroic group. I think that was very conscious and was a fun thing to do. It was interesting to see them in a completely different light.

**TLC:** *How did the SW6 Legionnaires come about?*

**TB:** One time Keith just called us up early in the run, and he said, "What would you think of the Legion fighting a clone Legion? Some villain or, somehow, somebody makes a bunch of clone Legionnaires and we have a big fight?" And it was like, "Well, that's cool. That would be neat." Then as Keith started exploring that idea, we more and more got into the notion of "Let's do something a little more than just have some disposable group that the Legion runs into and has a one-issue fight with." Eventually we started thinking of this group as a device that would allow us to do a couple of things. One would be to tell stories that recaptured the innocence and the fun of the original Legion, and also create the opportunity, if we eventually decided it was the way we wanted to go, to have a whole separate book starring this group. That wasn't the original intention. We were gonna run these kids through the motherbook, as we called it, and have them be characters in that book, and they might all get killed off, [or] maybe the other, older group would get killed off, or maybe half of each would get killed off, or [whatever]. We really were not committed to what would happen, but they were there and ready for use in the *Legionnaires* book if that became desired.

The *Legionnaires* book originally, in its very first conception, was going to be a series of spotlight issues retelling the ori-

gins of each character so that we could just progress the motherbook, and then have the readers get all the background they needed on each character by reading this other book. That was the original idea. Later on, when the timeline shifted, the next idea was, "Okay, we're gonna retell Legion history the way it's been shifted in the timeline in the *Legionnaires* book," and that was the next idea. Fairly close to preceding with that, we really had the first several issues outlined, and were gonna go ahead with that, [but] then at DC there was... edict may not be the correct word, but basically an advisory to editors that we were just spending too much time looking in the past and retelling past stories, and all books from now on should really go forward into the future. The editor at the time, Michael Eury, was told that he didn't have to apply that edict to *Legionnaires*. He could grandfather that and proceed as it was, but Michael thought that it really was a better idea to be consistent with the

direction of the entire company, and indeed go ahead and tell stories into the future, and luckily we had this SW6 Legion sitting right there available for that purpose. Michael said, "That is a good idea. Let's do that." And that's how that group ended up being in *Legionnaires* as a separate book.

**TLC:** *Was the point of that book also to appeal to people who didn't like the motherbook?*

**TB:** I think that was part of it. Keith never was under any delusion that his book was gonna please everyone, especially the old guard fans, and he had us there always reminding him that there was an old guard perspective that was worth considering. He knew that we would always be a little more fulfilled if we got to write something a little more in the tradition of the old Legion. So I think all of those factors were definitely part of the thinking of, "Wouldn't it be fun to tell a story about a young, relatively innocent kid Legion again?" So yeah, that was part of it. And Keith never wanted to say, "I'm the boss. I say how the *Legion* is, and everyone else is stuck with my *Legion*." He always understood and respected the fact that the *Legion* didn't belong to anyone, and the *Legion* was a gigantic, decades old thing that couldn't be controlled, and he respected the diversity that the history of the Legion encompassed. [He] was perfectly willing to put out multiple approaches that embraced that diversity.

**TLC:** *Do you think that the Legionnaires title did draw in new readers?*

**TB:** I think it brought in some. I don't think it brought in nearly as many as we would have liked. I think we really calculated it, and executed it as an entry level book that we wanted to be very aggressively put out there as something people could jump onto and read without a lot of background. We really tried to make every issue something you could just pick up and start reading and say, "Okay, in the 30th Century there's these heroes, they fight crime, and that's basically what you need to know." For whatever reason, I don't sense that a lot of

*Another Kent Shakespeare picture from the collection of Steve Mohundro.* Art © 2003 Jeff Moy; Kent Shakespeare TM and © DC Comics.

people did that. I haven't heard a lot of people say, "Oh, I started Legion with **Legionnaires** #1." I've heard ten times as many people say they started the Legion with **Legion** #1 of Keith's incarnation of the group, which was quite the opposite. It was an extremely dense, complicated book that was not really designed to be an easy entry level way to get started in Legion fandom. Although ironically, I think that because the book was so complicated, and threw so many things up in the air and in disarray, that in some ways the new readers actually had an advantage over the old readers. They didn't have to try to keep track of which character was which, who had which power, and who had what background because to them, Rokk was Rokk. He wasn't Cosmic Boy, he was Rokk, and they just accepted that. So in a lot of ways, I sense that the people who picked up the book right then kind of accepted the universe and just learned it and picked it up a little faster than the people who were trying to figure out exactly what it all meant and how it all tied together. Then, for some reason, **Legionnaires** never really picked up as an entry level book. I'm sure it could have been promoted and distributed and marketed a little differently, and maybe it would have been more successful on that front, but I haven't heard from a lot of people who said that they picked it up with **Legionnaires**.

**TLC:** *Eventually Keith left and the two of you were left on your own. The tone of the book changed about that time back to an old school, straight-forward super-hero comic. Was that your decision, or was that an editorial decree?*

**TB:** I think that that was kind of a combination. I think the editors at that point made it clear that they felt that would be a more productive direction to go in, and I don't think we felt capable of doing something with the denseness and sophistication of what Keith was doing. That was just Keith's genius and not ours, and so we were very comfortable throttling back a little bit on the ambitious nature of the book because that's not our *forte*. So I think it was a combination.

**TLC:** *Was the decision to reboot the title made while you were still on board?*

**TB:** We had no involvement in it. I think it was made behind the scenes, and a few people gave us a few gentle hints that it was coming, but that was something done

without our knowledge, and I think the assumption on the part of the people who were engineering that was that we wouldn't be very happy about it, and I'm sure they're right. It was just politically and interpersonally easier for them to just not tell us what was coming.

**TLC:** *Would you say that was a decision based more upon sales, or upon personal preferences on what the Legion should be? You did have an idea of how it was doing saleswise.*

*DC announces the changes to the Legion universe in this house ad from 1994.* © DC Comics.

**TB:** We had a pretty good idea. We didn't see sales figures every time. We knew basically how it was doing, and it was not a strong seller through the first couple of years. Certainly by the end of Keith's time on the book, the sales were getting lower than they wanted to see them, and then after Keith left, they took another hit, and it was drifting downward. By the time our run ended, it was not selling particularly well. By all means, their experiences with reboots had been that they do give you a surge. I think there was a combination

beyond doubt. If they were gonna reboot Legion history, that was gonna motivate sales. There was certainly a feeling, both from a commercial and creative viewpoint by the people that were making decisions at that time that the book was not a success, a feeling that there was a better direction for the book to take, and that better sales were possible. I think that coloring all of that was also personal preferences, personal taste on the part of the people who were not very appreciative of Keith's approach, not very appreciative of our approach, and when we were gone, it was time to bring in something different. Beyond all of that, there was a feeling of things had gotten too complicated and they needed to start over because people just couldn't figure out what was going on. And, of course, my feeling is that you don't resolve a complicated storyline by wiping out thirty-five years of continuity. You do it by having one issue that either explains away what the questions are, or you ignore the points of contention until people forget about them, or you do a plot twist to get rid of the undesirable elements, or whatever. I don't accept that the story had become so confusing that they had to wipe out the history. That, I think, is not a fair way of looking at the decision that was made. I certainly do recognize that we had a very complicated storyline, and a lot of people were confused about it, but I don't accept that you need to wipe out continuity to resolve that kind of confusion.

**TLC:** *You lasted on **Legionnaires** longer than you did on the mother-book...*

**TB:** Not really. We really were on the motherbook for fifty issues, and we were gone from **Legionnaires** by fifteen. We were on **Legionnaires** after we left the motherbook, if that's what you meant. We left the motherbook with issue fifty, and at that point I think **Legionnaires** was probably about five issues into its run—fairly early into it's run, so we had about another ten or so episodes of **Legionnaires** after we left the motherbook.

**TLC:** *So how were things coordinated between the two different books?*

**TB:** Initially, coordination was easy because we were writing both books, but once we were off the mother book, we just kind of did our stories and the mother book had its stories, and there wasn't much interaction. They just let us do our remaining stories, and they went on and did their stories until we were out of the picture.

**TLC:** *It sounds like it got depressing at the end there.*

**TB:** Yeah, I guess so. The perspective I always try to take is that we were able to do the Legion, and we really enjoyed it start to finish, to the very end for sure, but it was difficult and stressful at the end to be losing the assignment at the end of a dream come true experience for us. So it wasn't pleasant to lose it. And professionally, we're not good at selling ourselves and getting out there and getting the next assignment, so there was a cloud of, "How are we gonna put food on the table after these assignments go away?" But through various signals, we did know that we weren't going to be around for a long time after Keith left. There was a lot of advance warning that things were going in this direction. But yeah, it certainly was a very stressful time.

**TLC:** *You did get the chance to introduce some ethnically diverse characters in*

**Legionnaires** *before you left. Do you wish you had the chance to follow up more with those?*

**TB:** Yeah. We really enjoyed and liked all the characters. It was a pleasure to bring some overdue diversity that the group should have always had, and would have had in the Sixties if it was really a more open social climate for that sort of thing. That was fun, and we really do, without exception, love all the characters and enjoy working with them. Those particular characters that had ethnic diversity, we only got to skim the surface [of them], and that is frustrating. You do wish you could get deeper into them, and it's too bad that we really only got a couple issues on each character to start to explore them.

**TLC:** *Do you think that your run on the* **Legion** *was treated fairly by the fans?*

**TB:** Yes, in the sense that I don't really think the fans can be unfair about anything. As long as you pay your money, you're entitled to like it or dislike it, and express your opinion as you see fit. I think there were specific criticisms of the book that, in some cases, were inaccurate. There were people out there that got bent out of shape about certain things, [and] I don't particularly agree with their point of view, but by and large, I feel you put out a book and you let people react to it the way they do, and if you put out a book that really upsets them, you should put out a different book if you don't want to upset people. So I feel if the fans feel negatively about something, then that's their honest appraisal, and that's the way it should be. All the things that we did that were controversial and shook things up, I don't think the reaction was all that negative. I suppose the one thing that I will always try to amend when I hear somebody say it is, anyone who implies that the consensus is that era of the book just didn't work, that era of the book was a failure, that era of the book wasn't good, I will try to very persistently put out that a lot of people disagree with that evaluation,

and those people's opinions count as much as the people who didn't like it. I think we probably had a pretty split opinion out there. There were a lot of people who really disliked it. There were certainly people who really liked it. But I don't think one camp or the other can say, "Ah, history has proved that we're correct."

**TLC:** *Do you still follow the* **Legion** *today?*

**TB:** In the initial aftermath of us leaving the book, we just couldn't look at what followed, and that kind of inertia has continued to this day. I may have read a page here or there, or a panel or something, but no, we really have not read the **Legion** since then. It's been many years, but it seems like yesterday, and that kind of emotional negativity is hard to overcome, so it's not something that is inviting to us at the moment. But the thirty-five years of the book that preceeded our exit are still there, and are still treasured by us. We read the stories sometimes to our kids, and they make up their own little Legionnaires and so forth, so the Legion is definitely alive and well in our imaginations and in our family activities, but the current incarnation of the book is not part of that.

**TLC:** *If you had to do it all over again, would you make any changes?*

**TB:** I'd love to say, "No, no, we did it our way and we'll stick with it," but in retrospect, we certainly would have worked harder to try to somehow stay in favor politically better than we did. Every panel of every page, we'd be in there trying to make it just a little better if we could. We did a lot of learning in front of a wide readership, and it would be nice to go back and not have to make mistakes, to do that learning. So yeah, I think we would.

It was such a wonderful opportunity, and one we would have liked to have lasted as long as possible. I think if somehow we went back in a time machine, the thing we would do is put much more effort and heart into it. But all that said, I can't say I have regrets. I think we really did put our heart and soul into the work. I think we did the best we could at that time, and we produced a few stories there that I am immensely proud of. I hope if, somehow, we do end up in a time machine going back trying to redo it, we don't undo some of the really special issues that we were involved in.

*The new generation of Legionnaires takes charge in this portrait by Chris Sprouse. From the collection of Miki Annamanthadoo.* The Legion of Super-Heroes TM and © DC Comics.

# Steve Lightle

## Part Two

As mentioned elsewhere in this volume, the **Legionnaires** title had a very unique genesis. One of the participants involved was Steve Lightle, and his recollection of what went on behind the scenes appears below. The following is excerpted from the same conversation which resulted in the Steve Lightle interview which appears on page 171.

**TLC:** *Tell me about your involvement with the* **Legionnaires** *title.*

**SL:** [*laughs*] Well, there was no **Legionnaires** title, originally. To truly tell the story from the beginning, I'd have to go back to 1989, or something [like that], as the editor approached me with the idea that since sales were dropping, and had been plummeting on the **Legion** since they had gotten into the dark, grittier future, [he] was very interested in restarting everything, somehow regaining [what the **Legion** had lost]. We used to talk about the youthful Legion: "Let's make it the young Legion again." That was our key word for what we really meant was a hopeful Legion again. We wanted a heroic Legion again. So I was approached about doing that, and suddenly that editor dropped off the map. He ended up not editing that book anymore, and the idea disappeared. Later on, he came back to the book, and calls me again and says, "I know it's been a year, but I'm back on the **Legion** again, so let's do this thing. I want to do it, and I've talked to Dan Jurgens about it, and I've talked to you about it, and I'm thinking maybe you could alternate issues. You could draw one and he could draw the next." And that blossomed into the idea of restarting Legion continuity, and retelling the story from the beginning. The idea was to go back all the way to the beginning of Legion history and tell it with a Nineties sensibility. Instead of going back to the stories written for eight-year-olds that it had originally been, go back and tell it as though, "This is our palette. We still have all these things from the Legion's past, but let's tell it in such a way that people in today's audience can relate to it."

And it went back and forth, and this person was involved, and that person wasn't going to be, and this person might write it, and another person might like to

draw an issue, and it came about we were going to end up reintroducing the team, and Tom and Mary Bierbaum, now minus Keith Giffen, were going to write one book, and I was going to write and draw another, and we would have these two **Legion** books running consecutively. Mine was to be a mini-series, and my plan was do a mini-series, and then follow it up with another mini-series two months later. I saw it as a six-issue mini-series followed by another six-issue mini-series, followed by... who knows? Theirs was to be called **Legion of Super-Heroes**, and we finally settled on **Legionnaires** for the book that I was doing. I thought, to keep it separate so that we don't step on each other's toes all the time, I'll do a separate group of characters, and they'll be consistent in this book, and those Legionnaires will be consistent in that book, and they will interact, but it'll be like two separate sub-teams. This team will be led by Marla Latham, who was introduced way back when. I thought, "Okay, he's [R.J. Brande's] assistant. Maybe he still is. Let's see if these are within his duties." So he became the commander of this smaller team, and [was] trying to organize them.

If I remember correctly, I had chosen the characters Sun Boy, Quislet—I know, that defies all reasoning, because it's a character from much later in **Legion** history, but remember, we were restarting everything, so let's get the aliens in early since it's going to be a universe with aliens in it—a character I had created called Allegra (keep in mind, there was no drug called Allegra at the time. This predates that, and it was actually my wife's idea to call her this. It's based on the idea of the root being 'music played fast.' It's Allegro. Well, I just made it

Allegra because we'll feminize it a little bit, and make it a little more unique to this character). She becomes Allegra, and she was a descendent of Wally West, and raised briefly by the Flash [*Barry Allen* — **Ed.**]. I established all this detail about what kind of origin she might have, and how her life might have progressed. We also had a guy named Neutron in the group, and he was totally new, of my creation. Dream Girl, of course, was in it, and I wanted Ferro Lad in the book. Of all of them, the only one that I didn't tamper with was I had Ferro Lad looking just like he did when he was created by Curt Swan, or Jim Shooter, or whoever designed that costume. I kept wondering, "Maybe I should keep the classic costume design of Sun Boy." We had several different designs going for him. I don't know which one we would have settled on. But anyway, we had all these characters. They were this sepa-

Rheeta possesses the power of hyper-speed of super fast movement, but also accellerated per her behavior appear tic sometimes. Often Rhe her team-mates. sense when you consid tends to percieve and people around her still life. It a quires effort on her p pace of the rest verse.

In fact, u ached puberty, her m control. Who c raise a child that m at super-sonic

Fortunat tered by Barry and the only cou ca un tanding her unus Rheeta spen r ac ce i he household of her foster b er a ter on and Dawn Allen

Her costum ntury twist to it. speed, Allegra's activated, making her into a bolt of human g. It's a visual ho make this speedste from all the others in comics.

## Allegra ta Morales

Rheeta posse th wer of hyper-speed an of super fast mov t, also accellerated per her behavior appe rr sometimes. Often Rhe her team-mates. s m sense when you consid tends to percieve he wo and people around her still life. It ually quires effort on her p pace of the res verse.

In fact, u Rhee reached puberty, her m control. Who c d prope y raise a child that m at super-sonic eed?

Fortunatel Rheeta s fostered by Barry and the only couple apable understanding her unus Rheeta spent he adolesc re in the household of her foster bro er and si er, Don and Dawn Allen

Her costu e has a 30 century twist to it. speed, Allegra's costume is activated, making her into a bolt of human lightning. It's a visual ho e this speedster stand out from all the

*Lightle's original design of Allegra, now a member of Marvel's* **New Genix.** Art © 2003 Steve Lightle; Allegra TM and © 2003 Marvel Characters, Inc.

rate group of Legionnaires. And Karate Kid! How could I have forgotten! Karate Kid was gonna be on that team. I redesigned him. [*laughs*] I guess he had a mullet, or something. He had long hair in back and short on the sides, and he was definitely Asian. He was no longer Euro-Asian, or a European who said he was Asian. He was definitely an Asian character in this scenario. That was the team.

We actually had the first six issues scripted out, and we were ready to go ahead. I waited for three months for the go-ahead to actually start penciling the book. I had done mock-ups, I had done designs for the characters and everything, and I'd written the first six issues—and rewritten them a time or two—and I was told, "Any moment now we're gonna call you. It's gonna be the go-ahead. I'm just waiting for word from the higher-ups," was what my editor was telling me. Then I get a call on the twenty-fourth of December, after business hours. "I've got some good news and some bad news. The good news is, you got the go-ahead. Go ahead and start doing the book. Start drawing the issue." "Okay, what's the bad news?" "The bad news is we just need to tweak it a little bit again. I just need one little change." "What's that?" "Well, they've decided we can't restart continuity with the new char-

*Allegra and other New Genix members, along with some longstanding Marvel characters, from the cover of Marvel Comics Presents #175.*

Allegra and New Genix TM and © 2003 Marvel Characters, Inc.

acters, so these have got to be clones of the Legion. So instead of telling stories about the Legion, we're telling stories about clones of the Legion." At which point, the whole thing for me just caved in. I said, "No. Readers are not gonna swallow it. They're not gonna want anything to do with it. I don't want anything to do with it. I've put six or seven months worth of work into this, and now it's going to be stories about Legion clones?" So I said, "If this is not negotiable, if we cannot have this be the Legion, if it's gotta be clones of the Legion, then I'm out." And that's how I ended up not doing *Legionnaires* around '91, [or] something like that.

**TLC:** *Merry Christmas.*

**SL:** Yeah, Merry Christmas. That was a good one. [*laughs*] So the funny thing is, [with] that and other things like it, I've felt like I've been involved with the Legion even when I haven't been drawing the book. For one reason or another, [it seems like I've always been involved with the *Legion*].

Like recently, they had the idea that they wanted to do the **Legion** as an animated series. It had not been green-lighted by a studio or anything yet, it was just something that was brainstormed at DC. I'm told that Keith Giffen had something to do with the idea, so maybe that's another guy that's still preoccupied with the *Legion* even when he's not working on it. The idea was to make a *Legion* cartoon that would capitalize on the popularity of things like *Dragonball Z* and *Pokémon*. So what they wanted was for me to design these characters, because they'd had designs drawn up. I don't know if they were by Keith or by someone else, [but] they'd had designs drawn up already [that] they didn't like, so they came to me and said, "All right, we've got a paying job for you. Redesign the Legion, but we want you to design them for [children]. Think of them in terms of how you'd present them to a *Pokémon* audience. Each character has to have three designs,"—this was really bizarre— "because they change from one form to another. They evolve." [*laughs*] Kids really like that sort of thing, I guess. [*laughs*] "They evolve, so there's the human form,

which is a young teenager—a very young teenager—and there's the energized form..." Basically, they just described it as different stages. They become less human, or more super-heroic in the second stage, and in the third stage they became an entirely different entity, so that each stage had its own visual look.

So based on this, I came up with a few pages of designs. They said they loved them. I felt like I had almost betrayed the concept of the *Legion* by even taking such

*Allegra in a scene from Marvel Comics Presents.*

Allegra and New Genix TM and © 2003 Marvel Characters, Inc.

a job, and the good news is, I don't think it'll ever be seen. [*laughs*] But here I am, I can't entirely get away from the *Legion*, because even when I'm just trying to do advertising work, or animation work, here comes something to do with the *Legion*, so *Legionnaires*, back in the early Nineties, working on that, I really felt connected and like I was a part of the *Legion* team. Well I was, until I had to back out because of the clone thing—or felt I had to—and I still would not change that decision. Although I said I may regret my decision to have originally left the *Legion*, the idea of not doing a book about Legion clones—I still think that was a smart move. I'm glad I didn't do that. I'm only sorry that the work that I put into it didn't see the light of day.

# Mark Waid

A former editor and writer of the **Legion of Super-Heroes**, Mark Waid has been a Legion fan since childhood. Perhaps best known by the comic buying public for his stints on **Flash** and **JLA,** Waid was interviewed by fellow **Interlac** alum Chris Companik early in 2003. Special thanks go out to Companik for pitching in and helping out when help was needed.

**TLC:** *Growing up, what was your first encounter with the Legion?*

**MW:** The very first Legion story I ever read was **Adventure Comics** #353, the death of Ferro Lad. I was only five when I saw it, but even at that early age, having read comics for a year already, I knew heroes weren't supposed to die. Boy, was I surprised! It certainly taught me an early lesson: keep the readers guessing. Keep them on their toes. I read the Legion regularly thereafter, but I didn't become a huge Legion fan until the Mordru story.

**TLC:** *I didn't realize that you and I had begun reading the Legion with the exact same issue.*

**MW:** Man, Shooter/Swan/Klein really gets under your skin, doesn't it?

**TLC:** *Tell me about the impact on you of the "Luornu crawls through the sewers" scene.*

**MW:** The first chapter of the Mordru saga [**Adventure Comics** #369 —**Ed.**], I realized years later, is the template to this day for how I construct stories. That's how ingrained it is in my DNA. Everything about that story sang to me when I read it at age seven. Not only the shock ending of hopelessness, but that scene with Luornu crawling her way "home" through a tunnel while mourning her love for Superboy because she knew from her history lessons that they weren't destined to end up together.

**TLC:** *So how did you get involved in Legion fandom?*

**MW:** Same as most everyone—I read about **The Legion Outpost** in a **Superboy** letter column and sent mail away to Mike Flynn. Then, years later in the early 1980s, I'd moved to Texas, and at the comics shop [there] met a member of **Interlac** named Kevin Gould. Kevin introduced me to the APA and got me involved, and that really swept me up in Legion fandom. So many names I recognized from lettercols, like Mercy Van Vlack and Harry Broertjes and Ken Gale—it was like joining a club where I'd already been a lifelong member.

**TLC:** *Did you see it as a training ground for your future in comics?*

**MW:** Not really. I didn't grow up wanting to be a comics writer. I grew up wanting to be a comics editor. Still, in that sense, writing for **Interlac** and producing my own fanzines certainly helped me gain confidence in my writing ability.

**TLC:** *How did you wind up working on the Independent Comics Group/Eclipse **Legion** index series? Was it just knowing too many home planets of the Legion Subs?*

**MW:** I'd done the **Crisis on Infinite Earths** indices with fellow Texas fan Lou Mougin, so that established me with Eclipse. I no longer remember if I asked to do the **Legion** index or if they asked me to do it, but either way, it was a labor of love. I quite literally spent one month of my life, from dawn to midnight, poring through my collection, researching and indexing every single Legion appearance up to that time. And it was *fun*. I wrote what would have been twelve issues' worth, taking the series right up to #28 of the Baxter series, which was the current issue, but only five issues of the index saw print thanks to slow sales.

**TLC:** *Did you begin editing **Secret Origins** with #25, the retelling of the Legion's origin?*

**MW:** Actually, I began with the previous issue, "Blue Devil/Dr. Fate," which was

*Supergirl by George Pérez, courtesy of Spencer Beck (www.theartistschoice.com).*
Art © 2003 George Pérez; Supergirl TM and © DC Comics.

already in progress. The art assignment for the **Legion** story had already been made to Rick Stasi by former editor Barbara Kesel (then Barbara Randall). But I do remember working out the cover with Curt Swan and Murphy Anderson, that being the first of many, many dream assignments I was empowered to make as editor of **Secret Origins**.

**TLC:** *What about the Phantom Girl story? [**Secret Origins** #42 —**Ed.**] What it was like to go from seeing Dave Cockrum's work as a fan to handling "the real thing"?*

**MW:** It was terrific, but it also showed off my shortcomings as an editor. With all due respect to Tom and Mary Bierbaum, [who are] wonderful people, that story was, even after editing, about 20-25% too dense a script. Dave felt really stifled by the sheer verbiage of it, but he was a pro about it.

SECRET ORIGINS --
LEGION OF
SUPER HEROES
CLUBHOUSE

STORY-GERARD JONES
PENCILS-KURT SCHAFFENBERGER
INKS-TY TEMPLETON
LETTERER-ALBERT DE GUZMAN
COLORIST-TOM McCRAW
EDITOR-MARK WAID

I CAN'T BELIEVE IT! AT LONG LAST-- SMALLVILLE!

FUTURE HOME OF THE LEGION OF SUPER HEROES!

LISTEN, ARE YOU SURE YOU KIDS DON'T WANT TO THINK ABOUT THIS A LITTLE LONGER? WOULDN'T AN ORBITAL SATELLITE HEADQUARTERS BE JUST A LITTLE MORE... WELL... DRAMATIC...?

© DC Comics.

**TLC:** *You also gave the green light to the infamous Fortress Lad story.*

**MW:** Oh, yeah. But it was an eleventh-hour-and-fiftieth-minute job. Gerard Jones had written a whole 'nother script, illustrated by Kurt Schaffenberger and Ty Templeton, and it was completely done, ready for publication. But when the **Superman** editorial office vetoed it because it made reference to the Pocket Universe of Superboy, the entire thing had to be scrapped, and we had *no* idea what to do to replace it. "What the hell would the origin of the Fortress be if not that?" I asked aloud, and editor KC Carlson stuck his head in my door and made a joke about Fortress Lad. It stuck. At that point, I was both too amused and too desperate to let the idea go. Jones was game, so he turned around a new script based on KC's joke in no time flat. And the up side to it was that by then, Curt Swan was available to pencil. I still have the last page of that story, the original art, framed in my home. Minus, I might add, the **Superman** office-dictated patch that omitted Superboy from that last group shot of the Legion.

The very next issue of **Secret Origins** was devoted to "Dead Legionnaires," and Robert Loren Fleming wrote a dynamite Chemical King story that was one of the highlights of the series.

**TLC:** *Soon you were editing the **Legion** book itself...*

**MW:** Well, before that, walking in the door to DC editorial, I'd also been handed the

reins of **Who's Who in the Legion** because I was such a damn expert on the series. Barbara was writing it, but she needed help, so I ghosted a number of entries and ended up writing some of the lead features, as well. And that last cover? With three million head shots on it? I came up with that as a reaction to the drubbing I took over the cover to issue three, which had no Legionnaires on it at all. "You want Legionnaires?" I said to no one in particular, 'cause I was drunk. "*I'll* give you *Legionnaires*!" All those teeny head shots, all by different artists. Accounting had a meltdown and wanted me dead.

**TLC:** *From someone who had painted the **Legion** monitor board on his parents' garage door as a kid, it might have been my favorite cover.*

**MW:** The production department made me color it myself. True story. And I couldn't blame them.

**TLC:** *When you look back at your time editing the **Legion**, what are you now most proud of?*

**MW:** Not going to prison for murder. What a suicide assignment that book was. Jesus. I was told by management to let Keith Giffen go nuts, to let him have his head because, after all, he'd given us **Justice League** and had a well deserved track record for success. And I trusted Keith to entertain me and entertain the readers, and whatever vision he had, I just stepped back and let him run with it for better or worse. It was darker, denser, and far more complex than I would have preferred, and poor Tom and Mary Bierbaum, the scripters, paid the price because I was always nitpicking them to death and putting the burden on them for clarity, but at the end of the day, I felt good that Keith had a vision and was going places. And then the Superman Ripple Effect hit. Already the Legion continuity had been plagued by revisions in mainstream DC continuity. We'd been told we could no longer make reference to Rond Vidar as a Green Lantern; we'd been told, thanks to **Hawkworld** rebooting Hawkman, that Thanagarians could no longer be in continuity. There were other instances of similar madness, but what killed us, killed our momentum, and killed any chance **Legion Vol. 4** had for a linear narrative that might have actually brought readers in was the Superman Ripple Effect. Because of inter-office politics and machinations that make no sense to me to this day, it was decided that not only was there was no Superboy, but we weren't even allowed to reference him at *all*. We were not allowed to make reference to the Pocket Universe that he came from and we were ordered to rewrite Legion history to eliminate his presence from it altogether. Even Mon-El could no longer be called "Mon-El," we were told, because the "El" name belonged "exclusively to Superman." The disastrous long-

DRAMATIC, MAYBE. BUT-- NOT AS *FITTING*! WE WERE INSPIRED TO BECOME HEROES BY THE LEGEND OF SUPERBOY...

...AND IT WILL BE IN SUPERBOY'S LEGENDARY HOME TOWN THAT WE BEGIN OUR CAREERS!

WAIT A MINUTE. WE DON'T EVEN KNOW IF SUPERBOY EXISTED, REMEMBER? THERE ARE NO CONCLUSIVE RECORDS... A LOT OF PEOPLE SAY SUPERMAN DIDN'T GET STARTED UNTIL HE WAS FULLY...

NO, MR. LATHAM. WE *KNOW* THERE WAS A SUPERBOY. AND WE'RE GOING TO STAY HERE, WHERE HIS SPIRIT STILL LIVES.

*Top and above: Panels from the previously unpublished secret origin of the Legion clubhouse, courtesy of Kevin Gould. © DC Comics.*

term effect all this had on the Legion is felt to this day. The roots of the entire series were undermined, and from that point on, every story any editorial or creative team engineered as a "fix" just made things worse and more complicated.

**TLC:** *Was it easier when Keith was no longer plotting the book? Or was it past that point by then?*

**MW:** I was long gone by that time. I was out of DC editorial after issue five of the [relaunch], so I watched the rest of the tide of destruction clinging to a sandbar in the distance.

In retrospect, knowing what we know now, DC should just have cancelled the damn series at its peak, when Paul Levitz left. Not that creators afterwards didn't try to make it work, but by then everyone was building on shifting sand. The essential magic of the Legion was now gone, never to be recovered—the unique notion that, rather than maintaining an inviolate status quo, it moved forward in time. That readers could grow up *with* the characters, watch them change and mature.

There were also, by the way, two spin-off series proposed during my editorship that never got off the ground, which is a shame. Ty Templeton had done "The Secret Origin of the [Legion of] Substitute Heroes" for **Secret Origins**, and it was just about the most perfect comic book story I've ever seen. I asked Ty for it at the Chicago Convention of '88, and a few months later I opened an envelope to find 19 inked, lettered pages. This isn't the way comics are done. Scripts are written and approved, pencils are submitted and approved, *et cetera*. And I realized Ty hadn't bothered due process, but I didn't give a rat's ass, because the end result was *great*. My bosses flipped out—"Didn't you edit the script? Didn't you see the pencils?"—but who cares? It was *great*. So Ty wrote a pitch for a **Subs** mini and a first issue script based on that, and I remember very little about them other than that they were heart-stoppingly funny. Unfortunately, the Volume 4 [relaunch] didn't launch as hot as DC had anticipated, so plans for a **Subs** companion book were nixed.

Then, during the days of **Action Comics Weekly**—an unintentional double-edged name for a comic if ever there was one—I contacted Jim Shooter and asked him to pitch a "Legion Academy" serial for that book, figuring the ailing weekly could do a *lot* worse than to draw Legion fandom to

its door with a new Jim Shooter-written **Legion** series. But at the time, there were folks on staff who didn't want Jim at DC at all in any capacity, so that was scotched, too, in favor of the fabulously successful "Phantom Lady" serial, he said sarcastically.

**TLC:** *When the book was relaunched with* **Zero Hour***, were you hesitant or excited to now be writing it?*

**MW:** I was actually hesitant at first. Believe me, KC Carlson and co-writer/colorist Tom McCraw and I spent countless, countless hours in conference desperately trying to find some magic, continuity-driven way to "fix" the Legion's muddled history once and for all, but there was no way. Anything anyone came up with, from the "SW6 clones" to whatever, just made the series that much more inaccessible. I've always said that we didn't kill **Legion**. John Byrne's **Superman** relaunch was the bullet. We just pulled the plug.

Once it was decided to give the series a total, from-scratch reboot, *then* I was excited. And I have to tell you, in large part because of Tom McCraw—who structured the basic beats of **Legion** #0—that was one of the best comics I've ever been involved with, that relaunch issue. That was a really good comic. A really good relaunch. *And no one noticed.* We were told we couldn't restart the series with #1, so no one noticed. Everyone who wasn't already a faithful **Legion** fan just figured it was More Of The Same Confusing Stuff and stayed away from the reboot. Shame. More people should have seen that stuff. Tom really was the unsung hero of the reboot. So many of the ideas, from Rokk's corrupt manager to Imra's police background and more, were his, as I recall.

**TLC:** *Was dropping the "Lass" and "Kid" parts of the names your idea, his idea, or someone else's?*

*Another page from the unpublished origin of the Legion clubhouse, courtesy of Kevin Gould.* © DC Comics.

**MW:** KC Carlson's insistence, as I recall. KC had a lot of good ideas, and I think that Triad and Live Wire, to name two, are *much* improved names. On the other hand, KC also has to take the blame for sticking Kid Quantum in just to kill him off, which we did at his insistence specifically and only because "the X-Men killed off Thunderbird when they relaunched, and *that* worked." Then again, I'm the one who let Keith kill Blok, so we all have our crosses to bear. At the time of the Giffen relaunch, Keith wanted to pick a Legionnaire to kill—pick one by, literally, pulling a name out of a hat. That name was "Blok."

**TLC:** *And you got the angry letters from the "Blok's My Buddy" brigade.*

**MW:** Yeah. And they were right to be pissed. I've learned since then to have a healthier respect for other creators' characters even if—as with Blok—I don't particularly care for them.

**TLC:** *What was it like co-plotting with Tom McCraw? How did you work that?*

**MW:** Tom and I would knock ideas around on the phone and Tom would draft a plot outline that I would turn into a page-by-page plot to be given to a penciler. Then, depending on our schedules, either Tom would take a crack at dialoguing as well and I'd second draft it, or I'd dive into the first draft headlong. Tom was better at managing the little details of a plot, the issue-by-issue continuity threads and character development, while I was a little better at actual dialogue, so we made a pretty good team, I think.

**TLC:** *Was writing the* **Legion** *what you expected it to be?*

**MW:** In ways. I didn't and don't feel like I had the same creative freedom with it as I did on, say, **Flash** or **Impulse**. It was always a huge committee effort, what with Tom and KC and assistant editor Mike McAvennie all constantly in the mix. By and large, we all made the finished product better, but at the same time so many voices also tended to level out the moments of real inspiration somewhat. Still, there were some really delightful high points. The prison

PAGE 11-A

1. LEGIONNAIRES SHOW SUPERBOY CLUBHOUSE.
CAPTION:  Finally the great day came when the Legion journeyed to the mists of the 20th Century...
CAPTION 2:  ...to bring *Superboy* himself for a visit.
CAPTION 3:  They left it to him to guess its origin, but he never did.  And somehow, in the rush of events, it was never mentioned again.

2. "OLD" KRYPTON MONTAGE.
CAPTION:  Eventually the Legionnaires would be told that neither their clubhouse nor Superboy had truly come from their own past at all, but had crossed from another dimension...

3. "NEW" KRYPTON MONTAGE.
CAPTION:  ...a dimension far more colorful than their own, yet one which (at least, according to *current* theories) existed only in a tiny pocket of time.

4. LEGIONNAIRES TESTING NEW RECRUITS.
CAPTION:  None of them would have guessed it at the time. . None of them would have stopped to consider it.
CAPTION 2:  For the Legion was on a merry-go-round of action and expansion, and the clubhouse was the axis.

*The only unfinished page from the Legion clubhouse story, complete with accompanying script. For referring to Superboy and the pocket universe, the story was quashed. From the collection of Kevin Gould.*
© DC Comics.

break story, which came from a suggestion by Paul Levitz, was a great deal of fun and, to this day, I'm flattered and amazed that so many people come up to me and say that **Legionnaires Annual** #2, which was the big finish to our first year on the book, is their favorite comic book. Looking back, I think we did some good work.

My other memory of writing the book was that while Tom and I took pride in being prompt, it was always running late for whatever reason. *Always.* And I mean *hideously* late. To the point where I was literally having to peel art pages out of the fax machine and dialogue them *that moment*, two or three at a time and not necessarily in order, so we wouldn't miss shipping. That's why, for instance, the White Triangle villains were named "The White Triangle." Because I had, like, nine minutes to dialogue the page where they state their name, and the best I could come up with in nine minutes was that artist Stuart Immonen had put little white triangles on their tunics. Nine minutes. Sometimes I think it's a miracle those comics were any good at *all.*

**TLC:** *You did have a lot of great young new artists debut during your time as an editor and writer. Stuart Immonen, Chris Sprouse, Jason Pearson, Jeff Moy...*

*A 2000 commission of Blok by Steve Lightle, courtesy of the artist.*
Art © 2003 Steve Lightle; Blok TM and © DC Comics.

**MW:** Yeah. Stuart, in particular, was a dream to work with, and Chris Sprouse was my find—I put him on the Chemical King story in **Secret Origins** [#37 —**Ed.**] and he just shined. Jason, actually, was after my time.

**TLC:** *My last question is an age-old one. The current take on the book has moved so far from the "sense of wonder" that drew so many of us to the book and kept us there, I have to ask: Is there a place in today's comic for that to happen again?*

**MW:** Sure. Absolutely. At the risk of sounding self-serving, I push hard for that every month in **Fantastic Four**. Actually, I'm not sure I'd concur that the sense of wonder is gone from **Legion** these days. I thought the **Legion Lost** series, though dark, was very imaginative—a good combination of Silver Age ideas with a modern tone. That said—not that the current **Legion** series is necessarily guilty of this, but it is a trend elsewhere—I honestly believe that to ground fanciful, colorful characters in bleak, grim realism is to do them a disservice and make them something they're not.

**TLC:** *Finally, how far along are you on the* **Legion/Fantastic Four** *crossover?*

**MW:** Slightly less far than I am on my dream project, a Silver Age **Titans/LSH** team-up—something I'm saving for when I'm old and gray and can afford to do more vanity books.

BLOK

# K.C. Carlson

In a turn of events similar to those of the mid-Seventies, the editorial chair of the **Legion of Super-Heroes** became a hot seat again in the early Nineties, resulting in three editors in under five years. The third editor of the decade (fourth since the Giffen relaunch) was KC Carlson, an individual whose presence would be felt in perhaps the single most controversial decision in Legion history. Not just the editor of the **Legion of Super-Heroes**, Carlson would also edit the **Zero Hour** mini-series which rebooted the title, and whose effects are still felt in the **Legion** today. After nearly six years as editor, Carlson left the title in 1998 to pursue other options. He was interviewed by Glen Cadigan on April 17, 2003, and he copyedited the following transcript.

**TLC:** *The earliest place that I could find your name was in the pages of an old issue of **The Legion Outpost** [#2 —Ed.]. When did you start following the Legion?*

**KC:** When I was a kid, actually. I was buying it when it was in the **Adventure** run. In fact, I think that was one of the first series I actually started collecting. I actually remember making a really strange

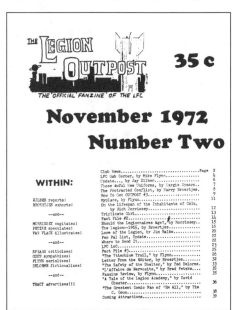

*From the pages of **Legion** fandom to **Legion** editor: KC Carlson's letter appeared in **The Legion Outpost** #2, November, 1972.*
The Legion Outpost © 1972 Harry Broertjes.

trade, 'cause I had a ton of **Walt Disney Comics and Stories**, but I traded them in to get back issues of **Adventure Comics**.

**TLC:** *Were you a steady **Legion** fan?*

**KC:** Pretty much, yeah.

**TLC:** *How did you get your start at DC?*

**KC:** I had been working in the business end of comics for about a decade before DC. One of the places I was working at was Capital City Distribution out of Madison, Wisconsin. From there I met Richard Brunning, who, at the time, was the editor of Capital Comics, which did **Nexus** and **Badger**. We became friends, and ultimately after Capital Comics folded and Richard ended up going to DC, he brought me in a couple of years after that. I actually worked at DC in two different stints, so I was there from '89 to about '90, and then I came back in mid-'92, and was there for another six years, I think.

**TLC:** *How did you go from the business end into editorial?*

**KC:** After I stopped working at Capital City Distribution I switched over to the Westfield Company, which is a big mail order firm out of Wisconsin. They did a monthly newsletter, which I wrote and edited. Instead of printing rumors in the newsletter about what we were hearing coming up, I started calling the publishers and saying, "We'd like to do a column about you every month. Can you give us some info?" This was long before most of the 'zines had started organizing. There was always **The Comic Reader** and things like that which had done news coverage back then, but we were trying to get something special going for the Westfield collectors. So I got in contact with a lot of the publishers, and mostly through DC I was talking with people like Peggy May way back when. The combination of them knowing who I was from my writing at Westfield in the marketing department, Richard's knowledge of me personally, and my interest in reading and things like that, kind of brought it all together.

I was originally called in to DC, and I don't remember what year this was, but I was brought in with about a half a dozen

*Another rare gem: Mon-El and Shadow Lass by Dave Cockrum. From the collection of Kevin McConnell. Mon-El and Shadow Lass TM and © DC Comics.*

other people from around the industry to interview for what ultimately became Piranha Press. DC was experimenting with the creator-owned thing. It didn't have a name at the time, but it was myself and a whole bunch of people that went on to bigger and better things, like Mark Waid and Brian Augustyn and Kevin Dooley, and several other people who I don't recall.

Actually, that wasn't my first time in the door at DC. I had been visiting there a few times before with the people at Capital City. At one point I actually switched from the Wisconsin branch and opened up one of their branches out in Connecticut, and I worked there for a half a year, and I would make trips into the city to represent the company at conventions and things. So over the years I ended up knowing a number of people at DC, and I didn't get the Piranha job, but a little while later Richard hired me to work with him, and pretty much all of us that interviewed for that job got hired eventually in some capacity at DC. So it was an interesting time. [*laughs*]

**TLC:** *Which comic did you edit first?*

**KC:** When I was first at DC, Richard was responsible for the graphic look of the

*Lightning Lad tries to enter the mystery rocket in another page from the secret origin of the Legion clubhouse.*
Courtesy of Kevin Gould. © DC Comics.

company. This was in the middle to late Eighties. You'll probably notice if you follow DC history they became a lot more graphically oriented back then, and it was a much bigger emphasis on how the comic books looked beyond just the stories. They talked about cover formats and designing pages for text, and this was the time they were experimenting with the upscale format books. This is when they started doing **Dark Knight Returns** and hardcover graphic novels like **Arkham Asylum** and things like that, so there were a lot of really exciting projects that Richard was looking after, both on a design level and manufacturing level, and I was assisting him in getting all these projects through the editorial offices, from the creators into the printers, and just making a lot of smooth transitions to make sure that nothing went wrong. I did that for about six months, and it wasn't exactly working out perfectly because I didn't have the exact design talent that Richard had, obviously. I was never educated as a designer or anything, but I had a feel for it, and Richard thought that I would be able to develop into something. The other thing that happened at the time is the collected books started developing—trade paperback

reprints and things like that— and I got heavily involved in that after a while, and started to assemble a number of the early collections at DC. Some of the early books that I remember working on are **V for Vendetta**, the **Prisoner**, and the first **Sandman** trade.

**TLC:** *So how did you get the* **Legion** *job?*

**KC:** During my first time at DC, I became friends with Mark Waid. He was the current editor of the **Legion** at that time, and that's when it was going through the relaunch where Paul Levitz had left the book and Keith Giffen was coming in and taking over as the main creative force. He brought in the Bierbaums. Mark Waid was editing it at that time, so Mark and I were friends, and he would show me all the stuff that was going on at the **Legion**, and it became well known around the offices that I was also a big **Legion** fan. Ultimately, I did all these odd jobs for a year and a half at DC, and then I got homesick, and there were some political things going on where my job was being phased out because Richard had decided to leave the company, and any number of things were going on. It was somehow corporate-wise very difficult for me to transition from where I was in the company into editorial. I still don't understand it to this day, but it's all business stuff.

I was getting homesick and I had decided to go back to Wisconsin for a while, and I went through about a two-year thing of the whole, "You can't go home again," because it wasn't the same when I went back, and I became bored. Ultimately, Mike Carlin called me. They had already gone through about three different **Legion** editors at that point. I think it was Waid, Dan Raspler, and Michael Eury, and Michael had decided to leave the company. I worked with Carlin quite a bit—I wrote a lot of letter columns for Carlin the first time I was around, and he and I were friends—so he called me up, and this was at the point where Carlin was actually transitioning to being the executive editor. Dick Giordano was leaving the company and going back to being a freelancer, and Carlin was taking the reins. He called me and said, "You want to edit the **Legion**?"

and I said, "Sure." [laughs] He made me promise that I would stay at least three years.

I had probably one of the strangest interviews ever, because my interviews took place with both Dick Giordano and Mike Carlin in two different cities, and it involved me driving about two thousand miles in about five days. It was just a very, very strange period of time. It also involved me going to a convention at Charlotte—there was a big **Legion** fan thing there, and I don't remember what the name of it was, but I was thinking about attending anyway [*"Reunion 2992,"* the Twentieth Anniversary of organized **Legion** fandom — Ed.]—and here I was going in probably going to be the next Legion editor, and I couldn't tell anybody at this convention. [laughs] Tom and Mary were there, and they were curious as to who their new editor was going to be. I don't remember if I told them or not at that convention, but it was a real strange transition. Basically, I drove down to Charlotte to see Dick at the convention, and Dick said, "It's not my choice. You gotta talk to Mike Carlin," so then I turned around the next day and I ended up driving up to New York and talking to Carlin, and he said, "No, it's Dick's call," and I said, "Okay, you guys get together, and let me know." So I went back to Wisconsin, and a couple of days later they said, "You got the job. C'mon, get out here as soon as you can." That's basically how that worked. It was very strange. I got the job because I had a reputation for knowing the Legion really well, and they wanted somebody who actually knew the Legion that could do something with it because they had had some problems before with some of the previous editors. They just didn't have a feel for it, I guess, is what they told me. I don't know. I thought they did a pretty good job.

**TLC:** *Your first few issues had a double credit between yourself and Michael Eury. Did the two of you work together for a time?*

**KC:** Not really. Michael was there for a couple of weeks, so there was a little bit of an overlap. Anytime there's an editorial switchover there's always two or three issues in the pipeline in various states, and there's never any really clear break as to somebody stops editing this issue, and this person takes over with the next one. Occasionally some people rewrite the credits because as soon as somebody comes in, they take the old name off and put their name in it right away, but the first few issues Michael had worked on quite a bit, and I was just coming in and basically being the traffic cop and getting them out the door. There's a point in the production of books where all the hard work is done and basically you're just making sure that it gets from one place to another on a timely basis. There were two or three issues there where I was just doing that kind of work, and DC wanted my name on the book, and I said, "Michael's name should be there also," to be fair, 'cause he did the hard work.

But there wasn't a lot of closeness. I mean, Michael and I were friends. We knew each other before I took over from him. The first time I was there in '89, Michael was editing the three-ring binder version of *Who's Who*, and I worked on a couple of issues with him. So we knew each other, and we both knew we knew the Legion, and I think Michael may have brought my name up as a person to talk to when he had decided to leave the com-

pany. Now that I think about it, Michael was probably another one of the "Piranha" guys.

**TLC:** *Almost immediately after you took over, the **Legion** went in a different direction. Was that your decision?*

**KC:** Not really. I came in at a very tumultuous time in the continuity. My first real issue of the *Legion* was the one where the Earth blew up, and for whatever reasons—I was never very clear on this—Keith Giffen had decided to leave the book at that time, or he thought he was gonna leave, and I think there was about a week or two-week period where he couldn't make up his mind if he was leaving or not. He wanted to see who the new editor was. I don't know exactly what Keith's thinking was. I was the new kid on the block, and Keith kind of scared me a little bit [*laughs*], 'cause Keith's kinda crazy. I was also working with Keith on *Eclipso* at the same time, and *Eclipso* was just an absolute nightmare, especially for Keith, because Keith pitched it as the scariest book that DC would be able to do and still be under the Comics Code, and what it eventually turned into was nothing like that at all. It turned into a real standard superhero book, and to cut to the chase, Keith got screwed. So he wasn't really thrilled with what was going on at DC anyway, and the *Legion* continuity was at a point where it felt like it was a good place for him to leave. So that's what happened there. I've always regretted not being able to work more with Keith on the project 'cause he's an immensely talented guy. He fires off a thousand ideas a minute, and he's a wild man. He's uncontrollable. You're very familiar with his work; you know how utterly unique it is. [*laughs*] So I always kind of regretted that, but Keith had all his protégés working with him on the projects, with Tom and Mary on the *Legion* and Robert Loren Fleming on *Eclipso*, so he didn't leave me in the lurch or anything. There were people in place to step in and work in Keith's footsteps at that point.

**TLC:** *How much interference did you get from the higher-ups when you were on the **Legion**?*

**KC:** Not a whole lot. It was a real interesting time. Like I said earlier, Mike Carlin was just coming in as the boss at the time. The *Legion* turned out to

be a controversial book from the get-go when Giffen started out, because there were all these continuity things with Mark Waid's run on the book. The *Legion* got off on the wrong foot, and I don't think it was anybody's fault, but it was just kind of a mess, because Carlin's thing was the *Superman* books, and he was very protective of all the Superman stuff. Of course, the Legion sprung out of Superman decades ago, and suddenly Keith was being asked to change things to protect the Superman continuity that the *Legion* office thought was okay to do since it was a thousand years in the future. That was one of the tough things about the *Legion*, because things needed to reflect what may have happened in the DC universe in the thousand years in between the two continuities. So that was occasionally an issue. But interference from the higher-ups, no, not really.

My mandate was to make the book good. They were sort of unhappy with it. I think they liked Keith's run, but it was so dense and dark, and it was unlike what the *Legion* had been, and it was certainly controversial among Legion fans at the time because it was so different from what had gone before. But there wasn't really anything actively going on. There was a thing with the Bierbaums coming in, because I don't think Mike Carlin liked the Bierbaums' work too much, and there may have been other people involved. I don't want to stick this to Mike in any way, but basically I was sort of pushed into possibly firing the Bierbaums right off the bat, and after I'd been there for a little while and I'd done my research, I realized that DC had just offered the Bierbaums a year long contract thirty days prior to this, and my sense of fair play kicked in. I said, "I can't fire somebody that you guys just signed a contract with. This is ridiculous. We gotta let 'em play out the contract. They haven't done anything wrong. They're just taking over on their own." It was hard because Tom and Mary were kind of put on notice as soon as they were taking over. It was really unfair to them, and put me in a weird situation, because I argued for them. They wanted some changes, but Mike ultimately trusted me to figure out what the book needed, and I don't think I got it right away. It took a little while to get to it, to where I was comfortable with the books.

The other thing was there were two Legion continuities at the time, because as I was coming in the *Legionnaires* book was starting up. I wasn't there at the time,

*Dreamer by George Pérez, courtesy of Spencer Beck at The Artist's Choice.*
Art © 2003 George Pérez; Dreamer TM and © DC Comics.

A Silver Age version of Chameleon Boy, courtesy of Steve Lightle. Art © 2003 Steve Lightle; Chameleon Boy TM and © 2003 DC Comics.

but from all the memos and stuff that were in the files when I got there, my understanding was that the **Legionnaires** book was a particularly tough birth, and had gone through three or four different incarnations before it was actually published. I think originally there was a false start. The "Legionnaires" entry that was in the three-ring binder **Who's Who** way back when stated that the original series was going to be tales of the Legion when they were younger, and that's the way that everybody thought it was gonna go for a while, and then that got killed, and they did this other thing. Eventually it became the adventures of the SW6 characters, which were the younger versions of the characters that Keith had created in the regular Legion continuity. So at that point I thought that the **Legionnaires** book was really cool, but then after a while I realized it was like there were two copies of every Legion character running around the Legion universe in the same continuity, and it was just confusing to me, and I think it became confusing to the readers. I just felt like it needed some housecleaning. That's what ultimately led to **Zero Hour**.

**TLC:** *How did Tom McCraw get the job as*

*Legion writer?*

**KC:** Tom was working as part of the creative team as the colorist for several years before I got there. I think he had started on the first issue with the Giffens and the Bierbaums, and they were a very close-knit team. Keith and Tom and Mary and Al Gordon, who was the inker, and Tom were all huge, huge Legion fans, and they were all pitching in ideas. It was very much a back-and-forth sort of thing. Tom is an incredible resource for the **Legion**. He's an incredible resource in general as a colorist because he's one of the few guys that, back in the old days when they were still color-coding comics, memorized all the codes for all the characters, so anytime you've got a book that had fifty different characters in it, Tom would get the job because he could just zing right through it.

He loved the Legion, he knew all the characters back and forth, and he was always pitching in good ideas. I was friends with Tom, and he kept pitching ideas to me, too, and I thought, "Well, let's give this guy a try." Ultimately, I don't think it worked out as well as possible. Tom did have plenty of great ideas, but he just didn't have the capability to structure a good story, and he required a lot of help from various people. I thought he did a great job. It was kind of a thankless job, because he was working on the book at a time where we knew **Zero Hour** was coming, and we knew there was going to be a major transition that Tom was gonna work toward. Ultimately we had X number of issues left, because I definitely knew that I wanted to bring in Mark Waid as the new writer of the **Legion** once we did the **Zero Hour** reboot. So it was a finite thing from the beginning, and I thought, "I'll give Tom a try out and see what happens." And there were some good stories, but like I said, it wasn't like he was given a blank slate. He had to kinda cram things around, given what was going on in the overall thread of the book. So it was an experimental time.

**TLC:** *There was a period there when the* **Legion** *went bi-weekly. How hectic did it get?*

**KC:** At that particular time it wasn't that bad, because it just happened to fall in the transition between the teams. Two of those issues were Tom and Mary's last issues, and then the other two issues that were involved in that bi-weekly period were by Tom McCraw, so Tom got going early. So

it wasn't that bad. There was some artistic juggling that we had to do. Any time you get something that you try to produce twice a month, you're gonna need fill-in artists. I don't remember it being that particularly hard.

**TLC:** *So why did the* **Legion** *go bi-weekly?*

**KC:** I think DC was experimenting with a number of titles at that point. Marvel was doing the same thing. They had a number of books that went bi-weekly during the summer. I think it was a publisher's experiment to see if people would like to see more issues of their favorite characters. Like I said, it was always kind of a tainted experiment because generally some of those issues weren't by the regular team, and so therefore they were probably weaker than normal issues, and that's what always happens when you try to do the bi-weekly thing. People are getting better at it because they're planning ahead nowadays, but back then it was just another thing. It was a numbers game. If you made X number of dollars per issue of **Legion** and you added two issues into the mix, you made that much more profit for the year.

**TLC:** *Marvel tended to reserve that for their better-selling titles, though.*

**KC:** Yeah. I don't know why **Legion** was picked, to tell you the truth. I may have volunteered for it. I did a lot of stupid things [*laughs*] on the **Legion**.

**TLC:** *What were the* **Legion** *sales like around then?*

**KC:** They were falling, but everybody else's books were falling, too. I can't tell you exact numbers, but I was always given good reports by my superiors at DC by saying that the sales weren't falling as fast as other titles. After we did the reboot, the sales stabilized and actually rose up a little bit. It didn't rise up as much as we hoped it would be, but it was a slowly descending spiral, just like the rest of the industry. It was the same time that sales were falling all over the place, and they told me that they thought the **Legion** was doing well because it wasn't falling as fast.

**TLC:** *When was the decision made to reboot the title?*

**KC:** Talking about the origin of **Zero Hour** is basically the starting point for the reboot. **Zero Hour** came about because I proposed doing a major DC crossover that actually involved time travel so the Legion could be involved, because there were several crossovers prior to *Zero Hour* that the Legion either wasn't involved in at all, or it was just some small tie-in. Since my mandate was to get the *Legion* noticed by the rest of the people who were reading DC comics, I wanted the Legion to be a big part of whatever the crossover was that summer. As I handed in my proposal, Mike Carlin kind of laughed and said, "You should read this," and he handed me another proposal that had come in from Dan Jurgens a week or so before, basically suggesting a time-travel crossover. So the two ideas got merged, and I was selected as the editor for the project, and Dan was the writer and artist. Things progressed from there, and we thought if ever we were going to reboot the Legion, this was the time to do it.

There were a lot of reasons why we decided to do it. One of the reasons I alluded to earlier is the fact that there were two separate versions of the Legion at the same time, and it just seemed confusing. Another reason was that the older characters were getting harder and harder to deal with because they had become less fantasy-like characters and more realistic in a lot of ways. Let me explain what I mean by that: I'll give it a TV analogy. If you follow sitcoms, the joke is whenever a couple has a baby on a sitcom, that kills the sitcom forever, because immediately the viewers care more about the baby, just because it's a baby. Nothing can happen because the viewers are always thinking, "Why is this going on? Where's the baby while this is going on?" With the *Legion*, we ran into that problem, because it was like while they were getting attacked by villains, people were thinking, "What's happening to the baby while this is going on?" We found we were constantly cutting to where the baby was.

It was a hard thing to lose, because the Legion was really unique. What Giffen and the Bierbaums had done was evolve the characters into a more adult situation. Most comic book series are locked into a fixed time, and the characters never age and they never grow, and that's what they were trying to get a hold of with the *Legion*. I'm not sure it was the best book to try that particular experiment with because of what happened. There were already a million characters, and when you started adding in all the other relatives and the babies and the relationships, it just got to be ponderous after a while. So there was that.

There was a feeling, especially among the people at DC, that the SW6 characters were ultimately going to be a lot more popular than the adults. They were cuter and more marketable and that kind of thing, and couldn't we do more stories about them? And we said, "Sure! We can do that." That led to the idea of, "Well, why not start the Legion over from scratch with the younger versions of the characters, but this time we'll tell the stories with a twist," or something like that. My feeling for the *Legion* overall was I thought that the *Legion* as a whole, as a series since the beginning of time, was basically created to be the ultimate kid's comic, and I don't mean specifically just for kids. It was such a great concept for an entry-level comic book, because as a kid you could walk into it and there were a million characters, and they all had super-powers, and they all had bright costumes, and they all had funny real names, and they came from weird planets, and you either got it instantly or you didn't.

I think part of the appeal for the *Legion* was that there were so many characters, and there were so many different combinations. On the one hand, because the characters weren't as fully developed as a series about a solo character, they were kinda blank slates, and I think that appealed to a lot of people, a lot of Legion fans especially, because they could make up their own stories and backgrounds about them. This is where fanfic comes into the whole thing, because there was a huge, huge amount of fanfiction around the Legion. Tom and Mary came out of that area initially, and that was kind of the overriding appeal to me about it. I loved what Tom and Mary and Keith were doing. It was very adult, it was very interesting, but I really did feel that the Legion needed to be more of a fun book, and a book that kids could read and be comfortable reading. This was at a time where DC was really getting into the grim and gritty stuff, and I remember having conversations with Mark Waid all the time, because it seemed like he and I were the only people trying to make fun comics at

DC. He was working on the *Flash* with Brian Augustyn, and we were trying to do fun stuff with the *Legion*. Eventually he got to do *Impulse*, and we were just trying to do books that we liked as kids. We knew that we ran the risk of being uncommercial about it, but we thought that we would still have enough of an audience there that just got tired of people shooting each other and doing bad things to each other all the time.

A lot of thinking went into it. The decision to change the whole thing and start it over from scratch probably went anywhere from nine months to a year before we actually got around to executing it, and we spent a lot of time going, "Do we really want to do this?" back and forth with the powers that be, the creators, and some of the key fans that we knew. It was really serious. We knew that it was going to be a really big deal, and there were a lot of people who were really going to be ticked off by it, but we thought and we hoped that there were going to be a lot more people

*An unpublished Legion cover by Stuart Immonen and Ron Boyd. From the collection of Royd Burgoyne.*
The Legion of Super-Heroes TM and © DC Comics.

that really liked the idea, and ultimately I still don't know exactly how it worked out. [laughs] A lot of people liked what we did, but nowadays I hear that people kind of just put up with it. I don't know. It's very hard to judge my place in **Legion** history, I think. [laughs]

**TLC:** *Who would have to sign off on a decision like that?*

**KC:** Mike Carlin as the executive editor was the person that I dealt with directly, and ultimately it would have been Jenette Kahn and Paul Levitz as the Publisher and Editor-in-Chief and President and all their various titles at the time. The situation with Paul was very interesting, because after he had stopped writing the **Legion** back then, he had backed away from it, and he wasn't really intimate with what Giffen and the Bierbaums were doing. He was kind of vaguely aware, but he wasn't reading the book at the time. I think his overall feeling was that it wasn't really the **Legion** that he wanted to see, either. I don't want to put words in Paul's mouth here, but this was just the impression that I got from the few conversations I had with him. I knew that there were a couple of things, one thing specifically about the

Giffen run that very much bothered him, because they took one of Paul's very personal characters and kind of warped it, and Paul wasn't very appreciative of that.

**TLC:** *Are you referring to Shvaughn Erin?*

**KC:** Yeah. Paul never told me to do anything specifically with the **Legion**. He would guide me occasionally if I did something wrong, or if I went in a wrong direction, he would kind of say, "Maybe we shouldn't have done it that way," that kind of thing. That was about all I got. He kind of backed away from it. It was really a weird situation for both of us. I had the feeling there were certain people at DC that thought since Paul was the big boss, his legacy on the **Legion** needed to be protected, and I agreed with that. I certainly wasn't gonna try to do anything bad to his version of the Legion, but I think that there were a number of people that were kind of zealous about it elsewhere in the company.

I think Paul would have been happy to have the **Legion** be the number one seller at DC. Obviously it was never going to be that, because Superman and Batman were so much stronger characters, and had been around forever. Paul loved the Legion. Paul wanted the **Legion** to always be published. The Legion was never in any position where it was going to be cancelled tomorrow, but it was never as big a success as it should be. It was like the ultimate cult comic for the longest time. It was one of the first Sixties Silver Age books to lose its own title, back in the **Adventure** days when it got booted into the back-up in **Action**, so it was tough going for the Legion for the longest time, and I think everybody wanted it to be a huge success, and it was occasionally frustrating because it wasn't.

Maybe the subject was just a little too esoteric for the average comic fan. That was the reaction I would get when I would go to conventions. Obviously the Legion fans would love to come up and talk to me, but I would try to initiate other people into talking about the Legion books when I was at the booth, and a lot of times the reaction was,

"Oh, yeah, the **Legion**. I don't *get* that book." So for some people it's just a tough sell. And it is an intimidating book, because of the characters, and especially in the Giffen era and the era that I worked on where the continuity became so intense. It was a tough book all around. You really had to put something into it to get something back.

**TLC:** *How much of a role did sales have in the decision to reboot the title?*

**KC:** Not that much. I think it was more of a decision of, "Let's go a different way and see what happens." There was never any kind of, "Well, we're gonna cancel this book if you don't change it." There was nothing like that. In some ways it was kind of a "gut" decision. As an editor, you have to try to anticipate that things may be going astray *before* you are told that you are going to be cancelled. I knew that some people at DC weren't happy with the way the books were going, and that certainly factored into the process, but it wasn't the *only* reason. It was just a matter of, like I said, the two different books with two different sets of characters was very hard to deal with, and we just thought it should be streamlined somehow, and that was the best way to do it. It probably wasn't the most gracious way of doing it. Obviously, each different group had its fans, especially the fans of the older characters, and they kind of got locked into deep freeze. But we really tried hard to do it in such a way that we weren't disavowing any of it. It's not like we threw the continuity away in terms of parallel stories and parallel universes and things like that. We did say very clearly in **Zero Hour** that all the stories that ever existed did exist at some point. And ultimately, that's what DC evolved into, the hypertime theory. We tried very hard to accommodate everybody, but we did feel that things needed to be changed a little bit.

**TLC:** *You said that you spent a long time making that decision. What other options were explored?*

**KC:** I don't recall anything specific, but we did discuss what seemed like dozens of options, but most of them led to creative dead ends. Mostly, we were working toward making this big change. We did try to think of ways to keep the books the same and to try to streamline them somehow, but we would have ended up turning the books into something that they weren't. For instance, we were talking ear-

*Legion girls by Jeff Moy. From the collection of Miki Annamanthadoo.*
Art © 2003 Jeff Moy; all characters TM and © DC Comics.

lier about the Tom McCraw run. We referred to it as the "Legion on the Lam" storyline, because they all went undercover, and they all got different identities, and things like that. That was an experiment, in a way, of one of the ways that we could have gone with it because DC was, at the time, trying to streamline the stuff. If you look at DC history, you've got all these dozens of characters that you have two or three or four different versions of, and to have two of them exist simultaneously is tough. They work it out between the Justice League characters and the Justice Society characters, but here the Legion fans are being presented with thirty different couples, basically [laughs], characters with the same name, and even when we were talking about characters around the office, it was just tougher talking to fans about it. "Oh no, I meant the SW6 Brainy." You'd have to qualify it all the time. That was pretty much it. I mean, we were scared. We knew it was gonna be a big change, and that's why we wanted to take our time in planning it. There's so many comics out there over the course of history that obviously wanted to take a big left turn because they thought they needed a jolt or sales boost, and they were so obviously not thought out that we wanted to cover as much of it as we could. We didn't want to be hasty in our decision about it.

**TLC:** *What kind of a reaction did you get?*

**KC:** Mixed. I think a lot of the older fans liked it because they liked the young Legion. That was what they grew up with. A lot of people who were fans of the Giffen era were horrified by it. I know that there's a number of people that stopped reading the book altogether, which I think includes Tom and Mary. In some ways, I can't blame them for that. It wasn't the book that they wanted. Every era that's ever been of the Legion has been in the situation where it's both alienated some people and actually brought in new people. A lot of people like the sophistication of the Giffen era, and they were really excited by that, and basically we cut their limbs out from under them. Of course they were mad, and rightfully so, because suddenly the book they loved wasn't around anymore. We turned it into this hybrid thing of something that was old and something that was new, and they didn't know what to think of it.

Like I say, the sales went up a little bit after the reboot. Not a huge amount, but enough to make everybody think that we had done the right thing, and that we were able to carry it on and do the storyline

from there. I don't recall getting any real death threats or anything. [laughs] We hoped we were on the right track. A lot of people were really cautious at the beginning, too. A lot of fans were, "Well, let's see how this works out," and they gave us the benefit of the doubt. Most of them stuck around, I think. A lot of the fans were very positive for it. I mean, there were a couple of years there where there were huge Legion gatherings at the major conventions, and fifty or sixty or seventy Legion fans would get together and take over the lobby of some hotel and just talk Legion all night long. It was amazing. There's always groups of people that get together to talk about comics, but people were commenting they'd never seen groups that large getting together and talking and not trying to kill each other. I always thought it was successful. I felt in my heart that it was, but I knew that there were people out there that didn't like it, and what can you do? You can't please everybody, especially Legion fans. [laughs]

**TLC:** *Which is more important to you: the concept of the Legion or the execution of that concept?*

**KC:** I think the concept is the ultimate goodness of the Legion. I just think that because it boils down so easily into "kids in space in the future." That says it all, I think, and that's basically what we were trying to get back to in our era, to the original feeling of awe and wonder and "space is great, and so is time travel, and this is so cool." In addition to that, I would also add on the character interaction and development is also a big, big part. I still think that's secondary to the concept, but once you get 'em hooked, then the characters have to be cool. That's a big part of it. The execution of the Legion over the years has been so much of a roller coaster up and down. Any Legion fan can look at it and find the great eras of the Legion, but there's also some really horribly bad ones, either artwise or writing-wise, and I'm not gonna say which ones are which. [laughs] Everybody knows, at least in their own heart, that not all the issues are great, even within a certain era. You try hard to do great work, and sometimes you just fall flat, but that's what you do when you have a monthly comic book. It's hard to make them all masterpieces.

**TLC:** *So you would see the age of the characters as an important part of the series?*

**KC:** Yeah. I think the Legion works because they're young. I believe, in terms of the characters and character

development, that the teenage years are the most angst-ridden and most rife for good storytelling in terms of you've got a whole bunch of boys and girls thrown together with raging hormones [laughs] and there's gonna be a lot of fireworks between characters. We probably never went as far as we could have with it. I always backed away from doing anything too salacious with the characters because I had a lot of respect for them. I didn't want to do teenage pregnancy stories and things like that, really.

**TLC:** *Why did you eventually leave the Legion?*

**KC:** I left the Legion because I left DC; I left DC because I left New York. I really got burned out in New York. I'd grown up in Wisconsin, and I was a Midwest kind of

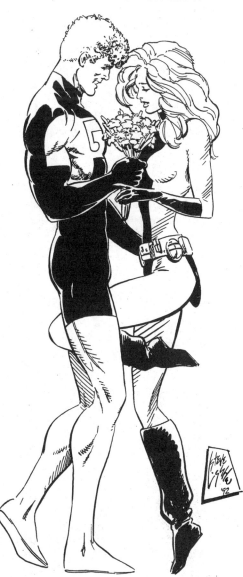

Art © 2003 Steve Lightle; Element Lad and Shvaughn Erin TM and © DC Comics.

person. I missed trees and clear air, and I got tired of the commuting lifestyle. I just got burned out by the whole thing. The other thing that happened that I really never told anybody at DC about at the time was that both my parents were dying, and I really wanted to spend some time with them. I knew that it wasn't going to go over well with me taking a bunch of time off. So it was a combination of a lot of things.

In some ways I also felt like I'd worn out my welcome a little bit on the **Legion**. It wasn't that we were out of ideas, but it got to the point on the book where I thought that maybe it was time for another creative shakeup in some way, and maybe it'd be better if a fresh editor came in and did the shaking up. It was a very bittersweet time, because I was going through all these personal things at the time, and I hated leaving the book. I loved the characters. It was the best job in the world. It was a headache and a nightmare on occasion, but I think it was some of the best work that I've done.

**TLC:** *Do you still follow the comic today?*

**KC:** Not as much as I should. I'm not a huge fan of more science-fiction than super-heroes, and that's kinda the way that the guys seem to be going. The current series seems too "Star Trek" for me. It's tough when you've been working on a comic and you have your own vision for what it should look like, and what it should read like, and when you see something different, it just doesn't click right for you. The new artist they brought in, Olivier Copiel, I thought was an incredible find for DC. He's an amazing talent, but I just thought he was really inappropriate for the **Legion** in any number of ways, and it made the book hard for me to look at at some point. I've always seen the Legion's future as being sort of "shiny" and "clean" and Copiel's stuff was pretty "dirty" and "scratchy." Too much Curt Swan influence, I guess. [*laughs*] The **Legion**'s kind of had a history of people leaving the book for various reasons and then just not following it afterwards. It's a book that people are very passionate about, and when they work on it, they put their very best work

into it, and it's hard to see somebody else doing it after you've worked so hard on it.

**TLC:** *So what are you up to these days?*

**KC:** I was managing a comic book store here in Richmond, Virginia, and I have some long-range plans to try to do some sort of archival or history project for comics, but I can't be more specific than that. I'm hoping that it might be something very good and useful for the industry. It's been in the planning stages for a while. Also, people keep telling me that I should try to write comics. Part of me thinks that I'm too old [*laughs*], 'cause I'm forty-five now. It might be a little too late to try to break in. I've written a couple of scripts here and there, but it's a young person's field, I think. I'd love to do more editing, but these days it seems like you are forced to live in big cities to do that, and I don't think my psyche is up for it anymore.

(L)

# Afterword

## by Glen Cadigan

At the end of any long journey, it is customary to give thanks. For the sake of convenience, I have divided the thanks-giving into sections, where each section represents an essential part of the book

- Thanks go out to all of the **Legion** creators who were interviewed for this volume, some of whom went even further and provided pictures to accompany their words. Thanks in particular go out to Steve Lightle for providing the piece which you see on the first page of this book, and to Dave Cockrum and Joe Rubinstein for providing its cover. While other artwork in this volume may be rare, those two pieces are exclusive to it.

- Thanks go out to all of the people who provided artwork from their own collections. While a complete list appears elsewhere in these pages, I would like to thank two people in particular: Miki Annamanthadoo and Steven Weill. Miki's collection is legendary amongst his fellow **Legion** fans, and he sent package after package as his collection grew. Steven's submission was the first one which I received, and from his collection

many rare pieces were found. I don't have to list them all here, as his name appears next to them in the book, but it was a bit like stumbling across buried treasure to see what he owned. Between the two of them the lion's share of artwork in this book was provided.

- Thanks go out to those who helped with the text portion of this book, especially Harry Broertjes for allowing so much material from the **Legion Outpost** fanzine to be reprinted here, and Jim Shooter for allowing us to use his introduction. Jim also sat down for an especially long interview, so his name and its connection with the **Legion** legend lives on. Thanks also go to Chris Companik, Peter Hansen, Neil Hansen (no relation), and John Pierce, all of whom made up the balance of the book. Chris filled in when it seemed like the dreaded deadline doom wouldn't allow for me to interview everyone on my list; Peter solved the mystery surrounding John Forte almost single-handedly; Neil was one of the few people to actually interview Curt Swan while he was alive (and from what I understand, it wasn't

as great a privilege as having him for a friend), and John's interview with E. Nelson Bridwell turned out to be interesting to more than just Captain Marvel fans. Together I like to think that it all made for one darn fine book.

- To those associated with the publishing end of things, thanks are also extended. From Adam Philips at DC to John Morrow at TwoMorrows and everyone in between, thanks. That includes Chris Day, who took all the packages which I could provide him with and glued them all together, along with the files which I sent him filled with words. It wasn't quite as simple as that, but you get my meaning.

- And to you, the reader, for buying this book. Don't sell yourself short; you're important, too. Without you, this would just be another idea in my head. If you're reading this in the store, bring it up to the counter and we'll be square. If you're reading it at home, then give yourself a pat on the back, because you've earned it.

— Glen Cadigan (06/27/03)

# THE TWOMORROWS LIBRARY

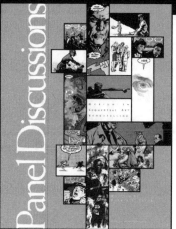

**EISNER AWARD WINNER! BEST SHORT STORY!**

## PANEL DISCUSSIONS
### TOP ARTISTS DISCUSS THE DESIGN OF COMICS

Top creators discuss all aspects of the **DESIGN OF COMICS**, from panel and page layout, to use of color and lettering:

• WILL EISNER • SCOTT HAMPTON
• MIKE WIERINGO • WALT SIMONSON
• MIKE MIGNOLA • MARK SCHULTZ
• DAVID MAZZUCCHELLI • MIKE CARLIN
• DICK GIORDANO • BRIAN STELFREEZE
• CHRIS MOELLER • MARK CHIARELLO

If you're serious about creating effective, innovative comics, or just enjoying them from the creator's perspective, this guide is must-reading!

(208-Page Trade Paperback) **$26 US**

## THE LIFE & ART OF MURPHY ANDERSON

Comics historian **R.C. Harvey** has compiled a lavishly illustrated autobiographical memoir of the man whose style defined the DC look for a generation of fans!!

• **MURPHY** discusses his career from the 1940s to today in a series of interviews!
• Covers his work on **SUPERMAN, HAWKMAN, ADAM STRANGE, ATOMIC KNIGHTS, BUCK ROGERS,** and more!
• Loaded with **ANDERSON ART,** plus behind-the-scenes anecdotes about **FINE, EISNER, SWAN, KANE,** and others!
• Includes a deluxe **COLOR SECTION** showcasing many of Murphy's finest cover recreations and paintings!

(176-page Trade Paperback) **$22 US**

## STREETWISE
### TOP ARTISTS DRAWING STORIES OF THEIR LIVES

An unprecedented assembly of talent drawing **NEW** autobiographical stories:

• Barry **WINDSOR-SMITH** • C.C. **BECK**
• Sergio **ARAGONÉS** • Walter **SIMONSON**
• Brent **ANDERSON** • Nick **CARDY**
• Roy **THOMAS** & John **SEVERIN**
• Paul **CHADWICK** • Rick **VEITCH**
• Murphy **ANDERSON** • Joe **KUBERT**
• Evan **DORKIN** • Sam **GLANZMAN**
• Plus Art **SPIEGELMAN,** Jack **KIRBY,** more!
Cover by **RUDE** • Foreword by **EISNER**

(160-Page Trade Paperback) **$24 US**

## "I HAVE TO LIVE WITH THIS GUY!"

Explore the lives of the partners and wives of the top names in comics, as they share memories, anecdotes, personal photos, momentos, and never-before-seen art by the top creators in comics!

• ALAN MOORE • WILL EISNER
• STAN LEE • GENE COLAN
• JOE KUBERT • JOHN ROMITA
• HARVEY KURTZMAN • DAVE SIM
• HOWARD CRUSE • DAN DeCARLO
• DAVE COOPER and many more!

(208-Page Trade Paperback) **$24 US**

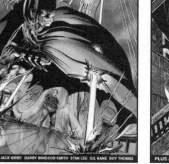

## ALTER EGO: THE CBA COLLECTION

Reprints the **ALTER EGO** flip-sides from the out-of-print **COMIC BOOK ARTIST #1-5,** plus **30 NEW PAGES** of features & art:

• Special color cover by **JOE KUBERT!**
• All-new rare and previously-unpublished art by **JACK KIRBY, GIL KANE, JOE KUBERT, WALLY WOOD, FRANK ROBBINS, NEAL ADAMS,** and others!
• **STEVE DITKO** on the creation of **SPIDER-MAN, ROY THOMAS** on THE **X-MEN, AVENGERS/KREE-SKRULL WAR, THE INVADERS,** and more!

(160-page Trade Paperback) **$20 US**

## FAWCETT COMPANION THE BEST OF FCA

Presenting the best of the **FAWCETT COLLECTORS OF AMERICA** newsletter!

• New **JERRY ORDWAY** cover!
• Index of ALL **FAWCETT COMICS!**
• Looks inside the **FAWCETT OFFICES!**
• Interviews, features, and rare and previously unpublished artwork by **C.C. BECK, MARC SWAYZE, KURT SCHAFFENBERGER, MAC RABOY, DAVE BERG, ALEX TOTH, BOB OKSNER, GEORGE EVANS, ALEX ROSS,** Foreword by **MARC SWAYZE,** and more!

(160-page Trade Paperback) **$20 US**

## THE COMIC BOOK ARTIST COLLECTION, VOL. ONE

Reprints the Eisner Award-winning **COMIC BOOK ARTIST #1-3,** plus over **50 NEW PAGES** of features and art:

• An unpublished story by **JACK KIRBY!**
• An interview with **NEAL ADAMS** about his **SUPERMAN VS. MUHAMMAD ALI** book (including unused art)!
• Unpublished **BERNIE WRIGHTSON** art!
• An unused story by **JEFFREY JONES!**
• Extensive new **ALAN WEISS** interview (including unpublished art), & more!

(228-page Trade Paperback) **$26 US**

**EISNER AWARD NOMINEE!**

## THE COMIC BOOK ARTIST COLLECTION, VOL. TWO

Second volume in the series, reprinting the Eisner Award-winning **COMIC BOOK ARTIST #5-6** (spotlighting 1970s DC and Marvel comics), plus over **50 NEW PAGES** of features and art:

• New interviews with **MARSHALL ROGERS, STEVE ENGLEHART, & TERRY AUSTIN** on their highly-acclaimed 1970s Batman work!
• An extensive look at perhaps the rarest 1970s comic of all, DC's **CANCELLED COMIC CAVALCADE,** showcasing unused stories from that decade!

(208-page Trade Paperback) **$24 US**

# READ EXCERPTS & ORDER AT: www.twomorrows.com

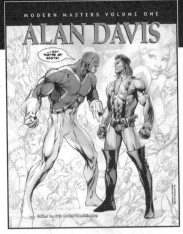

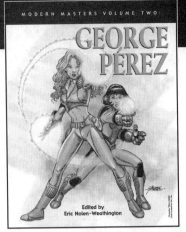

## COMIC BOOKS & OTHER NECESSITIES OF LIFE

A collection of **MARK EVANIER**'s **POV COLUMNS**, featuring a **NEW COVER** and **ILLUSTRATIONS** by **SERGIO ARAGONÉS**! Includes his best essays and commentaries, plus many never before published on:

• The state of the art form (as only Mark conveys it)!
• The industry's leading practitioners (including **JACK KIRBY** and **CARL BARKS**)!
• Convention-going and Mark's old comic book club (with unforgettable anecdotes)!

(200-page Trade Paperback) **$17 US**

## WERTHAM WAS RIGHT!

A second collection of **MARK EVANIER**'s **POV COLUMNS**, with a **NEW COVER** and **ILLUSTRATIONS** by **SERGIO ARAGONÉS**! Includes more of Mark's best essays and commentaries!

• Features many never-before published columns on comic book history, creation, and appreciation!
• Includes Mark's diatribe on comic book numbering!
• Essay on comics greatest villain, **DR. FREDRIC WERTHAM**!

(200-page Trade Paperback) **$17 US**

## MODERN MASTERS VOL. 1: ALAN DAVIS

First volume in a new book series devoted to the best of today's comics artists looks at the work of **ALAN DAVIS!**

• **ALAN DAVIS'** most **IN-DEPTH INTERVIEW** to date, including influences, and his views on graphic storytelling!
• **DELUXE SKETCHBOOK** section, & **HUGE GALLERY** of rare and unseen Davis art!
• Interviews with collaborators **PAUL NEARY** and **MARK FARMER**!

(128-Page Trade Paperback) **$17 US**

## MODERN MASTERS VOL. 2: GEORGE PÉREZ

Second volume focuses on **GEORGE PÉREZ**, from **THE AVENGERS** and **TEEN TITANS** to **CRISIS** and beyond!

• Contains rare and unseen artwork, direct from **GEORGE'S PRIVATE FILES**!
• Features a **COMPREHENSIVE INTERVIEW** with Pérez on his stellar career, including the JLA/Avengers series!
• **DELUXE SKETCHBOOK** section & **MORE**!

(128-Page Trade Paperback) **$17 US**

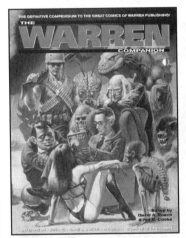

## CAPTAIN ACTION THE ORIGINAL SUPER-HERO ACTION FIGURE

**CAPTAIN ACTION** debuted in the wake of the '60s Batman TV show, and could become 13 different super-heroes. With over 200 toy photos, this trade paperback written by **MICHAEL EURY** chronicles his history (including comic book appearances) with historical anecdotes by the late **GIL KANE**, **JIM SHOOTER**, **STAN WESTON** (co-creator of GI Joe, Captain Action, and Mego's World's Greatest Super-Heroes), plus never-seen art by **GIL KANE**, **JOE STATON**, **JERRY ORDWAY**, **CARMINE INFANTINO**, and **MURPHY ANDERSON** (who provides a new cover)! Includes a color section!

(176-Page Trade Paperback) **$20 US**

## G-FORCE: ANIMATED THE OFFICIAL BATTLE OF THE PLANETS GUIDEBOOK

The official compendium to the Japanese animated TV program that revolutionized anime across the globe! Featuring plenty of unseen artwork and designs from the wondrous world of **G-FORCE** (a.k.a. Science Ninja Team Gatchaman), it presents interviews and behind-the-scenes stories of the pop culture phenomenon that captured the hearts and imagination of Generation X, and spawned the new hit comic series! Co-written by **JASON HOFIUS** and **GEORGE KHOURY**, this **FULL-COLOR** account is highlighted by a **NEW PAINTED COVER** from master artist **ALEX ROSS**!

(96-Page Trade Paperback) **$20 US**

## DICK GIORDANO CHANGING COMICS, ONE DAY AT A TIME

**MICHAEL EURY**'s biography of comics' most prominent and affable personality, who's done it all in comics: penciler, inker, editor, and more!

• Covers his career as illustrator, inker, and editor, peppered with **DICK'S PERSONAL REFLECTIONS** on his career milestones!
• Lavishly illustrated with **RARE AND NEVER-BEFORE-SEEN** comic book, merchandising, and advertising artwork!
• Extensive index of his published work!
• Deluxe color section!
• Comments & tributes by **NEAL ADAMS**, **DENNIS O'NEIL**, **TERRY AUSTIN**, **PAUL LEVITZ**, **MARV WOLFMAN**, **JULIUS SCHWARTZ**, **JIM APARO** & others!
• With a Foreword by **NEAL ADAMS** and Afterword by **PAUL LEVITZ**!

(176-pg. Paperback) **$24 US**

## WARREN COMPANION

**JON B. COOKE** and **DAVID ROACH** have compiled the ultimate guide to Warren Publishing, the publisher of such mags as **CREEPY, EERIE, VAMPIRELLA, BLAZING COMBAT,** and others. Reprints the Eisner Award-winning magazine **COMIC BOOK ARTIST #4** (completely reformatted), plus nearly 200 new pages:

• New painted cover by **ALEX HORLEY**!
• A definitive **WARREN CHECKLIST**!
• Dozens of **NEW FEATURES** on **CORBEN, FRAZETTA, DITKO** and others, and interviews with **WRIGHTSON, WARREN, EISNER, ADAMS, COLAN** & many more!

(272-page Trade Paperback) **$35 US**

Also available as a Limited Edition Hardcover (limited to 1000 copies) signed by **JIM WARREN**, with custom endleaves, 16 extra pages, plus a **WRIGHTSON** plate not in the Trade Paperback.

(288-page Hardcover) **$57 US**